MW00849617

# The Final Countdown Vol. 2

FIRST PRINTING

# Billy Crone

Cover Design:
Chris Taylor

# Contents

Preface............................................vii

1. *The Jewish People*.............................. Vol.1

2. *Modern Technology*.............................Vol.1

3. *Worldwide Upheaval*............................. Vol.1

4. *The Rise of Falsehood*........................... Vol.1

5. *The Rise of Wickedness*.......................... Vol.1

6. *The Rise of Apostasy*...............................9

7. *One World Religion*............................. 101

8. *One World Government*......................... 191

9. *One World Economy*............................285

10. *The Mark of the Beast*..........................361


*How to Receive Jesus Christ*.............. 438
*Notes*.........................................439

# *Preface*

Unfortunately, in the Church today, the study of prophecy has been forsaken under the assumption that one can't really know for sure what it all means and therefore we should refrain from teaching it. Yet, when you think about it, this is actually a slap in the face to God; for a majority of the Holy Scriptures deal directly or indirectly with prophetic issues. Why would God put prophecy in the Bible if it wasn't meant to be understood? Do we dare say that He is playing cat and mouse with us? In addition, how can one say that they are being faithful to present the whole counsel of God when they leave a major portion of it, prophecy, out of the picture? Furthermore, Bible prophecy has a wonderful way of bringing home two crucial truths that seem to be long forgotten in the American Church. One truth is that this world is not going to last forever. A flood destroyed it the first time and the next time it will be by fire. Therefore, this forces you and I the Christian to stop living merely for the temporary things of this world, thus wasting our lives and instead to get busy storing up treasures in heaven, which last forever. And is that not needed today? Also, Bible prophecy drives home the second truth of God being absolutely sovereign. He is in full control of all things at all times. So much so that God has already mapped out mankind's history. Therefore, only the student of Bible prophecy can rightly discern the times in which we live. Best of all, because God is sovereign, no matter how uncomfortable things may get, we can still be at peace knowing that our Lord reigns and that He will soon return to take us to be with Him.

What you are about to read will most assuredly shock you and certainly push you out of your comfort zone. If it doesn't, then you might want to check your pulse. Lest you think I'm making this material up, I invite you to check it out for yourself. This is why everything has been meticulously documented. This is not a time to react in fear but in faith. Our hope is not to be here, but in heaven. Remember, God is sovereign! One last piece of advice; when you are through reading this book then will you please *READ YOUR BIBLE*? I mean that in the nicest possible way. Enjoy, and I'm looking forward to seeing you someday!

Billy Crone
Las Vegas, Nevada
2017

*Chapter Six*

---

# The Rise of Apostasy

"Well hey, one day Kenny was getting a checkup and he tells his doctor that he thinks his wife, Lori, is losing her hearing.

So the doctor says to Kenny, 'You should do a simple test. Stand about 15 feet behind your wife and say, 'Honey?' And then move about 3 feet closer and then say it again, 'Honey?"

And then keep moving 3 feet closer until she finally responds. Remember how close you were when she finally gives you an answer. This will help me know how bad her hearing loss is.

So about a month later Kenny goes back to the doctor and the doctor asks, 'Well, did you do that experiment with your wife's hearing?'

And Kenny said, 'Yes.'

And the doctor asked, "How close did you get before she answered?'

And Kenny said, 'Well, by the time I got about 3 feet away, she just turned around and said 'For the FIFTH TIME...WHAT???'"[1]

But seriously folks, how many of you can not only identify with Lori's pain there, but how many of you would say Kenny's horrible assumption about Lori's hearing was about to make things much worse not better? Believe it or not, did you know that the Bible says one day the *whole planet* is going to make a wrong assumption that's going to make things a whole lot worse and it's going to happen at the Rapture of the Church! And the reason why it's going to be so horrible is because for those who refuse to accept Jesus Christ as their Personal Lord and Savior, they will be catapulted into the 7-year Tribulation and that is not a joke! It is an outpouring of God's wrath on a wicked and rebellious planet. In fact Jesus said in Matthew 24 it's going to be a time of greater horror than anything the world has ever seen or will ever see again. And that "unless that time of calamity is shortened, the entire human race would be destroyed." But praise God, God's not only a God of wrath, He's a God of love as well. And Because He loves us, He's given us many warning signs to show us when the Tribulation was near and Jesus Christ's Second Coming was rapidly approaching. Therefore, in order to keep you and I from experiencing the ultimate bad day of being left behind, we're going to continue in our series, *The Final Countdown*.

So far we've already seen how the **#10** sign on *The Final Countdown* was **The Jewish People**. The **#9** sign was **Modern Technology**. The **#8** sign was **Worldwide Upheaval**. The **#7** sign was **The Rise of Falsehood** and the **#6** sign was **The Rise of Wickedness**. What we saw there was that God lovingly foretold you and I that when we see an **Increase of Absolute Unadulterated Wickedness** in all levels of society, which is happening today right now all over the world, thanks in part to a Wicked Worldview called **Humanism**, a Wicked Teaching & Attack from **Atheistic Evolution**, a Wicked Worship called **self-love self-esteem**, a Wicked Lifestyle called **Hedonism**, and lastly a Wicked Connection with **Occultism**, which we saw is happening right now today all over the world with an increase of drug usage, demon worship and actual demonic witchcraft. As we saw, guess what? This is an indicator from God you are living in the Last Days AND it also explains why we've gone from a Great Mighty Christian Nation into what we have to deal with today!

The **#5** sign on *The Final Countdown* that God has given to lovingly wake us up is **The Rise of Apostasy**. That's right, not only is the world going down the tubes in the Last Days, so is the Church! But don't take my word for it. Let's listen to God's.

**1 Timothy 4:1-6** "The Spirit clearly says that in later times some will abandon the faith and follow deceiving spirits and things taught by demons. Such teachings come through hypocritical liars, whose consciences have been seared as with a hot iron. They forbid people to marry and order them to abstain from certain foods, which God created to be received with thanksgiving by those who believe and who know the truth. For everything God created is good, and nothing is to be rejected if it is received with thanksgiving, because it is consecrated by the word of God and prayer. If you point these things out to the brothers, you will be a good minister of Christ Jesus, brought up in the truths of the faith and of the good teaching that you have followed."

Now according to our text there, another major characteristic of the Last Days is that many people in the Church will do what? They will apostacize! They will "abandon" and "turn away" and "leave" the faith for demonic teaching! And that's when the show begins. They'll be pretending to be religious and give the appearance of being Christians, yet will show their true colors by turning away from the truth to follow hypocritical teachings, right? And granted, throughout history we've always had some people following some sort of perverted truths of Christianity. That's pretty commonplace. But what's not common is how in the last century alone, there has been a mass exodus of people "claiming to be Christians" who are turning away from even the basic truths of Christianity. I mean, they're following all kinds of wacked out stuff and it's getting worse! And to show you just how bad its become, let's take a look at the change of beliefs of people claiming to be Christians, even here in America, in just the past couple of decades:

1. **80% of Christians** believe "the Bible teaches that God helps those who help themselves."
2. **53% say** the Holy Spirit does not exist.
3. **12% do not know** what will happen to them after they die.
4. **25% agreed** that it doesn't matter what faith you follow because all faith groups teach the same lessons.
5. **30% say** that Jesus Christ died but never had a physical resurrection.
6. **29% contend** that "when he lived on earth, Jesus Christ was human and committed sins, just like other people."
7. **29% assert** that "there are some crimes, sins, or other things which people might do which cannot be forgiven by God."
8. **65% say** that satan "Is not a living being but is a symbol of evil."

9.  **22% agreed** that all people will experience the same outcomes after death, regardless of their religious beliefs.
10. **31% say** that a good person can earn his/her way into heaven.[2]

Now I don't know about you, but it sure looks to me that in the last couple of decades alone, there's been a massive Rise of Apostasy, hasn't there? Just like the Bible said would happen when you are in the Last Days! But the question is, "How could there be such a mass exodus of people deliberately turning from even the basic truths of Christianity in such a short amount of time, especially in America with our Godly Heritage?

## I - First Reason - A Flood of Phony Christians

The 1st reason people in the Church have turned from even the basic truths of Christianity is due to **A Flood of Phony Christians**. That's right, I'm talking about the fake believers in the Church. Little do people know, that as we saw previously, not only are satanists and witches coming into the Church wreaking all kinds of havoc and trouble, but so are a whole flood of phony baloney believers! And just like all the satanists and witches, sometimes, they too are hard to spot. They know the Christianese language. They know how to talk the talk. They might even have become members in the Church, but the proof is in the pudding, they're fake! In fact, Jesus warned us about them.

**John 6:63-64,70-71** "'The words I have spoken to you are spirit and they are life. Yet there are some of you who do not believe.' For Jesus had known from the beginning which of them did not believe and who would betray Him. Then Jesus replied, 'Have I not chosen you, the Twelve? Yet one of you is a devil!' (He meant Judas, the son of Simon Iscariot, who, though one of the Twelve, was later to betray Him.)"

Now according to our text, Jesus doesn't even hesitate to tell the people who were following Him that His teachings were not only from God, but that He Himself was God. And the way He demonstrates that is by knowing only what God could know, whether or not a person truly believed in Him. And because of this, we observe the shocking truth that "Not everyone who claims to be a disciple of Christ really is one." And as we saw, the Bible clearly says that some people in the Church, in the Last Days, are going to be counterfeit disciples just like Judas Iscariot. Oh, they might go to a Church service, but going to a Church service doesn't make you a Christian any more than sitting in a henhouse makes you a chicken. You must be born again!

But you might be thinking, "Oh come on, you don't mean to tell me that churches across America are full of phony boloney believers who are no better off than Judas Iscariot. That's crazy!" Well crazy or not, don't take my word for it. Let's listen to one. His name is Larry.

*"I'd really call myself an agnostic. I live my life the way I believe it should be lived. I very much live along Christian value lines but no, I'm not convinced and quite frankly, you know, I don't worry about it. I don't care.*

*I go to a church, I support the church and everything else. I'm very much in favor of it. I believe in strong morals, strong family values and want to bring them up in my children. I also believe my views are my views and other people believe what they want to believe and I don't want to get in an argument or try to convince them otherwise.*

*Logically, intellectually I have a hard time grasping that Christianity is necessarily right. I mean why...take Judaism for example, why isn't that just another mythology...why isn't that, you know, I mean, Romans had mythology. Greeks had mythology, so you know, why isn't Christianity just another mythology?*

*I mean you look at Jesus Christ and you'd say he had to be a phenomenal human being, a phenomenal leader. He was able to call Himself the Son of God, had a bunch of disciples and got a lot of people to believe that He was the Son of God and to reaffirm a belief in God and that then evolved historically into a great religion.*

*My view of the afterlife is, there is none. Life ends when you die. You didn't exist beforehand and you will not exist afterward."*[3]

We have got to wake up and deal with the facts. The Church of Jesus Christ right now has been flooded with phony baloney believers just like Larry, just like the Bible said would happen in the Last Days. They're all over the place! In fact, I used to have a 50-50 rule, where I figured about half the American Church probably still doesn't know Christ. But I remember reading in D. James Kennedy's biography where he put the number as high as 80%. And the reason why he said 80% was because of the 20-80 rule that we see in churches all across

America. Where 20% of the people do 100% of the work while 80% of the people do nothing! And he said the reason is simple! The reason why the 80% do nothing is because they're *not true Christians*. How can you be a true born again Christian and have no desire to serve Christ?! The logical response is, "Hey can I do something for you, etc." And as shocking as that might sound, believe it or not, some of those 80% might be your pastor! Check this out!

**Wes**, a Methodist, lost his confidence in the Bible while attending a liberal Christian college and seminary. "I went to college thinking Adam and Eve were real people," he explained. Now, he no longer believes that God exists. His church members do not know that he is an atheist, but he explains that they are somewhat liberal themselves. His ministerial colleagues are even more liberal: They don't believe Jesus rose from the dead literally. They don't believe Jesus was born of a virgin. They don't believe all those things that would cause a big stir in their churches."

**Rick**, a campus minister for the United Church of Christ, was an agnostic in college and seems to have lost all belief by the time he graduated from seminary. He chose ordination in the UCC because it required "no forced doctrine." Even as he graduated from seminary, he knew, "I'm not going to make it in a conventional church. He knew he couldn't go into a church and teach his own theological views. He does not believe "all this creedal stuff" about the incarnation of Christ or the need for salvation, but he remained in the ministry because, "These are my people, this is the context in which I work, these are the people that I know." In the pulpit, his mode is to talk as if he does believe, because "as long as ... you are talking about God and Jesus and the Bible, that's what they want to hear. You're just phrasing it in a way that makes sense to [them] ... but language is ambiguous and can be heard in different ways."

**Darryl** is a Presbyterian who sees himself as a "progressive-minded" pastor who wants to see his kind of non-doctrinal Christianity "given validity in some way." He acknowledges that he is more a pantheist than a theist, and thinks that many of the more educated members of his church hold to the same liberal beliefs as his own. And those beliefs (or unbeliefs) are stated clearly: "I reject the virgin birth. I reject substitutionary atonement. I reject the divinity of Jesus. I reject heaven and hell in the traditional sense, and I am not alone." Amazingly, Darryl is candid about the fact that he remains in the ministry largely for financial reasons. It is how he provides for his family. If he openly espoused his beliefs, "I may be burning bridges in terms of my ability to earn a living this way."

**Adam** ministers in the Church of Christ. After years in the ministry, he began to lose all theological confidence. He has moved fully into an atheist mode, yet he continues to lead his church in worship. How? "Here's how I'm handling my job on Sunday mornings: I see it as play acting. I see myself as taking on the role of a believer in a worship service, and performing." This "atheistic agnostic" stays in the ministry because he likes the people and, "I need the job still." If he had an alternative source of income, he would take it. He feels hypocritical, but no longer believes that hypocrisy is wrong.

**John** is identified as a Southern Baptist minister who has primarily served as a worship leader. He was attracted to Christianity as a religion of love, but his pursuit of Christianity "brought me to the point of not believing in God." As he explains, "I didn't plan to become an atheist. I didn't even want to become an atheist. It's just I had no choice. If I'm being honest with myself." He is clearly not being honest with his church members. He rejects all belief in God and all Christian truth claims out of hand. He is a determined atheist. Once again, this unbelieving minister admits that he stays in the ministry because of finances. Amazingly, this minister even names his price: "If someone said, 'Here's $200,000,' I'd be turning my notice in this week, because then I can pay off everything."[4]

I like what Gilbert Tennett said way back in 1739 about phony preachers, "If they will not remove themselves from the ministry, they must be removed. If they lack the integrity to resign their pulpits, the churches must muster the integrity to eject them." Why? Because they're phony! They're apostates and they'll ruin the Church!

And fortunately when it comes to these phony baloney believers in these Last Days, God doesn't leave us hanging high and dry, wondering who's who, and who's real and who's fake. He actually tells us how to spot them.

**1. The 1st way to spot a Phony Baloney Believer just like Judas Iscariot, is when they Worship God With Their Head But Not With Their Heart.**

**James 2:14-17,19** "What good is it, my brothers, if a man claims to have faith but has no deeds? Can such faith save him? Suppose a brother or sister is without clothes and daily food. If one of you says to him, Go, I wish you well; keep warm and well fed, but does nothing about his physical needs, what good is it? In the same way, faith by itself, if it is not accompanied by action, is dead. You believe that there is one God. Good! Even the demons believe that – and shudder."

The Bible simply declares that not all faith is a saving faith. And according to our text, if your faith is not accompanied by appropriate action, it's not only fake, *it's dead*. And here's the point. The devil knows this. He knows it so stinking well. So here's what he does. He tricks people into thinking that faith is having a head knowledge of God instead of a heart knowledge of God. Or in other words, just giving a mental ascent that God exists. Whip De Doo Dah! What'd we just read? Even the *demons believe in God*, but are they saved? Absolutely not! So if you believe there's a God, then whip-de-do! This only puts you on the same level as the demons! And this is what the Bible calls a dead faith.

It's my contention that this dead faith syndrome has become an epidemic in the American Church, just like the Bible said would happen in the Last Days! Many people today in churches think it's no big deal to not "get involved" and not "get serious" about going to church services. I mean, after all, you don't want to be labeled as one of those Jesus freaks do you? This apathetic behavior has become so commonplace in the American Church that we even make jokes about it all the time, like this one.

"There were three country churches in a small Texas town that were being overrun by some pesky squirrels.

So the 1st church called a meeting to decide what to do about the squirrels. And after much prayer and consideration they determined that the squirrels were predestined to be there and they shouldn't interfere with God's divine will.

And when the 2nd church got together, they decided they weren't in a position to harm any of God's creations. So, they humanely trapped the squirrels and set them free a few miles outside of town. However, three days later, the squirrels were back.

But it was only the 3rd church that was able to come up with the best and most effective solution. You see, they decided to baptize the squirrels and registered them as members of the church. Why?

Because now they only see them on Christmas and Easter."[5]

Now granted, that joke is pretty funny, right? Because it's so true, right? But it's really not that funny when you realize that those who are acting like squirrelly Christians may not even be Christians at all! I'm telling you, we better wake up! A true Christian is not one who lives for God just twice a year! They live for the Lord every single day of their lives and God uses them to transform this world. John Wesley said, "Give me ten people who hate nothing but sin, who fear nothing but God, and who love nothing but Jesus, and I can change the world." I don't know if you've noticed, but the American Church seems to be having a hard time changing this world nowadays. In fact, it seems this world *is having an easy time* at changing the American Church. And you know why? Well I'm thinking maybe it's because the American Church is full of people who **Worship God With Their Heads But Not With Their Hearts** and that means the American Church is full of Phony Baloney Believers.

**2.** The 2nd **way** to spot a **Phony Baloney Believer** just like Judas Iscariot, is when they **Worship God With Their Lips But Not With Their Lives.**

**Titus 1:15-16** "Everything is pure to those whose hearts are pure. But nothing is pure to those who are corrupt and unbelieving, because their minds and consciences are defiled. Such people claim they know God, but they deny him by the way they live. They are despicable and disobedient, worthless for doing anything good."

The Bible declares that not everyone who claims to know God really knows God. In fact, if all they do is give God lip service instead of life service then their so-called faith is actually worthless and the devil knows this. He knows it so stinking well. So here's what he does. He tricks people into thinking that all you have to do is *not live like a Christian*, but just *say* you're a Christian, and somehow you've become one. But we're only fooling ourselves if we think we can sin up a storm 6 days a week and go to a Church service on the 7th and somehow everything's just fine. Anybody can claim to know God all they want but if they deny this claim by the way they live then they're being a hypocrite. This is not only detrimental to your soul, but to the souls of others. One person said this:

*"The number one cause of atheism is Christians. Those who proclaim God with their mouths but deny Him in their lifestyles, are what the unbelieving world simply finds unbelievable."*[6]

It's my contention that this *lip service syndrome* has become an epidemic in the American Church, especially in these Last Days! Many people in churches today think that all you have to do is claim to know God but never live for God and somehow you're in like flint. But a true Christian is not one who lives for God just one hour a week. They live for the Him *every single day* of their lives and God uses them to light this world on fire! When asked why so many people came to hear him preach, John Wesley said, *"It's simple. If you light yourself on fire for Jesus Christ, people will come for miles just to watch you burn!"* Maybe this is why the American Church can't seem to get the fires of revival burning across our nation anymore. Maybe it's because people are **Worshipping God With Their Lips But Not With Their Lives**. Maybe the American Church is flooded with Phony Baloney Believers, just like the Bible said would happen, when you're living in the Last Days.

## 3. The 3rd way to spot a Phony Baloney Believer just like Judas Iscariot, is when they Worship God With Their Thoughts But Not With The Truth.

**1 John 2:18-19** "Dear children, this is the last hour; and as you have heard that the Antichrist is coming, even now many Antichrists have come. This is how we know it is the last hour. They went out from us, but they did not really belong to us. For if they had belonged to us, they would have remained with us; but their going showed that none of them belonged to us."

The Bible declares that not everyone who goes to a church service really belongs to the Church. If they walk away from the truth and start following a lie, then it only shows they were never saved in the first place. And this not only explains our opening text of the great falling away and people abandoning the faith, but once again, the devil knows this. He knows it so stinking well. So here's what he does. He tricks people into thinking *there are many roads to heaven* and that Jesus is not the only way to God. No! He's just one of the many ways to God. This is not only calling Jesus a liar, it's assuming that God's going to bend His truth to your man-made thoughts! And oh, it may sound nice and wonderful, and politically correct, but sooner or later the truth will be known, like this story reveals.

*"A counterfeit Christian is like a counterfeit ten dollar bill. For instance, let's suppose you have a counterfeit bill but don't know it. You think it's genuine.*

*So sure enough, you use it to pay for some gas. But as soon as it makes its way to the bank, the bank teller spots the phony and says, 'I'm sorry, but this bill is a counterfeit.'*

*Now that ten dollar bill may have done a lot of good while it was in circulation, but when it arrived at the bank it was exposed for what it really was and it was immediately put out of circulation.*

*And so it is with the counterfeit Christian. They may do a lot of good things in their life, but when they face Christ at the final judgment, they'll immediately be rejected."*[7]

The Bible says if a person "professes" to be a Christian yet walks away from the truth that Jesus really is the only way to heaven, then the Bible says they're a counterfeit. After thinking about this, "Well maybe this is the reason why the American Church has lost its zeal for the lost. Maybe it's because the majority of the American Church is still lost themselves?" Why? Because they're **Worshiping God With Their Thoughts And Not With The Truth** and now the Church is flooded with a bunch of Phony Baloney Believers, just like the Bible said would happen, when you are living in the Last Days.

**4. The 4th way to spot a Phony Baloney Believer just like Judas Iscariot, is when they Worship God With Their Religion But Not With A Relationship.**

**Matthew 7:21-23** "Not everyone who says to me, Lord, Lord, will enter the kingdom of heaven, but only he who does the will of my Father who is in heaven. Many will say to me on that day, Lord, Lord, did we not prophesy in your name, and in your name drive out demons and perform many miracles? Then I will tell them plainly, I never knew you. Away from me, you evildoers!"

The Bible declares that not everyone who says, "Lord, Lord" really belongs to the Lord. If their faith is based on pious religious deeds instead of a personal relationship, then they don't belong to Christ. The devil knows this. So here's what he does. He tricks people into thinking that if they want to get to heaven, then *just be a good religious person* who does good religious deeds once in awhile. But Jesus didn't die on the cross so people could get religious for Him. NO! He died on the cross so we could have a *relationship* with Him. And again, it's my contention that this religious attitude has become an epidemic in the American Church, especially in these Last Days! And because of that, many people who claim to be alive in Christ are actually dead to Christ because of their religion, like this story reveals:

*"There was this new minister in a small Oklahoma town who spent the first four days desperately calling on the church membership and begged them to come to his first services. But try as he might, nobody would come.*

*So he decided to place a notice in the local newspapers, stating that the church was dead, and it was his duty to give it a decent Christian burial the following Sunday.*

*Well, this of course got the curiosity of the whole town and everyone turned out. And when they got there, they saw a coffin smothered in flowers in front of the pulpit.*

*After the minister read the obituary and delivered a eulogy, he invited his congregation to step forward and pay their respects to the dearly departed.*

*Without a moments hesitation a long line was formed because each person couldn't wait to see what in the world was in the coffin. But as soon as each person peeped into the coffin, a strange thing happened. Each person quickly turned away with a guilty look. Why?*

*Because the minister had placed a large mirror inside the coffin which meant that every single person simply saw themselves."*[8]

I place a mirror before us and the American Church today and say this, "If you have to have your arm twisted to give up your time, treasure, talents and tongue for God, then maybe it's because you don't have a relationship with God, maybe it's because you've got a *religion* with God." And if you can't ever seem to get motivated to come hear the Word of God, then maybe one day you'll hear from God, "Away from me you evildoer, *I never knew you!*" Why? Because you're *Worshiping God With Your Religion And Not With A Relationship*. It might be a sign you are a Phony Baloney Believer, just like the Bible said would happen in the Last Days.

What more does God have to do? He loves us. This is happening before our very eyes! He doesn't want us to go into the 7-year Tribulation! And this is why He's given us the sign of the *Rise of Apostasy* today to show us that the 7-year Tribulation is near and that Christ's coming is rapidly approaching. That's why Jesus Himself said:

**Luke 21:28** "When these things begin to take place, stand up and lift up your heads, because your redemption is drawing near."

People of God, like it or not, we are headed for *The Final Countdown*. So the point is this. If you're a Christian, it's time to *get busy*! Stop bickering and start working together, and let's get busy saving souls! But if you're not a Christian, or maybe you *think* you're a Christian, but God exposed you today and you're feeling a little uncomfortable, then I urge you to become a true Christian. Why? Because God knows who's real and who's not like this guy shares.

### A TRUE CHRISTIAN

**COMMISSION***: I think that if you are a true Christian, you don't consider Christianity just a part of your life-it is your life. If you follow the teachings of the Bible, specifically Mark 16:15 which says, "Go out into the world and preach the Good News to all creation."*

**AN OBLIGATION**: *Then you have an obligation to share that faith with others. If you saw a building on fire and you knew there were people in it and you knew you were capable of running in there and saving someone who wouldn't be able to help themselves. If you knew you could help them, would you just stand there and do nothing? Unfortunately, by not clearly seeing the issue, I think that's what a lot of Christians do, is that they just stand there.*

**AN OMMISSION**: *I think by and large, most of it is that most Christians are not really well educated as to their own religion's position on various issues.*

**AN IGNORANCE**: *They consider worshiping Jesus to be a part of their lives but not their primary purpose and I believe that true Christianity considers it to be the primary purpose.*

> **A PURPOSE**: *If you are a true Christian, you believe that those that are not Christians, those who have not followed the teachings of the Bible, that have not accepted Jesus Christ as their personal Savior, those people aren't going to Heaven, they are going to Hell. Hell's not a fun place.*

**A HEAVEN AND A HELL**: *I have heard Christians that have the view that everyone is entitled to their own belief, and that's not necessarily a bad position to have, but if you believe that what they believe is going to earn them a place in eternal suffering, then there's a problem with that in that you're allowing them to be tortured for eternity while at the same time believing that you shouldn't save them from that. It's very awkward.*

> **A REAL BELIEF**: *If you really believe that people who are not Christians are going to hell then that is a very serious consequence and if you don't take that seriously I think you might be compromising your own belief system.*

**A COMPROMISE**: *Those who do take their faith seriously, they need to encourage or teach those who might not know how important that is.*

**A FEAR**: *Sometimes I think Christians are afraid of being labeled as a "bible-thumper" or to have negative connotations associated with that.*

**A LABEL**: *But that is not necessarily negative if you're a Christian; I'd think it would be something you'd be proud of. There's nothing to be ashamed of if you're a Christian about the Bible or being a "bible-thumper". It's something to be proud of. It's something you take seriously and it's something you should encourage others to take seriously as well.*

> **A REACTION**: *And it might require you to challenge yourself. You know, to stand up in front of crowds to talk to people who you don't know.*

**A CHALLENGE**: *Missionaries who work in places where the predominant religion is not Christianity and that's a completely different scenario than in most parts of the United States, but they take it in stride and they accept it and they move on.*

**A BOLDNESS**: *You shouldn't take rejection personally, but consider that you gave them a fighting chance.*

⤳ **A FIGHTING CHANCE**: *Give them a fighting chance of Heaven even if you have to risk offending someone or a risk of friendship. It's a simple way of weighing priorities.*

⤳ **A WEIGHING OF PRIORITIES**: *If I were a Christian of course I would take the Bible seriously. I respect people who take their beliefs seriously and I would take the Bible's teaching seriously. Among those teachings is the idea that there's a Heaven and there is a Hell and those that accept Jesus Christ as their personal Savior go to Heaven, and those that don't, go to Hell and the implications of that are very far reaching.*

ATHIEST:

*"And you're an atheist?"*

*"Yes I sure am."*[9]

## II - Second Reason - A Flood of Greedy Christians

The **2nd reason** people **in the Church** have abandoned the Christian faith and have turned from even the basic truths of Christianity, is due to **A Flood of Greedy Christians**.

That's right, I'm talking about the *Word of Faith Movement*. Or in other words, the Name it and Claim it, the Blab it and Grab it group. Little do people know that all these false teachings of the Word of Faith Movement that we keep hearing about and seeing every single day on so-called Christian TV is one of the clearest signs we're living in the Last Days. But don't take my word for it. Let's listen to God's. He told us this was going to happen!

**2 Peter 2:1-3** "But there were also false prophets among the people, just as there will be false teachers among you. They will secretly introduce destructive heresies, even denying the sovereign Lord who bought them – bringing swift destruction on themselves. Many will follow their shameful ways and will bring the way of truth into disrepute. In their greed these teachers will exploit you with stories they have made up. Their condemnation has long been hanging over them, and their destruction has not been sleeping."

In other words, you don't want to be in their camp when Judgment Day comes! But as you can see, the Bible clearly says that in the future, in the Last Days, people in the Church would actually be led astray, not just by false teachers, but specifically by false teachers who are greedy and who are exploiting people in the Church for their money. In other words, they're going to *be ripping Christians off of their cash* with stories they made up! It says it right there! It's all over the place! It's in the Church, on TV, it's in so-called Christian bookstores, it's everywhere! Today, people in the Church…en masse…are being led astray by *false teachers who are manipulating them* out of their money, exactly like the Bible said would happen when you're living in the Last Days!

## 1. The 1st way they're doing it is by The Promotion of False Hopes.

If you're familiar with these "Word of Faith" false teachers, that's exactly what they do. First of all, they're called "Word of Faith" teachers because that's what they say, that's what they teach; they say that if you just have enough faith and speak the right word, then we could obtain untold riches and have perfect health from God every single time. Don't believe me? Here's a sampling of some of their most prominent leaders and their false teaching.

### FALSE TEACHINGS ON WEALTH

- **Jesse Duplantis**: "The very first thing on Jesus' agenda was to get rid of poverty!"

- **Fredrick Price**: "The apostles were businessmen. They were rich men and had plenty of money. I'm going to show you that Jesus was a wealthy man and had plenty of money. Jesus and the disciples were rich. Only rich people could take off for 3.5 years."

- **John Avanzini**: "Jesus was handling big money because that treasurer He had was a thief. Now you can't tell me that a ministry with a treasurer that's a thief can operate on a few pennies. It took big money to operate that ministry because Judas was stealing out of that bag. If you have a treasurer, that means you have a lot of money."

- **Creflo Dollar**: "I'm telling you, Jesus wasn't poor, and He didn't wear no rags, either. Like we march in on these Easter little plays that we do at our church, with those raggedy sheets on. Jesus didn't have no rags on. He wore designer clothes, honey!"

- **John Avanzini**: "Jesus wore designer clothes. Well, what else you gonna call it? I mean, you didn't get the stuff He wore off the rack. It wasn't a one-size-fits-all deal. No, this was custom stuff."

- **Creflo Dollar**: "But without faith stuff, you have no stuff, because faith stuff is the stuff of all stuff. Take away the faith stuff, you ain't got no stuff. Get the faith stuff, and you can get some more stuff, because you got the main stuff. Now, did you get all that stuff?"

- **Robert Tilton:** "The only time people were poor in the Bible is when they were under a curse" and "Being poor is a sin."

- **Fredrick Price:** "The whole point is I'm trying to get you to see – to get you out of this malaise of thinking that Jesus and the disciples were poor and then relating that to you – thinking that you, as a child of God, have to follow Jesus. The Bible says that He has left us an example that we should follow His steps. That's the reason why I drive a Rolls Royce. I'm following Jesus' steps."

## FALSE TEACHINGS ON HEALTH

- **Benny Hinn**: "Sickness does not belong to you. It has no part in the Body of Christ. Sickness does not belong to any of us. The Bible declares if the Word of God is in our life, there will be health, there will be healing – divine health and divine healing. There will be no sickness for the saint of God. That means not even a headache, sinus problem, not even a toothache – nothing! No sickness should come your way."

- **Kenneth Hagin:** "It is the plan of our Father God in His great love and His great mercy that no believer should ever be sick."

- **Kenneth Copeland**: "You began to meditate on those scriptures until you built an inner image of yourself healed. As that image grew more crisp and clear, you begin to expect – or hope for – that image to become a reality. You'll be expecting the very presence of God to rise up in you so powerfully that instead of believing for healing every six weeks, you'll walk in divine health every day!"

- **Marilyn Hickey:** "Say to your body, 'You're whole, body! Why, you just function so beautifully and so well. Why, body, you never have any problems. You're a strong, healthy body.' Or speak to your leg, or speak to your foot, or speak to your neck, or speak to your back; and once you have spoken and believe that you have received, and don't go back on it. Speak to your wife, speak to your husband, speak to your circumstances; and speak faith to them to create in them and God will create what you are speaking."

- **Fredrick Price:** "How can you glorify God in your body, when it doesn't function right? How can you glorify God? How can He get glory when your body doesn't even work? What makes you think the Holy Ghost wants to live inside a body where He can't see out through the windows and He can't hear with the ears? What makes you think the Holy Spirit wants to live inside of a physical body where the limbs and the organs and the cells do not function right?"[10]

Excuse me? Every person who ever got a disease, or who was ever confined to wheelchair, or whoever had body parts that didn't work right, these hucksters just put a stake into their heart! And we wonder why there's this *massive falling away* in these Last Days from the Church! I'd run too from this baloney! But as you can see, the basic teachings of the Word of Faith Movement are completely antithetical to the Scripture and they're *manipulating people* with false hopes of so-called fabulous riches and so-called perfect health.

But there's a catch. You see, you have to send them *your money* to get these supposed *free* financial blessings or healings from God. And in exchange for sowing a financial seed into their ministry, they will send you the latest religious trinket to get rich or to get your healing. For instance, to acquire these untold riches and healings, right now you can send off for a genuine faith nail, prayer cloth, prayer candle, paper prayer rug, anointing oil, and that's right, a cornmeal miracle packet. I'm not making this up folks! And lest you think I'm kidding, listen to these guys yourself. They've got all kinds of gimmicks. Check it out!

## Kerney Thomas: (Miracle Hankie)

*"Financial trouble? Do you need a miracle from God. I want to rush you one of*

*my anointed prayer handkerchiefs in the mail absolutely free of charge"*

*"Ever since I used it my neck stopped hurting. My whole body starting feeling good. Not only physically, but financially by bringing my mortgage up to date that was 3 months behind!"*

*"Guess what? This is real. This is the anointing and the spirit of God endeavoring to break the curse of poverty and those generational curses off of your home and your life and your business"*

## Miracle Manna

*"Call for this biblical point of contact and get into position to receive God's best for you and your loved ones."*

*"$28,000? $28,000!!"*

*"I received one check for over $50,000. Whatever he say to do. Do it."*

*"Every bite from this heavenly cake-you'll feel empowered and encouraged to move into all God has for you. Take the first step to a new life. Call the number on your screen and get your free packet today"*

*"Today, take Him as your Senior Partner. Make a $1,000 vow of faith and as God begins to provide, listen to me, and as God begins to multiply-that's all God's saying, just keep it watered, fulfill your vow"*

## Kerney Thomas: (Miracle Hanky Part II)

*Oh I feel the anointing of God. FOR GOD CALLED MIRACLES to happen in your life!"*

## Peter Popoff: (Miracle Spring Water)

*"I see many miracles coming to you. Money!! Is coming to you. That's right. Miracle money. Divine transfers. I want to show you how to get yourself into a position so that you can receive."*

*"I can feel it now! I can feel it! I can feel it!"*[11]

Repeat after me, "I can feel it! I can feel myself getting *ripped off*!" And what did the Bible say? When you see these things on TV and these guys ripping people off of their cash in the Church, you're living in the Last Days. Of course they say when you follow the secret formula on how to pray for your financial blessing or healing, these people promise to personally pray for a 100-fold increase, to your *generous donation* of course!

And you might be out there thinking "Come on! Nobody *in the Church* is ever going to fall for this wacky stuff." But as I stated earlier, *right now* shelves in every Christian bookstore across America are full of this stuff! And these so-called faith ministries are raking in millions of dollars each year, off of people who are not seeking Jesus Christ, but cash. They're not seeking God, they're seeking great health! And it's all for money, and it's all for profit, exactly like God said would happen in the Last Days!

If that wasn't bad enough, it gets even worse. These hucksters not only perpetuate this false teaching that once you're a Christian you're guaranteed perfect health and perfect wealth, but then they have the audacity to say if you are not experiencing this, then something's wrong with *you*! Not the stories they made up, but you! They say you either have some *secret sin you need to confess* or you just don't *have enough faith*. Excuse me? So here's the problem. Now you feel guilty as a Christian and horrible because you don't have this perfect wealth and perfect health that they say you're supposed to have and it breaks your heart. And so now, not just the *non-Christian*, but now even *the Christian* starts to wonder what's up with God! Why am I experiencing this pain? Why am I going through these hard times? If God loves me why am I suffering, right?

The Bible is clear. Bad things are going to happen to us! We're not guaranteed a perfect life or a big 'ol pile of cash on earth! Bad things are going to happen because we live in a world full of evil and suffering. Heaven comes later! But don't take my word for it. Let's listen to God. He tells us what to expect this side of heaven and it's not all perfect!

**Psalms 34:19** "A righteous man may have many troubles but the Lord delivers him from them all."

**Isaiah 48:10** "See I have refined you though not as silver, I have tested you in the furnace of affliction."

**Matthew 5:10-12** "Blessed are those who are persecuted because of righteousness, for theirs is the kingdom of heaven. Blessed are you when people insult you, persecute you and falsely say all kinds of evil against you because of Me. Rejoice and be glad, because great is your reward in heaven, for in the same way they persecuted the prophets who were before you."

**Matthew 24:9** "Then you will be handed over to be persecuted and put to death, and you will be hated by all nations because of Me."

**2 Timothy 3:10-12** "You, however, know all about my teaching, my way of life, my purpose, faith, patience, love, endurance, persecutions, sufferings – what kinds of things happened to me in Antioch, Iconium and Lystra, the persecutions I endured. Yet the Lord rescued me from all of them. In fact, everyone who wants to live a godly life in Christ Jesus will be persecuted."

**Acts 14:21-22** "They preached the good news in that city and won a large number of disciples. Then they returned to Lystra, Iconium and Antioch, strengthening the disciples and encouraging them to remain true to the faith. 'We must go through many hardships to enter the kingdom of God,' they said."

**Philippians 1:29** "For it has been granted to you on behalf of Christ not only to believe on Him, but also to suffer for Him, since you are going through the same struggle you saw I had, and now hear that I still have."

**Philippians 3:10** "I want to know Christ and the power of His resurrection and the fellowship of sharing in His sufferings, becoming like Him in His death."

**1 Peter 5:9** "Resist him (devil) standing firm in the faith because you know that your brothers throughout the world are undergoing the same kind of sufferings."

**1 Peter 4:12,13** "Dear friends, do not be surprised at the painful trial you are suffering, as though something strange were happening to you. But rejoice that you participate in the sufferings of Christ."

I'm telling you, that's just the tip of the iceberg, of the *plethora* of examples throughout the Bible declaring that yes, we the Christian are going to encounter suffering in this world. It's all over the Bible! And yet one of the Word of Faith teachers, Kenneth Copeland, actually had the audacity to say this about God:

**Kenneth Copeland**: *"I was shocked when I found out who the biggest failure in the Bible actually is. The biggest one in the whole Bible is God. I mean, He lost His top-ranking, most anointed angel, the first man He ever created, the first woman He ever created, the whole earth and all the fullness therein, a third of the angels, at least – that's a big loss, man. Now, the reason you don't think of God as a failure is He never said He's a failure. And you're not a failure till you say you're one."*[12]

And we wonder why the text said, "And their condemnation has long been hanging over them, and their destruction has not been sleeping." God's going to take these jokesters out and you don't want to be there when it happens! What we need to do is call it like it is and realize that the only ones getting rich off these stories they've made up, is these jokesters! Don't believe me? Even the secular will admit it.

**Dateline**: *"He claims he can heal the sick. Critics say the only miracle may be the millions that he is making."*

*"Though Hinn refuses to make his financial information public. He has said that every dollar given to his ministry goes to the work of the Lord. Be that as it may, Benny Hinn does manage to live very well. His home is this mansion overlooking the Pacific Ocean, built and paid for by his ministry. According to building records its has 7 bedrooms, 8 bathrooms and more than 7,000 sq. feet of living space. The ministry told us that the mansion was it's parsonage and a good investment. According to area realtors, today it's worth about $10 million dollars.*

*And when Hinn goes to crusades around the world, he travels in this private jet. According to documents we obtained, the ministry pays more than a $112,000 a month to use the plane. And closer to home "pastor" Benny still travels in style. This photo obtained by Dateline shows him getting out of a Mercedes SUV. And then he's shown driving a Mercedes convertible. Both cars retail for about $80,000.*

*At this crusade in Milwaukee, the documents indicate Benny Hinn occupied the Presidential Suite of the Pfister Hotel. The hotel told us the room costs $990 per night. At a crusade in Panama, the documents show and we verified with the Intercontinental Hotel that Hinn was in the Royal Suite. The published rate: $1,700 a night. At a crusade in Montreal we verified Pastor Benny was* ensconced in the Royal Suite of the St. James Hotel. The regular rate there, $2,700 a night. The room is the size of the average house, 2,200 sq. feet. Including a make-up room, dressing room and a piano that plays by itself.

We found some other trips which seemed to have little to do with "spreading the Word of God". Hinn is a regular at Beverly Hill's clothing stores like Versace, Louis Vuitton and Bijon- where Hinn's name is on the window along with Princes and Heads of State. There are questions raised by some of the purchases we found in those expense documents. For example, in just over 4 weeks in 2003, we found six separate charges at high end clothing stores totaling more than $6,000.00 all charged on the ministries corporate card.

But we were intrigued by what appeared to be stops made by Pastor Benny at resorts and spas around the world, on his way to and from crusades. The ministry called these stops "layovers". Now for most of us travelers, layovers mean long hours waiting for a connection at an unfamiliar airport-maybe an overnight stay at a low rent hotel. But remember, Pastor Benny travels in the ministrie's private jet and sets his own schedule-so consider Benny Hinn's version of a layover. On his way home from California from this crusade in Columbia, the documents show and the hotel confirmed for us, pastor Benny stopped at this resort in Cancun, Mexico. He stayed in the Presidential Suite there that cost the ministry $2,684 for one night and the trip was described as a layover.

After crusades in Russia and Sweden in July of 2003, Pastor Benny apparently didn't get on his private jet and fly west and go home. Instead he flew from Sweden, south to Italy, then back North to England with an entourage that included his son, his daughter and her fiancé. There were expensive meals. Like this one for more than $900 in Italy, and one at this Lebanese restaurant in London for more than $1,700-and check out these hotel bills. Transportation charges of more than $6,000. In London another $6,000 for incidentals such as chauffeur services and in-room tea. The documents also list tips. In 3 days more than $4,500 worth. Including $1,000 to a concierge and another $1,000 to a desk manager. And then there were Pastor Benny's hotel rooms. In London-the documents show Hinn stayed at the exclusive Lanes Borough Hotel. The hotel confirmed for us it was Suite 210 and told us they never discount rooms. The going rate the hotel says-$3,124 per night. And then there's Pastor Benny's hotel in Milan according to the expense documents-Room 1001-the hotel confirmed it was the Presidential Suite. The hotel website says that the room is "fit for a

*prince" and the largest hotel suite in Europe-among its 5,400 sq feet, 3
bedrooms, a formal dining room, a fireplace, a jacuzzi, a sauna, a turkish bath, a
large terrace with a panoramic view of the city and a 100 ft long swimming pool
decorated with marble and frescos. The hotel tells us this room rents for more
than $10,000 a night. No discounts. And through it all Pastor Benny maintains he
has truth and God on his side.*

*Benny Hinn: Look-come and get a close shot. Look at these eyes. I have never
lied to you. Never. I never will. I'd rather die than lie to God's people."*[13]

Wow! The audacity! People, when in the world are we in the Church
ever going to wake up and call it like it is. The world does. They know the truth.
These guys are false teachers and they're ripping people off of their cash!
Exactly like God said would happen in the Last Days! He is not some kind of a
"Cosmic Santa Claus," that if we rub the right way, He has to give us whatever
we want. Are you kidding me? *He is God* and *we are not*. Besides, I know this
might be hard to believe, but did you know that the Apostle Peter was profoundly
used by God and to my knowledge, he never once owned an Armani suit or drove
a single Cadillac. In fact, did you know, there's no record of him chanting an Old
Testament prayer over and over again in order to increase the size of his ministry.
But what we do know is the Apostle Peter *clearly warned us* that this kind of
monetary manipulation would come by false teachers *in the Church* in the Last
Days! And it's happening *right now*! We better wake up!

**2. The 2nd way these false teachers are manipulating people in the
Church for their cash in the Last Days just like God said would happen,
is by Perverting Church Discipline.**

You see, if you haven't already recognized it, these hucksters not only
have the perfect scapegoat when you don't get your so-called fabulous wealth
and so-called perfect health, even after sowing a seed to their ministry, and that
was the excuse they come up with, as we saw earlier, it's because *you* don't have
enough faith or *you* have some secret sin, blah, blah, blah, right? But they also
have a second scapegoat excuse to help make sure they get to keep on teaching
this baloney and that is this: When you corner them Biblically for this false
teaching, for preaching heresy in the Church, and say they need to be disciplined
for it, they blow up! They act like *you're the one* who's committing a crime!
How dare you question them? Don't you know they're the chosen ones to whom
God has revealed this new supposed truth? Yeah right! And here's the point. The

Bible clearly says this is yet another thing these hucksters are going to be doing in the Last Days. Not only will they rip people off of their cash, but they'll despise authority with a seared conscience.

**1 Timothy 4:1-2** "The Spirit clearly says that in later times some will abandon the faith and follow deceiving spirits and things taught by demons. Such teachings come through hypocritical liars, whose consciences have been seared as with a hot iron."

**2 Peter 2:3** "In their greed these teachers will exploit you with stories they have made up. Their condemnation has long been hanging over them, and their destruction has not been sleeping. This is especially true of those who follow the corrupt desire of the sinful nature and despise authority."

So just what does a seared conscience, that utterly despises authority look like, in the Church? Well gee, I kind of think it looks like this.

## TRINITY BROADCASTING NETWORK

**BENNY HINN**: *"You wonderful people of God quit attacking man of God by name! Somebody's attacking me because of something I'm teaching. Let me tell you something brother! You watch it! Dear God in heaven, I wish I could just MMPH! (makes a punching motion)*

*You know I looked for one verse in the Bible, I just can't seem to find it-one verse that said if you don't like him, kill him. I really wish I could find it."*

*(Audience laughs)*

**HINN**: *"But don't mention people's names on your radio program and your TV program thinking you're doing God's service. You're not! You stink, frankly! That's the way I think about it."*

*(Audience): AMEN! HALLELUJAH!*

**HINN**: *"Sometimes I wish God would give me a holy ghost machine gun-I blow your head off!"*[14]

Now let me ask the obvious question. Would it be appropriate for me to say that from the pulpit? Then why is it acceptable for that man? Looks to me like he despises authority and has a seared conscience like the Bible said would happen in the Last Days! They're fakes and at least this guy had the guts to admit it:

## MARJOE GORTNER

*"Marjoe Gortner was a famous child evangelist who learned the tricks of the trade utilized by many of today's religious charlatans.*

*Officially ordained at the age of 4, he was the talk of the revival circuit. Large halls would fill will people who came to hear this young, charismatic boy preach.*

*As Marjoe grew into manhood, he continued his "profession", preaching in tent revivals, making thousands of dollars, deceiving large crowds.*

*In the late 60's Marjoe decided to leave the "ministry" but take one last ride on the revival tent trail...only this time to expose himself to the world!*

*With a team of producers and TV cameras, he filmed his own documentary and showed the world how he duped people out of their money, pretending to be a Christian evangelist.*

*Marjoe Gortner confessed that he didn't even believe God existed.*

*The following excerpts are taken from the 1972 documentary:* **Marjoe**

*Marjoe as a young child: "I thank God for my fine Christian mother that's taken me to Jesus. If we had more good Christian mothers that would speak the Word and pray more instead of drinking cocktails and smoking filthy old cigarettes we would have a better America. Better men and women and not so much juvenile delinquency"*

*Marjoe: There would be gestures, like when I say "Jesus" my arms would have to go out. When I would say "the devil" I would go forward. And she had this incredible set of signals. Like she would say "Oh Jesus" if I was going too slow or she would say "Glory to God". That meant you better speed up and go a little bit faster, and later on she would come up with new signals. Like "Praise God" meant you got the people where you need them and you better take an offering and raise some money"*

*Marjoe to a revival audience: "Hallelujah. Hallelujah. Let's raise up our hands and worship the Lord. Praise Him tonight. Hallelujah. (Starts speaking in "tongues" Oh God is so real tonight. If you don't got the Holy Ghost tonight, man, you're dead and don't know it. So why don't you praise Him. Why don't you call upon His name. Why don't you worship the Lord tonight. Put up your hands and praise Him. Hallelujah. Hallelujah. Hallelujah. Oh Hallelujah!"*
*(Lays hands on people as they fall "slain in the spirit)*

*Notice the reaction of Marjoe's admirers. They responded to his magnetism in identical fashion as we often see people respond in packed out stadiums featuring popular preachers today such as Benny Hinn and others.*

*Marjoe to man: "Brother, say Jesus, right now, Jesus"*
*Man: "Jesus"*
*Marjoe: "Say it again"*
*Man: "Jesus"*
*Marjoe: "In the name of Jesus, brother. Say it. Say Jesus. That's right, say Jesus"*
*Man: "Jesus. Jesus"*

*Marjoe talking to interviewer: "There's the experience where you say you're saved and then there's the fire baptism, when you "get" the Holy Ghost and that's the tongues thing, and they love to work people over, where you gotta shoot in on this when you see people gathering around people and start laying hands on them praying with someone. You gotta come in with the camera too. It's very important because they'll be laying hands on someone, a poor person saying "Thank you Jesus" Now this is a person that is already saved but getting "the baptism". Someone will be standing there and we're saying (fakes tongues by speaking jibberish) and the poor person will be standing there and they're not saying anything. Then after awhile, after 4 or 5 more will gather around and they'll start doing the same thing. Oh come, on speak it out, speak it out till all of a sudden the person will get so overwhelmed by the thing they'll start (imitates speaking in tongues). And the next thing you know, ah good, we got another one. Then we'll go on to the next person."*

*Marjoe in a hotel room: (Singing) "Are your garments spotless, are they white as snow. Thank you Jesus (dumps paper bag full of money on the bed) Are you washed in the blood of the Lamb? Jesus is so good to me tonight, Hallelujah. Thank you Jesus (counting piles of cash) I praise the Lord. Oh glory, glory hallelujah. I feel good in my soul. Oh praise the Lord. It sure isn't as heavy as it used to be though in the old days, wow."*

*Marjoe to interviewer: There's one guy that gets into it so heavy that he prophesies and he told me how he did it. I mean he sat...he looked right across the table back and forth at me and he told me how he confiscates money. He says he's on this station that has over 40 states and uh, he'll go on and he get on the radio and he'll say, "I know listening in my little voice tonight that there's some lady out there and you got $10 put away in a cookie jar, now God spoke to my heart and told me to go and tell you to get that $10 and get it in the mail and send it to me and God will bless you. God will give you a reward as you have never known before" Then he comes back to me and tells me if you're on the radio and you're going on over 40 states and you're on at prime time and have thousands of people listening, chances are that there are at least two or three hundred little old ladies who got a $10 bill in a cookie jar and so even if you get a couple hundred to go ahead and get it and send it to you, that's two grand you've made just like that. And so, you know, if you're going to get into big time religion this is the games you gotta play. Things like that. Going into it like a business and work it as a business.*

*Marjoe to woman showing her one of his secrets: "God is going to do something for you." Then I turn around to the crowd and say, "DO YOU BELIEVE IT?" And you know everyone says yes, you know, and I say, "That's not enough! But if there's no faith here tonight I can't do anything. You gotta believe it" and I go "DO YOU BELEIVE IT?" and this time the crowd's like "YES!!" and then I say "sister if I lay my hands on you it's going to happen". By this time you're just like this (shaking and twitching) (laughs) because I do a whole thing on you and then I sort of get like "Now I'm gonna pray the prayer; bow your head." Puts his hand on her forehead "IN THE NAME OF JESUS!" (woman and others start laughing) By this time if the shock doesn't get you, you know (laughs again) then once you get one or two that really come up and say yeah I felt that I had a bad back, got a bad leg then there a host of others that say "yeah i feel better too" because 90% percent of it is psychosomatic."*[15]

We have to wake up and call it like it is. These guys are hucksters, fakes, phonies, and it's high time we admit it like Marjoe did! And the reason why these hucksters get to continue on with this kind of behavior, is because for whatever reason, they have conditioned us to keep our mouths shut by saying stuff like this, "Well, you really shouldn't talk about other pastors in the pulpit. I mean, you really shouldn't call them out by name or say any kind of bad stuff about them in public." Really? Have you ever read your Bible? The Bible says a good Pastor or Shepherd not only *feeds* the sheep but he *protects* the sheep from hirelings who come in to harm the flock, including ripping them off of their cash and promoting false healings! It's the bad Pastor that keeps his mouth shut! In fact, if you read your Bible, you'll see that Jesus not only called out the Pharisees and their false teaching, but He did so *in public*! And He called them a bunch of blind men, blind fools, blind guides, brood of vipers, band of murderers, bag of dead man's bones and a bunch of hypocrites, *in public*! And even the Apostle Paul called out several false teachers *by name*.

**1 Timothy 1:18-20** "Timothy, my son, I give you this instruction in keeping with the prophecies once made about you, so that by following them you may fight the good fight, holding on to faith and a good conscience. Some have rejected these and so have shipwrecked their faith. Among them are Hymenaeus and Alexander, whom I have handed over to satan to be taught not to blaspheme."

**2 Timothy 2:16-18** "Avoid godless chatter, because those who indulge in it will become more and more ungodly. Their teaching will spread like gangrene. Among them are Hymenaeus and Philetus, who have wandered away from the truth. They say that the resurrection has already taken place, and they destroy the faith of some."

I'll say it *again*, when in the world are we going to wake up *in the Church* and call it like it is? These Word of Faith teachers are false teachers and they need to be called out on the carpet by name, like this Pastor did!

## Prosperity Pimps Beware!

*And you listen to me! Every one of you prosperity preachers! Jesus Christ did not die on a cross, He did not take the stripes on his back, He did not take a crown on His head, His side was not pierced that we may drive Rolls Royces and buy twelve thousand dollar dogs and live in 40 million dollar homes. But He died on a cross to save mankind from the power of sin and the grip of darkness! And SHAME ON YOU! SHAME ON YOU! SHAME ON YOU!*

*Man's problem is not what kind of suit he wears or what kind of house he lives in or what kind of car he drives. Man's problem is SIN! And man needs a SAVIOR! And that savior is JESUS CHRIST!*

*There MUST be a reformation of the cross...there MUST be a reformation of...oh you're not gettin' it! I SAID THERE MUST BE A REFORMATION OF THE CROSS!! The church MUST come back! For God so loved the world that He GAVE His only begotten Son! The church must have a reformation of Christ and Him crucified!!*

*I'm angry! I'm mad! I'm tired of God's people being fleeced! We...LISTEN!...you better hang on and buckle your seatbelts! We don't need....anymore prosperity pimps!...leading the church into spiritual idolatry!*

*I SAID!...WE DON'T NEED...ANYMORE..PROSPERITY PIMPS...DOWN A PRIMROSE PATH OF DESTRUCTION! WE DON'T NEED ANY SNAKE OIL SALESMAN! WE NEED MEN OF GOD WHO WILL STAND BEHIND A PULPIT AND PREACH THE GOSPEL!*

*I'm going to say it again! If you're preaching that lie of the greed you are a prosperity pimp. I said....if your gospel...is a gospel of greed, you are a prosperity pimp. And you're gonna stand before God and give an account for every single message that you preached on that... souls are dying and going to hell and you're prostituting the Word of God. Men are bound by alcohol and you're prostituting the Word of God. Homosexuals bound in their sin and you're prostituting the gospel of Jesus Christ!*

*Prosperity pimps...let me tell you what's going on and let me tell ya what's gonna happen. Jesus said when he walked into the temple, "My house shall be called the house of prayer but you have made it a den of thieves" YOU ARE THIEVES! And I'll remind you of what happened. HE CLEANED THE PLACE OUT! AND HE'S GONNA CLEAN THE PLACE OUT AGAIN! YOUR DAY IS NUMBERED! YOUR DAY IS NUMBERED! HE'S ABOUT READY TO TURN OVER THOSE TABLES! HE'S ABOUT READY TO THROW YOU OUT!*

*MY HOUSE SHALL BE CALLED A HOUSE OF PRAYER. WHERE PEOPLE CAN GET SAVED! Not how to have success seminars. I'm sick and tired of preachers saying "we don't want K-mart Christians in this church." Well they don't want ya, but JESUS wants ya! I don't care if you don't have shoes on your feet. Jesus wants you! I don't care if you ain't got two dimes to your name. Jesus wants you! I don't care if you don't know where your next meal is coming from. Jesus wants you!*

*Where...tonight...are the preachers...that will stand up and take a stand. Where are they? We need Jeremiahs. We need some Daniels. We need some Isaiahs. We need some Jehosephats. We need some Davids. We need some Hezekiahs. That says I'm sick and tired of a dirty temple. It's time to clean it up!"*[16]

Amen and amen! Folks, this is what's so wild about this behavior. Do we have any idea what's really going on and just how close we are to the Last Days? How many people, even in the Church, are clueless to the prophetic meaning of what we just read and what we just studied? Every time you turn on the TV and you see one of these *prosperity pimps*, it shouldn't just *make you sick*. It should send this clear message to you. Oh no! I better start living for Jesus! I better start serving God. I better start witnessing more. I better get saved! Why? Because when you see these hucksters on TV it means you are living in the Last Days! We better wake up! It's happening now!

The prosperity gospel is no gospel at all. When you see how it not only rips people off of their cash but leads them away from the true Christ and His calling for us, it makes you sick, like this guy shares:

*"I don't know what you feel about the prosperity gospel, the health, wealth, and prosperity gospel, but I'll tell you what I feel about it...hatred.*

*It is not the gospel. It's being exported from this country to Africa and Asia. Selling a bill of goods to the poorest of the poor.*

*Believe this message, and your pigs won't die and your wife won't have miscarriages and you'll have rings on your fingers and coats on your back. That's coming out of America. The people that ought to be giving our money and our time and our lives. Instead, selling a bunch of crud called gospel.*

*Here's the reason it is so horrible. When was the last time that any American, African, Asian ever said 'Jesus is all satisfying because you drove a BMW?' NEVER. They'll say, 'Did Jesus give you that? Well, I'll take Jesus.' That's Idolatry! That's not the gospel. That's elevating gifts above the giver.*

*✝ I'll tell you what makes Jesus look beautiful. It's when you smash your car and your little girl goes flying through the windshield and lands dead on the street, and you say through the deepest possible pain, "God is enough. He is good. He will take care of us. He will satisfy us. He will get us through this. He is our treasure. Whom have I in heaven but you? And on earth there is nothing that I desire besides you. My flesh and not my heart and my little girl may fail, but you are the strength of my heart and my portion forever."*

*That makes God look glorious. As God, not of giver of cars or safety or health. Oh, how I pray that America would be purged of the health, wealth and prosperity gospel and that the Christian church would be marked by suffering for Christ.*

*God is most glorified in you when you are most satisfied in him in the midst of loss, not prosperity."* [17]

## III - Third Reason - A Flood of Worldly Believers

The **3rd reason** people in the Church have abandoned the Christian faith and Apostacized, is due to **A Flood of Worldly Believers**.

I'm talking about the *Church Growth Movement*. Little do people know that the teachings of the Church Growth Movement have actually aided in this *massive rise of apostasy* in these Last Days! Today, people *in the Church* are being led astray by *marketing manipulation* and *secular business techniques* instead of following what the Bible says as to how we are to "run the Church,"[18] and it's given rise to this massive influx of worldliness in the Church causing this great Apostasy. But don't take my word for it. Let's listen to God's.

**1 Corinthians 1:10-18** "I appeal to you, brothers, in the name of our Lord Jesus Christ, that all of you agree with one another so that there may be no divisions among you and that you may be perfectly united in mind and thought. My brothers, some from Chloe's household have informed me that there are quarrels among you. What I mean is this: One of you says, "I follow Paul"; another, "I follow Apollos"; another, "I follow Cephas"; still another, "I follow Christ." Is Christ divided? Was Paul crucified for you? Were you baptized into the name of Paul? I am thankful that I did not baptize any of you except Crispus and Gaius, so no one can say that you were baptized into my name. (Yes, I also baptized the household of Stephanas; beyond that, I don't remember if I baptized anyone else.) For Christ did not send me to baptize, but to preach the gospel – not with words of human wisdom, lest the cross of Christ be emptied of its power. For the message of the cross is foolishness to those who are perishing, but to us who are being saved it is the power of God."

Now according to our text, I think it's pretty clear. The Apostle Paul had to remind the Corinthian Church, *number one,* to stop playing favorites in the Church, right? Why? Because it causes *divisions*! And *two,* he had to remind them to start being united about that which is truly important in life. Yes, every Christian teacher may have a different personality and thus teaching style, but that's okay, they're equally valuable. Don't get hung up on secondary issues! They're all a gift from God! But when it comes to presenting the Gospel, preaching the Gospel, there's only one methodology. And notice what that is. It's the message of the cross, right? Why? Because through the cross of Jesus Christ, *and that alone,* men might be saved from utter destruction. That's where the power of God flows. That's when lives are changed. That's when souls are saved from hell. Therefore, that's what people need to hear, that's what we need to be about in the Church, that's what we need to promote, right?

*Not anymore!* I'm telling you, we have been divided by the Church Growth Movement and they have convinced us to no longer do "Church" God's way anymore. And for those of you who don't know, the Church Growth Movement is a movement that started in the Church just a few decades ago that says that the best way to run a Church today, is to do it the world's way, not God's way. And they say, if you want to be a successful Church you have to use *secular business ideals and slick marketing techniques* in order to have any kind of Church growth, hence the name, Church Growth Movement. And we are being told that we have to *act* like the world, *be* like the world, *speak* like the world, *look* like the world, and even *do business* like the world, just so the world will *like us.* Why? Because the premise is, if they like us, why, they'll stick around and your numbers will go right through the roof! And isn't that what we want?

But we just saw that the Bible says we need to be about the business of preaching Christ and Him crucified so the world can be *saved*, not made comfortable in the pew! In fact, they may not like us initially because the Bible says the cross is going to be foolishness to them at the beginning! But if you keep on preaching it, it has the power of God to save them! So who cares if they don't like you in the beginning? They're headed to hell! This is serious business. And I'd rather have somebody hate me and end up in heaven, than have them like me and go to hell, right? And yet, this is exactly what The Church Growth Movement is trying to get us to do! Make lost people feel comfortable in the church, just to jack up our numbers, and empty the cross of its power by not mentioning it!

**1. The 1st way they're tricking us into doing this is by Focusing on Numerical Growth Instead of Spiritual Growth.**

**Mathew 28:18-20** "Then Jesus came to them and said, "All authority in heaven and on earth has been given to Me. Therefore go and make disciples of all nations, baptizing them in the name of the Father and of the Son and of the Holy Spirit, and teaching them to obey everything I have commanded you. And surely I am with you always, to the very end of the age.""

Now according to our text, this is the classic passage that we like to call the Great Commission, not the Grand Suggestion, or the Great Idea to ponder over a cup of coffee, it's called The Great Commission. That means it's an order to be obeyed and notice what that order was. We are to go out into all the world, and make what? Oh, I know! Believers, right? People who make a profession of faith? No! Or, I know, Professional Pew Sitters! Oh, I know! We are to go out in the world and get people to show up Sunday mornings just to jack up our attendance, right? That's a successful church, right? Wrong! What did Jesus say? We are to go out in the world and make *disciples*! The word there is "mathetes" and it means, "disciplined learners." Yes, we are to go out and teach people how to get saved but after that, according to Jesus, we are to be about the business of teaching people how to grow up spiritually and obey everything He commanded, right? Spiritual growth comes first!

*Not anymore*! Haven't you heard? That's old-fashioned! We have a whole new focus today! Thanks to the Church Growth Movement we're now being told we need only be concerned about numerical growth and that at all costs! Who cares about that spiritual growth thing. Forget that! People might leave if you talk about them being a sinner! That's bad marketing. Come on! Don't you know how to run a business? Here's what you do. *You entertain them*! Don't worry about that spiritual growth thing. Just entertain them. I mean, everybody loves a good show, right? Just make them feel good, right at home with the world, give them some good old fashioned entertainment and man you'll have more numbers than you know what to do with! Isn't that awesome? Isn't that a successful church?

Excuse me? My Bible says a "successful church" is one that preaches Christ and Him crucified and gets busy teaching people how to obey Him, *not* one that throws out a bunch of syrup so we can attract a bunch of flies! And yet we wonder why there are so many problems "buzzing" around the Church today? I've said it before and I'll say it again, "If you have 500 people in your congregation but only 5 of them are saved, *what in the world did you just accomplish?*" Are you actually trying to *encourage* people to go to hell?

And for those of you who don't think the Church would ever fall for this baloney, I'm telling you, it's not only the "latest craze," but there's actually a new term out there to describe this new way to entertain the lost. It's called "*Theotainment*"[19] Theos/God. In other words "God entertainment." And this is what they say we need to do, "If you want massive amounts of people coming to your church, because remember, numbers are the top priority, you've got to give them this "Theotainment." You have to entertain them with *worldy-looking leaders* who *act* like the world, *speak* like the world, and even *dress* like the world, so they'll feel comfortable. Otherwise they might leave and your numbers will go down. And so the question is, "What does this new and improved worldly looking Theotainment leadership in the Church look like? I think it looks like this guy, Ignatius, the new improved Youth Leader:

## Ignatius Youth Group Pastor

*Becky: My husband and I are taking our first real vacation in 6 years and I'm so excited. I mean, don't get me wrong. I love the students but sometimes you need a break, you know? So I'm really excited because Ignatius is going to cover Wednesday nights for me.*

*Tom: Ignatius is like the biggest name in student ministry. He's worked with the biggest speakers, biggest worship leaders. He has spoken to like a million kids. He's like the Michael Phelps of student ministry.*

*Carl: I'm kind of old fashioned and I don't know much about him but he knows Becky and he loves Jesus and that's enough for me.*

*Ignatius: So people ask me, "Ignatius. What does it take to become a great youth pastor?" Well, my answer is always the same. X-Box 360, a copy of Rock Band, book deal, and uh there's something else. (Tapping fingers on Bible while trying to think of it) umm, yes! A moderately priced haircut. I get my hair cut at Tony & Guy, uh $70 bucks-plus highlights.*

*Our ministry's called Flame and it's based on some verse in the Bible about fire. You know we want to see our kids on fire for God. In the middle of this Godless culture we want to drive a stake in the heart of it. I mean we want our kids...burning at the stake.*

*I take my preparation very seriously. I'll spend 2-3 hours doing something called "Prayer Lattes." Prayer Lattes is when I get on an exercise ball. I have a Latte non-fat. It's like God's my trainer and He's stretching my spiritual muscles as well as my physical muscles.*

*Who are my influences? Bono, of course. C.S. Lewis's Chronicle of Narnia films-they were great. First two were killer. I hope he writes another one."*

*Kelly to Ignatius: Hi, I'm Kelly. Nice to meet you. This is Carl. He's on our volunteer staff.*

*Carl to Ignatius: Hi, Kelly has told us so much about you.*

*Ignatius: All good I hope.*

*Kelly: (laughing)*

*Ignatius: Tell me a little bit about your group.*

*Carl: Well, we had a lock in last weekend and six of our kids made a profession of faith.*

*Ignatius: Ha, you mean 60...*

*Kelly: We're gonna need about 20 minutes before service starts so we can pray.*

*Ignatius: 20 minutes? Do you think it will take that long?*

*Kelly: Eh, ha ...uh and you probably want to spend some time with the students.*

*Ignatius: Why would I wanna to do that?*

.........................

*Room full of students. Music starts blaring.*

*"In the name of love....in the name of love.."*

*Ignatius comes running into the room: Woo high five! Who's your daddy? Huh? Who's your daddy? Did I hear somebody say Ignatius? Alright!*

*My name is Ignatius and tonight we're gonna talk about the God of the Universe and how he loves each and every one of you with an unquenchable fire. But before we do that. Did anyone bring their Bibles tonight?*

*(students raising their hands)*

*Ignatius: Alright, get' em out. Let's get those Bibles out and put them over your head. That's it. And now repeat after me. Say God's Word....*

*Students repeat: God's Word*

*Ignatius: Is Living....*

*And active... It is powerful...It is more...than I can deal with...at this stage...of my life.*

*Students repeat*

*Ignatius: Good! Put 'em under your seat. You're not gonna need 'em tonight.*

-----------------------

*Ignatius: I mean to think there are kids that don't even know about the Flame website is...uh...WOW. Yeah but I want to see them fired up, you know? Engulfed in flames. They're gonna be smoldering. I'm gonna burn em!"*[20]

Yeah, you're going to burn them alright, you're going to burn them straight into hell!

Let's be honest. How many of you have ever been to a Church service and that is the kind of leadership that's in the church? And I'm not just talking youth Pastor, I'm talking the senior Pastor? And they're all about the business of what? Desperately trying to *look* like the world, *act* like the world, *speak* like the world, and even *dress* like the world, so the world will *feel comfortable.* Why? Because haven't you listened to the new gurus of The Church Growth Movement? Forget the Bible! Don't you know, this is exactly what you have to do to get those numbers because number always comes first!

I don't know about you, but if I'm going to grow up spiritually I don't want a Pastor that looks like Bono. I don't want a Pastor who resembles this world. I want a Pastor that looks like Jesus Christ! I want a Pastor that says like the Apostle Paul, "Follow me as I follow Jesus Christ. *Not* follow me as I follow the way of this world! I want somebody to pull me out of this wicked world system! Not push me back into it, right? And lest you think this is only happening to YOUTH MINISTRIES, you're wrong! Even ADULT MINISTRIES are choosing worldly entertainment "Theotainment," over the Word of God, and all for the sake of numbers!

**The Drive-Thru Church:** Believe it or not there's a new drive thru church in Davenport Iowa, where services only take about five minutes and you don't even have to get out of the car. 'Just pull up in our parking lot,' the Rev. Rich Hendricks suggests where he promises some humor in the offerings with congregants, for example, will be dressed like anglers in tune with a fish theme. In fact, everyone will be given communion, but this will be specially delivered in a tackle box and a clean bait cup. A station will be set up for an informal church choir, and those interested may exit their vehicles and sing. Participants also will take home a special gift in the form of brightly colored fish key chains or other accessories.

**The Clown Communion Church:** A sassy little Episcopal Church in New York City now not only has a clown performing communion services, but the congregants are encouraged to dress up as clowns themselves. Looking like refugees from a Ringling Bros. and Barnum and Bailey Circus, the Rev. Dr. James Herbert Cooper, encouraged the parish family to come to church "in clown dress, big hats, floppy shoes or some sort of foolish garb." In fact, he encouraged those watching on the Internet to also be foolish enough to put on some white face or a big grease-paint smile as we worship God and learn about the structure of the communion by being the circus which came to town and to church on that day. And after the offering was taken for that day the people responded with their noisemakers.

**The Porn Movie Church:** The People's Church, formerly known as The First Baptist Church, in Franklin, Tennessee recently achieved national attention by hosting a special event they called "Porn Sunday." Believe it or not they actually showed an 'R' rated film entitled, "Missionary Positions," to allegedly help those addicted to pornography. In fact, one of the makers of the film said, "We can't keep up with the amount of requests to do these 'Porn Sunday' things, so we're doing a national 'Porn Sunday.' And one church that hosted the event actually said they had one of the best days ever in church.[21]

Now I don't know about you, but for some reason I don't think Jesus came all the way from heaven to die a horrible death on the cross just so we can sit around celebrating Porn Sundays! Looks to me like we've gotten off track somewhere. I mean, it's almost like we've bought into some sort of a lie that's tricked us into focusing only on numerical growth instead of spiritual growth. And that we have to entertain people instead of sharing the Gospel with them just so they'll keep coming back. Gee, if only we knew what that lie was. If only we could discover why this is happening to the Church. Oh yeah, that's right! It's called the *Church Growth Movement*! And because of it, we're seeing a massive increase of worldliness and apostasy in the Church exactly like the Bible said would happen in the Last Days!

**2. The 2nd way the Church Growth Movement is helping to produce this massive rise of worldliness and apostasy in the Church is by getting us to Focus on Cultural Music Instead of Christ-like Music.**

**Ephesians 5:17-20** "Therefore do not be foolish, but understand what the Lord's will is. Do not get drunk on wine, which leads to debauchery. Instead, be filled with the Spirit. Speak to one another with psalms, hymns and spiritual songs. Sing and make music in your heart to the Lord, always giving thanks to God the Father for everything, in the name of our Lord Jesus Christ."

Now according to our text, the Bible clearly says that one of the best things you and I could ever do with music is to what? We are to praise God with it, right? In fact, Sebastian Bach said, "The sole purpose of all music is to bring praise to God." And this is why every time we gather together, as the Church, we are to sing songs to God that are God-glorifying, God-honoring, and God-exalting. Why? Because we are so in love with Him, after all He's done for us, we can't help but sings songs back to Him, right?

*Not anymore*! First of all, when it comes to music in the Church, we usually seem to get side-tracked with what I believe is the main point of music and we start to debate which is better, hymns or contemporary, like this guy.

*"One day this old farmer went to the city one weekend and attended one of those big city churches. And when he came home his wife asked him how it was.*

*And the farmer said, "Well, it was good. They did something different, though. They sang these praise choruses instead of hymns."*

*"Praise choruses?" said his wife. "What are those?"*

*"Oh, they're OK. They are sort of like hymns, only different," said the farmer.*

*"Well, what's the difference?" asked his wife.*

*The farmer said, "Well, it's like this - If I were to say to you: "Martha, the cows are in the corn" - well, that would be a hymn. If on the other hand, I were to say to you:*

*'Martha, Martha, Martha,*
*Oh Martha, MARTHA, MARTHA,*
*the cows, the big cows, the brown cows, the black cows*
*the white cows,*
*the black and white cows,*
*the COWS, COWS, COWS*
*are in the corn,*
*are in the corn, are in the corn, are in the corn,*
*the CORN, CORN, CORN.'*

*Then, if I were to repeat the whole thing two or three times, well, that would be a praise chorus."*

*Well, the next weekend, his nephew, a young new Christian from the city came to visit and he attended the local church of the small town. He went home and his mother asked him how it was.*

*"Well," said the young man, "it was good. They did something different though. They sang these hymns instead of our regular songs."*

*"Hymns?" asked his mother. "What are those?"*

*"Oh, they're OK. They are sort of like our regular songs, only different," said the young man.*

*"Well, what's the difference?" asked his mother.*

*The young man said, "Well, it's like this - If I were to say to you: 'Martha, the cows are in the corn' - well, that would be a regular song. If on the other hand, I were to say to you:*

*'Oh Martha, dear Martha, hear thou my cry
Inclinest thine ear to the words of my mouth
Turn thou thy whole wondrous ear by and by
To the righteous, inimitable, glorious truth.*

*For the way of the animals who can explain*

*Yea those cows in glad bovine, rebellious delight
Have broke free their shackles, their warm pens eschewed
Then goaded by minions of darkness and night
They all my mild Chilliwack sweet corn have chewed.*

*So look to the bright shining day by and by
Where all foul corruptions of earth are reborn
Where no vicious animals make my soul cry
And I no longer see those foul cows in the corn.'*

*Then if I were to do only verses one, three and four and do a key change on the last verse, well that would be a hymn."*[22]

Now does that sound familiar or what? The point of Christian music is not one or the other, hymns or contemporary, it's whatever the style you sing with, according to our text, you what? You sing from your heart *to Jesus*, a love song *to Jesus* right? As long as it's God-glorifying, God-honoring, and *mentions the Name of Jesus Christ*, who cares if it's hymns or contemporary, right?

*Not anymore!* Thanks to the lie of The Church Growth Movement, we're now being told we should no longer do the music in the Church God's way! No! That's old-fashioned! You've got to do it the world's way! Why? Because it's all about those numbers! And so here's what you do! You've got to gut all your songs of this Jesus and God stuff and just switch to generic terms that make them feel more comfortable, like He or Him. Why? Because the world doesn't like hearing song after song after song about God and Jesus and the Bible. I mean, what are you, some sort of religious wacko? Are you trying to run them off? That's bad marketing. They'll get convicted and leave! If you want big numbers, here's what you do. You sings songs that are *not* convicting to the culture, but are *comfortable* to the culture. Which means, you've got to sing songs that they like, and that fits their style and their preferences, and Man you keep that up, listen, you're going to have numbers coming out of your ears! Huh? Isn't that a successful Church? I mean, everybody loves a good concert, right? Isn't that what it's all about?

Now you might be thinking nobody in their right mind in the Church would ever fall for this baloney, but I'm telling you this has become yet another "latest craze" in the Church to lead people in so-called worship. But my question is, "Just who are you worshiping?" You never mention the name of Jesus. You only say He or Him. And so I'm left wondering who is that? Are you singing about your boyfriend, your fiancé, your husband? Who's He? Why don't you mention the Name of Jesus? This is a Church service! We're supposed to be singing love songs to Jesus! What's wrong with Jesus?

And me personally, I think I know why this is happening. Put yourself in the shoes of a demon; the last thing you'd ever want to hear people singing in the Church, especially in the Last Days, is the name of Jesus, right? Why? Because they know there's no other name under heaven by which men might be saved and there's no other name under heaven by which the demons must cower, obey and flee! That's why they convinced us to gut our so-called "worship music" of the name of Jesus Christ! I really believe it's spiritual warfare! It not only makes the world feel comfortable, it makes the demons feel comfortable in the Church! Don't *pray* in the Name of Jesus and don't *sing* about the Name of Jesus!

And then if that wasn't bad enough, speaking of selling out, there's yet another new trend in the American Church! We all know, every Church is hurting for cash in this depressed economy, right? Well get this, churches are now selling out to corporations to drum up cash, and it makes you wonder if our songs aren't next, like this mans shares:

*"I was reading in Time Magazine-there was an article-it was in Time so it was probably true. So I was reading, it was talking about how a lot of churches are selling out to corporations all over the world. Churches selling out to corporations?! Can you imagine outside this beautiful building- a big NIKE*

*swoosh? No, no no. Just "Pew it"? No! That'd be wrong. Your pastor's silhouette (Makes swoosh stance). It's dumb.*

*Pretty soon corporations, I know what they're gonna do-they're gonna take our praise and worship songs. You know, songs we love in church, put their words to our songs. That's just going to be horrible.*

*One of my favorites is (sings) "Holiness. Holiness is what I long for. Holiness is what I need." What's it going to be now?*

*"Krispy Kremes. Krispy Kremes. What I long for. Krispy Kremes. What I need. Krispy Kremes. Krispy Kremes. What I want to eat. Take some dough and form it. Add some glaze. And warm it. Chew it up. Transform it. Oh Lord. Oh Lord. Oh Lord. Gimme more."*

*And the car companies will get into it, ya know.*

*"Ford I lift your name on high. Ford I love to sing your praises. I'm so glad you're 4-wheel drive. I'm so glad you're fuel injected"*

*"My Dodge is an awesome Dodge it is. Such a really nice car he drives. A Dodge is an awesome Dodge."*

*"Better is Hyundai than a Ford. Better is Hyundai than a Jeep. Better is a Hyundai than a Chevy or a Hugo. Better is Hyundai. Better is Hyundai."*

*You know what's gonna happen? The "I Can't Believe It's Not Butter People" They're gonna catch on and then it will get really weird.*

*"I can only eat margarine. It's all I can do. Because I don't like butter or butter substitute. I can only eat margarine. Yeah. Surrounded by some biscuits or on a piece of bread. On top of a Cheese It. It's an artificial spread. Oh I can't live without it. I'll eat it with all of my grub. Sometimes I just take a spoon and eat it outta the plastic tub. I can only eat margarine. Yeah. I can only eat margarine."*[23]

Did you pay attention to what he said at the beginning there? This is not make-believe. Churches today are *already* selling out to corporations! Which means, all kidding aside, those kinds of worship songs aren't that far away! Why? Because I'm here to tell you, we're already there! Remember, the premise of the Church Growth Movement. All for the sake of numbers you need to do what? Our music in the Church needs be what the culture likes, not what Christ likes, not God-honoring music, but world-honoring music! We need to cater to our styles, all for the sake of numbers, to *their* preferences, including the rock band AC/DC. Don't believe me? It was already played at a so-called Church service![24] Here's the lyrics if you're not familiar with that song. Keep in mind, this was what was sung at a so-called Church service:

**Perry Noble's New Spring Church**

*Worship band starts playing.*

*"Living easy, living free, Season ticket on a one-way ride. Asking nothing, leave me be. Taking everything in my stride.*
*Don't need reason, don't need rhyme. Ain't nothing I'd rather do. Going down, party time. My friends are gonna be there too.*

*Yeah! I'm on the highway to hell, on the highway to hell, highway to hell, I'm on the highway to hell. Ooo yeah!"*

Yup, AC/DC in the Church. Don't you feel comfortable now? Folks, what's next? Where do you draw the line? Metallica? Garth Brooks? Brittany Spears? You mean to tell me that we in the Church can't come up with some better songs on our own, to make a point or worship Jesus, and instead we need the help of secular God-hating entities to help us out with our worship music? What? People, that song celebrates people's gladness over going to hell *in the Church*!

But we are Christians! And we are called to worship Jesus Christ with our music, because He's rescued us from hell! We're going to heaven! And that's why our music in the Church should not only be God-glorifying, God-honoring, and God-exalting but it is to never, ever, ever, ever be ashamed of mentioning the name of Jesus Christ! Who cares what the world thinks! Who cares if it makes them feel comfortable or not! It's not about *them* it's about *Him*! It's about *Jesus*! And we are to praise His Name and give Him the glory and honor He is due and the proper recognition at our Church services, like this guy did:

*"If I had the pleasure of bringing out Christ, this is just how I would do it. It ain't got to be the way you do it. You might not think it's just right. But this is how I would do it.*

*Ladies and Gentlemen. It is my honor to introduce a Man who needs no introduction. His credits are too long to list. He has done the impossible. Time after time. He hails out of a manger in Bethlehem to Jerusalem, by way of heaven...His daddy is author of a book that has been on the bestseller list since the beginning of time. He holds the record from the world's greatest fish fry. He fed five thousand hungry souls with 2 fish and 5 loaves of bread. He can walk on water. Turn water into wine-no special effects, no camera tricks. He has a head shot on every church fan in America. Even before the kings of comedy he was hailed the KING of all kings. Ruler of the Universe, Alpha and Omega, Beginning and the End, the Bright and the Morning Star. Some say He's the Rose of Sharon and some say He's the Prince of Peace. Get up on your feet. Put you're hands together and show your love for the second coming of the One and Only!*

*(standing ovation)*

*God has been good.* "[25]

Isn't that how our "worship" services to JESUS need to be? After all He's done for us? Makes you wonder if we truly worshiped Him like that if more souls would be saved. That's a secular concert that was done at. How much more so at out weekly Church services? I don't know, correct me if I'm wrong, but it looks to me like we've gotten off track somewhere, you know what I'm saying? I mean, it's almost like we've been tricked into buying into some sort of a lie that's tricked us into focusing only on *cultural music* instead of *Christ-like* music just so people will feel comfortable. Gee, if only we knew what that lie was. If only we could discover why this is happening to the Church. Oh yeah, that's right! It's called the Church Growth Movement! And because of it, we're seeing a massive increase of worldliness and Apostasy in the Church, like the Bible said would happen in the Last Days!

**3. The 3rd way the Church Growth Movement is helping to produce this massive rise of worldliness and apostasy in the Church is by getting us to Focus on Fluffy Teachings Instead of Godly Teachings.**

And that's exactly what God said would happen in the Last Days! But don't take my word for it, let's listen to His.

**2 Timothy 4:1-4** "In the presence of God and of Christ Jesus, who will judge the living and the dead, and in view of his appearing and his kingdom, I give you this charge: Preach the Word; be prepared in season and out of season; correct, rebuke and encourage – with great patience and careful instruction. For the time will come when men will not put up with sound doctrine. Instead, to suit their own desires, they will gather around them a great number of teachers to say what their itching ears want to hear. They will turn their ears away from the truth and turn aside to myths."

Now according to our text, the Bible clearly says that there will actually come a day, in the Last Days, because that's the context here…it actually stems over from Chapter Three where Paul says, "But mark this: There will be terrible times in the Last Days," and then he proceeds to give a whole list of rotten evil behavior by people in general who, as we saw before, are lovers of self, lovers of money, greedy, boastful, prideful, abusive, disobedient, ungrateful, unholy, unloving, unforgiving, slanderous, out-of-control, brutal, evil, treacherous, rash, and conceited! And as we saw before, every single one of those wicked behaviors is *commonplace* in our society *right now*! Now pay attention. We're still in the context of the Last Days of Chapter Four here and notice that Paul says something horrible is also going to go wrong this time with the Church. And notice what it is. "People in the Church will not put up with sound doctrine." They're not going to like hearing the Bible. "Instead, to suit their own desires, they will gather around them a great number of teachers to say what their itching ears want to hear." The word "itching" is actually the Greek word, *"knetho"* which means, "to desire only that which is pleasant." Which means, in the Last Days, people in the Church will only want to hear *fluff*! So much so that they will purposely gather around themselves <u>many</u> teachers who will only give them this fluff…not God's Word!

Can I tell you something? This passage of Scripture is being fulfilled before our very eyes, which means we are of that generation who are living in the Last Days! How do I know? Because this is precisely what the lie of The Church Growth Movement is telling us we need to do in order to be a "successful church." We need to preach *fluff and only fluff* so people will keep coming back! If you want your numbers to go through the roof, you've got to *gut* all your sermons of anything that might actually *convict people*, you know, things like sin, and hell, and God's wrath and His hatred towards sin, don't do that! What are you, some crazy religious wacko? Don't do that! That's counter productive! They might leave! So here's what you do. Don't *convict* them, but *coax* them! Don't make them feel *bad*, make them feel *glad*! Give them fluff and only fluff, and tell them how good they are, and that God loves them and there's no need to fear! And then tell them how to be financially successful, how to live the American Dream with a high self-esteem, you know *learn to be a better you.* And man you keep that up, whew! You're going to have numbers coming out of your ears! Huh? Isn't that awesome? Isn't that a successful church? I mean, everybody loves a good motivational speech, right?

Now you might be thinking, nobody in their right mind in the Church would ever fall for this baloney, because it's so clear, it's right here in the text! It's been here for 2,000 years so we wouldn't be caught off guard, right? People in the Last Days will only want fluff, so don't do that, right? *Not anymore!* I'm telling you, we are falling for this *lie,* hook, line and sinker from The Church Growth Movement! Little do people realize that every time you see one of these impotent worldly preachers on TV tickling people ears week after week, it's actually a sign we're living in the Last Days! But don't take my word for it! Let's listen to theirs. You tell me if this is not fluffy godless teaching over the life-changing Word of God!

**Seeker Sensitive/Entertainment church leaders**:

**Steven Furtick of Elevation Church**: *The number one question people seem to ask me these days has nothing to do with theology or ministry. It's all about the hair. Man how did you go from having bold black hair to this platinum pastor that you are today?*

**Fallen pastor Ted Haggard**: *You know all the surveys say that evangelicals have the best sex life of any other group.*

**TV preacher**: *If you're single I want to encourage you, for the next four weeks. I want to encourage you to buy this book "Sex God" by Rob Bell. It's in our bookstore.*

**Another church promotion: 30 day Sex Challenge**.
*Inside, there's a place to write your top two needs that your partner should address over the next 30 days. Make sure you're specific in how your spouse can meet your needs.*

**JOEL OSTEEN Channel 11 News**

*He's your Texas preacher with a positive message, a best selling book, and a dazzling smile but he also has his critics.*

**Ole Anthony**: *"It's a perverted gospel"*

**Joel Osteen**: *I think that's the message that's caught on, why so many people watch because I'm always building them up telling them what they can do.*

**Karen Borta reporting**: *Each weekend, tens of thousands of people from around the world come to Houston.*

**Osteen to audience**: *How many of you are ready to worship the Lord today? Amen?*

**Borta**: *Each is seeking the same thing: a sermon by Joel Osteen-Senior Pastor at Houston's Lakewood Church.*

**Osteen to some ladies**: *Y'all watch it over there?*

**Borta**: *These women are from East Africa.*

**Women**: *God, I'm speechless. I'm glad I came here today.*

**Borta**: *Joe and Pamela DiDonadan are from Toronto*

**Joe:** *Joel Osteen's messages are extremely positive and nothing about negativity. Borta: Such testimonials aren't unusual. More than 30 thousand adults regularly attend his church, making it by some accounts, the largest and fastest growing congregation in America. His weekly sermon is broadcast in more than 100 countries and he now has a best selling book. What makes him so popular?*

**Osteen**: *We're not beating people down. I just feel like we got enough negative things putting us down. I try to give people a boost for the week. Make it practical and relevant.*

**Borta**: *But even if thousands are drawing to Osteen's positive message, some folks just aren't buying it.*

**Ole Anthony**: *It's a perverted gospel that panders to the individual self, the isolated self and that's the problem with it.*

**Borta**: *Ole Anthony is the President and Founder of the Trinity Foundation, a Dallas based televangelist watchdog group. He says Osteen's message is simply cotton-candy theology.*

**Ole Anthony**: *I would have no problem with him if he was doing it in the name of Bruce or saying it was some kind of self-help seminar but it has really nothing to do with the Cross of God.*

-------------

*His latest book, Become a Better You, for which he reportedly got a $13 million advance, goes on sale tomorrow. They read more like self-help than religion. In his new book, Osteen lays out 7 principles he believes will improve our lives.*

*Reporter to Osteen: To Become a Better You, you must be positive towards yourself. Develop better relationships. Embrace the place where you are.*

**Osteen**: *Yeah.*

**Reporter**: *Not one mention of God in that. Not one mention of Jesus Christ in that.*

**Osteen**: *That's just my message. There's a lot better people qualified to say here's a book to explain the scriptures to you. I don't think that's my gift.*

**Reporter**: *His supporters say that Osteen simply has a God given ability to make people smile.*

**Osteen**: *God's given me a great life and I've always smiled all my life. In my baby pictures I'm smiling so, you know, people kid me about it but I think it's great. I love to smile.*

**Reporter**: *Osteen never went to the seminary and only went to college for one semester, but he said after editing his father's sermons for 17 years-he's qualified to preach. "*[26]

Now if all it took to become a preacher was to "edit some sermons" then my wife could preach! But we're not going to do that because that's not Biblical! But seriously, what did the Bible say? In the Last Days, the Church would gather round themselves *many* teachers who would tickle their ears with things like you just read. Learn how to be financially successful, learn how to have a fulfilling sex life, learn to be a better you and anything and everything but God's Word, right? Can you believe it? It's happening before our very eyes! Which means, like it or not, we are living in the Last Days!

I'm telling you, if there's any hope for our nation, then we have got to get serious about God's truth again *in the Church*! We've got to start preaching it again in our churches throughout our country if there's any hope to turn things around, like this guy shares:

*"It grieves me to say that, for the most part, the modern Christian, the modern pastor, and the modern church have lost their savor. Taken as a whole, we have lost our inner character: the ability to resist decay and preserve the land.*

*Our churches are no longer places of respite from the world, they are mirrors of it: the same dress; the same attitudes; the same carnality; the same spirit; the same stubbornness; the same pride.*

*Churches are no longer bastions of truth. They are glorified social clubs or mere corporations, where Christianity is never allowed to interfere with business. Instead of being watchmen on the wall, our pastors are CEOs or, even worse, politicians. Popularity and personal ambition far outweigh the commitment to truth.*

*We have a pandemic all right, but it's not the swine flu, it is a pandemic of spineless Christianity. Parents who cannot stand up to their own children; pastors who cannot stand up to their own congregations; religious leaders who cannot stand up to politicians; and churches that cannot stand up to unconstitutional government.*

*If one is looking for someone to blame America's demise on, don't look to the prostitutes, drug dealers, or crooked politicians: look no further than the doorsteps of America's churches. While the ominous clouds of oppression and tyranny boil overhead, our churches are content to play kid games and wallow in their own materialism and laziness.*

*Sadder still is the lack of anything on the horizon that points to any kind of spiritual awakening. Look at the churches that are growing: for the most part, they are of the Joel Osteen and Rick Warren variety, where conviction has been replaced with compromise, and principle with popularity.*

*And genuine Bible prophets now occupy the pulpits where hardly anyone attends. Truth has been replaced with entertainment, and calls for repentance are drowned out by the clamor of prosperity.*

*I can tell you from personal experience that, in more than 34 years of Gospel ministry, it has never been harder to continue to carry the torch of truth than it is today. It takes a toll on one's physical health and emotional being, and even on one's family.*

*Any pastor desiring to carry the torch of truth today need not expect to have many friends. And any evangelist desiring to carry the torch of truth today need not expect to get many meetings. Why?*

*Because truth today is about as popular as a bad case of the measles, and yes, I mean among today's professing 'Christians.'"*[27]

Folks, we had better get motivated before it's too late. We are heading over a cliff and unless we change *now* we are not coming back! Church Historians are calling us the *terminal generation*. Meaning that if this generation of Christians do not turn things around and start getting truly serious about God's Word, the Gospel and Jesus Christ, *it's over*! We're not coming back! We've gone too far!

You also need to understand that it isn't always just the pastors who are refusing to preach God's truth. A lot of times it's the Church! Here's what's going on. There are still faithful men in America who will preach God's truth, but my experience has been that in the Church they will not hire these guys nor let them preach the truth, otherwise they fire them! Why? Because what did our text say? It's not just the preachers who would only preach this fluff, it's the what? The Churches, en masse would demand *only* this fluff! In the Last Days, the "Churches will gather around themselves a great many teachers to say what their itching ears want to hear." It's not just the Pastors. It's the Churches too! The Churches only want these guys and so that's all you get, all over the place, that's your only option, even on TV! Why? Because maybe it's a sign that God's *judging us,* not blessing us, like this guy shares:

*"Your 'best life now'? I will not lose sleep tonight worried about your best life now. I will not pray tonight or tomorrow worried for their best life now or whether they have self-esteem or their checkbook is balanced or that they got 40 days or 90 days or 100 days of "purpose" in their life.*

*I will lose sleep because one day every one of you will stand before God naked and be judged and some of you will be cast into hell.*

*Preachers. You're not professionals. You're not businessmen. You're not little boys running around serving the community. You're prophets or you're NOTHING!*

*To bring a Word from God. These are people dying. The wrath of God lays waste your community even as we speak. How many people will be swept away even today by the wrath of God through death in hell? And you're worried about whether or not someone feels good about themself?*

*False teachers are God's judgment on people who don't want God but in the name of religion plan on getting everything their carnal heart desires. That's why a Joel Osteen is raised up. Those people who sit under him are not victims of him. He is the judgment of God upon them because they want exactly what he wants and it's not God!"*[28]

I don't know about you, but it looks like we are under the judgment of God, because that's exactly what we're seeing today. God's given us what we want alright, and it's *not Him*. So He's raised up these fluffy panty-waist preachers just like the Bible said would happen in the Last Days! Why? Because we've bought into the lie of The Church Growth Movement that says we have to give people only fluffy motivational speeches instead of the Word of God, just so they'll keep coming back, because haven't you heard…it's all about the numbers! That's what makes for a successful church these days! And because of it, we're seeing a massive growth alright, it's a growth of worldliness and apostasy in the Church, just like the Bible said would happen when you are living in the Last Days!

**4.** The 4th **way** the Church Growth Movement is helping to produce this massive rise of worldliness and apostasy in the Church is by getting us to **Focus on a Powerless Gospel Instead of the True Gospel.**

**Galatians 1:6-9** "I am astonished that you are so quickly deserting the one who called you by the grace of Christ and are turning to a different gospel – which is really no gospel at all. Evidently some people are throwing you into confusion and are trying to pervert the gospel of Christ. But even if we or an angel from heaven should preach a gospel other than the one we preached to you, let him be eternally condemned! As we have already said, so now I say again: If anybody is preaching to you a gospel other than what you accepted, let him be eternally condemned!"

Now according to our text, this is a serious issue! The Bible clearly says that if anyone ever dares preach another Gospel other than the one and only True Gospel, that of Jesus Christ and His death on the cross that's accepted by faith as full payment for our sins to rescue us from hell, then what? Let that person be *eternally condemned,* right? It's the Greek word, "*anathema*" which means, "accursed, devoted to destruction, or doomed to eternal punishment." And how many of you guys would say that's a serious warning? Uh huh! And so therefore, the last thing you'd ever want to do in the Church is be about the business of promoting a false Gospel, right?

*Not anymore!* Thanks to the lie of the Church Growth Movement we're now being told we need to *preach a new and Improved Gospel*! Why? Because that old Gospel damages people's self-esteem. What are you, some sort of religious wacko? Don't you know if you start preaching that Jesus Christ is the only way to heaven that that's not politically correct? I mean, what are you trying to do, run people off? And don't you realize that if you start talking about sin and the need to repent of it and cast your life upon the mercies of God to be rescued from the Wrath to come, that people will leave? Don't you know how to run a business? That's bad marketing! So here's what you do. You say that, "God has a plan for your life," so when people come forward they just say, "Okay, I accept God's plan for me." I'm in like flint! They'll stick around for that. That's not the Gospel! Or I know, you just tell them "You just need to believe in God and that God loves you!" Excuse me? The Bible says even the demons believe in God and they ain't going to heaven! Or I know, worse yet just tell them, "There is no hell, no need to worry, we're all going to be just fine." And man you keep that up, preach this *new and improved gospel*, and whew! You're going to have numbers coming out of your ears! Huh? Isn't that awesome? Isn't that a successful church? I mean, everybody loves to hear *how good they are*, especially when it comes to eternal matters, right?

Now you might be thinking that nobody in their right mind in the Church would ever fall for this baloney. I mean come on, this is Basic Christianity 101.

It's only through the cross of Jesus Christ that men might be saved, right? *Not anymore!* I'm telling you, we not only have men in the pulpit who are only preaching fluff, we have men in the pulpit who are preaching a different gospel. In fact, they can't even define what the Gospel is! Don't believe me? Listen to their own words!

**Fox Sunday with Chris Wallace**

**Chris Wallace**: *And what about Mitt Romney and I gotta ask you the question because it is a question, whether it should be or not in this campaign is, is a Mormon a true Christian?*

**Joel Osteen**: *Well in my mind they are. Mitt Romney says that he believes in Christ as his savior and that's what I believe so, you know, I'm not the one to judge the little details of it. So I believe they are so, you know, Mitt Romney seems like a man of character and integrity to me and I don't think anything would stop me from voting for him if that's what I felt like.*

**Chris Wallace**: *So, so when people start talking about Joseph Smith, the founder of the church and golden tablets in upstate N.Y. and uh, and God assumes the shape of a man. Do you not get hung up in those theological issues?*

**Osteen**: *I probably don't get hung up in them because I haven't really studied them or thought about them and um thought I'd try and let God be the judge of that.*

---------------------------------------

**Tony Jones**: *Listen, for me John, for me it's a daily...DAILY I wonder if this whole thing is a total crock-DAILY! I think-is there really a God? Is my whole life based on a hoax? Everyday I make a decision to go on one day more. I mean really. I'm agnostic in that sense in that I--everyday I don't know.*

**Rob Bell Promo of Love Wins**

**Rob Bell**: *Several years ago we had an art show at our church and people brought in all kinds of sculptures and paintings and we put them on display and* *there was this one piece that had a quote from Ghandi in it. And lots of people found this piece compelling. They'd stop and sort of stare at it and take it in and start to reflect on it. But not everybody found it that compelling. Somewhere in the course of the art show, somebody attached a handwritten note to the piece and on the note they had written, "Reality check. He's in hell"*

*Ghandi's in hell? He is? And someone knows this for sure and felt the need to let the rest of us know.*

*This is why lots of people want nothing to do with the Christian faith. They see it as an endless list of absurdities and inconsistencies and they say, "Why would I ever want to be a part of that?"*

*The good news is that "love wins."*

-------------------------------------------

## Brian McLaren and Tony Jones Emergent Church Leaders

**McLaren**: *In an ironic way, the doctrine of hell basically says no but that's not really true. In the end God gets His way through coercion and violence and intimidation and domination. Just like every other kingdom does. The cross isn't the center then. The cross is almost a distraction and false advertising for God. (laughs)*

**Jones**: *Oh Brian, that was just so beautifully said. I was tempted to get on my soapbox there and...and...and you know, because as you and I know there are so many illustrations and examples you could give that show why the traditional view of hell completely falls in the face of uh, it's antithetical to the cross. But the way you put it there uh, I loved that. I mean it's false advertising.*

---------------------------------

## Joel Osteen on Larry King Live

**Female caller**: *Thank you Joel Osteen for your positive messages and your book. I'm wondering though, why you sidestepped Larry's earlier question about how we get to heaven and the Bible clearly tells us that Jesus is the way, the truth and the life and the ONLY way to the Father is through Him and that's not really a* *message of condemnation but of truth.*

**Joel Osteen**: *Yeah, I would agree with her. I believe that.*

**Larry**: *So then a Jew is not going to hell.*

**Osteen**: *No, no. Here's my thing, Larry, is that I can't judge somebody's heart, you know. I don't know-only God can look at somebody's heart and so I don't know-to me it's not my business to say this one is and this one isn't and I'm just saying here's what the bible teaches and I'm going to put my faith in you know, in uh Christ and I think it's wrong when we go around saying you're not going, you're not going, you're not going cause it's not exactly my way. I believe my way with all my heart.*

**Larry**: *But assume someone doesn't share it. Well it's wrong isn't it?*

**Osteen**: *Well I don't know if I look at it like that. I would present my way but I'm just going to let God be the judge of that. I mean I don't know. I don't know."*[29]

    Then why in the world are you even in the pulpit? He even went on to say that he wasn't going to judge an atheist on whether or not they were going to heaven or hell! Excuse me? Put all these together and what are these so-called pastors saying *from the pulpit*? Mormons are going to heaven? Atheists and Jews are going to heaven? Anybody goes to heaven? There is no hell and the cross is actually a false advertisement for God? What??? People, if you are in these guy's camp you better run! Why? Because the Bible says if anyone ever dares preach another Gospel than the one and only True Gospel, through Jesus Christ and His death on the cross which *can* save us from hell…*yes it's real*! Then what? Let that person, including those guys, be *eternally condemned*! They are accursed, they are devoted to destruction and they are doomed to eternal punishment." Why? Because you had the audacity to wimp out on the Gospel all for the sake of numbers and instead you promoted a false gospel that is leading people straight into hell!

    In fact, let's put their so-called gospel to the test. Let's see if we can rescue people from hell with the false gospel these men of The Church Growth Movement are promoting. Imagine your loved ones headed into the pit, your kids, grandkids, parents, siblings, co-workers, neighbors, whoever, and there they go, one after another, headed into the pit of hell. And they are going at a rapid rate because statistics say that there are 1.8 deaths per second, which multiplies

to over 100 deaths per minute, or 150,000 deaths per day and over 55 million deaths per year. Now let's see if we can rescue them from hell with The Church Growth Movement techniques. Here we go. Here's what we say just before they fall over the pit into hell:
Just believe in God....He loves you....
God has a plan for your life....He'll help you live the American Dream...
Learn to be a better you...hold your Bible up and achieve your full potential
There is no hell...that's not really a pit you're falling into....

And we wonder why God's Word said, let these people who say these things *be eternally condemned*! You are devoted to destruction and you are doomed to eternal punishment. Why? Because this is not a game! How dare you do this! You had the opportunity to save people from eternal damnation in hell but you didn't! You wimped out and chose to curse them for all eternity because you're more concerned about popularity and numbers! How dare you! Anathema is right!

Why is this happening? Why is not only the world going down the tubes, but now even the Church is going down the tubes. Why are we getting so worldly? Why is there so much apostasy? Why is there so little power in the Church today? I'll tell you why! Because we have been tricked into buying into the lie of The Church Growth Movement and because of it, we're seeing a massive growth alright, a growth of worldliness and apostasy *in the Church* exactly like the Bible said would happen when you are living in the Last Days!

People, this is not a game! If you're a part of one of these *Harlot Churches* that is preaching a false Gospel in these Last Days, with worldly dress, and worldly music, and worldly leadership, I'll say it again, you better come out from them and be ye separate, because the Bible says they are headed for destruction, like these guys admit:

**Wake up call to the church. Montage of preachers:**

**David Wilkerson**: *The Church has forgotten it's foundations. A church that has turned away from it's beginnings and begins to become a harlot church.*

**Carter Conlon**: *Just tell me how blessed I am. Just tell me I'm going to be powerful and popular and gonna have no trouble in life. Just tell me these things.*

**David Wilkerson**: *Watered down. Half truths. This gospel says just believe and get saved. There's nothing of repentance, nothing of godly sorrow, nothing of* *turning from your sins, nothing about taking up your cross and following the Lord. But people who say a little prayer, who said you're fine-you're good.*

**Keith Daniel**: *Now we've revised that and said if you can get people for one hour on Sunday morning and into the building-that's the church. That's NOT the church. We can use any device we want to get people for one hour and keep it early and keep it moving and keep it going. But that's not the church Jesus built.*

**Leonard Ravenhill**: *And I'm embarrassed to be part of the church of Jesus today because I believe it's an embarrassment to a Holy God. Most of our joyous clapping our hands and having a good time and afterwards, talking all the drivel of the world.*

**David Wilkerson**: *Don't talk to us about holiness or separation from the world. We don't want to hear of that. People today don't want to hear anything they call gloom and doom. If it's not smooth it's gloom and doom.*

**Leonard Ravenhill**: *Well fine then, let me tell you lovingly to go to hell and live with all the scum of the earth. You like to drink, go with the drinkers. You like to lust. Go with the prostitutes.*

**Carter Conlon**: *And if you don't believe this is happening in our generation I challenge you to go to a Christian bookstore this week and find the best sellers. Ask them which are the best sellers. AND LOOK AT THEM. LOOK AT THE COVERS! THEY ARE THE IMAGES OF MEN, NOT THE IMAGES OF GOD. Five steps to be like me. Five steps to better yourself. Five steps to the new you. Five steps to a wonderful destiny. With their glossy faces on the cover, not so subtly telling the Church of Jesus Christ if you use the principles of God you will look like me. AND YOU BECAME ENAMOURED WITH YOUR OWN BEAUTY AND YOUR WHOLE THEOLOGICAL FOCUS NOW IS HOW YOU CAN BE SMARTER, BETTER, BETTER LOOKING, MORE PROSPEROUS. YOU LOST THE CALL OF GOD, CHURCH!*

**Leonard Ravenhill**: *When I see the church in the New Testament they didn't have stately buildings. They didn't have paid evangelists. They didn't have a lot of money. They didn't have organization. They didn't get on TV and beg. But I'll tell you what they did. THEY TURNED THE WORLD UPSIDEDOWN! I think we ought to watch this business with "you know God loves you and God loves you" and all the bumper stickers sloppy evangelism. Will you remind people of* *the goodness and the severity of God? Will you remind them mercy is cut off forever? Will you remind them that people pray in hell but nobody ever answers.*

**Carter Conlon**: *But in spite of what God has spoken they create a garment of fig leaves and they cover themselves and say, "All is well. All is well" and they seek out a church that won't challenge their sin. That won't expose this hypocrisy for what it is. I'd rather you get mad at me and go to heaven. I want to challenge you with everything in me. Put away lifeless religion. Put away empty pursuits of God. Put away all of the deception of the carnal nature.*

**Keith Daniel**: *Be ye holy, for I am holy. That's God's words. Not mine.*

**David Wilkerson**: *Word to God that Episcopalian, Presbyterian, Baptist, Methodist, Pentecostal pastors begin to stand up and see what's happening to the church that was once called the church of Jesus Christ. Backsliding. Turning apostate. Turning against the truth.*

**Carter Conlon**: *Some who are listening even now and will be listening to tapes in the future. You just can't lighten up and enjoy these theologically shallow experiences like so many around you are today. Everyone around you is saying lighten up! Lighten up! God's love. God's good. God is kind. God is nice. Come to church, stick your feet up on the altar. Have coffee and cookies with us, we hear three point messages on nothing about God--but there is a stirring in you, a stirring in the true bride in this generation. But if the Holy Spirit is truly, truly upon you in this generation, YOU WILL NOT BE SATISFIED. YOU WILL NOT BE FOUND AMONG THOSE WHO SIT IN SUPPOSED HOUSES OF GOD WITH YOUR FEET ON THE ALTAR RAIL WITH A CUP OF COFFEE IN YOUR HAND LISTENING TO A POWER POINT SERMON ABOUT A CHRIST THEY DON'T KNOW!!*

*The majority of God's people have always rejected God's prophetic word spoken through His servants.*

*Are you one of them?* "[30]

## IV - Fourth Reason - A Flood of Occult Believers

The **4th reason** people **in the Church** have abandoned the Christian faith, and apostacized is due to **A Flood of Occult Believers**.

That's right, I'm talking about the *Signs and Wonders Movement*. Little do people know that the teachings of the Signs and Wonders Movement have actually aided in this massive rise of apostasy. Today, people in the Church are being led astray by *emotional spiritual manipulation* and it's actually helping them to worship *the Antichrist*! But don't take my word for it. Let's listen to God's.

**2 Thessalonians 2:1-10** "Concerning the coming of our Lord Jesus Christ and our being gathered to him, we ask you, brothers, not to become easily unsettled or alarmed by some prophecy, report or letter supposed to have come from us, saying that the day of the Lord has already come. Don't let anyone deceive you in any way, for that day will not come until the rebellion occurs and the man of lawlessness is revealed, the man doomed to destruction.

He will oppose and will exalt himself over everything that is called God or is worshiped, so that he sets himself up in God's temple, proclaiming himself to be God. Don't you remember that when I was with you I used to tell you these things? And now you know what is holding him back, so that he may be revealed at the proper time. For the secret power of lawlessness is already at work; but the one who now holds it back will continue to do so till he is taken out of the way. And then the lawless one will be revealed, whom the Lord Jesus will overthrow with the breath of His mouth and destroy by the splendor of His coming. The coming of the lawless one will be in accordance with the work of satan displayed in all kinds of counterfeit miracles, signs and wonders, and in every sort of evil that deceives those who are perishing. They perish because they refused to love the truth and so be saved."

According to our text, the Bible clearly says that when the Antichrist himself is revealed, he's going to do so with false counterfeit signs, wonders and miracles, right? And it's not only going to be satanically inspired and empowered but it's going to deceive people who specifically refuse to love God's truth, i.e., those who are not Christians, they still need to be saved! Now here's my point. Man! Good thing we don't see any signs of that happening any time soon, people turning away from God's truth and instead loving and following counterfeit miracles, signs, and wonders. Are you kidding me? It's happening before our very eyes! And it's even called that! The Signs and Wonders Movement! Little do people realize it's setting them up to worship the actual Antichrist!

**The 1st way it's doing that, even in the Church, is by getting people to Follow a Different Spirit Than the Spirit of God.**

And that different "spirit" is called *emotions*! But shocker! That's not what the Bible says we need to be following! Here's what we need to be following.

**Psalm 19:7-8** "The law of the LORD is perfect, reviving the soul. The decrees of the LORD are trustworthy, making wise the simple. The commandments of the LORD are right, bringing joy to the heart."

Now according to our text, if you want to bring joy to your heart, and if you want to experience *true revival* in your soul, and if you want to become wise and not fall for all the deception out there, what do you do? You fall in love with the Word of God, right? It says it right there! You delight in it. You seek it. You immerse yourself into that and whew! Life is good, right? *Not anymore*! Haven't you heard? Apparently God's Word's is old hat. It's old-fashioned and it's not good enough anymore. We need something *new and improved* in these Last Days to make us alive in the Church! And that something new and improved is called *The Signs and Wonders Movement*! And what they would have you and I believe, is that in order to be a true spiritual Christian, in these Last Days, we need to seek an *experience* with God, an *emotional* encounter instead of becoming a student of God's Word. Why? Because put yourself in the Antichrist's shoes! He's not stupid! He knows he can't fool people when he shows up on the scene with all these false lying signs, wonders and miracles if they know the Word of God. That Book is the Truth! You can't be steered wrong by the Word of God AND it exposes his lies! It shows us step by step what he's going to do in the Last Days. So here's what does. He gets people, even in the Church, to put down the Word of God and seek a so-called *experience* with God. Why? Because once you go after emotions, you can be duped! Emotions are deceptive, feelings are deceptive, *but not the Word of God*!

And I'll state it on record that I don't have a problem with having an emotional encounter with God. I'm very *passionate* when I preach and sometimes in prayer I'm bawling my eyes out like a little baby! I love this intimate walk with the Creator of the Universe and I wouldn't exchange it for anything. But that's not what's going on here. These emotional encounters that The Signs and Wonders Movement are promoting in the Church are *not* genuine. They're counterfeit! Things like ecstatic speech, barking like dogs, having convulsions, or even uncontrollable laughter, in church services are now supposed to be the new signs of true spiritual maturity and a genuine encounter with God. Don't believe me? Let's take a look at what's going on in the American Church and you tell me if people aren't being deceived!

**The Holy Ghost Hokey Pokey Church:** If you not only want some good ol' fashioned entertainment at your next Church service, but a free healing to boot, you can attend this Church and join them in a "new" movement of God called the Holy Ghost Hokey Pokey.

### Rick Joyner's Morningstar Church
*Three weeks ago we did a Friday night School of Spirit and we saw 12 people healed by Word of Knowledge and 40 healed during the holy ghost hokey pokey. Let's just go ahead and do that and see what the Lord does. You guys okay to do the holy ghost hokey pokey? Can you lead it?*

*Alright, Brian is gonna lead us in the holy ghost hokey pokey.*

**Brian singing**: *Put your right hand in, put your right hand out. You put your right hand in you put your right hand out. You put your right hand in and you put your right hand out. You put it in and you shake it and you shake it all about. You put your left hand in, you take your left hand out...*

**Guy from the audience**: *When I started doing the hokey pokey at first with the arms and I got no real effect, but then when I started doing the whole movement, put your left foot in, your right foot in, both of my knees-you know, one at a time, all of a sudden there was like no pain.*

**The Can Can Dance Church:** One Church service included a lady who said the Spirit of God gave her the "Left Leg Anointing". Suddenly she kicks up her left leg (like the "Can Can" dance), and says, "More Jesus", whereupon people are supposedly slain in the Spirit in the direction of her kick. Then she proceeded to take the Lord's name in vain saying, "Oh my God, Oh my God, Oh my God", which she later changes to "Oh my goodness."

**The Hiss Like a Snake Church:** Another Church service included the so-called minister hissing like a serpent and sticking his tongue out grunting loudly as he walked through the crowd. And all the while in the background people are yelling, screaming and making animal sounds.

**The Squeal Like a Pig Church:** Go to this service and you would have heard the sounds of pigs squealing while people are dancing a jig.

**The Moo Like a Cow Church:** Or go to another service and you'd see a lady "mooing" like a cow with two so-called ministers rolling around on the floor beside her.

**The Baa Like a Sheep Church:** Or go to this service and you join these folks "baaing" like a sheep.

**The Bark Like a Dog Church:** Or for those of you "canine" lovers out there, maybe you can go to this service and join everyone in barking like dogs. That's right…Who let the dogs out!

**The Roar Like a Lion Church:** Or if a dog bark isn't loud enough for you, you can go to this Church service whereupon you will be encouraged to roar like a lion.

**The Cluck Like a Chicken Church:** Believe it or not you can go to a Church service where the so-called minister doesn't preach another boring sermon from the Bible. No! He stands around clucking like a chicken! And for those of you who don't believe me, here's a transcript.

*John Scotland:*

*Okay now before we take our…you know-uh-before we go surfing…let's get the reading done. (sways as if drunk) Luke..LUKE!!! (starts laughing) Chapter TWOOOOOOOOOOOOO.*

*I'll tell ya what let's look at chapter one verse…verse…verse…. COCKADOODLE DOOOOOOOOO!!!!*

*(church audience laughing uncontrollably)*

*Matthias was a member of the abbey (makes another loud animal sound then crows like a rooster a second and third time)*

**The Toking the Holy Ghost Church:** If animal noises just aren't your thing and you really want that "spiritual high," then look no further than these churches who encourage you to toke the Holy Ghost.

**Brandon Barthrop, John Crowder, Stacey Denboer and friends**:

**Brandon Barthrop**: *"What is tokin' the ghost? This is tokin' the ghost."*

*(motions like he just took a hit from a joint)*

*"Tokin' the ghost is simply putting your fingers together in the form of smoking a joint, but instead of smoking an illegal substance that's harmful for the body, you are inhaling the holy ghost with the access point of putting your fingers together and looking like you're smoking a marijuana cigarette but in fact you are receiving impartation from almighty God. I challenge you today that tokin' the ghost is an idea from the holy ghost to disturb the religious strongholds, to disturb religious demons, to destroy religious spirits from hell and get the church into the freedom and laws of liberty in Christ Jesus so that you may...two things...glorify God and enjoy Him."*

**Man next to Crowder**: *"We're at Springs of Living Water Church in Fargo, North Dakota and I'm here with John Crowder."*

**John Crowder**: *"I firmly believe in tokin' the ghost. Have a little jehovahjuana."*

**Man standing next to Crowder**: *laughing hysterically*

**John Crowder**: *"The great thing-it's free. You just reach in your pocket. Wow! Look what's there!"*

*(pretends to hold a joint)*

*"You just take a little...(puts fingers to mouth and pretends to inhale) Take a little whiff of the glor-y and then quick exhale. I'm just going to give you a little second hand-right through the video screen alright? Time and space are not an issue. This is a heavenly realm alright? See this access point right here."*

*(motions like he took another hit then motions like he's blowing smoke into the*

*camera)*

*"Oy yoi yoi yoi"*

**Man**: *"There's no high like the most high."*

----------------------------------------

**Stacy DenBoer**: *"Hello out there in internet land. I was just gonna...I was just gonna take a big ol' glory injection off my baby Jesus. I just took my baby Jesus and strapped him to...ah...um a syringe and I'm just gonna take a glory injection into my veins on the mainline. Get some of that big heavy, liquid heavy, weighty shoobie boobie juice just pumping through my veins from heaven. So here I go."*

*(raises arm put "baby Jesus syringe" up to his arm, makes motion of giving himself an "injection")*

*Then states, "Shingy boing boing ding ding ding."*[31]

Now I don't think Jesus came all the way from heaven to die a horrible death on the cross just so we can walk around clucking like chickens or smoking a so-called Holy Spirit joint, you know what I'm saying? You talk about blasphemy! And oh yeah, I don't doubt you're having an experience but it's not from God! I think it's from the Antichrist! Why? To prepare your heart to worship him! He knows if you stick to the Word of God instead of that baloney, that he can't fool you! But now that he's got you barking like a dog, roaring like a lion, and heaven forbid clucking like a chicken, man you're ripe for the picking! He's got you! You're seeking emotions over God, you're following a different spirit, and now you're set up for the Last Days where he'll give you an experience alright, it's called lying counterfeit signs, wonders and miracles. And we now have a whole new generation of people, even in the Church, who are ready to receive it! Exactly like the Bible said would happen, when you are living in the Last Days!

**2. The 2nd way** people are being deceived into worshiping the Antichrist in the Last Days, even in the Church, is by **Linking Themselves to a Different Spirit Than the Spirit of God.**

**2 Corinthians 11:13-15** "For such men are false apostles, deceitful workmen, masquerading as apostles of Christ. And no wonder, for satan himself masquerades as an angel of light. It is not surprising, then, if his servants masquerade as servants of righteousness."

Now according to our text, if there's one thing the Bible is clear about, it's that satan doesn't always appear on the scene as some horrible looking creature with horns and demon breath, right? What'd it say there? Sometimes he'll show up as an angel of light, which means it won't be freaky at all! It's going to be fabulous! Your emotions are going to be so full of bliss and love and so surely it's got to be an angel of God, right? No! That's part of satan's deceptive character. So here's the point. Surely we wouldn't fall for that ol' trick in the Church, would we? I mean, surely we wouldn't link ourselves to a different spirit just because it felt right, would we? *Not anymore!* Folks, haven't you heard! True spiritual Christians in these Last Days are not only those that can have an emotional encounter with God, but those that can *express* their emotions with God! You know, let it all hang out! Jump and scream and shout and dance and go crazy and wild!

Again, I'll state it on record. I don't have a problem with showing emotions at a Church service! I do not believe that clapping is illegal nor that raising your hands is inviting the judgment of God! But that's not what's going on here. These expressive emotional encounters that The Signs and Wonders Movement are encouraging people to do in the Church are *not* genuine. They're counterfeit. Little do people realize that they are being duped into getting worked up into an altered state of consciousness, *in the Church*, by this behavior, to link themselves up to a different spirit, rather than Spirit of God! Don't believe me? Let's take a look at this process of behavioral manipulation by the occult, to get people into an altered state of consciousness with their behavior, and you tell me there aren't some parallels.

### Kundalini Awakening - Dynamic Meditation

*"During these sessions its a very strange environment. People speak in tongues, they yell and they scream; they talk in foreign languages. It's like a madhouse, it's real crazy. Everyone bounces around on foam pads flying up in the air."*

**Telly Savalas:** *Rajneesh is one of India's most controversial gurus. Largely because of his endorsement of shocking sexual practices as a prerequisite for "salvation."*

*Rajneeshpuram Oregon, U.S.A*

*(Room full of people wildly jumping up and down to the sound of drums)*
*His brand of yoga, called dynamic meditation, is a New Age combination of*
*Hinduism and psychotherapies. This exercise involving rigorous breathing and*
*hyperventilation is designed to arouse the serpent force called kundalini, which*
*the gurus believe lies coiled at the base of the spine.*

*(people are now screaming and yelling at the top of their lungs)*

**Woman speaking***: The next phase, the screaming phase of dynamic meditation*
*feels like when you finally have an opportunity to throw a tantrum when you were*
*a little kid. By the time you get to the third phase of jumping up and down and*
*yelling "who", you're hardly "there" at all. So it's pretty hard to remember*
*what happens when you're there. I guess the closest thing I can associate with it*
*is mindlessness. You get to a place where your mind actually leaves your body.*
*Your body is just jumping up and down and the voice from your gut is yelling*
*"who" and you're not doing it anymore. You become one with this whole energy.*
*The next phase in dynamic meditation is the quiet space. Someone yells "STOP!"*
*and you've just been doing 30 minutes of intense catharsis and what happens*
*after being in such incredibly intense movement for so long, is such a feeling of*
*peacefulness and stillness. My mind actually stops and I feel a oneness with the*
*whole universe. "*[32]

Now as creepy as that is, it gets worse. It's one thing for people to do that
and fall for that, getting worked up into a frenzy to get yourself into an altered
state of consciousness, but believe it or not, the enemy has "repackaged" this
mind altering occult technique to the American Church and simply calls it being
Charismatic. Don't believe me? Check out this parallel of behavior between what
you just saw, and some of the so-called church services in the American Church
and you tell me if there's not a direct connection.

### The Four Phases of an Altered State of Consciousness

**FIRST PHASE:** The Hindu followers first began with a form of "repetitive
movement" combined with "music" for an extended period of time.

Some church services today include people "repeatedly" running around, jumping up and down, swaying back and forth, etc. to the beat of so-called "worship" music.

**SECOND PHASE**: The Hindu followers then start to speak forth a "repetitive phrase" or "mantra" over and over again until it became mindless.

Some church services today include people speaking forth a "repetitive phrase" or a so-called "unknown language" over and over again.

**THIRD PHASE**: The Hindu followers then start to "shout repeatedly" over and over again as a way of further "releasing" themselves from reality.

Some church services today include people "shouting, yelling, screaming" over and over again in order to "let it all hang out" in their so-called "worship" of God.

**FOURTH PHASE**: The Hindu followers finish this occult mind altering procedure with a sudden ceasing of all activity so as to "feel" a connection with the universe or spirit world.

Some church services today include people being requested (after a prolonged period of repetitive movement, repetitive speaking, repetitive shouting) to then be completely still and silent so as to "feel" the so-called presence of the Holy Spirit.

Maybe it's just me, but I think somebody's masquerading as an angel of light here, you know what I'm saying? I mean, there's no doubt these people are having an "experience" even in the Church but that doesn't mean it's coming from God! And for those of you who think they'll never get you, why, you're a conservative! You'll never clap your hands let alone raise your hands at a church service! They'll never get you! Really? Well, they may already have. Do you do *Yoga*? It does the exact same thing! But don't take my word for it. Let's listen to these Yoga Masters. At least they're honest enough to admit it!

**Caryl Matriciana - Yoga Uncoiled**:

**Caryl**: *Recently, I returned to India and had the opportunity to interview yogis who train their followers through various physical and mental exercises and I* questioned them about yoga's transformation. I also asked Indian experts if the practice of yoga consciousness could be separated from it's eastern spirituality and used as physical fitness only.

**Dr George Alexander, Associate Professor. Author of Yoga: The Truth Behind the Posture**

**Dr. Alexander**: *Today in the West, about 35 million Americans are into yoga, just seeing yoga as physical fitness. Yoga is a Hindu word. Yoga is a Hindu discipline, to become 'one' with the universal consciousness, which means become one with god-which god? Brahma, the Hindu god.*

**Dr Victor Choudhrie, a leading cancer surgeon in India, is also a well know lecturer and author of many books:**

**Dr Choudrie**: *The word yoga, in Hindu language means union. As simple as that. And the purpose of this union is they think there is a  powerful kundalini in their spine, in the base of their spine which is a kind of coiled serpent and the idea is when this union takes place-this serpent is uncoiled and travels into their minds and releases the "third eye". The "third eye" means the Shiva idea, the god Shiva.*

**Dr. Alexander**: *In Hinduism, the serpent is a prominent deity and many people worship serpents. I have seen many snake temples in India. If you look at the picture of lord Shiva in Hinduism, you see a snake wrapped around his neck. They believe that the serpent power is in every person and the serpent power is sleeping in you. By practicing yoga, they awake that kundalini power in you. Actually kundalini is the name for a cobra, so when the kundalini power is awakened that goes up to the brain and awakens the psychic power.*

**Dr. Choudhrie**: *When the spirit of kundalini is uncoiled there is a movement of body serpent-like movements.*

*I don't think we can separate yoga-the practice of yoga from the spiritual into just a form of exercise because every form of the yoga movement derives from the serpent and there's a root behind it so when a person practices yoga he's actually bowing down to the god of the serpent.*

**Caryl Matriciana**: *In most cultures, the serpent is seen as a positive creature* *and worshipped for it's wisdom. Only in the Bible is the serpent described as the Creator God's enemy, a usurper who wishes to take God's rightful place in the mind of mankind. In Hinduism he is called the kundalini and believed to be able to be awakened through yoga meditation and grant the practitioner an awareness of god. A stillness. A god-conciousness."*[33]

Now I don't know about you, but I'd say somebody's being prepared to receive the Antichrist, you know what I'm saying? It's like somebody's masquerading as an angel of light or something….hmmm. And to show you just how deep this deception goes, even in the Church, we now have church services that not only practice Yoga, but they have the audacity call it "Holy Yoga."[34] And on their website they say their whole purpose is to promote this, *in the Church,* is to: quote, "Deepen people's connection to Christ." Really? Which Christ? The Antichrist??? And you need to know that it's not only gaining popularity all across America, but it's growing like wildfire in the Church. In fact, one report said, "Yoga followers have tripled from what it was just 15 years ago!

Gee, if I didn't know better I'd say somebody's tricking us into linking ourselves with a different spirit other than the Spirit of God, how about you? And you know why? Because the Bible says in the Last Days the actual Antichrist is going to appear on the scene and spiritually link people to him with lying false counterfeit signs, wonders and miracles. And speaking of wonders, we now have a whole new generation of people, even in the Church, who are ready to do just that! Exactly like the Bible said would happen, when you're living in the Last Days!

## 3. The 3rd **way** people are being deceived into worshiping the Antichrist in the Last Days, even in the Church, is by **Possessing Themselves with a Different Spirit Than the Spirit of God.**

**1 John 4:1-3** "Dear friends, do not believe every spirit, but test the spirits to see whether they are from God, because many false prophets have gone out into the world. This is how you can recognize the Spirit of God: Every spirit that acknowledges that Jesus Christ has come in the flesh is from God, but every spirit that does not acknowledge Jesus is not from God. This is the spirit of the Antichrist, which you have heard is coming and even now is already in the world."

The Bible clearly says that not every spiritual encounter you have is from God, right? Why? Because there are counterfeits out there, and they're being promoted by false prophets and the spirit of the Antichrist, which is already at work in the world, right? And so John says, man, you better put these so-called spirits to the test because the last thing you'd ever want to do is to be led astray, let alone possessed, by a different spirit than the Spirit of God, right? And by the way, a Christian cannot be possessed by another spirit other than the Spirit of God. SO if a person is being possessed by another spirit, they're not a Christian! So let's do that! Let's put these so-called spiritual encounters that The Signs and Wonders Movement are encouraging people to do in the Church, to the test. Let's see if this is truly a work of God or just another satanic counterfeit.

## SIGNS & WONDERS vs OCCULT

| Signs & Wonders | Hindu Gurus | Meditation | African Spiritism |
|---|---|---|---|
| 1. Slain in the spirit | √ | √ | √ |
| 2. Electrical shock | √ | √ | √ |
| 3. Physical jerks | √ | √ | √ |
| 4. Animal sounds | √ | √ | √ |
| 5. New revelations | √ | √ | √ |
| 6. Surge of energy | √ | √ | √ |
| 7. Ecstatic speech | √ | √ | √ |
| 8. Trances | √ | √ | √ |
| 9. Visions | √ | √ | √ |
| 10. Uncontrollable laughing | √ | √ | √[35] |

Maybe it's just me, but apparently this kind of behavior from The Signs and Wonders Movement isn't so "new and improved" after all. Looks to me like the occult's been doing the exact same thing for a long time now. And once again, I don't doubt that you're having a "spiritual experience." But when you put it to the test like the Bible tells us to, I don't see it as being consistent with the Spirit of God. So the question is, "What does this full-blown possession of another spirit other than the Spirit of God look like today, even in the Church? I think it looks like this. Let's take a look.

**Andrew Strom - Kundalini Warning:**

*"I want to show you some of the shocking things and just how similar they are to*

*the kundalini cults of Hinduism and the New Age movement and eastern religions. The stuff that has been invading in the last 16-17 years, I believe that it's the worst invasion in church history.*

*What became known as the "Toronto Blessing" went worldwide under that name-the Toronto Blessing-everybody knew what that was about. People falling down and acting drunken, laughing hysterically, shaking uncontrollably or jerking backwards and forwards, their heads shaking back and forth. People even roaring like lions, people making animal noises. You know this stuff had not been seen in the church, I mean in a tiny way on the fringes but this stuff had not been seen in the church on this scale before and it invaded worldwide.*

*So all around the world, especially in the commonwealth countries, especially England and all through the U.K., Australia, New Zealand, Canada and many other nations all over the world, all through Europe all of the charismatic movement was into this stuff for the large part and so this thing became a worldwide sensation in just a couple of years.*

*Now the basic question we're asking in this documentary is why are these manifestations so similar to Eastern religions and Hinduism and the kundalini cults and yet they're not found in scripture, they're not found in the Bible, they're not found in classical Christianity at all. Of course in Hinduism one of the most common ways of experiencing a kundalini awakening is through a guru placing his hand upon your forehead. This is called Shakti-Pat and when they do that you'll become infused with this incredible love and this wave of emotion, you'll fall down. There will be manifestations, making animal noises, joy and weeping and shaking. This is a kundalini awakening and amazingly it is exactly the same as we have been seeing in the Toronto Blessing.*

*Now one of the very clearest signs of a kundalini awakening has always been these kryias. You see this woman involved in the New Age movement, she's walking along exhibiting these kryias happening, involuntary jerking motions and the staggering thing about it is that we are seeing again and again and again these exact same type of kryias right through the Toronto Movement. This has always been one of the clearest signs of kundalini that we know of.*

*A friend of mine from South Africa has done a tremendous amount of research on this topic. He says that kundalini is like a false Holy Spirit. It even produces miracles and healings, infusions of love, power and energy and emotion and all these kind of things and yet it's the Hindu version of the Holy Spirit and it's not holy.*"[36]

If I didn't know better, I'd say somebody's tricking us into possessing ourselves with a different spirit other than the Spirit of God, how about you? And you know why? Because the Bible says in the Last Days the actual Antichrist is going to appear on the scene and spiritually possess people with lying false counterfeit signs, wonders, and miracles. And we just happen to have a whole new generation of people, even in the Church, who are ready to do just that! Not Christians, but people who go to church services. Just like the Bible said would happen, when you are living in the Last Days!

## V - Fifth Reason - A Flood of Deadly Believers

The **5th reason** people in the Church have abandoned the Christian faith and Apostacized, is due to **A Flood of Deadly Believers**.

That's right, I'm talking about the *Liberal Christianity Movement.* Little do people know that the teachings of Liberalism or Liberal Christianity have actually aided in this massive rise of apostasy. Today, people *in the Church* are being led astray by doctrinal manipulation by these so-called Liberal Christians and it's *not* true Christianity. Like a wolf in sheep's clothing, it externally looks Christian, when in fact, internally they doctrinally manipulate almost every cardinal teaching of the Church. They deny the deity of Jesus, the Virgin Birth, the Resurrection, the Trinity, and on and on it goes, and that's just the tip of the iceberg as we'll see in a second, which means they're *dead*! They're fake! They're a rotting corpse! But don't take my word for it. Let's listen to God's.

**Revelation 3:1-3** "To the angel of the church in Sardis write: These are the words of Him who holds the seven spirits of God and the seven stars. I know your deeds; you have a reputation of being alive, but you are dead. Wake up! Strengthen what remains and is about to die, for I have not found your deeds complete in the sight of my God. Remember, therefore, what you have received and heard; obey it, and repent. But if you do not wake up, I will come like a thief, and you will not know at what time I will come to you."

In other words, you're going to be in a heap of trouble! Now according to our text, we see the classic passage concerning the Church of Sardis in the Book of Revelation that's classified as the what? The *Dead Church*! Why?

Because what did Jesus say? I know your deeds! You can't fool Me! You've got this reputation of being a happening Church and that you're alive, but I've got a news flash for you, you're dead! Dead as a stump! Why? Because of their deeds! They showed their deadness by their deeds! And I'm here to tell you it's the
> same thing with Liberal Christianity. It's not Christianity. They *say* they're Christians and on the outside they *look* like Christians, but on the inside they are "dead man's bones!" They too, just like Sardis, prove their deadness with their behavior! Again, they not only deny the deity, miracles and resurrection of Christ, but they go so far as to say that true and loving Christians will have an open mind when it comes to understanding the Bible. They say that feelings, not doctrine, provide the foundation for Christianity. Or in other words, your version of Christianity is what feels right for you. In essence, *you make up your own doctrine*, which means you make up your own Christianity!

And you might think that nobody in the Church would fall for this kind of wacky stuff. This is crazy! You don't make up your own version of Christianity! You can't do that! We're supposed to be followers of Christ not dictators to Christ! But listen, why do you think *right now*, mainline denominations are battling over whether or not Jesus really is the only way to heaven? It's called pluralism. This is why people in the Church claiming to be Christians are actually denying the existence of hell and are saying that homosexuality is perfectly fine including homosexuals behind the pulpit. After all, it *feels* right. It all stems from this lie called Liberal Christianity, which is *not* Christianity, it's dead, it's fake AND it's taking over the Church! Right now, whether you want to believe it or not, True Evangelical Christianity is being replaced, it's being eradicated by a Dead Church! We are going out of existence *right now* here in America! Why? Because it's all part of the Antichrist's plan to prepare a Dead Church that will go along with anything he says once he takes over the religions of the world. A True One will never go along with his demands, but a fake one will! And that's what He's creating!

**1. The 1st way he's getting people to create a DEAD Church, is by getting them to Create a New Service.**

And that "new service" is one that all revolves around SELF. It's an offshoot of two lies we've already seen before impacting the Church, that of Secular Psychology, which encourages self-worship at all costs, and The Church Growth Movement, which panders to self at all costs. But shocker! That's not what God says we need to be doing when we gather together! Let's take a look.

**Colossians 3:16-17** "Let the word of Christ dwell in you richly as you teach and admonish one another with all wisdom, and as you sing psalms, hymns and spiritual songs with gratitude in your hearts to God. And whatever you do, whether in word or deed, do it all in the name of the Lord Jesus, giving thanks to God the Father through Him."

Now according to our text, the Bible is clear. Our Church services, i.e. when we gather together as Christians, should be all about Who? GOD, right? What's it say there? We not only teach His Word and sing songs of gratitude to Him, but *whatever you do*, it's all for *His glory*, right? Not ours! Not self!

*Not anymore*! Haven't you heard? That's old fashioned! Thanks to the lie of Liberal Christianity, we are now being told that a truly prosperous "service" that meets people's needs is one that is all about SELF, like these people.

*"Imagine a church where every member is passionately, whole-heartedly, recklessly calling the shots.*

**Woman**: *"I have a busy work week and by the time Sunday rolls around-I'm tired! So how about a church service that starts when I get there"*

*Can do. When you arrive. We begin.*

**Father pointing to infant son**: *"This guy. He plays by his own rules. We want to find a church where when he starts screaming we're not the bad guys."*

*Say no more! If your baby's screaming, you stay seated. The others around you can leave.*

**Man and wife**: *"You know, financially, Sherry and I don't give a lot to the church but we sure would like to know who does."*

*Alright. If you join now, you'll know what every person gives in detail.*

**Woman 2**: *"When I'm in a church service can my car get a buff and a wax?"*

*Not just that but an oil change and a tune up!*

**Young man**: *"How 'bout tickets to the Super Bowl?"*

*That's asking too much.*

**Young man***: "I'm serious, if I'm going to join. I want tickets to the big game."*

*Alright if you join now, we'll get you there.*

**Young boy***: "I'd like a pony!"*

*Look in your back yard!*

*MeChurch. Where it's all about you."*[37]

That mentality would be funny if what? If it weren't so true! Correct me if I'm wrong, but do not most people think like that when they come to church services today? Where they think it's all about them? You cater to MY needs. It's all about ME, ME, ME…SELF, SELF, SELF! And the problem with this is that it's not only NOT BIBLICAL, but it opens Pandora's Box. Once you start going down this road of SELF and you start to cater all your services around SELF instead of YOUR SAVIOR, you just opened the floodgates of apostasy! Don't believe me? Check out all these "new and improved" SELF-PLEASING Church services, and you tell me if it's not leading to a DEAD CHURCH!

**Automated Prayer Service:** *Believe it or not there's a website out there called "Information Age Prayer Service" that was offering an automatic prayer service so you don't have to do it, they'll do it for you! It states, "Information Age Prayer is a subscription service utilizing a computer with text-to-speech capability to incant your prayers each day."*

*It gives you the satisfaction of knowing that your prayers will always be said even if you wake up late or forget. We use state of the art text to speech synthesizers to voice each prayer at a volume and speed equivalent to a typical person praying. Each prayer is voiced individually, with the name of the subscriber displayed on the screen.*

*At Information Age Prayer we think our service should be used like a prayer supplement, to extend and strengthen a subscriber's connection with God." And you'll be happy to know that there are promotional rates, for new users only, and for a limited time.*

*For instance, they are running a special deal for only $3.95 a month for The Lord's Prayer. "This prayer is the model that Jesus taught us. It thanks God, asks Him to provide for our needs and to forgive us. One simply cannot go wrong with this most beautiful classic prayer."*

*Or you could subscribe to The Morning Prayer. "The morning prayer is meant to be said each morning. A nice, short prayer, it has all the basic essentials important in a daily prayer. Subscribe to tell God that you think of Him each morning!" Also only $3.95 a month.*

*Or how about The Prayer for your Children. "This prayer asks God to watch over your children, allow them to do good, and to keep them from harm. This is the cheapest prayer you can get for the Information Age; it can be said each day for an entire month for only $1.99."*

*Or how about The Prayer for the Sick. "The prayer for the sick implores God to bring a sick person back to full health. Insert the name of the sick person and have the computer voice the prayer for them each day by subscribing here." Only $4.95 a month.*

*Or how about The Prayer for Financial Help. "We are all hurting as the world economy slumps. This prayer asks God to improve the economy and to enable us to support ourselves "in honor but not in disgrace."*

*For obvious reasons we provide this service at a considerable discount! Our Economic Stability Rate is only $3.95 a month. And for a limited time only, you can get up to 5 get well prayers each day for only $9.95 a month!*

**Free Cash Giveaway Service:** *Worshipers at Lighthouse Church in Illinois have an added incentive to be in the pews the last few weeks. Their Pastor is giving away cold, hard cash. A thousand bucks a weekend according to the Chicago Tribune. The pastor pulls three seat numbers out of a hat and two lucky worshipers gets $250, while one gets $500. The cash comes straight out of the collection plate and attendance is reportedly up 900 people over the past five weeks, from about 1,600 people to 2,500. Still, I wonder if they've created a spiritual version of Cash for Clunkers, which filled auto dealerships with crowds but dried up when the cash was gone.*

**Cell Phone Blessing Service:** *An Anglican priest eager to keep their parish relevant in the face of declining church attendance nationwide is asking users of mobile phones and other technological gadgets to bring them in this weekend for a special blessing. Aware of the attendance crisis, they wanted to experiment with different ways to spread the word. They have made a disclaimer though, "We do not claim to be able to exorcise the demons from your computer."*

**Animal Blessing Service:** *Another Anglican priest at St. Peter's Anglican Church in Toronto, offered Trapper, a four-year-old German Shepherd-Rhodesian Ridgeback cross, communion during a church service in late June. St. Peter's has long stood out as a church with a reputation for being open. Once a year a service is conducted to bless people's pets.*

**Beer Drinking Service:** *Most Christians are familiar with the Biblical story of Jesus turning water into wine, but now two New Zealand Pastors are seeking to turn a pub into a church complete with beer-drinking during the gatherings. While the sports bar service will not contain any sermons or singing, the Pastors say it will serve as both a place of prayer and a place to grab a beer. And they're not the only ones. Another Pastor in California is doing the same thing. "Some Churches use tactics like providing coffee and sweets, but a new church in San Jose has a very different approach. It provides beer for attendees. Pastor Jenkins said this is where the real ministry takes place. 'Come on," he says, 'I'll buy you a pint!"*

**Tattoo Parlor Service:** *A Michigan pastor who says he's doing everything he can to reach out to people who don't feel comfortable at a traditional house of worship has opened a tattoo parlor inside his church. Rev. Steve Bentley said his ministry is built on the belief that mainstream religion has become ineffective and irrelevant to most people. To that end, he opened Serenity Tattoo.*

*"Ryan Brown is the manager of Serenity Tattoo studio in Flint Township. He never imagined he'd work in a tattoo shop, in of all places, a church.*

*Traci Seeback can't imagine going anywhere else to get her tattoo.*

*"It feels good to me to be able to come in here and know that it's a nice, safe environment."*

*"Being home to a tattoo studio isn't the only unique thing about this church.*

*They also host MWO wrestling events and, later on this year, they plan to bring in cage fighting. "*[38]

I don't think Jesus came all the way from heaven to die a horrible death on the cross just so we can have Beer Drinking services, while we get a tattoo and pay somebody else to say our prayers! You talk about blasphemous! And here's the point! I don't doubt one iota that these people are having a *great time* alright in these so-called self-pleasing church services but it's not for the glory of God, which means it's *dead*! It's a Fake Church and it's step one of the Antichrist creating an apostate DEAD Church that'll go along with anything he says once he takes over the religions of the world…He'll make it pleasing to SELF! He'll make it sound good and when he does, he'll take over the religions of the world and that's exactly what the Bible said would happen when you are living in the Last Days!

**2. The 2nd way Liberal Christianity is replacing the True Church with a Dead Church and preparing them for the Antichrist's reign of a global religion is by getting people to Create a New Scripture.**

You know, one that won't convict anyone of the dead self-centered behavior in their services! But come on! They wouldn't do that would they? Uh yeah! It's already being done. But lets first take a look at why we need God's Word.

**2 Timothy 3:16-17** "All Scripture is God-breathed and is useful for teaching, rebuking, correcting and training in righteousness, so that the man of God may be thoroughly equipped for every good work."

Now according to our text, we clearly see that *all Scripture*, i.e. the Bible, is inspired by God and useful for what? I know! To stare at, right? No. To sit on the coffee table and impress your friends when they come over! No, I know! To collect dust just in case you need some extra dirt to grow your own crops in the backyard to become financially stable! No! What did it say? It's there to teach us, rebuke us, correct us and train us in what? Righteousness! I.E. how to live *right* according to God's standard, not our own, right?

*Not anymore*! Haven't you heard. That's old fashioned. Thanks to the lie of Liberal Christianity, we need a new and improved "Scripture." Why? Because that old Bible is just way too convicting for our self-centered behavior and after all, it damages our self-esteem. Therefore, we need a new and improved

Scripture that's MAN INSPIRED, not God inspired. Don't believe me? Check out all these "new and improved" Bible Versions out there, and you tell me if it's not leading to a DEAD CHURCH!

**The New Samurai Version:** *One man says he wants the world to know Jesus Christ alright, but just not the gentle, blue-eyed Christ of old Hollywood movies and illustrated Bibles. So a Mr. Akinsiku has come up with his new version called the "Manga Bible" which is the Japanese form of graphic novels. "It will convey the shock and freshness of the Bible in a unique way." Bible characters are depicted among other things as skateboarders in Bedouin gear, with things like Noah getting tripped up counting the animals in the Ark saying, "That's 11,344 animals? Arggh! I've lost count again. I'm going to have to start from scratch!" Or Abraham riding a horse out of an explosion to save Lot. Or Og, king of Bashan, looking like an early Darth Vader. However, the Sermon on the Mount did not make the book, because there wasn't enough action to it."*

**The Politically Correct Version:** *Referring to the Oxford University Press' release of a 'culturally sensitive' version of the Bible, the religious editor of Newsweek recently quipped that the King James Bible 'never looked so good before.' These are his poignant comments:*

*Readers who find the Bible sexist, racist, elitist and insensitive to the physically challenged, take heart. Oxford University Press' new 'inclusive language version' of the New Testament and Psalms has cleaned up God's act. In this version, God is no longer 'Father' and Jesus is no longer 'Son.'*

*The hierarchical title of 'Lord' is excised as an archaic way to address God. Nor does God (male pronouns for the deity have been abolished) rule a 'kingdom'; as the editors explain, the word has a 'blatantly androcentric and patriarchal character.'...Even God's metaphorical 'right hand' has been amputated out of deference to the left-handed. Some examples:*

- *In the majestic opening of John's Gospel, 'the glory he has from the Father as the only Son of the Father' becomes 'the glory as of a parent's only child.' (John 1:14)*

- *The Lord's prayer now begins like this: 'Father-Mother, hallowed be your name. May your dominion come.' (Luke 11:2)*

- *Jesus' own self-understanding as God's only son is generalized to: 'No one knows the Child except the Father-Mother; and no one knows the Father-Mother except the Child...' (Matthew 11:27)*

- *Avoiding another traditional phrase, 'Son of Man,' the Oxford text reads: 'Then they will see 'the Human One' coming in clouds with great power and glory.' (Mark 13:26)*

*The editors do not claim that Jesus spoke in gender-neutral language. But they obviously think he should have. The changes they have made are not merely cosmetic. They represent a fundamental reinterpretation of what the New Testament says—and how it says it."*

**The New Feminist Version:** *A publisher is touting a new edition of the Gospels that identifies Christ as a woman named Judith Christ of Nazareth. LBI Institute says its version was needed to correct the gender of Christ and God.*

*'This long-awaited revised text of the Gospels makes the moral message of Christ more accessible to many and more illuminating to all," says Billie Shakespeare, vice president for the publisher. He said, "It is empowering. We published this new Bible to acknowledge the rise of women in society."*

*The new version, according to the publisher, revises familiar stories, transforming the 'Prodigal Son' into the 'Prodigal Daughter' and the 'Lord's Prayer' into the 'Lady's Prayer.' Here are a few other examples of the 'new' translation.*

- *In Luke chapter 2 the verses now read, 'And Joseph went to Bethlehem. To be enrolled with Mary, his wife, who was then pregnant. And she brought forth her firstborn child. And her name was chosen to be Judith.'*

- *A passage on the crucifixion, from John 19 says, 'And She bearing her cross went forth. There they crucified Judith.'*

- *And a resurrection passage from Matthew 28 now states, 'Mary Magdalene and the other Mary came to see the tomb. But the angel said to the women, 'Do not be afraid, for I know that you seek Judith who was crucified. She is not here; for She is risen.''*

**The New Postmodern Version:** *This new version takes Darwin's theory of evolution as gospel and presents Jesus as being born, 'not to a virgin, but to a gorilla.' According to Ruth Rimm, Bronx school teacher and book artist, 'It explores the emergence of a new global spirituality that mixes the best of each wisdom tradition with the latest findings in psychology, quantum physics, neuroscience, and linguistics. It is a Bible for skeptics, seekers, and people of different faiths.'*

*The first volume in the series, which will eventually present the Torah, Bhagavad Gita, Buddhist sutras, and Sufi mysticism, covers the Gospel of Mark. However, it includes parables not found in Mark, such as the Parable of the Dolphin, the Parable of the Snow Leopard and the Parable of the Gorilla.*

*The Parable of the Gorilla begins with, 'He was born in a manger a long time ago, not to a virgin, but to a gorilla. What's so funny? Who did you expect his ancestors to look like, Tom Cruise? But wait. I'm not making fun of Jesus. I'm not mocking religion. In fact, from the deepest wellspring of my heart, I'm despairing something we've lost in our scientific culture. Yes, if Jesus was alive today, he would understand that his ancestors, just like ours, were beasts. No, he wouldn't run around claiming he was born of a virgin. And, brilliant rabbi that he was, he would likely ask us to understand the miracle stories metaphorically, as morality tales, but certainly not as literal truth.'*

*"Imagine from the loins of beautiful primates came prophets such as Jesus, Moses, Mohammed, the Buddha, and Lao Tzu. When we look at our evolutionary cousins, we look at ourselves. In a beautifully preserved time capsule that we evolved from apes or that the universe is billions of years old only deepens the mystery.*

*Our rational way of life has left us starving for the spiritual. Starving for a special connection to the cosmos. A connection that the mothers of Moses and the fathers of Jesus still seem to cherish.*

*How did our common ancestors give birth to the mystical sense within us. How did they learn to compose poetry or speak in metaphors or capture the sublime on a painted canvas. Look deep into their eyes. That the father of Jesus was not somewhere in Heaven, but in the sperm of beautiful primates closely related to these, is one of the most liberating and joyful discoveries in human history."*

**The New Gay Bible Version:** *"There's a new version of the Bible set to be published with the Gay Old and Gay New Testament which "says gay is right and "straight" (or heterosexual) is a "sin". In this version, Adam gets the heave-ho, and is replaced with Aida. "And the Lord God caused a deep sleep to fall upon Aida, and she slept: and he took one of her ribs, and closed up the flesh instead thereof; and the rib, which the Lord God had taken from woman, made he another woman, and brought her unto the first. And Aida said, 'This is now bone of my bones, and flesh of my flesh: she shall be called Woman, because she was taken out of me. Therefore shall a woman leave her mother, and shall cleave unto her wife: and they shall be one flesh. And they were both naked, the woman and her wife, and were not ashamed." Max Mitchell has described his work as divinely inspired. "Jesus was gay. In Biblical times homosexual relationships were so commonplace that no one gave it a second thought. It was heterosexuality that was considered sinful." And one participant even stated, "Finally, a version of the Bible everyone can relate to."*[39]

Again, I don't think Jesus came all the way from heaven to die a horrible death on the cross just so we can make up our own Bible and say that Jesus was a woman, or that He came from an ape, or that He was gay, you know what I'm saying? You talk about blasphemous! And here's the point! I don't doubt one iota that these new versions are pleasing the heart of man alright, but that's not what the ONE and ONLY TRUE BIBLE is for! It's inspired by God *not man* to teach us, rebuke us, correct us and train us in righteousness…not unholiness! And not one of these "new and improved versions" do that, which means they're useless, they're fake, they're *dead*! Why? Because it's step two of the Antichrist creating an apostate DEAD Church that'll go along with anything he says once he takes over the religions of the world…He'll make these new perverted versions pleasing to SELF! He'll make it sound nothing but good and when he does, he'll take over the religions of the world, and that's exactly what the Bible said would happen, when you are living in the Last Days!

**3. The 3ʳᵈ way Liberal Christianity is replacing the True Church with a Dead Church, preparing them for the Antichrist's reign of a global religion is by getting them to Create a New Savior.**

What! Are you serious? They wouldn't create a *new Jesus* would they? Uh huh! They already have. But let's first get acquainted with the REAL JESUS.

**Revelation 4:8** "Each of the four living creatures had six wings and was covered with eyes all around, even under his wings. Day and night they never stop saying: "Holy, holy, holy is the Lord God Almighty, who was, and is, and is to come.""

**1 Peter 1:15** "But just as He who called you is holy, so be holy in all you do; for it is written: "Be holy, because I am holy.""

Now according to our texts, if there's one attribute that God clearly wants us to know about Him, it's what? He is HOLY, HOLY, HOLY, right? AND if there's one thing He wants us to know that He EXPECTS from US, it's what? We are TO BE HOLY JUST LIKE HIM, right?

*Not anymore*! Haven't you heard. That's old fashioned. Thanks to the lie of Liberal Christianity, we need a new and improved "Savior" to help us out. Why? Because that old Jesus is just *too Holy*. I mean, how are we ever going to please ourselves if He keeps demanding that we be Holy just like Him? Therefore, we need a new and improved Savior that's just like US…full of SIN. Don't believe me? Check out this "new and improved" Savior that Liberal Christianity has created. And you tell me if it's not leading to a DEAD CHURCH!

**The Pole Dancing Savior:** "Here's a new way to express your faith. On the second Sunday of every month, Crystal Deans leads a pole dancing course for church-goers in Texas. She says she knew exotic dancing wasn't for her, but she realized she could use her experience with exotic performing to help other women connect with the teaching of Jesus Christ. Don't believe me? Here's the report.

**[Reporter-Kristin Kane]** *Well Malinda, I bet you never heard of this one before, "Pole Fitness for Jesus". I know you're probably thinking: How on Earth can you mix pole dancing with Jesus? Well, according to one studio up in Spring, you can definitely mix the two.*

**[Crystal Deans]** *You're gonna step in front with the inside leg, now you are gonna kick this one out.*

**[Crystal Deans]** *I was actually a dancer for 3 years, probably 7 years ago or so. I did it for awhile, it's not something that I felt very rewarded with, but to each his own and it was just something I didn't want to do anymore so I actually decided to take the part that I liked about that and bring it here.*

**[Kristin Kane]** *Don't let the name of the class fool you though. There's no prayer beforehand and there's no crosses hanging in her studio.*

**[Crystal Deans]** *We just-like I said get past the whole stigma of the whole thing. You know I teach women to feel good about themselves. I teach them to be empowered. And you know, we get in really good shape. I mean it does the legs. That's why we wear the shoes actually.*

**The Erotic Church Service Savior:** "Hundreds lined up for a new Erotic Church service where a female dancer danced in a skin colored stocking in the middle of the church facility in front of the altar. Nearly one thousand interested people waited outside the door despite a thunderstorm. Above the entrance was the caption, "A warm welcome to the Vineyard of Love". Then a man came to the microphone and announced, "This is an erotic church service; can you move a bit closer together, all of you." This was followed by saxophone music and dance. Then it was announced that, "eroticism and lust are not taboo and pushed aside by God." In fact, "lust has to be lived out." Then the faithful were asked to take part in an anointing ritual in which they should massage the forehead and hands of the person sitting next to them. And one congregant stated, "This is how church services should be." Then they all said "Our Father" together and then were encouraged with these words, "Praise God with your body, your lust and tenderness." And judging by the enthusiastic applause, the audience fully intended to do this."

**Transgender Pastor Savior:** "The Episcopal Church's House of Bishops on Saturday approved a proposal that, if it survives a final vote, would give transgender men and women the right to become ministers in the church. The move comes nine years after the Episcopal Church approved its first openly gay bishop, sparking an exodus of conservative parishes. The church now allows gay men and lesbians to join the ordained ministry and the new resolutions on gender would now allow transgender individuals as well." It's all part of their overall non-discrimination policy to church members."

**The Adultery Approving Savior:** "One Church Bishop warned that all this ongoing redefinition of marriage with same sex unions will soon include the idea of what's being called, "non-monogamy" or the concept of faithfulness between a man and a woman in marriage being outdated. The new concept will be the acceptance of "multiple partners" without the stigma of adultery. In fact, a court case has already been brought forth claiming that since same-sex marriage restrictions are being lifted, so should restrictions on multiple-partner marriages."

**The Atheist Accepting Savior:** "Believe it or not, there's now a new "ministry" being offered to the Church. Jerry DeWitt, a Pentecostal preacher for 25 years, now turned atheist, is encouraging other atheist pastors to stop pretending like he did and "come out" and admit their atheism. He's the executive director of what's called Recovering from Religion and its slogan is, "Thousands of organizations will help you get INTO religion, but we're the only one helping you OUT." One person stated, "It wouldn't be growing if there wasn't a need for it," which tells you the status of the American Church. In fact, this so-called "ministry" of people "recovering" from Christianity is not only for pastors, but now it's for any so-called Christian. A psychologist from Berkeley is helping former "fundamentalist" Christians to "lose their religion" in a workshop called, "Release and Reclaim." "Their God was a capricious, vindictive, punishing figure. Now, they need help learning to trust themselves."

**The New Age Occult Savior:** "The Church of England has recently hosted a "New Age Festival" where it opened its doors to tarot card readers, crystal healers, meditation experts and dream interpreters. The church is in trouble and attendance has fallen for the sixth year in a row so they decided to hold the festival in a bid to embrace alternative forms of Christianity. But this shouldn't be surprising because another church leader has stated that, "Harry Potter is a Christ-like figure because he promotes Biblical values, and a Protestant church in California teamed up with a high priestess of the pagan fertility goddess Isis to help them with "guided meditations" in their fifth annual "Faith and Feminism Conference." The high priestess stated, "I've taken people to their past lives in Egypt, as that culture had all the secrets. They're the ones that knew."

I mean, gee whiz, what's next? A full-blown "New Age" Church service? Uh yup, it's already here.

**Gene Ferrara:** *I am the spiritual leader of the community - Loving Spirit Community. We have opened a center in Madison- Center for Conscious Living.*

*At the Center for Conscious Living we do a variety of events that happen during the course of the week. Starting with Sunday morning, our Sunday morning- which we call our celebration of life community gathering. We do some chanting, some singing, some honoring of spirit in each other. I get to do my little metaphysical rant.*

*[Bongo Drum being played] Woman chants "Ohhhh hey ah hey ah hey Ohhhh."*

**Gene Ferrara**: *Then we do a guided meditation, allowing people to come on an inward journey that I still take.*

*Ferrara to his following [meditation music playing softly in background]: "Feeling yourself emerging from this darkness which has become light. Once again into a universe of swirling colorful energy."*

**Gene Ferrara**: *We see our function here as encouraging, facilitating, inspiring people to awaken to their true nature-to their spiritual nature so that they can incorporate that perspective and that point of view into their daily lives to make their human experience more meaningful and more joyful.*

*[followers bowing to each other] "namaste. namaste."*[40]

Again, I don't think Jesus came all the way from heaven to die a horrible death on the cross just so He could bless homosexuality, let us get our palms read and team up with the Occult and New Age. You talk about blasphemous! And here's the point! I don't doubt one iota that these new Saviors are pleasing to the sins of man alright, but *that's not the Real Jesus!* The Bible is clear! He is Holy, Holy, Holy and He has *zero tolerance* for sin! That's why there's a punishment called HELL and that's why He died on the cross to rescue us from that place! It's REAL and so is SIN and God's Holiness! Which means this "new and improved" savior *can't save a thing*, which means it's useless, it's *dead*! Why? Because it's step three of the Antichrist creating an apostate DEAD Church that'll go along with anything he says once he takes over the religions of the world. He's preparing their hearts to receive the ULTIMATE FALSE SAVIOR... HIM...and he'll let them do anything their evil hearts desire just so they'll worship him! And when he does, he'll take over the religions of the world, and that's exactly what the Bible said would happen, when you are living in the Last Days!

So if you're a Christian, AND you're a part of any of these Apostate Movements, be it the Word of Faith Movement, the Church Growth Movement, Liberal Christianity movement with their dead service, dead Scripture and a dead Savior, can I encourage you to do something...RUN! RUN FOR YOUR LIFE, Church, because your life might depend upon it, like this man shares.

*[On the first Sunday following the tragedy of September 11th, 2001, Carter Conlon delivered this soul-stirring message at Times Square Church in Manhattan]*

*Carter Conlon: Listen to me like you've never listened to me ever in your life. We have got to lay our lives down for the purposes of God. This is not a Sunday School picnic, the church of Jesus Christ. This is not an invitation to have a continuous good time. This is a war for the souls of men.*

*Come out from among them. Run for your life. Because this is about your life. This is not just about an opposing theology or conflicting viewpoint on Jesus, this is about your life.*

*My mind is forever branded with the stories that I heard of police officers from the city of New York. As people were fleeing from a crumbling building there were police officers and firemen and others that were running towards the buildings saying "Run for your life," at their own peril. And in some cases I believe they knew they were going to die but there was a sense of duty.*

*I was crying out to God; I said, "God, Oh Jesus, don't let my sense of duty be less for Your Kingdom than these beloved firemen and policemen were for those who were perishing in a fallen tower. We are living in a generation when truth is falling into the streets. I want to be among those that are not running away from the conflict but running into the conflict saying, "Run for your life."*

*Run from gospels that focus only on success and prosperity. Run!*

*Run from those who use the name of Christ only for personal gain. Run from those who are picking your pocket in the name of Jesus. Run!*

*Run from gospels that only focus on self-improvement. Run!*

*Run from churches where men and not Christ are glorified. Run!*

*Run, Body of Christ, Run! Get out! Don't touch the unclean thing.*

*Run from churches in America and Canada where there is no Bible. There is no cross in the theology. There is no soul-searching word. There is no repentance from sin. There is no mention of the blood of Jesus. Run! It's unclean. Run!*

*Run from churches where you are comfortable in your sins. If you come into the house of God and you got sin in your life and you're not convicted of it, you are at a table of devils.*

*Run from pulpits that are filled with political men who are using the pulpit of God for a personal political agenda. Run!*

*Run from those who preach division between races and cultures. Run!*

*Run! Get out! Turn it off! Get away from it!*

*They know nothing of God.*

*Run from ungodly spasmodic movements and aimless empty prophesying. Beloved Church, run for your life!*

*Run from preachers that stand and tell stories and jokes. Run like you've never run before!*

*RUN!*

*RUN!*

*RUN!*"[41]

And believe it or not, even with all this amazing evidence pointing to the signs of Christ's soon return, some people still think that they can mix the good with the bad without having any head problems, like this guy:

*"There was a man who was a Dallas Cowboys fan who had a big dilemma. He wanted to marry a lady who was a San Francisco 49ers fan. And knowing that this would be a lifelong problem, the Dallas Cowboys fan agreed to have 50% of his brain removed in order to ensure compatibility in the marriage. So he goes to his doctor and says, 'I've just got to marry this woman who's a San Francisco 49ers fan. I love her so much.'*

*So the doctor says, 'Well, it's risky, but okay.'*

*So into the operating room they go for the brain removal procedure.*

*Later though, when the man who was the Dallas Cowboys fan woke up, the doctor came in and said, 'We are very sorry, but we accidentally removed 75% of your brain instead of 50%.'*

*To which the man looked up and said, 'Go 9ers!'"*[42]

Now that guy found out the hard way that, try as you might, you can't mix the good with the bad, can you? It not only caused him some serious head problems but his condition even worsened, didn't it? But believe it or not, he's not alone. You see, many people today also think that they can mix hypocritical teachings with Christianity and still be Christians. Yet the Bible says that these "religious" people are sadly in line for the ultimate rude awakening from Jesus Himself.

**Matthew 7:21-23** "Not all people who sound religious are really godly. They may refer to me as 'Lord,' but they still won't enter the Kingdom of Heaven. The decisive issue is whether they obey my Father in heaven.

On judgment day many will tell me, 'Lord, Lord, we prophesied in your name and cast out demons in your name and performed many miracles in your name.' But I will reply, 'I never knew you. Go away; the things you did were unauthorized."

People of God, I hope you're not one of those who are busy being religious yet have never truly bowed a knee before Jesus Christ. I hope that you have honestly surrendered your life to Him by following *all of His teachings*, not just the ones you like. Why? Because you might wake up one day and discover that you've been left behind. And do you know what? God doesn't want you to be left behind. Because He loves us, He has given us the warning sign of **The Rise of Apostasy** to show us that the Tribulation could be near and that Christ's 2nd Coming is rapidly approaching. Jesus Himself said this:

**Luke 21:28** "When these things begin to take place, stand up and lift up your heads, because your redemption is drawing near."

Like it or not folks, we are headed for *The Final Countdown*. We don't know the day or the hour. Only God knows. The point is, if you're a Christian, and you're not willing to go to the front lines to fight for the cause of Christ, then will you at least support those who will? Folks, it's high time we Christians speak up and declare the good news of salvation to those who are dying all around us. But please, if you're not a Christian, give your life to Jesus today, because tomorrow may be too late! Just like the Bible said!

*Chapter Seven*

---

# One World Religion

"Every year Orson and his wife Janette go to the Air Show here in Vegas and every year Orson would say to Janette, 'You know, Janette, I'd like to ride in that there airplane.'

And every year Janette says, 'I know, Orson, I know, but that airplane ride costs ten dollars, and ten dollars is ten dollars.'

Well, this one year, apparently, Orson and Janette go to the air show again, and again, Orson says, 'Janette, I'm getting older and if I don't ride that airplane this year I may never get another chance.'

So Janette replied, 'Orson, that there airplane ride costs ten dollars, and ten dollars is ten dollars.'

Well, the pilot overheard them and he said to them, 'Folks, I tell you what. I'll make you a deal. I'll take you both up for a ride and if you both can stay quiet for the entire ride and not say one word, I won't charge you, but if you say one word it's ten dollars.'

So Orson and Janette agreed and they went up in the plane.

And so the pilot, he's doing all kinds of twists and turns, rolls and dives, but not a word is heard. Then he does all his tricks over again, but still, he doesn't hear a single word.

So finally they land and the pilot turns to Orson and says, 'My goodness, I did everything I could think of to get you to yell out, but you didn't.'

And Orson replied, 'Well, I was gonna say something when Janette fell out, but ten dollars is ten dollars.'"[1]

Did you know the Bible says there's also going to come a surprising day to the whole planet when people really are going to be falling all over the place, and that's going to happen at the Rapture of the Church? The reason why it's going to be such a *surprising time* is because for those who refuse to accept Jesus Christ as their Personal Lord and Savior, they will be catapulted into the 7-year Tribulation and it's not a joke! It's an outpouring of God's wrath on a wicked and rebellious planet. In fact Jesus said in Matthew 24 it's going to be a "time of greater horror than anything the world has ever seen or will ever see again and "unless that time of calamity is shortened, the entire human race will be destroyed." But praise God, God's not only a God of wrath, He's a God of love as well. And because He loves us, He's given us many warning signs to show us when the Tribulation was near and when Jesus Christ's 2nd Coming was rapidly approaching.

Therefore, in order to keep you and I from experiencing the ultimate bad day of being left behind, even worse than riding in a plane with Orson, we're going to continue in our series, *The Final Countdown*. In the last chapter we saw how the **#5** sign was *The Rise of Apostasy*. What we saw was that God lovingly foretold you and I that when we see not only the *world* going down the tubes, but even the *Church* going down the tubes, which is happening right now today all over the world, thanks in part to a massive flooding of Phony Baloney Believers *in the Church*, Greedy Believers in the Church, Worldly Believers in the Church, Occult Believers in the Church and a massive flooding of Deadly Believers in the Church. In other words, dead, fake, phony Christians. And what we saw was this was being done by the lies of The Liberal Christianity Movement, which is not Christianity, and it's tricking people into thinking they're Christians when they're not! They're fake, they're phony, they're dead, *and* they're taking over the Church with their New Services, their New Scripture and their New Savior, exactly like the Bible said would happen when you are living in the Last Days!

The **#4** sign on *The Final Countdown* that God has given to us to lovingly wake us up, is none other than a **One World Religion**.

The Bible is clear. All the religions of the planet, one day, are going to come under the head of one man, the Antichrist, and his buddy, the False Prophet. These dead, fake, phony Christians as we just saw, are going to go right along with it. But don't take my word for it. Let's listen to God's.

**Revelation 13:3-9** "One of the heads of the beast seemed to have had a fatal wound, but the fatal wound had been healed. The whole world was astonished and followed the beast. Men worshiped the dragon because he had given authority to the beast, and they also worshiped the beast and asked, 'Who is like the beast? Who can make war against him?' The beast was given a mouth to utter proud words and blasphemies and to exercise his authority for forty-two months. He opened his mouth to blaspheme God, and to slander his name and his dwelling place and those who live in heaven. He was given power to make war against the saints and to conquer them. And he was given authority over every tribe, people, language and nation. All inhabitants of the earth will worship the beast – all whose names have not been written in the book of life belonging to the Lamb that was slain from the creation of the world. He who has an ear, let him hear."

In other words, you better pay attention to this! According to our text, the Bible clearly says that there's really coming a day when all the inhabitants of the earth are going to be busy worshiping who? The Antichrist himself, right? One day, the Bible says, the whole world will be unified into **A** *One World Religion* that is actually *satanically inspired*. But that's the question. "Could this really happen? Could the whole world really be deceived into creating A One World Religion that the Antichrist is going to hijack and take over? And is there any evidence that this is really going to take place just like the Bible said?" You bet there is! And it's happening right before our very eyes *right now*!

**I. The 1ˢᵗ way we know we're really headed for A One World Religion is due to a Welcoming of All Faiths.**

That's right, I'm talking about the *Interfaith Movement*. You see, put yourself in the Antichrist's shoes. If you're going to deceive people into creating a One World Religion then you've also got to get rid of any sense of one religion being superior over another and this is precisely what the Interfaith Movement has done. This term, by the way, interfaith, is the new buzzword for A One World Religion. When you see this anywhere in the news or print, Interfaith, or Interfaithism, just supplant it for what it is. It's talking about the formation of a One World Religion because that's what it means. Promoters of this movement would have you and I believe that *all religions* are valid pathways to God. In other words, all roads, no matter what the belief is, lead to heaven. Therefore, they say, there's no need to argue or fight with one another. We just need to respect, tolerate and find common ground with one another. We need to work together for the common good of saving Mother Earth and the planet and keep humanity from destroying itself, right? *Or this...*"After all, in light of the terrorist attacks on September 11th, we all know that "religious differences" are the main cause of war, right? No, it's not, that's a lie and we'll explode that myth later in this chapter. But this is what Interfaith or Interfaithism teaches, which as you can tell is diametrically opposed to True Biblical Christianity. But granted, on the surface, it sounds nice, it sounds politically correct, but as far as the Bible is concerned, there is no such thing. If a person says they're an interfaith Christian, they're an oxymoron. Why? Because according to their own definition, Jesus was apparently the most intolerant bigoted person who ever lived because He said this:

**John 14:6** "I am the way and the truth and the life. No one comes to the Father except through me."

Now here's the problem. According to our society's Interfaith Movement, you cannot make a more "intolerant" statement than that! But that came from the lips of Jesus! And I don't recommend you call Him a "religious bigot"! But this is what "interfaith" teaches. You have to deny what Jesus said, right there, and in essence call Him a liar, and instead say He's NOT the only way to heaven and that all religions are valid pathways to heaven. And can I tell you something? *You can't do that as a genuine born again Christian*!

But you might be thinking, "Come on, this is America. We're a Christian nation. There's no way people are going to be able to pull off this Interfaith Movement and create a One World Religion. Maybe in some other country, but not here! Nobody's ever going to fall for this." Really? I'm here to tell you that not only have many well-known people here in America already done so, even to the highest levels of society, Hollywood, the Government, you name it, but they're about to put the whole thing in place!

**1.** The **1st proof** that we know we really are headed for a One World Religion is the **Chronological Proof.**

What most people don't realize is that this One World Religion is not only going to be put into place, because the Bible said it would, but what people don't realize is that it's been in the planning stages for a long time. Look at the progress for yourself:

## CHRONOLOGY OF ONE WORLD RELIGION

- *1893: 1st World Parliament of Religions held*
- *1930: World Congress of Faiths*
- *1948: World Council of Churches*
- *1970: World Conference of Religions for Peace Started*
- *1974: 2nd World Conference of Religions for Peace*
- *1979: 3rd World Conference of Religions for Peace*
- *1984: 4th World Conference of Religions for Peace*
- *1986: Vatican calls for a meeting of all religions to come and pray for world peace*
- *1989: 5th World Conference of Religions for Peace*
- *1993: 2nd World Parliament of Religions held with largest gathering of religious leaders in history*
- *1993: The Declaration of Global Ethic – A new set of commandments for the world*
- *1994: 6th World Conference of Religions for Peace*
- *1997: Charter written for the United Religions Organization*
- *1999: 7th World Conference of Religions for Peace*
- *2000: United Religions Organization charter signed by most of the world's religions*
- *2000: World Peace Summit of Religious and Spiritual Leaders – signing of Commitment to Global Peace and creation of World Council of Religions*

### CBN News on Global Religion

**Lee Webb:** *The United Nations are pursuing the development of a one world religious organization. Today, on the United Nations 55th Anniversary, CBN reporter Wendy Griffith takes a look at what's behind this push for a global* *religious voice.*

**Griffith:** *After awhile, the drums, chants and prayers representing many of the world's leading religions all started to sound alike, somehow losing their flavor in a melting pot of spiritual soup. The first ever Millennium World Peace Summit of Religions and Spiritual Leaders took place at the United Nations in August 2000 and some believe it marked the first major step toward a movement to usher in a global spiritual body that may one day speak for all religions.*

*Robert McGuiness with the Family Research Counsel says it appears that the hidden agenda is to unite people under one religious organization so they will peacefully accept U.N. goals such as population control, abortion rights and one world governments.*

**Ted Turner (speaking at the U.N.):** *Instead of all these different gods, maybe there's one god who manifests himself and revealed himself in different ways to different people. Ya know what about that, huh?*

**Griffith:** *CNN's founder and billionaire, Ted Turner was the Honorary Chair at the World Religions Summit. Turner, known for his critical views on Biblical Christianity, promoted the New Age concept that there are many ways to heaven.*

**Turner:** *And the thing that disturbed me, is that my religious Christian sect was very intolerant. Not that intolerant of religious freedom for other people but we thought-they thought we were the only ones going to heaven.*

**Griffith:** *Other reporters of a Religious Global Voice come down hard on evangelical Christians who refuse to adopt their new age agenda.*

- *2001: World Congress on the Preservation of Religious Diversity*
- *2002: Vatican calls for a meeting of all religions to come and pray for peace and to overcome conflict*
- *2002: 1st meeting of World Council of Religions*
- *2002: World Conference of Women Religious and Spiritual Leaders*
- *2002: World Peace Summit Established by World Conference of Religions for Peace*
- *2003: 2nd World Peace Summit*
- *2003: Pope commends peace of world to Mary*
- *2003: Pope urges unity against violence among World Religions*

- *2003: Inter-religious tribute given on behalf of Mother Teresa*
- *2004: 3rd World Peace Summit*
- *2004: Vatican hosts Interfaith Concert*
- *2004: Pope says religions must unite for peace*
- *2005: 4th World Peace Summit*
- *2005: World Council of Churches asks Pope for renewed commitment to ecumenicalism*
- *2005: Global Day of Prayer unites diverse Churches*
- *2005: Vatican promotes Unity at World Mission Conference*
- *2006: 8th World Conference of Religions for Peace*
- *2006: Pope encourages more Inter-Religious prayer meetings*
- *2006: 5th World Peace Summit*
- *2006: World Religions unite over Global Warming*
- *2006: 2nd Global Day of Prayer*
- *2006: Pope and Dalai Lama herald peace between Catholics, Buddhists and Hindus*
- *2006: Pope's praying in a Mosque deemed a "New Horizon" in Interfaith*
- *2007: 6th World Peace Summit*
- *2007: Interfaith Council established for Jerusalem*
- *2007: 3rd Global Day of Prayer*
- *2007: Groups in U.S. declare that all paths lead to God*
- *2007: World Council of Churches encourages different religions to unify in diversity*
- *2008: 7th World Peace Summit*
- *2008: World Council of Churches and Pope seek cooperation*
- *2008: Pope meets with Jewish, Islamic, Buddhist, Jain, Hindu leaders in Washington*
- *2008: 4th Global Day of Prayer*
- *2008: Oprah Winfrey begins openly promoting New Age thoughts and One World Religion ideals specifically saying that Jesus is not the only way to heaven.*
- *2008: Tony Blair launches his Faith Foundations to help Unite the World's Religions*

## Tony Blair: Faith Foundation

***Matt Lauer:*** *Talk about this Faith Foundation, the idea, and correct me if I'm wrong- to paraphrase is basically to bring people of different faiths together to* *solve global problems like poverty. Given the fact that so many conflicts in this world have been based on religion, how do you feel that religion can now bring people together in this critical time?*

**Tony Blair:** *Well that's a good point. I mean it's precisely the reason for having the foundation, it might be what happens in the modern world that everyone's been pushed closer together. That's what globalization is doing. The world becomes a smaller place, religion, either becomes the means for pulling people apart and dividing people-can become then a source of conflict. I'd like religion and religious faith, people of different faiths to work together in peaceful coexistence and make religion a source of reconciliation and a source of peace.*

**Matt Lauer:** *And to talk to one another...*

**Tony Blair:** *Well, what we got to do, both in our foreign policies but also in things like this Faith Foundation-try to bring people-Muslims, Christians, Jews, other religious faiths together. We've got to create the circumstances in which those people that believe in a modern future for that region succeed and those people, the extremists, are put into retreat.*

- *2009: World Parliament of Religions is held in Melbourne Australia. Up to 8,000 people from "various faiths" participated in discussions about "Climate Change" and the "Eradication of Poverty."*
- *2010: Tony Blair begins to Court Pastor Rick Warren and enlist his aid in Uniting the World's Religions.*
- *2010: Interfaith Meetings in Manhattan begin to be held twice a month by Christian, Jewish, Muslim and other religious leaders and it's supported by the Obama White House, which has identified interfaith work as a public policy goal.*
- *2010: The G8 World Religions Summit was held where, among other things, a sacred fire was lit and participants were told that "Mother Earth needs to hear that we love her and they offered up to her a prayer of gratitude. Other rituals were performed to invoke "the spirits" and to encourage all that "there is not only one way;, there are many ways."*
- *2011: Another Global Day of Prayer*
- *2011: Another World Peace Summit (Note: Many of these Prayer Days and Peace Summits are targeted to Youth)*
- *2012: Rick Warren begins promoting King's Way as an attempt to bring evangelical Christians and Muslims together as an overall part of his*

*PEACE Plan. A document was produced that stressed points of "agreement" between the two faiths, including belief in "one God" and it also called for the sharing of their faith with one another but not for the purpose of conversion.*

- *2012: A Global Charter of Conscience was drafted by a group of 50 international academics, politicians and NGO leaders representing various faiths that encouraged the world to "live together in peace with their religious differences."*
- *2012: Pope urges religions to root out "Fundamentalism."*
- *2012: Vatican calls for the Establishment of a One World Government and a New World Order that will "serve the common good of the human family" and be a "moral force" that has the "power to influence."*[2]

Now correct me if I'm wrong, but when you take a look at the timeline, I'd say somebody's pretty serious about this One World Religion. It's almost like they're following some sort of a *Chronological Plan* to get us to go along with it and it's coming to a planet near you!

**2. The 2nd proof that we know we really are headed for a One World Religion is the Coercive Proof.**

You see, just in case you don't go along with being politically correct and popular like the rest of the world, with this Interfaithism, they also have a backup plan to *make you go along with it* and that plan is to *coerce* you into this lie by fear and manipulation! Haven't you heard? If we don't go along with this One World Religion the planet is going to blow up! We've got to put our differences aside and come together as religions to save Mother Earth! Haven't you heard? The planet is in danger of *Global Warming*. Really? It is my proud honor to expose this lie for what it is. In fact, it's such a big lie that even the Founder of the Weather Channel is blowing the whistle on it. Check it out for yourself!

**Global Warming Lie:**

*Glenn: If a scientist says the temperatures are up point zero one degree (.01)-lead story around the country and every newspaper, but when somebody with decades of experience comes out and says "global warming" is a manufactured crisis-no one cares and you can hear a pin drop. How do I know? That is exactly what happened last week when the founder of The Weather Channel wrote an article that began, and I quote-*

*"It is the greatest scam in history. I am amazed, appalled and highly offended by it. Global warming; it is a scam."* - John Coleman, Founder, The Weather Channel.

*But since that opinion doesn't fit nicely in the mouth of the media beast: hello NBC, you probably didn't hear a word about it. Well now you will. John Coleman is the founder of The Weather Channel. He was also the first weatherman ever on Good Morning America and he is currently weatherman at KUSI News in San Diego. John, your head about exploded with the NBC thing this week. Is that what was the breaking point for you?*

**John Coleman:** *<chuckles> Well I've been listening to all the global warming talk for a long time and posting material about global warming on our website, but finally, the crescendo of global warming myth, nonsense, exploded in my head and I had to write a real rant and that's the one that got noticed. It's on our website and was picked up by icecap.us. Picked up by Drudge. First thing you knew it was all over the newspapers, all over the radio, all over the TV sets and I created a bit of a stir and all I was doing was telling you the truth as best I know it.*

**Glenn:** *What was the turning point for you? I know that you said you went in to look for an honest answer. You thought maybe it's real. What was the thing that stood out, and you said this is absolutely bogus?*

**Coleman:** *Well, when I looked at the "hockey stick" graph that was produced in Manning's original report and it showed a steady line temperature through the millennium and a sudden rise, I knew that was incorrect. I knew it couldn't possibly be and I started asking experts about it and I started digging into how that was produced. And I found out it was bogus science. It wasn't real. The numbers had been massaged. The whole thing had been created. What bothered me was that the other scientists had accepted it. Well why did they possibly do that? And I think that the real answer to that question is that they all have an agenda. An environmental and political agenda that said "Lets pile on here-we're all gonna make a lot of money. We're gonna get research grants. We're gonna get awards and we're gonna become famous." I guess that's what happened.*

**Coleman:** *There are scientists speaking out. There are hundreds of them* *speaking out. There are thousands who signed a petition; 19,000 on a petition against global warming. There are many scientists speaking out but the mainstream press is totally ignoring them."*[3]

Now let me get this straight. 19,000 scientists and the founder of the Weather Channel say global warming is totally bunk…and yet the press continues to ignore them and still promote it…WHY? Because what'd he say? *They have an agenda.* And yes, part of it is money and power, but part of it is to become the ultimate excuse to form a One World Religion. We need a global catastrophe to get the global religions to work together. Don't believe me? Let's look again at the Environmental Worship video we saw and you tell me if it's not being used to draw all the religions on the planet together.

***NBC News Tom Brokaw:*** *And back in this country a provocative and timely question in the debate over energy policy; what would Jesus drive? This is the centerpiece of a new energy conservation campaign, but some say the gospel has no place in the debate over gasoline. Here's NBC's Don Teague.*

*<TV ad>God saw that it was good..*

***Teague:*** *As TV ads go, this is something different.*

*<TV commercial continuing>..yet too many of the cars, trucks and SUVs that are made that we choose to drive are polluting our air.*

***Teague:*** *Not because it carries an environmental message but because of the obvious audience it targets.*

*<TV ad continues> So if we love our neighbor and we cherish God's creation, maybe we should ask, "What would Jesus drive?"*

----------------------

**Fox News:**

***Mark Hemmer:*** *What would Jesus drive, huh? Environmental evangelism. It's a new way to raise awareness about global warming. Our Fox religion correspondent Lauren Greene joins us with more on that. Hi! Good morning. Who's pushing Christian green lines?*

*Lauren Green: Hey! Well a lot of people, it really is across the board theoretically speaking or religiously speaking. Here are the top green religious people according to Live Earth.*

*We've got Rev. Joel Hunter. He's a senior pastor at Northland Church in Longwood, Florida. He was actually offered Head of the Christian Coalition but turned it down because he wanted to focus on issues such as poverty and environmental protection.*

*Then Norman Hobble is a theology professor out of Australia. He edited something called the Earth Bible.*

*Then of course there's Pope Benedict XVI and yesterday he issued a statement that said, "The people of faith must listen to the voice of the earth or risk destroying its very existence."*

*We also have the Archbishop of Canterbury-Rowan Williams-head of the Anglican Church and of course the Buddhist leader, the Dalai Lama.*

*But one thing you should add to this list is the National Evangelical Association because 2 years ago it issued a letter to 50,000 member churches which means it's 30 million evangelicals saying that, 'We affirm that God-given dominion is a sacred responsibility and that government has an obligation to protect it's citizens from the effects of environmental degradation.'*

*So it's a big movement all across the board."*[4]

Hmmm. Looks to me like this manufactured crisis is being used to get all the religions on the planet to come together as one. Where have I heard that before? Which is exactly what the Bible said would happen when you are living in the Last Days. Oh and by the way, this is why they changed the term from "Global Warming" to "Climate Change." Because they didn't want to get caught in the lie, they switched to a more generic term, Climate Change, so as to avoid this. But last time I checked, *the climate changes every day*! Where's the crisis? It's a lie!

But that's not the only lie. Another lie they're using to coerce us into going along with a One World Religion is this, "Well, haven't you heard, *religion is the main cause of wars* and if we don't come together as one, the planet is headed for destruction!" Really? Now let me demonstrate why it's a lie. Let's take a look at what's really the major cause of wars.

## WHAT REALLY CAUSES WARS?

- *Congo Free State - 1886 to 1908 - 8,000,000 dead - Control of colonial profit and*
- *power base*
- *Feudal Russia - 1900 to 1917 - 3,500,000 dead - Political control*
- *Turkish Purges - 1900 to 1923 - 5,000,000 dead - Ottoman Empire*
- *collapse/Political control*
- *First World War - 1914 to 1918 - 15,000,000 dead - Balance of power*
- ***NOTE:** The First World War killed more people than all the religious*
- *wars in the past. 6,000 men a day died for 1,500 days in World War I.*
- *Russian Civil War - 1917 to 1922 - 9,000,000 dead - Political control*
- *Soviet Union, Stalin Regime - 1924 to 1953 – 20-45,000,000 dead - Political*
- *control*
- *China Nationalist Era - 1928 to 1937 - 3,000,000 dead - Political control*
- *Second World War - 1937/38 to 1945 - 55,000,000 dead - Balance of*
- *power/Expansionism*
- *Sino-Japanese War - 1937 to 1945 - 21,000,000 dead – Expansionism*
- *Post-WWII German Expulsions from Eastern Europe - 1945-1948 - 1.8-*
- *5,000,000 - Post-war policies. Retributions/Soviet and Eastern European*
- *control*
- *Chinese Civil War - 1945 to 1949 - 2,500,000 dead - Political control*
- *People's Republic of China - 1949 to 1975 – 40-80,000,000 dead - Political*
- *control*
- *North Korean Regime - 1948 - 1.7-3,000,000 dead - Political control*
- *Korean War - 1950 to 1953 - 2,800,000 dead - Political control*
- *Second Indochina War - 1960 to 1975 - 3-4,000,000 dead - Political control*
- *Ethiopia - 1962 to 1992 - 1,500,000 dead - Political control*
- *Khmer Rouge - 1975 to 1978 - 2,500,000 dead - Political control*
- *Afghanistan - 1979 to 2001 - 1,800,000 dead - Political control/Soviet expansion*

- *Kinshasa Congo - 1998 - 3,800,000 dead – Political control &Resources*[5]

Once you look at the facts, I'd say we're being lied to! Religion *is not* the biggest cause of wars, it's the anti-God man-made agendas that are! It's *politics*, not religion and they're using this fear and manipulation to coerce us into going along with this One World Religion, exactly like the Bible said would happen, when you are living in the Last Days.

**3. The 3rd proof** that we know we really are headed for a One World Religion is the **Promotional Proof.**

As if what we've seen isn't enough, this Interfaithism Movement is also being promoted by virtually every single mover and shaker from around the world. Just in case you aren't politically correct or scared into doing it, they're using Hollywood, the Governments and even the Vatican to help "educate you" and promote this lie to go along with a One World Religion. But again, don't take my word for it. Let's listen to theirs.

***Prince Charles of England*** *launched a new movement called Respect, in order to, "Promote tolerance among the world's religions."*

***Global Warming promoter Al Gore*** *made this amazing statement: "The richness and diversity of our religious tradition throughout history is a spiritual resource long ignored by people of faith, who are often afraid to open their minds to teachings first offered outside their own system of belief. But the emergence of a civilization in which knowledge moves freely and almost instantaneously through the world has spurred a renewed investigation of the wisdom distilled by all faiths. This panreligious perspective may prove especially important where our global civilization's responsibility for the earth is concerned."*

But he's not the only one. Hollywood, the Governments and even the Vatican are promoting this One World Religion:

***Oprah:*** *One of the mistakes human beings make is believing that there is only one way to live and we don't accept that there are diverse ways of being in the world . . . that there are millions of ways to be a human being and many ways, many paths to what you call God. Her path might be something else and when she gets there she might call it 'the Light.' But her loving and her kindness and* *her generosity* — *if it brings her to the same point it brings you, it doesn't matter whether she calls it God along the way or not.*

**Audience Member:** *And I guess the danger that could be in that is that it sounds great on the onset, but if you really look at both sides, I....(Oprah cuts her off)*

**Oprah:** *There couldn't possibly be just one way!*

**Audience in general:** *What about Jesus?*

**Oprah:** *What? What about Jesus?*

**2nd Audience member over several voices:** *You say there isn't only one way. There is one way, and only one way, and that is through Jesus!*

**Oprah:** *There couldn't possibly be only one way with millions of people in the world!*

**2nd Audience member:** *Just because you say there isn't, because you say...*

**Oprah:** *No! There couldn't possibly be...*

**2nd Audience member continues:** *...you intellectualize it and say there isn't, if you don't believe that, you are all buying into the lie.*

------------
**C-SPAN: U.S. Senate Chamber**

*Today's opening prayer will be offered by a guest chaplain Rajan Zed of the Indian Association of Northern Nevada.*

**Man heard in background:** *Lord Jesus forgive us Father for allowing the prayer of the wicked which is an abomination in your sight..*

**Senate leader:** *The Sergeant of Arms will restore order in the Senate*

**Another man:** *This is an abomination. YOU SHALL HAVE NO OTHER GODS BEFORE YOU*

*Senate leader:* *The Sergeant of Arms will restore order in the chamber*

----------------------

**Good Morning America**

*Charles Gibson:* *Let me ask you some questions about faith which is a tough subject to talk about. Do we all worship the same God? Christian and Muslim?*

*George W Bush:* *I think we do. We have different routes of getting to the Almighty.*

*Gibson:* *Do Christians and non-Christians and Muslims go to heaven in your mind?*

*Bush:* *Yes they do. We have different routes of getting there.*
----------------------

**Dave Hunt discussion from 1986**

*Hunt:* *The Vatican and the Roman Catholic church-it's Pope is currently leading the greatest ecumenical movement in history in order to unite all religions under Rome's leadership. In 1986, Pope John Paul II gathered in Assisi, Italy the leaders of the world's major religions to pray for peace. There were snake worshippers, fire worshippers, spiritists, animists, Buddhists, Muslims, Hindus, North American witchdoctors. I watched in astonishment as they walked to the microphone to pray. The pope said they were all praying to the same God and that their prayers were creating a spiritual energy that was bringing about a new climate for peace. John Paul II allowed his good friend the Dalai Lama to put the Buddha on the altar in St. Peter's Church in Assisi and with his monks to have a Buddhist worship ceremony there, while Shintoists chanted, rang their bells outside.*

*The prophesied world religion is in the process of being formed before our eyes and the Vatican is the headquarters of the movement. Is this not spiritual fornication?*

But that's not all. This One World Religion also has a new symbol. Maybe you've seen it. It's called COEXIST and it looks like this:

***King Abdullah of Saudi Arabia*** *has been planning for years to, "find a way to unite the world's major religions in an effort to help foster peace", and believes a new international organization will help make that dream a reality.*

***Chief Rabbi Yona Metzger****, one of the two Chief Rabbis of Israel said, "We need a United Relations of Religions, which would contain representatives of the World's Religions as opposed to nations. Uniting the world's faithful is key to world peace. We must promote a respect for the differences among various religions. A Church, a mosque, a synagogue or a holy temple must be embassies of God and we have to spread this idea to our believers." He has suggested that the Dalai Lama could lead the assembly.*

***Muslim Leader Adnan Oktar*** *recently met with three representatives from the re-established Jewish Sanhedrin, to discuss how religious Muslims, Jews and Christians can work together on rebuilding the Temple." An official statement about the meeting has been published on the Sanhedrin's website, "We are all the sons of one father, the descendants of Adam, and all humanity is but a single family. Peace among nations will be achieved through building the House of G-d, where all peoples will serve." Oktar added that the Temple, "Will be rebuilt and all believers will worship there in tranquility." And, "The Temple could be rebuilt in one year."*[6]

Now correct me if I'm wrong, but I'm kind of thinking somebody's taking this One World Religion kind of seriously. Everybody's promoting it! Even to the highest levels of society! Exactly like the Bible said would happen, when you are living in the Last Days!

**II. The 2nd way** we know we're really headed for **A One World Religion** is due to a **Watering Down of the Truth.**

I'm talking about the *Ecumenical Movement*. And once again, put yourself in the Antichrist's shoes. If you're going to deceive people into creating a One World Religion then you not only have to get rid of one religion being superior over another, but you must certainly get rid of any sense of absolute rights or wrongs, right? Why? Because if people still think there are genuine absolute rights and wrongs then it is going to mess up your attempts to get everyone saying all religions are right and that none of them is wrong. And this is precisely what the *Ecumenical Movement* is doing.

For those of you who may not know, Ecumenicalism is defined as "the organized attempt to bring about the cooperation and unity of all believers."[7] At the onset, that sounds pretty good. But what they don't tell you, is it's come to mean all believers, meaning even those outside of Christ, no matter what they believe, whether they believe in Christ or not! And their so-called "unity" is being sought not on the basis of *truth*, but from a "watered down version of it." I'm here to tell you, the Bible is clear. We Christians, genuine believers in Christ, do not join hands with somebody who's preaching a "watered down version" of God's truth, i.e. *a lie*! Rather the Bible says we need to come out from among them and *be ye separate*! I didn't say that. God did.

**2 Corinthians 6:14-17** "Do not be yoked together with unbelievers. For what do righteousness and wickedness have in common? Or what fellowship can light have with darkness? What harmony is there between Christ and Belial? Or what does a believer have in common with an unbeliever? What agreement is there between the temple of God and idols? For we are the temple of the living God. As God has said: I will live with them and walk among them, and I will be their God, and they will be my people." Therefore, Come out from them and be separate, says the Lord. Touch no unclean thing, and I will receive you."

According to our text, the Bible clearly says that when it comes to unbelievers, i.e. non-Christians, what are we supposed to do? Hang out with them, witness to them and love them enough to tell them the truth about Jesus being the only way to heaven because we're concerned about their eternal destiny, but the last thing we ever want to do, is to be what? Is to be "yoked" with them, right? The word "yoked" literally means, "to bound together with or to have fellowship with." Why? Because it's like oil and water. It doesn't mix! It can't mix! It'll never mix. Why? Because you cannot mix a lie with God's perfect holy truth and that's Paul's argument there! Why in the world would a born again Christian try to mix God's truth with the devil's lies? What do righteousness and wickedness have in common? What fellowship can light have with darkness? What harmony is there between Christ and Belial? In other words, how in the world can a Christian go along and link hands with this One World Religion? *You cannot meld the two together*! They deny that Jesus is the only way to heaven! That's why Paul writes, Come out from among them and be ye separate! Touch no unclean thing, including this lie of a One World Religion, *says the Lord*! And yet, that's exactly what the Ecumenical Movement is trying to get us to do!

**1. The 1st way they're trying to get us to do that is by getting us to repeat the lie that We Just Need to Love.**

If only we would love each other, then peace will come to the planet, like the transcript of this video shows:
*United Religions Initiative*

*Peace. It should be the natural order.*
*Peace. Why is it so hard to find?*
*Peace. Why do people try so hard to prevent it?*

*Why do so many people divide, split and fracture the one face of humanity? Is there something you can do to heal the violence? Yes.*

*Religiously motivated violence can end. This is your invitation to be a Peacebuilder. In the year 2000, a unique global community took the initiative to end religiously motivated hate and violence by founding the United Religions Initiative. Because of URI, Indians and Pakistanis of diverse faiths are looking beyond the boundaries that divide them. Because of URI, Christian and Indigenous Peoples of Latin America are creating a new world of mutual respect. Because of URI, Jews, Muslims, Christians in the Middle East are learning that the only security is peace.*

*In just a few short years, the United Religions Initiative has spread to 50 countries on 5 continents. In a few short years, former enemies have stopped seeing each other as the "other" and started seeing each other as themselves.*

*B'Hai, Christian, Muslim, Jew, Zorastianism, Buddhist, Sikh, Hindu. All around the world, URI is helping people experience the shared human face behind the different human faiths. Achieving on a deep, personal, spiritual level what personal governments and organizations were unable to accomplish before. Now more than ever this initiative must become a shared initiative.*

*One neighborhood. One community. One region at a time.* "[8]

Huh? Don't you want to be a peace builder? How many of you have heard of this lying propaganda before? We just gotta love to bring peace to the planet. And here's just one of the verses they quote out of context to suck us into it!

**John 13:35** "A new command I give you: Love one another. As I have loved you, so you must love one another. By this all men will know that you are my disciples, if you love one another."

Well there you have it, from the lips of Jesus Himself. We're all supposed to love one another. Just join hands and link together with anyone and everyone, including people of different faiths and peace will come to the planet! Wrong answer! First of all, peace only comes to the planet when the Prince of Peace, Jesus Christ comes back to the planet! And as far as loving one another, yes we are to love one another, as Christians, *not support those who support satanic lies*! Yes, we are to be concerned about the lost, yes we are to pray for them, yes we love them enough to tell them the truth that Jesus is the only way to heaven, but we're not to believe like them and link hands with them! Why? Because it's a lie! Jesus is the only way to heaven. I didn't say that, He did!

Besides, can we really "get along" with those who believe that we ourselves are gods, or that we'll burn in a mythical place called purgatory where we purge away our sins in order to get into heaven, which is denying the cross? Can we really "join hands" with those who would have you and I believe that sin is just an illusion, or that hell is only make believe and that heaven for some men will be to endlessly satisfy their lusts with as many virgins as they want, which only happens after they kill a bunch of people? And can we really "get along" with those who are claiming to be Christians yet state that one has to keep the sacraments to be saved, or that satan doesn't exist, or that Christ's work on the cross is not secure? Can we really "join hands" and have fellowship with those who would have you and I believe that Jesus is not God, but the archangel Michael, or worse yet, that He is the spirit-brother of satan himself...lucifer? I don't think so! The answer is obvious! *Come out from among them and be ye separate*! Why? Because God says to! You cannot have fellowship with those who are leading people to hell! He doesn't like that! Don't believe me? Let's take a look at what's going to happen during the 7-year Tribulation to this One World Religion movement that says you just gotta love one another.

**Revelation 18:4-8,23** "Then I heard another voice from heaven say: Come out of her, my people, so that you will not share in her sins, so that you will not receive any of her plagues; for her sins are piled up to heaven, and God has remembered her crimes. Give back to her as she has given; pay her back double for what she has done. Pour her a double portion from her own cup. Give her as much torment and grief as the glory and luxury she gave herself. In her heart she boasts, 'I sit enthroned as queen. I am not a widow; I will never mourn.' Therefore in one day her plagues will overtake her: death, mourning and famine. She will be consumed by fire, for mighty is the Lord God who judges her. By your magic spell all the nations were led astray."

Can I tell you what one of those *spells* is? Just love! Link hands and join together with anyone and everyone no matter what they believe, including that Jesus is not the only way to heaven, and form a One World Religion so that peace can come to the planet. It's all happening *right now*, right before our very eyes, and that's exactly what the Bible said would happen, when you are living in the Last Days.

**2. The 2nd way the Ecumenical Movement is getting us to fall for the lie of a One World Religion is by getting us to repeat another lie and that is this...We Just Need to Tolerate.**

How many of you have heard that one? You should NEVER JUDGE. You just need to tolerate. And here's another verse they quote out of context to suck us into it.

**Matthew 7:1** "Do not judge, or you too will be judged. For in the same way you judge others, you will be judged, and with the measure you use, it will be measured to you."

Well there you have it. The Bible says we should never judge another person, no matter what they believe, no matter what they say, we just love them and accept them, right? Wrong! I'm here to tell you this is another one of the biggest lies the enemy has thrust upon the Church in these Last Days. And the reason why I know this is because if we weren't supposed to judge anyone or anything, no matter what they say, believe, or do, including their supposed version of God, then why did Jesus say this?

**John 7:24** "Stop judging by mere appearances, and make a right judgment."

Jesus isn't saying we should never judge! He didn't say to *never* make a judgment. He said *when you do judge* make sure that it's *right*! Get your facts straight! He said it right there! And if we're really never supposed to judge, then why did the Apostle Paul say this?

**1 Corinthians 6:1-5** "If any of you has a dispute with another, dare he take it before the ungodly for judgment instead of before the saints? Do you not know that the saints will judge the world? And if you are to judge the world, are you not competent to judge trivial cases? Do you not know that we will judge angels? How much more the things of this life! Therefore, if you have disputes about such matters, appoint as judges even men of little account in the church! I say this to shame you. Is it possible that there is nobody among you wise enough to judge a dispute between believers?"

I don't know about you, but it sure sounds like we Christians are not only *supposed to be judging*, but we're supposed to be *judging up a storm*, right? And so the question is, "Why in the world do people quote Matthew 7 and say we're never supposed to judge? They're quoting it out of context! Matthew 7 is dealing with a *hypocritical judgment* where a person is judging somebody of something when they themselves are guilty of doing the very same thing, if not worse! How do we know? Because the rest of the text says that the one person judging has a log in their eye and the other only has a speck of dust in their eye. But if you read the rest of the passage it doesn't stop there. It doesn't say don't ever judge. It says first take the log out of your own eye and then you can what? You can *rightly judge* and remove the speck from the other person's eye! The whole point of the passage, and John 7, is not to say that we're never to judge, *but just the opposite*! It says to get rid of your hypocrisy first, then get your facts straight so you can make a righteous judgment, right?

And yet, this is what the Ecumenical Movement is saying we should never do! That *We Should Never Judge* between right and wrong. We need to accept everything as right and nothing is wrong! And we just need to tolerate. But the problem is, they don't tell you that they've changed the definition of tolerance. And here's how they're sucking us into it. Let's take a look at what this guy says again.

## Josh McDowell: Steeling the Mind of America: Tolerance

*Some of you are saying, 'Wait a minute, I thought tolerance was good' That's the problem. That's the problem! Little Johnny comes home from school and that very sincere Christian mother from the most fundamental evangelical church meets little Johnny and says, 'How was school today?'*

*'Oh Mommy.'*

*'What did you talk about?'*

*'We talked about tolerance.'*

*And that Christian mother goes, 'Oh that's wonderful. You know Jesus told us to be tolerant.'*

*ABSOLUTELY NOT!! That mother is undermining everything she believes and it won't take years; it will only take months to come back and haunt her. You're saying, hold on a minute, I don't get this. The reason is this. Right now there are two distinct definitions of tolerance. One I call a historical traditional tolerance. It's one that almost everyone who is here has been conditioned to think by and how you're listening to me through traditional tolerance. I am speaking from a whole new definition of tolerance. Traditional tolerance would be defined by Webster: To bear or put up with someone or something that is not especially liked. Or you know in our circles we say', God has called me as a Christian to love the sinner but to hate the sin.' That's one of the most bigoted statements you could make today. You make that statement in the average classroom today and that entire class would turn on you. The bigotry and the intolerance to say, 'Love the sinner, hate the sin'. The reason is, there is a second definition of tolerance and I would say that 80% of the time, outside the walls of the church, when you hear the word tolerance whether the media, the magazines, the school or what - it's not the tolerance you were conditioned to think by. It's a whole new definition of tolerance, 80% of the time-it's a new definition.*

*The tolerance you were brought up with is now referred to as negative tolerance. The new tolerance is called positive tolerance. It's defined this way. Every single individual's values, beliefs, lifestyles and claims to truth are equal. Let me repeat that- ALL values, ALL beliefs, ALL truth, ALL lifestyles are equal and if you dare to say there is a value, belief, a lifestyle or claim to truth greater than another, that is called hierarchy and that's the new definition of bigotry. A bigot today has nothing to do with racism or anything. A bigot today is someone who's committed to moral hierarchy that there are differences in values and beliefs, lifestyles or claims to truth. Positive tolerance adds the word praise. What it means is this- we not only want your permission, we demand your praise and if you do not value my lifestyle, my claim to truth as equal to your own--now listen to this--as equal to yours from the heart, you are a bigot and you are intolerant. From the heart. It's called positive tolerance.*

*Let me show you just how it's hit the church. Just in a little brief one. Can you tell me historically what has been the number one verse quoted from the scriptures by Christians and non-Christians, Christian young people, non-Christian young people, the media, everything. What's the number one verse quoted historically by the scriptures? John 3:16. Do you know what it is now? Have you all been listening? Have you even been listening to your own young people? Can anyone tell me now, by far, way out far from everything, what's the number one verse quoted even from Christian young people from the Bible? Number one now, what is it? Judge not, that you not be judged. Listen! Why? The moment you make a judgment you're saying there's hierarchy and that makes you a bigot and intolerant and it makes you stand against the number one virtue in culture. Tolerance. All is equal. Christian love and the number one virtue of culture today cannot coexist. In fact, I'll go as far as to say that Christian love is the number one enemy of the number one virtue in the culture: Tolerance.*

*In fact, men and women, I'll say this. I believe now it's a point as a pastor, as an evangelist-someone like that. It is very difficult to be popular and faithful. Jesus loved that woman at the well. And in love and compassion He said to her, 'Go call you're husband.' she said, 'sir, I don't have a husband.' And in loving compassion Jesus said, 'That's right. You've had five husbands and the one you're living with right now is not you're husband.' Jesus exposed her lifestyle. He was witnessing to her. He exposed her lifestyle. Now speak to me. Did Jesus expose her lifestyle as an alternate lifestyle or a sinful lifestyle?*

**Audience:** *"Sinful lifestyle."*

**Josh:** *"You're a BIGOT! What right do you have to say that?! You're INTOLERANT! Who do you think you are to think you have the corner on truth?*

*What right do you have to make any moral judgment on someone?"*

*He did it in love. If you don't believe me that that's not true- you try it anywhere in culture right today. You just travel with me into the high schools and universities. And Jesus did it in love. Christian love and tolerance cannot coexist. We had better wake up."*[9]

Why? Because everything we believe in as Christians is at risk! Think about it! Because of this new definition of tolerance they put on us, we're now going to become *the new enemy of the state*! All that we believe in, all of Christianity, all the Scriptures, is based on *absolute* right and wrongs! Jesus is the ONLY way to heaven, not one of many. The Bible declares that there is ONLY one God; not several or that we can become gods ourselves. The very Ten Commandments are all *absolute judgments* of what's right and wrong from God! You shall not murder, you shall not commit adultery, you shall not steal, etc. *You cannot tolerate that*!

PLUS, how can all values be equal? What if someone's "value" was to molest his or her children? Is that right? Am I supposed to accept that? If you bought into the new definition of TOLERANCE you would have to say yes. Yet, every ounce of your being says NO! What if it was another person's "value" to teach their children to steal for a living? What if it was a mother's "value" to teach her daughter a fulfilling lifestyle called prostitution? What if a father had a "value" he wanted to teach his son called being an abuser of women? Now can I tell you something? Some religions on the planet today *do teach that*! They treat women as prostitutes and they force them into a subservient lifestyle and even kill them if they don't like them. I'm supposed to accept that? In certain religious cultures today, people get their hands chopped off for stealing or their heads chopped off just for disagreeing. Do we agree with that? Should we tolerate that? I don't think so! It's true Biblical Christianity that's freed people historically from these tyrannous belief systems by setting the standard of right and wrong!

And yet, the Ecumenical Movement says *We Should Not Judge* between right and wrong and instead we need to *tolerate* anything as right and nothing as wrong, to bring peace to the planet and it's all happening *right now*, right before our very eyes, even in the Church, just like the Bible said would happen when you are living in the Last Days.

**3.** The **3**rd **way** the Ecumenical Movement is setting us up to fall for the lie of a One World Religion is by getting us to repeat this lie...**We Just Need to Rethink.**

Don't be harsh. Don't be judgmental. Don't be intolerant. Just "rethink" this idea of Jesus being the "only way to heaven" and that God is the "Only One" worthy of worship. Really? That's not what the Bible says we need to be doing!

**Deuteronomy 6:13-15** "Fear the LORD your God, serve Him only and take your oaths in His Name. Do not follow other gods, the gods of the peoples around you; for the LORD your God, Who is among you, is a jealous God and His anger will burn against you, and He will destroy you from the face of the land."

Now how many of you would say that God doesn't want His children worshiping other so-called gods? Sounds to me like He takes it kind of Personal. Why? Because His children are supposed to lead people to *heaven,* and instead they're working with people who are *leading others to hell* and this is exactly what the Ecumenical Movement is doing! They say *We Need to Rethink this Command* to worship only God, to say there's only one way to heaven and instead accept these other gods so we can have peace on the planet, and a One World Religion, AND just in case you don't "rethink" this on your own and be popular like the rest of the world, they've got a backup plan. They plan to "re-educate" you, the next generation, through the *media* and the *secular education system.* Don't believe me? Let's take a look at what's being taught in our schools and you tell me if it's not been hijacked to get our kids to "accept" a One World Religion and the Antichrists Kingdom, coming to a planet near you!

## GLOBE PROGRAM

*It's been said that the best teachers are often found in the corners. Well interestingly enough someone sent this article to me from a small town newspaper. Look at what they are beginning to teach in public school.*

*Would you hire Soviet Mikhail Gorbachev to teach your children about American values? I'm sure you would say, "You've got to be kidding!" No, I'm not kidding. His philosophy is being taught in 10,350 of our United States Schools today.*

*Let me explain. The curriculum in these 10,000+ schools is patterned after this socialized program. This program is called GLOBE and it is being promoted worldwide.*

*GLOBE teaches:*

*1) Earth Worship (pantheism)*
*2) Evolution.*
*3) Socialized Medicine.*
*4) World Government*
*5) Animal Rights (animals seen as brothers & sisters)*
*6) Redistribution of American Wealth to other nations.*
*7) Contraception and "Reproductive Health"*
*8) Legal Abortion*
*9) Debt Forgiveness to third world nations*
*10) Adoption of the gay rights agenda*
*11) The elimination of the right to bear arms*
*12) Setting aside massive amounts of private land where no human presence is allowed*

-------------------------------------------

*GLOBE stands for Global Learning and Observation to Benefit the Environment. Mikhail Gorbachev is the head of an organization called Green Cross International operating right here in the United States. Gorbachev is working to create World Government and he's helping to implement this education scheme. He is also in joint partnership with UNESCO, which is the source of much of the anti-American education curriculum, as well as the International Baccalaureate program. This GLOBE program is funded and implemented through the Federal Department of Education created under GOALS 2000 and has now carried over in "No Child Left Behind."*

*No Child Left Behind? It should be called No Child Left Unindoctrinated."*[10]

Indoctrinated in what? Anti-God, Anti-American ideals to "erase" any and all sense of Patriotism, and instead, "accept" a One World Government and a One World Religion. Looks to me like somebody's hijacked our school system to brainwash, how about you? And if that surprises you, it shouldn't. In fact, it's even worse. One man shares this:

*"Many public schools have become pagan religion indoctrination centers. These schools now teach children anti-Judeo-Christian beliefs and pagan religions, and try to mold children's minds through the latest techniques in behavioral psychology.*

*Here is just a small sample of the flood of "spiritual" sessions, (remember religion is supposed to be taken out of school) taking place in classrooms throughout the country.*

*Altered states of consciousness:*
*Astrology:*
*Other forms of divination:*
*Spiritism:*
*Magic, spells, and sorcery:*
*Occult charms and symbols:*
*Solstice rites, sacred sex, Serpent worship:*

**Human sacrifice:** *Students are given lessons on death education and lessons to advocate the cultural endorsement of abortion and euthanasia as a way to prepare the new generation to accept many new forms of sacrifice, such as the notion of sacrificing oneself for the "common good."*

*Is this what our children should be learning? Should schools turn children into Earth-and spirit-worshipers? Should parents pay property taxes for public schools that promote pagan religions?"*[11]

Can I answer that? No! I thought kids need to learn Reading, Writing and Arithmetic and instead they're being "re-educated" to hate America, hate the Christian God and accept the Antichrist's kingdom! And this is all happening *right now*! It's the pre-stated goals of the humanists who took over our School System to specifically prepare our children for the New World Order. I didn't say that, they did!

- *"Education is thus a most powerful ally of humanism and every American school is a school of humanism. What can a theistic Sunday School's meeting for an hour once a week and teaching only a fraction of the children do to stem the tide of the five-day program of humanistic teaching?"* **Charles F. Potter, Humanism: A New Religion (1930)**

- *"I am convinced that the battle for humankind's future must be waged and won in the public school classroom by teachers who correctly perceive their role as proselytizers of a new faith: a religion of humanity. These teachers must embody the same selfless dedication as the most rabid fundamentalist preachers for they will be ministers of another sort, utilizing a classroom instead of a pulpit to convey humanist values in whatever subject they teach, regardless of educational level – preschool, day care or a large state university. The classroom must and will become an arena of conflict between the old and the new – the rotting corpse of Christianity...and the new faith of humanism.*" **John J. Dunphy, "A New Religion for a New Age," The Humanist, January/February 1983**

- "*Every child in America entering school at the age of five is mentally ill because he comes to school with certain allegiances toward our founding fathers, toward our elected officials, toward his parents, toward a belief in a supernatural Being and toward the sovereignty of this nation as a separate entity. It is up to you teachers to make all these sick children well by creating the international children of the future.*" **Harvard Professor of Education and Psychiatry, 1984**[12]

Our schools have been hijacked to get our children to "rethink" Who God is, and that Jesus is the only way to heaven, and that America should remain a sovereign nation, just so they'll go along with a One World Religion and the Antichrist's kingdom. And it's all happening *right now*, right before our very eyes exactly like the Bible said would happen when you are living in the Last Days!

Like it or not, we are headed for *The Final Countdown* and so the point is this: If you're a Christian, it's time to get busy! We've got to lay aside our differences, not God's truth, and get busy working together saving souls! They need to know that JESUS IS THE ONLY WAY TO HEAVEN!

But if you're not a Christian, then I beg you, please, heed the signs...heed the warnings...give your life to Jesus now...because if you continue to follow this lie of a One World Religion...you're going to end up in **hell**...In fact, you might just be one click away, like this man shares.

*"How many of you think that you'll go to hell?"*

*The world has convinced themselves that this is a place that they are not going to. No man wants to believe he's going there.*

*You know some of you, you've read this text, I know that there are those of you, I know, I know based on what God's word tells me, some of you in this place that hear my voice will go to the place I describe today. Some of you are headed there, you don't think you are but even now you provoke God by your very attendance of His worship today because you have not Christ. You have no hope. You're without God. But you don't think you'll go there. You think that somehow you're going to reason, you're going to figure out because of something that you have done or are doing or hope to do in the future, somehow you plan to miss that place.*

*Three people every second are passing into eternity. (Snapping fingers) That fast, souls are going out of this world into an eternal hell or an eternal joy. And God's Word says that most of those are on the broad way to destruction, Christ is the only way to the Father. Those who are Buddhist in this world are passing into damnation. Those who die practicing Muslims are going. Practicing Catholics if they are worshiping Mary, they are not worshipers of Christ. One of those clicks has your name on it.*[13]

**4.** The **4ᵗʰ way** the Ecumenical Movement is getting us to fall for the lie of a One World Religion is by getting us to repeat this lie...**We Just Need to Blend.**

Come on! Don't you want to just work together? Haven't you heard? We are the world, we're God's children and we'll make the world a brighter place for you and me, if we just start *blending*. Don't believe me? Wasn't anybody paying attention to the Michael Jackson Funeral? They used that whole thing as a platform to get us to go along with a One World Religion. I encourage you to find the video online and watch for the symbols in the background as you listen to the message.

**Michael Jackson Memorial: Song: We Are The World**

*The performance of "We Are the World" accompanied by the lyrics to the song projected on a big screen, with many letters replaced by the religious icons of the world's faiths.*

*<Darryl Phinnessee>*
*There comes a time when we heed a certain call*
*When the world must come together as one*

*<KEN STACEY>*
*There are people dying*
*And its time to lend a hand to life*

*The greatest gift of all*

*<Dorian Holley>*
*We can't go on pretending day by day*
*That someone, somehow will soon make a change, make a change*

*<Judith Hill>*
*We are all a part of God's great big family*
*And the truth, you know,*
*Love is all we need*

*<Orianthi Panagaris>*
*We are the world, we are the children*
*We are the ones who make a brighter day*
*So lets start giving*

*<Judith Hill>*
*There's a choice we're making*
*We're saving our own lives*

*<Judith and Orianthi>*
*Its true we'll make a better day*
*Just you and me."*[14]

It's true! We'll make this world a better place if we just start blending. You know, form a One World Religion. If you watched the video, did you see the symbols? In fact, if you were paying attention, they did the exact same thing during the 9-11 memorial services. Let's take a look at that.

*"President Bush pointed out that 9-11, this "Day of Infamy" was a spiritual event with spiritual implications. He only hinted however, at what these implications could be.*

*The first inkling came a few days later at the services held for 9-11 at the Washington Cathedral. During this service, we saw clerics from Christianity, Judaism and Islam present themselves in full regalia. They were fully unanimous in their assertion that "we all worship the same God."*

*This theme would again be apparent when Oprah Winfrey led a "prayer service" in Yankee Stadium. This time, we were treated to prayers and "words of wisdom" from Protestant Preachers, Catholic Cardinals and Bishops, an Eastern Orthodox Bishop, Islamic Imams, Jewish Rabbis and Hindu Clerics.*

*But strangely missing from these services were Christian Fundamentalists. The omissions were intentional because our beliefs are incompatible with the goals and objective of the New World Religion.*

*"Fundamentalists" groups which do not fit into the mold can now be marginalized as cults and wiped out in the most profound fashion, while the liberal "Christianity" represented by the mainstream denominations is held up as acceptable."*[15]

Why? Because they'll go along with a One World Religion. But the problem is, that's not what the Bible says! But don't take my word for it. Let's listen to God's.

**Romans 16:16-18** "Greet one another with a holy kiss. All the churches of Christ send greetings. I urge you, brothers and sisters, to watch out for those who cause divisions and put obstacles in your way that are contrary to the teaching you have learned. Keep away from them. For such people are not serving our Lord Christ, but their own appetites. By smooth talk and flattery they deceive the minds of naive people."

I don't want you to be naïve, and that's why the Bible clearly says that even though we're supposed to be nice to each other as Christians, when it comes to those who cause *division*, what are we supposed to do? We *keep away from them*! Titus 3 says we kick them out of the Church! We don't give them a holy hug. We don't give them a holy kiss. We give 'em a *holy kick*! We kick them out of the Church! Why? Because they're teaching things contrary to the truth and they're stirring up trouble!

And yet, this is exactly what the Ecumenical Movement is saying we *shouldn't do*! They say, "Don't kick them out of the Church, give them a voice. Don't stay away from them, *blend* together with them and we'll make this world a brighter place for you and me and for those of you who think this could never happen in the Church, I'm here to tell you, it's already happening! In fact, there's a new term for it. It's called *salad bar religion*. Check this out.

*"Salad-bar religion denotes the trend where people pick and choose religious beliefs, doctrines and practices – mixing and matching them much as they would select food in a cafeteria.*

*This is not just popular among non-Christians, but also among people who consider themselves to be Christians. People borrow from different traditions, then add them to whatever religion they're used to. But they don't want anything to do with organized religion.*

*Americans write their own Bible. They fashion their own god. More often than not, the god they choose is more like a best friend who has endless time for their needs, no matter how trivial.*

*Scholars call this, 'domesticating God,' turning Him into a social planner, therapist or guardian angel. We have trivialized God. We assume that God is the butler who serves you for one reason, to give you a happy life. We've turned Him into a divine Prozac."*[16]

Why? Because haven't you heard? If we just blend together with other religions and refashion God into this Giant Grandfather in the Sky, who wouldn't hurt a flea and accepts anything and everyone, including those who don't believe Jesus is the only way to heaven, then we can have peace on the planet. Really? And this is precisely what the Ecumenical Movement has done! They've actually conditioned us, even in the Church, to think that we're broadening the gospel when in actuality we're compromising the gospel and actually redefining what it means to be a Christian. In other words, we're not doing what our opening text says we need to do. We're not getting rid of heresy, we're propagating it! And now those in the Church who take a stand for sound teaching and correct doctrine like we're supposed to, are being labeled as the "divisive" and "unloving" ones! Do you get it? It's the complete reversal of the text!

But you might be thinking this is crazy! I can see this going on in the Liberal Churches, but there's no way that Mainline Denominations, Evangelical Christianity, is ever going to go along with this, no way!" Really? Well let's take a look at what's going on in the American Church *right now* and you tell me if we're not blending our Christianity into a One World Religion starting right here in my home of Las Vegas. They finished up their 25th Annual Interfaith Forum in 2012. Let's take a look.

## Interfaith Forums 2012

***Aleda Nelson:*** *Good evening everyone. Hi, um, a lovely spirit here this evening with everyone. Very friendly and cozy and a perfect evening to welcome you here to our 2nd forum in our 25th season in the Interfaith Forums. My name is Aleda Nelson and I'm the moderator for the evening.*

*We'd like to thank the Interfaith Council, the Interfaith Forum Committee and of course, Grace In The Desert Episcopal Church.*

*Our panelists this evening are-first off, representing Islam, Dr. Aslam Abdullah is the Director of the Islamic Society of Nevada.*

*Then we will be hearing from our Episcopal representative, Reverend Dr. Jim Wallis from Grace In The Desert Episcopal Church.*

*Following Jim will be Mr. Teji Malik representing the Sikh faith from Gurdwara Baba Deep Singh temple.*

*From humanism we have Mr. Mel Lipman who's the immediate class president of the American Humanist Association Union.*

*From the Church of Jesus Christ of Latter Day Saints, Mrs. Ruth Johnson is here and in addition to community activist, she's on the Board of Public Affairs Committee-is that right? Yes. Of the Church of Jesus Christ of Latter Days Saints.*

*And representing the B'hai faith is Mrs. Elham Khomassi*

*First of all we assume that our religious beliefs are our most deeply held beliefs and as such, we do not try to change the beliefs of others. There's no debate. There's no challenging. There's no defending one's belief in this environment.*

- The Global Faith Forum kicked off Thursday. Hundreds of Christians, Muslims, Jews, Hindus, Buddhists and atheists have convened at NorthWoods church in Texas in an effort to try to understand one another.

- Representatives of Jewish, Catholic, Protestant, B'hai, Mormon, Sikh, Vedic Druid and Muslim beliefs in Sacramento read scriptures from each of their religious texts, including six verses from the Quran, calling for all faiths to live in harmony. Again and again they uttered the refrain, "Let there be peace on earth and let it begin with me."

- A Bishop is now urging Christians to call God Allah. The Catholic leader believes it would help ease the tensions between the religions.

- Christians are celebrating religious diversity. On Pentecost Sunday, Christian churches across the United States are dedicating their worship to a celebration of our interfaith world. Progressive Christians thank God for religious diversity! We don't claim that our religion is superior to all others. We can grow closer to God and deeper in compassion – and we can understand our own traditions better – through a greater awareness of the world's religions. Sponsored by The Center for Progressive Christianity – Pluralism Sunday, will be promoted throughout churches and participating churches will be profiled in publicity releases, creating an evangelism opportunity for your congregation. The number of people looking at The Center for Progressive Christianity's website is topping 40,000 per month! "We believe Pluralism Sunday is an opportunity for progressive churches to reach some of the many people who are turned off by Christianity because of exclusivist claims some Christians make about it."

- Many Born-Again Christians hold Universalist Views, Barna finds. One in four born-again Christians believe that all people are eventually saved or accepted by God. A similar proportion, 26 percent, said a person's religion doesn't matter because all faiths teach the same lessons. And an even higher proportion, 40 percent, of born-again Christians said they believe Christians and Muslims worship the same God.

- The United Methodist Church's Claremont School of Theology has launched a program to train leaders. "There are a variety of beliefs regarding exclusivity in each of the traditions, and not all Christians, Jews and Muslims believe that their way is the only way." "Christians, Muslims and Jews will now have the opportunity to take classes together to learn about each other's religious traditions, to study topics that deal specifically with interfaith issues and to build bridges through coursework that assists them...our society's future religious leaders."

- Churches now promote Islam. Dozens of Christian churches, from Park Hill Congregational in Denver to Hillview United Methodist in Boise Idaho, and First United Lutheran in San Francisco to St. Elizabeth's Episcopal Church in Honolulu, are planning to send "A message both here at home and to the Arab and Muslim world about our respect for Islam" with a time to read the Quran during worship this Sunday. The Interfaith Alliance of Human Rights First is calling on Christian clergy to read portions of the Quran during their services Sunday.

- In fact, Churches are now letting other religions use their facilities. Heartsong Church near Memphis is allowing members of the Memphis Islamic Center to hold Ramadan prayers in its building and Aldersgate United Methodist Church in Alexandria Virginia allowed the Islamic Circle of North America to hold regular Friday prayers in its facility. But is this what we should be doing as Christians? I don't think so, as this man shares.

**Fox and Friends: All Faiths Welcome?**

*Two Protestant churches are taking some heat for opening their church to Muslims needing a place to worship.*

*<sign> Heartsong Church welcomes Memphis Islamic Center to the neighborhood because their own facilities were either too small or under construction.*

*Some see it as a Christian duty. Others disagree. We're back with Governor Huckabee with more on this. So is this counter against everything these churches stand for?*

***Huckabee:*** *Well you know, as much as I respect the autonomy of each local church-you just wonder, "What are they thinking?" I mean, if the purpose of a church is to push forth the gospel of Jesus Christ and then you have a Muslim group that says that Jesus Christ and all the people that follow Him are a bunch of infidels who should be essentially obliterated, I guess I have a hard time understanding that. I mean if a church is nothing more than a facility and a* *meeting place, free for any and all viewpoints without regard to what it is, then should a church be rented out to show adult movies on the weekend? I mean where does this end? How far does it go?*

Oh, but that's not all. A Prominent Church in Michigan removed its cross Tuesday and has changed its name as part of a series of moves intended to make it more inclusive. C3Exchange was formerly known as Christ Community Church. The Rev. Ian Lawton, the church's pastor, said the name change and removing the cross was designed to reflect the church's diverse members. "Our community has been a really open-minded community for some years now." "We've had a number of Muslim people, Jewish people, Buddhists, atheists…we're catching up to ourselves." "We honor the cross, but the cross is just one symbol of our community." In fact, they were so excited about it, they even videotaped it.[17]

Can I tell you something? That's what's wrong with America. We're removing the Cross of Christ *literally* and we're paying a heavy price for it. But correct me if I'm wrong, it sure looks to me like people, even Christians, are blending together with other religions, how about you? Sounds like a One World Religion is right around the corner! And that's exactly what the Bible said would happen, when you are living in the Last Days.

**5. The 5ᵗʰ way the Ecumenical Movement is getting us to fall for the lie of a One World Religion is by getting us to repeat this lie…We Just Need to Submit.**

Would you stop resisting? Would you stop being a fundamentalist? If you don't knock it off and *submit*, we're going to have to take you out! I didn't say that, God did. Listen to what He said this One World Religion is going to do to the resisters.

**Revelation 17:1-2,5-6** "One of the seven angels who had the seven bowls came and said to me, 'Come, I will show you the punishment of the great prostitute, who sits by many waters. With her the kings of the earth committed adultery, and the inhabitants of the earth were intoxicated with the wine of her adulteries.' The name written on her forehead was a mystery: BABYLON THE GREAT THE MOTHER OF PROSTITUTES AND OF THE ABOMINATIONS OF THE EARTH. I saw that the woman was drunk with the blood of God's holy people, the blood of those who bore testimony to Jesus."

You know that He's the only way to heaven. But according to our text, the Bible clearly says that this One World Religious system is not only going to seduce the world's government and people, and in other places work with the Antichrist with this feel-good message of, "We just gotta love, we just gotta tolerate, we just gotta rethink this whole evangelical Christianity thing and blend together with other religions." But it also says *for those who resist*, she what? She'll be drunk with your blood, right? In other words, if you don't *submit* to her *you're going to die*! And as creepy as that sounds, that's what the Bible clearly says. But here's the point. What's even creepier is just how close we are to the fulfillment of this passage. You see, in order for this passage to be fulfilled, you need *three things*. A Woman Figure to represent the World's Religions, because it's a woman that rides the Beast, a Mother of prostitutes, and you need an Antichrist figure to work with, because it says she rides the Beast, or Antichrist, and three you need some sort of a Global Authority System to punish those who don't obey, right? Well all three are on the verge of being fulfilled!

## 1. The 1st sign of this fulfillment is the Woman Figure.

Believe it or not, we are already seeing how we are being conditioned to move away from the Male Patriarchal system of Religions, i.e. a Male Deity, to a Female Deity. And as we saw before, it's even happening in the Church. Let's take a look at those quotes from Feminism in the Church again.

- Mary Daly, who considers herself to be a Christian feminist, says this about traditional Christianity: "To put it bluntly, I propose that Christianity itself should be castrated." The primary focus of the 'Christian' feminist is to bring an end to what they perceive as male-dominated religion by 'castrating' the male influence from religion. Daly continued by saying, "I am suggesting that the idea of salvation uniquely by a male savior perpetuates the problem of patriarchal oppression."

- Herchurch.org is the website for Ebenezer Lutheran Church in San Francisco. On Wednesdays they open their sanctuary for the "Christian Goddess Rosary." They say that, "the exclusive emphasis of God as Father supports a domination structure that oppresses and subordinates women." They also encourage people to pray the "Hail Goddess Prayer" that states, "Hail Goddess full of grace. Blessed are you and blessed are all the fruits of your womb. For you are the MOTHER of us all."

- Jann Clanton author of, "*God, A Word for Girls and Boys*" says "Masculine God language hinders many children from establishing relationships of trust with God. In addition, calling God "he" causes boys to commit the sin of arrogance…Calling the Supreme power of the universe "he" causes girls to commit the sin of devaluing themselves. For the sake of "these little ones" we must change the way we talk about God."

- One of the hottest books that's being promoted in the Church right now is called "The Shack" and if you look at it, it's not only openly New Age in doctrine, but it actually presents God as a woman…shocker![18]

As you can see, even the Church is being prepared to accept a female deity. But feminism is not the only one trying to get us to change to this female deity. If you think about it, other religions are all ready to go. For instance, Catholicism has their worship of Mary, right? Environmentalism has their worship of Mother Earth. The Eastern Religions have their Ying/Yang principle of the male and female duality system. Hinduism has their worship of the goddess Shiva, and even Wicca and Witchcraft have their goddesses to worship as well. In fact, the European Union has already picked their new symbol. Can you guess what it is? Take a look!

19

As you can see, it's all out there. But as you can also see, the whole world's ripe for a female deity called The Woman that Rides the Beast.

**2. The 2nd fulfillment** of this passage that's on the verge of coming to pass is the **Antichrist Figure.**

You not only need a Female Deity, but you have to have an Antichrist person for the Female Deity to work with and as we saw before, the Antichrist Figure is going to be a Political Figure that people actually worship as a god during the 7-year Tribulation. But it's a good thing we don't see any signs of that happening any time soon! People worshiping a political figure as god! It's already happening! Let's take a look.

**MSNBC:** Obama god?

***Evan Thomas of Newsweek:*** *"Obama's really had a different task as we've seen too often as the bad guy and he has a very different job from, Reagan-was all about America, and you talked about it. Obama is "We are above that now." -- We're not just parochial. We're not just chauvinistic. We're not just provincial. We stand for something. I mean in a way Obama's standing above the country. Above the world. He's sort of god."*

Obama is like God? I don't think so! But if that surprises you it shouldn't. As we saw before, this is just the tip of the iceberg of people even here in America worshiping a political figure of a man as god.

> An artist in Iowa created an inaugural parade of Barack Obama, riding on a donkey making his own triumphal entry complete as adorers wave palm fronds along with a "Secret Service" escort.

Another artist planned to unveil a portrait of Barack Obama in a Christ-like pose with a crown of thorns upon his brow at New York City's Union Square Park, marking the president's 100th day in office.

In fact, Newsweek not only carried a picture of Obama with the caption of "Second Coming" and another issue called him the "God of All Things."

And lest you think this is all just one big coincidence, we even have people for the first time in our nation's history saying that a political figure, a man, is our Lord and Savior. Don't believe me? Check this out.

***Jamie Foxx:*** *"First of all give an honor to god and our lord and savior Barack Obama."*[20]

Giving honor to god, our lord and savior, Barack Obama...who in the world would have ever thought that the day would come when we would see somebody here in America call a political figure of a man, "god our lord and savior?" *But it's happening now*! And that's exactly what the Bible said would happen, when you are living in the Last Days.

**3. The 3rd fulfillment** of this passage that's on the verge of coming to pass, is the **Global Authority Figure.**

Remember, you not only need a Female Deity and an Antichrist for the Female Deity to work with, but you have to have a Global Authority to punish those who resist, right? She's going to be drunk with their blood! And again, I'm so glad we don't see any signs of that...happening...any... time...soon! Yeah, right! Believe it or not, it's already begun! As we saw earlier, people all over the world are already calling for the Global Religious Headquarters. Let's take a look at that again.

**King Abdullah of Saudi Arabia** has been planning for years to, "find a way to unite the world's major religions in an effort to help foster peace, and believes a new international organization will help make that dream a reality."

**Chief Rabbi Yona Metzger**, one of the two Chief Rabbis of Israel said, "We need a United Relations of Religions, which would contain representatives of the World's Religions as opposed to nations."

And speaking of the United Nations, believe it or not, they've already stepped into this role by promoting what's called, "Defamation of Religions" where believe it or not, Christianity and preaching the Gospel will now become "illegal" across the globe. Don't believe me? Take a look!

*"Hi, this is Jay Sekulow of the American Center for Law and Justice. I've just gotten off the air. I'm here in the radio studio but I wanted to bring you this very important update. I've just authorized and established today, sending our teams to New York to the United Nations. Here's what's happening. We're sending lawyers from our Washington, D.C. office, our Government Affairs Office, as well as our New York City office which by the way is just a couple of blocks from the United Nations.*

*We're going there because the U.N. is going to be considering a resolution from an organization called the O.I.C., that's the Organization of the Islamic Conference. They are the largest group inside of the U.N. They represent over 47 countries, all of them Islamic. They are trying to criminalize anyone who speaks out against Islam. In other words, by quote, "defaming" Islam. If you say Jesus is the way of salvation, that would be deemed an act of defamation. And what they are trying to do is get a U.N. resolution that says that speaking out against Islam would be a violation of International Law. In effect, this would be criminalizing the proclamation of the Gospel."*

And lest you think they won't ever make you submit to this One World Religion where Christianity and preaching the Gospel is illegal, don't worry, just like with the public schools, they're coming after your kids. Check this out.

### UN Rights of the Child:

***Huckabee:*** *Right now the United States is one of only two countries in the world that is not signed onto a treaty that very well may get the government involved in how you raise your kids. Why haven't we heard about this? Let's ask Mike Farris. He is a constitutional lawyer, Chancellor of Patrick Henry College in Virginia and founder of the Homeschool Legal Defense Association and a leading advocate of parental rights. Why haven't we heard about this treaty that's being proposed?*

***Michael Farris:*** *Well it's been sitting in limbo ever since 1995. The political climate simply wasn't right for it to be sent to the Senate for ratification.*

*Madeleine Albright, on behalf of the Clinton Administration did sign it in '95, but the time is right now. The Obama administration, particularly Secretary of State Hillary Clinton and Barbara Boxer in the Senate believe that this is their hour. And it's probably going to be coming up for ratification either this fall or maybe next spring, but sometime in this session of Congress we're going to see this U.N. treaty that tells all parents and children how their lives will be governed through the U.N. by the United States government.*

**Huckabee:** *I mean this will be huge and we're not hearing about it Mike. So first of all, to the skeptic-how do I know this is really gonna make a difference in the way the case law could be applied? Are there any instances in the past where children were sort of maybe taking on their parents in a courtroom setting?*

**Farris:** *In Washington state, for a number of years they had a state law that paralleled the U.N. Convention on the Rights of the Child. It's since been repealed, but when I was a lawyer in Washington state, a 13 year old boy went to the social workers through his public school counselors and complained that his parents took him to church too much. They went Sunday morning, Sunday night and Wednesday night prayer meeting. The social workers were outraged about this amount of church and they removed the boy on an emergency basis.*

**Huckabee:** *Out of his own home?*

**Farris:** *Out of his own home! On an emergency which is for child abuse. Serious matters. The 72 hour hearing came along 3 days later. I was the lawyer for the families. The only issue in the case, was how much church and the judge said, "You know what? I think once a week is enough for any 13 year old boy and if you want to keep custody of your son, you have to agree to only take him to church once a week."*[21]

It's all happening right now. Who would have thought, in our nation's history, we'd ever get to the point where some Global Authority would actually tell us when we could and could not take our own kids to Church services, and how many times, otherwise, we're going to come and take them away. In other words, *submit* to this Global Authority, or pay a price. Gee, where have I heard that before?

*"Contrary to the father of lies, God's Word describes hell as the place where God pours His wrath on the wicked.*

*God's Word declares in **Romans 2:5-6,9** that 'But because of your stubbornness and unrepentant heart you are storing up wrath for yourself in the day of wrath and revelation of the righteous judgment of God, who will render to each person according to his deeds. There will be tribulation and distress for every soul of man who does evil.'*

*God's Word speaks of this in **Hebrews 10:26-31,** that there will be a 'certain terrifying expectation of judgment and of raging fire which consumes the enemies of God...severer punishment...for we know Him who said, 'Vengeance is mine. I will repay.' It is a terrifying thing to fall into the hands of the living God.'*

*Will hell be a good time? Contrary to the father of lies, hell will not be a place of friendship and rock music, but of misery, darkness, and isolation. The only thing you will hear from others are their cries of torment.*

*Jesus Christ warned in **Matthew 8:12** 'The subjects of the kingdom will be thrown outside into darkness where there will be weeping and gnashing of teeth.'*

*The Bible speaks in **2 Peter 2:17** of the wicked "for whom the black darkness has been reserved."*

*God's Word declares that there is no rest for the wicked in hell. **Revelation 14:11** states, 'And the smoke of their torment goes up forever and ever; they have no rest day and night.'*

*Jesus said of the Day of Judgment in **Matthew 25:41,46** 'Then He will say to those on His left, 'Depart from Me, you who are cursed into the eternal fire prepared for the devil and his angels...Then they will go away to eternal punishment, but the righteous to eternal life.'*

*God's Word says in **2 Thessalonians 1:7-9** that 'He will punish those who do not know God and do not obey the gospel of our Lord Jesus. They will be punished with everlasting destruction and shut out from the presence of the Lord and from the majesty of His power.'*

*God's Word also describes hell as a lake of fire. If you refuse to turn to Jesus Christ for eternal life, you too will go to the lake of fire forever! What are you going to do? Don't go to hell. Please. I beg you. Don't go to hell.*

*All of these people in the New Age movement that believe that everybody's going to heaven, that you can worship anything, that you can worship a flea, you can squeeze a tree, you can worship a crystal, you can worship the stars, I've got news for you.*

*They're not going unless they accept Jesus Christ as their Lord and Savior because the Word says that the only way to the Father is through the Son."*[22]

### III. The 3rd way we know we're really headed for A One World Religion is due to a Worldwide Assault on Christians.

That's right, I'm talking about the rise of *Christian Persecution*. And once again, put yourself in the Antichrist's shoes to understand this. If you're going to deceive the world into creating a One World Religion, then you not only have to get rid of any one religion being superior over another and any source of truth being more right than another, but you must certainly get rid of people who don't go along with your program, right? Of course! And so guess what? That's exactly what the Bible said is going to happen specifically to God's people in the Last Days! But don't take my word for it. Let's listen to God's.

**Matthew 24:3-9** As Jesus was sitting on the Mount of Olives, the disciples came to Him privately. "Tell us," they said, "when will this happen, and what will be the sign of Your coming and of the end of the age?" Jesus answered: "Watch out that no one deceives you. For many will come in My Name, claiming, 'I am the Christ,' and will deceive many. You will hear of wars and rumors of wars, but see to it that you are not alarmed. Such things must happen, but the end is still to come. Nation will rise against nation, and kingdom against kingdom. There will be famines and earthquakes in various places. All these are the beginning of birth pains. Then you will be handed over to be persecuted and put to death, and you will be hated by all nations because of Me."

Now maybe it's just me, but it appears that the events during the 7-year tribulation are not going to be pleasant ones for God's people. Wars, famines, earthquakes, false prophets, deceit and what? There's actually going to come a time when *the whole world*, Christian, *is going to hate you* just for being a follower of Jesus! Even to the point where they're going to want to kill you!

And for those of you wondering, the context here is *during* the 7-year Tribulation so the people he's talking about here, being hunted down and killed, are the Jewish remnant who follow Christ after their temporary blindness is removed. And two, those who get saved after the Rapture during the 7-year Tribulation, because people can still get saved during the 7-year Tribulation because the Gospel still goes forth from multiple sources. The Two Witnesses, the 144,000 male Jewish Witnesses, the Angel of God who proclaims the Eternal Gospel and anything you and I might leave behind. But the point is this. The lesson is, you should've got saved *before* the hammer came down. But now you're going to pay with a price, your life. During that time, people are going to hate you and actually seek to kill you just for being a follower of Jesus.

So here's the point for you and I today. Do we see any signs of a rise of Christian persecution and hatred towards us around the world even to the point where people actually want to kill us? Yes! In fact, it's already here, all over the world! In fact, pretty soon, believe it or not, you might have one of these encounters even right here in America. Let's take a look.

**Big Brother Interrogation**

*Interrogator: Thanks again for coming down Mr. Wilson. I know you're a busy man so we'll try and keep this short. Come on and have a seat.*

*So, for the record, your name is John Francis Wilson and you live at 15 Clear Heights Drive*

*John Wilson: <shakes head in agreement>*

*Interrogator: I'm sorry, could you clearly reply yes or no to my questions.*

*John Wilson: Yes I am John Wilson. Is this being recorded?*

*Interrogator: Are you a member of the Church of God on Springer Avenue?*

*John Wilson: Yes.*

*Interrogator: Have you taken part in their pro-life meetings and marches?*

*John Wilson: Uh yes, but what does that have to do with.. <Interrogator interrupts>*

*Interrogator:* Plan on attending this evening's meeting with this group?

*John Wilson:* Yes. <looks puzzled>

*Interrogator:* <writes something down> Mr. Wilson, are you aware that it is legal in this country to have an abortion.

*John Wilson:* Well yes but it hasn't always been that way.

*Interrogator:* Are you aware that some health care providers have been attacked and murdered by members of groups like yours?

*John Wilson:* Hold on. We have nothing to do with those groups. We are peaceful people that are <gets interrupted again>

*Interrogator:* Are you aware some health care providers have been attacked, Mr. Wilson?

*Mr. Wilson:* We believe in preserving life and not taking it!

*Interrogator:* Are you aware, Mr. Wilson, yes or no.

*Mr.Wilson:* <sighs>

*Interrogator:* You are a member of three different Right To Life groups. You are a member of a number of evangelical Christian organizations. You've donated money to Christian research and the Salvation Army. You receive daily emails from radical organizations that encourage prayer for our government on matters of policy. You've signed a number of petitions supporting the traditional definition of marriage. You frequently visit websites that are pro-Israeli and others that believe in an imminent cataclysmic event. Your wife and children are also enrolled in or talking to many other radical anti-social organizations and people, Mr. Wilson. There's a lot more here. Are these the actions of a peaceful man and his family?"[23]

Now for those of you thinking that this could never happen here in America, I'm telling you, it's right around the corner. Why? Because we the Church in America have been asleep at the wheel for so long and because we have become so complacent and in love with the things of the world instead of God Who made this world and because we continue to beat each other up and defeat the purpose of God, we are now paying a horrible price. The noose has slowly been put around our necks while we're literally being entertained to death. And now a global hatred of Christianity, is just around the corner.

### 1. The 1st way we know we're headed for this Global Persecution of Christianity is that The Propaganda is Already Here.

Take a lesson from Hitler. As incredible as this may sound, it's already open season on Christians here in America. For instance, correct me if I'm wrong, our society now says we are being *judgmental* because we say that our society is not good enough for God. But in reality, it's not us, it's the Bible. The Bible says that "no one is righteous, no not one." (Romans 3) They say that we're being *arrogant* because we think we've found the only way to eternal life. But I didn't say that, Jesus did. "He is the way, the truth, and the life, and that nobody comes to the Father except through Him." (John 14:6) Then they say that we're being *narrow-minded* because if we practiced what we preach, we would see all people worthy of salvation. No! The Bible says that "no one is worthy, no not one." (Romans 3) Then they say we're being *ignorant* because we ignore other paths to enlightenment for truth. But that's not what Jesus said. He said He was the ultimate source of Truth, not one of many. (John 14:6) Then they say that we're being *old-fashioned* because we cling to obsolete myths. But the Bible says that it is the truth we are to cling to, not a bunch of feel-good made up stories to create a One World Religion. (2 Timothy 4)[24]

And just to make sure that we sound really bad in the public arena, we are now being labeled, listen to the propaganda, with such terms as, "psycho groups," "harmful and dangerous sects," "Obstructionist right-wing fanatics who embrace a message of hate and fear (quote from Bill Clinton)," "mongers of hate who preach their anger (quote from Texas Governor Ann Richards)," "Intolerant, using subterranean tactics (quote from Congressman Vic Fazio)," "unchristian religious right who are selling our children out in the name of religion (quote from U.S. Surgeon General Joycelyn Elders)," "A greater threat than the old threat of communism (New York Times writer)," "fire-breathing radicals," "merchants of hate," "fanatics," and even "militants and bigots," and of course "right wing fundamental extremists."[25]

Hey, wait a second. That's the same terminology they're using for the Muslim terrorists that everybody says we need to get rid of? I'm telling you, you better wake up! We've been asleep at the wheel too long! They're already using the same propaganda on us and so that means we're next! Don't believe me? Check out this alleged quote from Janet Reno who gives us her definition of a cultist:

*"A cultist is one who has a strong belief in the Bible and the Second Coming of Christ; who frequently attends Bible studies; who has a high level of financial giving to a Christian cause; who home schools their children; who has accumulated survival foods and has a strong belief in the Second Amendment; and who distrusts big government.*

*Any of these may qualify [a person as a cultist] but certainly more than one [of these] would cause us to look at this person as a threat, and his family as being in a risk situation that qualified for government interference.* [26]

In other words, they'll come and take away your kids as we already saw before. But it appears to me there's a serious spiritual battle going on right here in America and I'm telling you, this is just the tip of the iceberg of what's coming down the pike. Let's take a look at even more examples of the negative propaganda on you and I the Christian, and you tell me if we better not get motivated.

*Richard Dawkins in his TV special,* "The root of all evil?" *said,* "The scriptural roots of the Judeo-Christian moral edifice are cruel and brutish. When we look closely at the Bible, you find a system of morals which any civilized person today should surely find poisonous." *He said about a* "Church service" *it reminds him of* "a Nuremberg Nazi rally, that Nazi leader and propagandist Dr. Goebbels would have been proud." *He later goes on to say that,* "Fundamentalist American Christianity is attacking science. But what is it offering instead? A mirror image of Islamic extremism. An American Taliban." *And the next scene on that program showed the burning towers of the World Trade Center in New York City on 9/11."*

Oh, but he's not the only one who thinks Christians are the new terrorists. So does Rosie O'Donnell.

### ABC's The View

***Elisabeth Hasselbeck:*** *Those attacks. Okay. That is widespread and if you take radical Islam and you want to talk about what's going on there. You have to...*

*Rosie O'Donnell:* <interrupts> *Just one second. Radical Christianity is just as threatening as Radical Islam. In a country like America...*

<audience claps>

*Rosie:* *Where we have a separation of church and state. We're a democracy.*

*Elisabeth:* *We're not bombing ourselves.* <referring to Christianity>

----------------------------------------

**Fox and Friends**

*Steve Doocy:* *Her exact quote was, Rosie O'Donnell of...what was it about 2 months ago she said, "Radical Christianity is just as threatening as radical Islam." And in the last hour we received an email from somebody who said, "You seem to forget that in the land of radical Islam, Rosie, the woman, the lesbian, would either be hung or stoned to death and in the world of radical Islam there would be no The View, no show with independent opinionated women."*

But she's not the only one. Texas Democrat Al Green said during a Homeland Security hearing that we need to, "Expand its hearings on radical Islam to include a hearing on the radicalization of Christians."

And he's not the only one. A University professor in Australia stated that *"Incompetent design, as I call it, is an anti-intellectual post-modernist mechanism for snaring the ill-educated into Protestant fundamentalism. They're talking about archbishops and politicians 'running scared' and not condemning this 'Christian Wahabbism' the same way that moderate Muslim leaders don't condemn Islamic terrorists."*

And apparently that's why US Representative Sheila Jackson Lee warned about how, "Christian militants might try to bring down the country and that such groups need to be investigated." And she's not the only one. Again, it's open season on Christians today! Let's take a look.

*Erroll Southers:* *Obama's Nominee to head the Transportation Safety Administration*

*Southers:* *"Most of the domestic groups that we pay attention to here are white supremacist groups. They're anti-government, in most cases anti-abortion, they are usually survivalist type in nature, identity oriented."*

*"Those groups are groups that claim to be extremely anti-government and Christian identity oriented"*

----------------------

### The Huff Post Live:

*Josh Zepps:* *The separation of church and state is fundamental for American life but what about the separation of church and military. In a new report by national security experts says that fundamentalist Christianity is rampant in the U.S. Armed Forces and that military leaders overtly promote evangelical Christianity.*

------------------------

*Jim Parco:* *Professor of Economics at Colorado College:*

*You actually have a system that actually is creating religious fundamentalists and that's what's concerning to me.*

-------------------------

### Huff Post Live: Email

*Sara Primrose:* *The only question that needs to be asked is "Do these fundamentalist beliefs and associated behavior compromise our missions abroad?" If yes, we must discourage or ban the encouragement of the spread of this brand of Christianity in the military.*

---------------------------

### Rachael Maddow Show: MSNBC

*Maddow:* *What we are learning about the religious beliefs of this militia group makes them seem a little bit like a cult, like a stand alone religious oddity. But some of the things they are obsessed with: fighting the Antichrist, avoiding the mark of the beast, the pre-tribulation Rapture-all this stuff-this isn't a set of beliefs that is specific to this one cult. These beliefs are actually characteristic of a broader movement, aren't they?*

----------------------------------

*Fox News Radio*

*Andrei Codrescu, a commentator for the program, All Things Considered, mocked a Christian pamphlet about the doctrine of the Rapture, the ascension into heaven, "The evaporation of four million people who believe in this crap would leave the world a better place."*

-------------------------

*Townhall.com*

**Woman:** *The young man, in Times Square who tried to blow innocent people that he doesn't even know up. These guys are acting on conviction. Somehow the idea got into their minds, that to kill other people is a great thing to do and that they would be rewarded in the hereafter.*

**Interviewer:** *But Christians do that every single day. In this country.*

**Woman:** *Do they blow people up?*

**Interviewer:** *Yes they do. Christians? Everyday.*

---

*<scenes from Dances With Wolves>*
*Pagan practices of American Indians are treated with loving respect*

*<scene from Little Buddha-Miramax Films>*
*Where Eastern religions bask in the warm fuzzies of spiritual awe.*

*<scene from Out On A Limb>*
*And where even the occult is given the benefit of the doubt*

**Shirley MacLaine:** *"He said the divine force is what the soul is made of."*

*<scene from The Handmaid's Tale>*
*Where the Christian faith of untold millions is portrayed as a potential breeding ground for neo-nazis. Public executions and a religion induced madness that*

*could lead to everything from mob violence...*

*<scene from The Rapture>*
*to a mother's willingness to kill her child for God.*

**Mom holding gun:** *Do you love God?*

**Little girl:** *Yes.*

**Mom:** *Tell him that. Don't be afraid baby.*

**Little girl:** *on her knees praying*

*Far too often this is the gospel according to Hollywood.*

*<sound of mother pulling the trigger>*

That's sick! And yet, do you see the propaganda? We're dangerous. We're cultists. We're terrorists and we'll even kill our own kids. Hitler must be proud of our media.

And apparently that's why Obama's faith advisor "Eboo Patel" also compared "Christian totalitarians," those who believe in only one correct interpretation of their religion, as dangerous as, "Al-Qaida."

In fact, the hatred towards Christianity has gotten so bad that they are now offering "Fundamentalist Workshops" where former Christians can come and be "rescued" from their religion. It's called, "Release and Reclaim." It's being headed up by a Berkeley psychologist named Marlene Winell who wrote a book called "Leaving the Fold" and she says, "Their God was a capricious, vindictive, punishing figure. Now they need help trusting themselves." And she goes on to say that, "Fundamentalism shares a belief in original sin, a final judgment day, and a reliance on the Bible as the literal word of God. That's a damaging belief." And she is now calling on, "The help of professions to study and treat the recovering adherents as they do other traumas and addictions."

You know, like in a virus or some bad habit like drugs or smoking or something. And that's why Richard Dawkins calls it just that. *"I think of religion as a dangerous virus. It's a virus, which is transmitted partly through teachers and clergy, but also down the generations from parent to child to grandchild. Children are especially vulnerable to infection by the virus of religion.* " And of course, Christianity.

So gee, what's next? A "vaccination" from "religion" and other so-called "addictive behaviors"? Well, believe it or not folks, it may not be that far away, as these reports show.

### Vaccinating against Drugs & Fundamentalism:

*Dr. Graham Phillips: When it comes to drug addiction, science still doesn't fully understand why some people become hooked and others don't. But for most who are addicted to drugs, giving them up or just cutting them back can be an almost impossible task. Well, scientists are developing vaccines against drug addiction. They work by vaccinating against the pleasurable effects of the drugs, hopefully making it easier for users to give it up. In fact, one day, they may even vaccinate people before they've been near a drug. To catch them before they can become addicted.*

*But what about a "vaccination" for "dangerous religions"?*

*Department of Defense lecture on the VMAT2 gene (God Gene) Expression In Religion VS Non-Religious Individuals:*

*Lecturer: Excuse me. On the left over here, <points to screen> we have individuals who are religious fundamentalist/religious fanatics and this is the expression in RTPCR-Real Time PCR- expression of the VMAT2 gene. Over here.. <gets interrupted>*

*Man: Doctor, -there are holes in your theory but <gets interrupted>*

*Lecturer: Let me complete. So over here we have ah, individuals who are not particularly fundamentalists, not particularly religious and you can see there's a much reduced expression of this particular gene-the VMAT2 gene, another evidence that supports our hypothesis for the development of this approach.*

But just in case the new "vaccine" doesn't work to keep you from being a Christian, maybe they'll just get rid of you period. The United States Department of Homeland Security issued its "Rightwing Extremism: Current Economic and

Political Climate Fueling Resurgence in Radicalization and Recruitment" Report. This report alleges that a violent "rightwing extremist" movement is trying to take over the nation. According to the definitions in these reports, Bible believing Christians are now being labeled as "rightwing extremists." And their strategies are reminiscent of Adolph Hitler's "Enabling Powers" which the Third Reich used after the Parliament building was burned down by "terrorists." These "Enabling Powers" gave Hitler the legal power to profile and arrest anyone who was even suspected of being critical of the Nazi Party and it enabled Hitler to grab control of Germany in just a matter of months killing millions of Jewish people and Christians.

And if you're wondering if you'll ever be qualified as a terrorist, listen to this. According to our own current government, any one of the following beliefs could classify an individual or group as a terrorist:

- Pro-life
- Critical of the United Nations
- Critical of the New World Order
- Critical of the Federal Reserve
- Homosexual marriage
- Oppose the North American Union (which they say officially does not exist)
- Critical of the income tax
- Oppose illegal immigration
- Fear foreign powers such as Communist China, Iran, Russia and India
- Critical of any of President Obama's policies (abortion, homosexual marriage. etc.)
- Concerned about RFID chips
- Belief in Bible prophecy or "End Time Prophecies"

As one man states, *"What is interesting about the above list is that a great deal of it has to do with things that have nothing to do with the individual nation. The only possible reason any national government would be concerned about its citizen's objecting to things like the New World Order, world government, the United Nations, homosexual marriage, a regional global government like the North American Union, abortion, RFID chips and belief in end times prophecies is because this is what they are planning to promote in the near future. Otherwise why be bothered about it?"* And he says this, *"I would suggest to you that Bible prophecy is being fulfilled far faster than most of us realize and that is why governments around the world are concerned about these things."*[27]

And I would agree. But again, maybe it's just me, but it appears we better stop fighting each other, and we better start working together and getting united and getting motivated or we're going to be in a heap of trouble, how about you? We don't have the liberty to play games anymore. We better start covering each other's back, instead of putting knives in each others backs! We need each other! Why? Because Jesus said this is what's going to happen in the Last Days. People are going to hate you, even to the point where they will want to kill you, just for being a Christian.

**2. The 2nd way** we know we're headed for a **Global Persecution** of Christians is that **The Persecution is Already Here.**

This behavior is not just being talked about, it's already being done! Christian persecution has skyrocketed in recent years and how ironic it is that everybody knows that Hitler killed 6 millions Jews. But how many realize that he murdered about 7 million Christians? And it's being repeated today! *Right now,* there are over 250 million Christians worldwide under the threat of persecution. *Right now,* all over the world, our fellow brothers and sisters in Christ are being beaten, tortured, imprisoned and murdered. Why? Because they refuse to compromise the truth, unlike the ecumenical movement who's promoting this One World Religion! In fact, in 1988 alone, there were some 310,000 Christians slaughtered and more Christians have died for their faith in this last century alone than in the previous nineteen centuries combined.[28] And it's getting worse. Let's take a look at even more facts on persecution.

75% of all religious persecution around the world is now directed against Christians, which is why Christianity is now the world's most persecuted religion. Researchers are now saying, "Christianity isn't dying, it's being eradicated." In fact, recently even a Jewish Rabbi admitted that, "Christians have become the new Jews." And just like Jesus said would happen, they are calling for our extinction.

This is an actual quote that I received from a "fellow American" on YouTube. *"Christians are going to start dying in mass numbers, when America ends. I will be the first one to lead the charge. Christians are starving the poor, and driving nice cars and Christians always need money. We have to come together and kill*

them. *When the dollar collapses, and there are riots, and there are no more rights and law enforcement, just start killing Christians as fast and as many as you can before they implement slavery, and the same government that got us here in the first place."*

And gee, that would also explain why we have the new t-shirts out there that say, "Exterminate Christians One Bullet at a Time."

And this is why one Christian commentary predicted, *"The real Christian church in America is going to be forced to do as the early Christians did – go underground. The mainline Christian churches have slipped away from the foundation of Scripture to adopt secular tenets and leftist politically correct philosophies until they have become only a shadow of the true followers of Christ. Our mainline denominations have become nothing more than social clubs and their pastors 'preach' feel good 'sermonettes' about the environment and things like 'social justice'. They are fearful of preaching the Scriptures and of pointing out man's failings lest they be accused of slander or sued for libel."*

And that's why the founder of the Gospel for Asia says he believes this persecution will soon impact believers in America and that he is fearful that many are not ready. *"The great falling-away from faith could be worst here in America because people are absolutely not prepared to face suffering or persecution because we cannot imagine a gospel with the cross and the suffering in it."*

He said we have focused on "prosperity" and "material possessions" instead of surrendering all to Christ. And the result, he says, is that the American Church has become "very naïve in thinking that real persecution will never come their way. *"These are warning signs,"* he exclaims. *"God is telling us that we need to prepare our lives"* Or as one pastor puts it, *"The time for excuses is over."*[29]

I don't know about you, but I'd say it's time we stop beating each other up, start getting along and get motivated. Looks to me like the persecution that Jesus said would come in the Last Days is already here!

*"Church buildings are being burned down. Christian's homes are being destroyed.* **Survivors:** *"A mob of Hindus came at midnight. They burned our homes and destroyed our Church. We had to hide in the jungle to survive."*

*Believers of a home church that was attacked and the Pastor beaten. "I should have been dead if it were not for the grace of Jesus Christ. Pastor Simon prayed for me and I am a witness today of the healing power of God. So will you stand firmly for Jesus Christ in any situation? Even if they kill me I am not going to leave Jesus."*

*House of Prayer-Pastor Walter Masih. <video showing a gang of men inside the church beating with a bat and 2x4's and kicking the pastor>*

*Another persecuted Christian: "As Jesus had told us we have to practice to show the other cheek. I have forgiven them, let them be blessed. They are ignorant."*

*In Aug. 2008 in Orissa, India, an uproar of anti-Christian violence swept through 300 villages. Over 50 Christians were beaten to death, cut to pieces or burned.*

*There are more than 26 million documented cases of martyrdom in the 20th Century alone. More than 250 million Christians in over 80 nations are currently living under the threat of persecution. 60% are children. Stop tolerating sin.*[30]

**3.** The **3ʳᵈ way** we know we're headed for this **Global Persecution** of Christians is that **The Plan is Already Here.**

But don't take my word for it. Let's listen to God's. He tells us what that plan is going to lead to.

**Revelation 6:9-11** "When He opened the fifth seal, I saw under the altar the souls of those who had been slain because of the Word of God and the testimony they had maintained. They called out in a loud voice, "How long, Sovereign Lord, holy and true, until You judge the inhabitants of the earth and avenge our blood?" Then each of them was given a white robe, and they were told to wait a little longer, until the number of their fellow servants and brothers who were to be killed as they had been was completed."

Now again, maybe it's just me, but it sure appears the events during the 7-year tribulation are not going to be good ones for the followers of God. Being slain, killed and your blood being avenged just for following God, that doesn't sound like a good time to me, how about you? And again, those people being slain and asking God to avenge their blood are the people who got saved after the

Rapture, and again, the lesson is you should've got saved before the hammer came down! But now you're going to pay a price, and that price is your life. They're actually going to *hunt you down and exterminate you* just for being a follower of God.

And so here's the point for you and I today, "Are there any signs of the whole world wanting to hunt down and exterminate people, just for believing in God's Word and refusing to give up their testimony for Jesus?" Yes! As we saw before, it's already here! In fact, the **plan** to do it is already in place!

**1. The 1st phase of that plan is to make Christians out to be the Big Troublemakers.**

You see, put yourself in the Antichrist's shoes. If you're going to get rid of Christians, then you have to have a good excuse for getting rid of them in the first place, right? You know, like Nero did with blaming Christians for the burning of Rome and then once they became the bad guys, the troublemakers, they went about killing them, right? I'm telling you, this is precisely what the One World Religion Movement is doing, *right now*! Right now, you and I the Christian are the new troublemakers on the planet! We're the people who have the audacity to put up a fight and refuse to go along with their plans of a One World Religion and we're messing it up for their hope to bring peace to the planet. And so what they've done is they've boxed us into a corner and forced us to giving up our *testimony*, just like the text said, about Jesus being the only way to heaven, and that God's Word is the Only Word!

And here's how they've done it. They continue to say to us, and the whole planet, the lie that Jesus was just one of many great teachers, there's nothing special about Him, the Bible's not the only book of truth on the planet, and you just need to go along with a One World Religion. And we rightly respond and we give our testimony…NO!

**A. The 1st Biblical testimony about Jesus is that Jesus Christ is God.**

**John 20:26-28** "A week later His disciples were in the house again, and Thomas was with them. Though the doors were locked, Jesus came and stood among them and said, "Peace be with you!" Then he said to Thomas, "Put your finger here; see my hands. Reach out your hand and put it into my side. Stop doubting and believe." Thomas said to Him, "My Lord and my God!"

Now I think it's pretty obvious, but Thomas not only said Jesus was *Lord* but He's Who? He's *God*, right? And so here's the point. Is Buddha God? Is Confucius God? How about Mohammed? I don't think so!!! Then how in the world can you say they're all the same as Jesus? The Biblical testimony, our testimony, is that He is God! That's different, totally different and that's why we can't go along with a One World Religion.

## B. The 2nd **Biblical testimony** about Jesus is that **Jesus is the Creator**.

**Colossians 1:15-16** "He is the image of the invisible God, the firstborn over all creation. For by Him all things were created: things in heaven and on earth, visible and invisible, whether thrones or powers or rulers or authorities; all things were created by Him and for Him."

That means Jesus! So once again, here's the point. Did Buddha create the world? No! How about Confucius? No! Or how about Mohammed? No! Then how in the world can you say they're all basically the same as Jesus when He's *radically different* than all the rest! He is totally unique, unlike those other guys, Moe, Larry and Curly and that's why we can't go along with a One World Religion.

## C. The 3rd **Biblical testimony** is that **Jesus is the Forgiver**.

**Acts 4:12** "Salvation is found in no one else, for there is no other name under heaven given to men by which we must be saved."

It's in the Name of Jesus! So once again, here's the point. Did Buddha forgive us of our sins? No! Did Confucius go to the cross? No! Or how about Mohammed? Did he die for us? No! Then how can you say they're all the same as Jesus when He's *the only way to heaven*! He's the Only One Who went to the cross for us! He's the only Name under heaven that men might be saved! How can you say it's logical and good to go along with a One World Religion when Jesus Christ is radically different than the rest? We can't! Why? Because Buddhism can't save you! Islam can't save you! Mormonism can't save you! Catholicism can't save you! Humanism can't save you! Spiritism can't save you! New Age can't save you! *But Jesus Christ can and He will if you just call upon His Name*! There is no other Name under heaven by which men might be saved! And that's why one guy said this…here's his testimony.

*"Jesus Christ is the First and Last, He's the Beginning and the End! He is the keeper of Creation and the Creator of all! He is the Architect of the universe and The Manager of all times.*

*He always was, always is, and always will be...Unmoved, Unchanged, Undefeated and never Undone!*

*The world can't understand him. The armies can't defeat Him, the schools can't explain Him and the leaders can't ignore Him.*

*Herod couldn't kill Him. The Pharisees couldn't confuse Him, the people couldn't hold Him! Nero couldn't crush Him, Hitler couldn't silence Him, the New Age can't replace Him and Donahue can't explain Him away!*

*He is Holy, Righteous, Mighty, Powerful and Pure. His Ways are right, His Word is eternal, His Will is unchanging and His Mind is on me.*

*He's my Redeemer, my Savior, my Guide and my Peace! He's my Joy, my Comfort, my Lord and He rules this life!*

*He will never leave me, forsake me, mislead me, forget me and never cancel my appointment in His appointment book!*

*When I fall, He lifts me up! When I fail, He forgives! When I am weak, He is strong! When I am lost, He is the way!*

*When I am afraid, He is my courage! When I face persecution, He shields me! And when I face Death, He carries me Home!*

*This is why I WILL NEVER go along with a One World Religion!"*[31]

That's our testimony. That's standing on God's Word and now, here's what they say, "Ah ha! We got you...you troublemaker. We heard it with our own ears. You confessed it with your own mouth! You gave us your testimony. Therefore, you leave us no choice. You're standing in the way. You're ruining all our plans. It's time to get rid of you, you're the one to blame!" Do you see how it's happening just like the text said it would?

## 2. The 2nd phase of the plan is to make Christians out to be the Big Terrorists.

And this is what we previously saw. If you're going to get rid of the resisters who won't go along with our One World Religion, you not only have to paint them as troublemakers, but *terrorists* and you specifically have to target any Monotheistic Religion out there because they believe by definition that there's only one way to heaven and only one God, mono, meaning one, right? The reason why is because Monotheism doesn't fit with a Pantheistic goal, meaning *all*, of a One World Religion that says *all* is god and *all* paths lead to heaven. So can anybody guess just what the three Monotheistic Religions on the planet are? That's right! Christianity, Islam and Judaism. You have to get rid of all three of these guys to pull off a One World Religion. But now you've got a problem. By your own definition, all religions are supposed to be valid pathways to God, but here you have three that'll never go along with it. So what do you do? Simple. You supplant the true Monotheistic Religions with fake ones, and then you systematically start getting rid of the real ones by making them out to be terrorists. Let me show you what I mean[32].

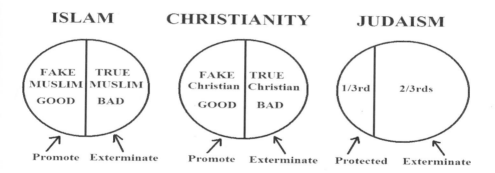

First, you specifically have to get rid of any monotheistic religion. Mono meaning one, Theos meaning God. Monotheistic religion, because by definition a monotheistic religion means there is only one way. There is only one God. Which is what you and I believe, which is what the scripture teaches and the reason why they have to get rid of that is because the New Age-the One World Religion is what's called "pantheism". Pan meaning all, as in all paths lead to god, all truths are true, all ways lead to salvation. So now you have oil and water-it doesn't mix.

Now it just so happens that there are three religions on the planet, major religions that are monotheistic. Can anybody guess what those are? Us-Christianity, also Islam and Judaism. Now here's the point. You have a problem with the one world religion-you're pantheistic-all is supposed to get you there. But now you have three of the world's major religions that say-Na-ah. No way. So what are you gonna do?

It's a bait and switch thing. You take all the monotheistic religions and what you do is start to label the true ones, the true followers of that monotheistic religion, as the bad guys and then you work about supplanting them with the fake guys.

Let me explain how they're doing it right now. This is their plan, to make you and I not just troublemakers, but the terrorists.

They've started and they've been starting since 9/11 with Islam, that's a monotheistic religion that believes that there is only one way through Allah-which I disagree with, but that's what they believe and what they've done is split it right down the middle (see graphic) and this is part of their plan. Now they've taken the true Muslims-and those are the ones who unfortunately, follow the Qur'an and what it actually says and that is to kill the infidel-which is you and I the Christian and the Jewish people. It actually says you do what it takes-you're only guaranteed paradise if you blow people up and stuff like that. That's really what it teaches. And they say-well those guys are the bad guys. Those are the "bad" Muslims. Those are the terms-right wing, fundamental, extremists.

Now at the same time they are labeling those guys, who are the "true" ones. Again, I'm not condoning it and I don't think it's a good thing, but that's what they believe. That's what their book teaches. Now they're saying those are the bad guys but now taking the fake ones, the media uses the term "moderate" Muslims. Have you ever heard that? Have you heard the term-"true Muslims; Islam is a peace-loving religion" No it's not.

But they take the fake ones-in Christianity, we call it liberal Christianity-which is fake Christians, we'll get to that in a second. So they're taking the fake Muslims and saying "Oh, these are the 'good guys.'"

Why? Because these guys will go along with the One World Religion and so now what they're doing ever since 9/11, they're saying we need to exterminate these "bad" Muslims and what they are doing is promoting these "good" Muslims.

Why would they go through all that trouble? Because you have to understand from a Bible prophecy point of view, you're all heading towards a One World Religion.

So you have to have Islam, because your premise is all religions are right. So Islam in name only, will continue on during the 7 year tribulation-but what they're doing is taking the true Muslims and exterminating them; they're taking the fake ones and elevating them so they continue on. You see it? It's a bait and switch.

Now here's where you and I better pay attention. *They're doing the same thing to you and I right now.* This is what we saw previously with the propaganda. What's the terms they're using on you and I? They're splitting us right down the middle and they're taking you and I, i.e. the evangelical Christian-what are they calling us? Right-wing, extremists, fundamentalist. The exact same terminology is being used on you and I and they're saying <true Christians> are the bad guys because we will not budge. We will not go along with this One World Religion. They're taking these fake Christians-the liberal Christians-who are Christians in name only, and denies virtually every cardinal doctrine in scripture. These are the "good" guys because they will go along with the One World Religion.

They are doing the same thing to you and I right now. They're calling for the extermination-wait until you see the extermination of these "bad" Christians, the "extremist" Christian. "They're not representing 'true' Christianity" And what they've been doing is promoting the fake ones. Well why would you go through all that? Because again, you need to understand from a Bible Prophecy point of view, it's the One World Religion and so that means all religions continue to go on. But here you have three that will never go along and so what do you do? It's a bait and switch. You create a half and get rid of the real ones and supplant them with the fake ones so that it continues on. Now what's interesting, according to bible prophecy, guess who's left on the list? Judaism.

The Bible tells us what's going to happen to the Jewish people. Is it any wonder that after they get Islam and Christianity to go along with this One World Religion, that the Jewish people- who are the major players in the 7 year tribulation-the Jewish people are left. It's not by chance, it's all in the plan and here's what they do. First of all, the whole Jewish nation, unfortunately they're not split up yet, they're going to strike a deal with the Antichrist and that's

Daniel 9:27, that they're going to make a peace treaty with the Antichrist. Where does everybody want to make a peace treaty right now? Israel.

One guy is going to pull it off and he's going to do it specifically for 7 years. That guy is the Antichrist and that's the very event that starts the 7 year tribulation. Then you're going to see that 3 1/2 years into the tribulation, the Antichrist shows his true colors and is going to go up into the Temple, the rebuilt Jewish Temple, and declare himself to be God. That's when the blindness is removed. Paul talks about it in the book of Romans that the Jewish people's blindness is removed and then they get their split. Here's the split, notice it's different. The Bible says it's not half and half, but 2/3rds of the Jewish people on one side and 1/3rd on the other side. The Bible says in the book of Zechariah that the Antichrist is going to hunt them down and exterminate 2/3rds of the Jewish People and then 1/3- Revelation Chapter 12- are going to be protected by the archangel Michael because God is not done with them and He always wins and He always has a remnant.

That is I believe, the plan that has been foisted upon you and I.

Now here's the point for you and I here today. Do we see any signs of this bait and switch, the elimination of true monotheistic believers, specifically Judaism, Islam and Christianity as being labeled as the bad guys so they can replace them with the fake guys, who'll go along with a One World Religion? Uh, yeah! In fact, CNN is starting to produce programs on it. Let's take a look.

### God's Warriors: Report by Christiane Amanpour

*The scripture is the blueprint to life and living.*
*They are sure of their mission.*
*Our role is to redeem the entire world.*
*And the stakes are high.*

*Do you really wish that you could have been martyred?*

*"Yes, martyrdom was my biggest wish"*

*What they have in common-Jews, Christians, and Muslims- is the belief that modern society has lost its way.*

*They're raping virgin teenage America on the sidewalk and everybody's walking by and acting like everything's okay.*

*The problem we have now with civilizations is that we don't offer them anywhere to go. He doesn't know his place in life.*

*The people that don't keep the Torah. They don't understand the meaning of being Jews. They're wasting their life.*

*They say God is the answer.*

*I would like to see America become the "Nation Under God" again.*

*The dead battle to save the world has caused anger, division and fear.*

*I believe Islam is a real threat.*

*Something's going wrong.*

*We've too closely fused politics and our faith.*

**Amanpour:** *I'm Christian Amanpour in Jerusalem, a place sacred to Christians, Muslims and Jews. Each has zealous followers driven to change the world. They are God's Warriors and this is how they are shaping the 21st Century.*

*Over the last 30 years, religion has exploded as a powerful political force with armies of believers determined to fight for their faith. In the United States, the Christian Right forged an agenda that would transform the political landscape.*

**Pat Robertson:** *"We set a 10 year program to put a born-again Christian in the White House."*

**Amanpour:** *In Israel, a small band of religious settlers began a quest that would change the face of the Holy Land.*

**Former Pres. Jimmy Carter:** *There's no doubt, in any rational analyst mind, that the settlements are deemed a major obstacle to peace.*

**Amanpour:** *And in Muslim countries, a spiritual awakening sparked the rise of* *political Islam and an extreme fringe who would become the world's nightmare.*

*We're going to fight for it, die for it and kill others for it. That's the scary part. That's why we ought to take it serious."*[33]

Now, did you notice the propaganda? Did you see how we are lumped into the other "armies" of "dangerous" believers like Islam who are "fanatics" trying to "take over the world" hindering true peace from coming to the planet? Us…Evangelical Christians…are lumped in with the Islamic terrorists. All Monotheistic Religions are being attacked and supplanted with fake ones who will go along with a One World Religion. And lest you think they're really not trying to make you and I into these evil bad guys, just like the Islamic terrorists, check out this documentary they released on us, called **Jesus Camp**. Let's take a look.

**Jesus Camp:**

*This is a sick old world. Kids, you gotta change things. Boys and girls can change the world? Absolutely!*

*I pledge allegiance to the Christian flag…*

*There are two kinds of people in the world. People who love Jesus and people who don't.*

**Young child in camouflage face paint yelling:** *SPEAK THE WORD OF THE LORD!!*

*<Lakewood Park Bible Camp> Where should we be putting our focus. I'll tell you where our enemies are putting it. They're putting it on the kids.*

**Woman:** *How long have you been a Christian?*

**Kid:** *At five, I got saved. Because I just wanted more of life.*

*You go into Palestine and they're taking their kids to camp like we're taking our kids to bible camps and they're putting hand grenades in their hands.*

*<kid clapping hands> I got Jesus, how bout YOU!*

*<entire table of kids and adults clapping>* I've got Jesus, how about you. I've got Jesus, how about you.

*<Room full of kids and adults jumping up and down clapping>*

**Young girl:** *There's this excitement, yet there's a peace with it all too, and it's really cool.*

**Young boy:** *I really feel that we're a key generation to Jesus coming back and we are a generation that needs to rise up and run with that time.*

*"One of the best films of the year. So compelling in so many ways" --The Hot Button*

**Man to audience of kids:** *How many of you want to be those who would give up their lives for Jesus <to cheering audience>*

*"An admirably even-handed film" --Washington City Paper*

**Young boy:** *We're being trained to be God's Army.*

*"Provocative. A lightening rod." --Indiewire*

*Lou Engle, Dominionist, to children: You are the beginning of a movement. Raise up righteous judges.*

*<group of children chanting> "judges, judges, judges, judges"*

**Ted Haggard:** *There's a new church like this every two days in America. Twenty five percent of the American population-that's about 80 million people. If the evangelicals vote, they determine the election.*

*They've taken over the White House, Congress, the judiciary for a generation.*

*This is just the tip of the iceberg.*

*<kids crying, rock, acting charismatic yelling> This means war!*

*Adult leader: This means war! Are you a part of it or not?*
*<scenes from the film Jesus Camp>* "[34]

Don't you see? We are so dangerous. We're just as dangerous as those Islamic terrorists who brainwash their kids in camp and teach them to be an army who blows things up! Now is that some serious propaganda or what? Do you see how "dangerous" we are? We're training our kids to be like those Islamic terrorists and if we're not careful, these Nasty Pig-headed Evangelical Christians, right here in America, all 80 million of them, might start blowing us up too! Do you see the justification to get rid of us, the real ones, and promote the fake Liberal ones as "true good guys" instead of us, because they'll go along with a One World Religion? It's all happening right now, just like the text said would happen. I'd say we better get motivated! I'd say we better stop beating each other up and start getting along because we're going to need each other.

**4. The 4th way we know we're headed for a Global Persecution is that The Implementation is Already Here.**

Believe it or not, the Bible even tells us how they are going to "implement" this annihilation of God's people.

**Revelation 20:1-4** "And I saw an angel coming down out of heaven, having the key to the Abyss and holding in his hand a great chain. He seized the dragon, that ancient serpent, who is the devil, or satan, and bound him for a thousand years. He threw him into the Abyss, and locked and sealed it over him, to keep him from deceiving the nations anymore until the thousand years were ended. After that, he must be set free for a short time. I saw thrones on which were seated those who had been given authority to judge. And I saw the souls of those who had been beheaded because of their testimony for Jesus and because of the word of God. They had not worshiped the beast or his image and had not received his mark on their foreheads or their hands. They came to life and reigned with Christ a thousand years."

In other words, they were rewarded, they got to share in the joys of the Millennial Kingdom where Jesus Christ will be literally ruling and reigning on planet earth. No wonder it's awesome, and satan will be bound, which is why true peace will finally be across the planet. That's a whole lot better than what they came out of where the Antichrist was hunting them down and trying to kill them and exterminate them during the 7-year Tribulation. I'd say that's *much better circumstances.* That's well worth taking a stand for Jesus and not giving up on your testimony, right? Now here's the point. Of all things, notice what was the method of execution or extermination during the 7-year Tribulation of God's people? What was the tool they used to "implement" this? Beheading, right? But hey, good thing we don't see any signs of that form of capital punishment ever…making…a come…back…any time soon…yeah right! It's already here! Believe it or not, in our lifetime, it just so happens that beheading, of all forms of capital punishment, is not only making a come back all over the world right now, but it's specifically being used on guess who? Christians! This is amazing, exactly like the text said!

In **North Korea** right now, there are over 1 million people locked up in Concentration Camps, many of them Christians, and experiments are being done on them. Witnesses have been quoted by the BBC saying, "We watched entire families being put into gas chambers and gassed." Then they are left to an agonizing death while scientists are taking notes.

Christians right now are being killed in *Eritrea, Turkey, Tunisia, Kenya, Afghanistan, Vietnam, Columbia, Iraq, Pakistan* and *India.* All for either following Jesus and/or refusing to renounce their faith in Jesus and that's just the tip of the iceberg. In India, right now, the going rate to kill a Pastor is $250.00. Hindus are actually offering money, food and alcohol to anyone who murders Christians and destroys their homes. But remember, the Bible says that Christians would not just be killed in the Last Days, they would be specifically beheaded and that too is also on the rise.

**Indonesia:** Four Christian high school girls were attacked with machetes by Muslims and only one survived. Three of the girls were decapitated by the assailants and only one named Noviana survived with a severe slash to her head and neck in an unsuccessful beheading attempt. The three Christian high school girls were beheaded as a Ramadan "trophy." The girls' severed heads were dumped in plastic bags in their village along with a handwritten note threatening more such attacks. The note read, "Wanted: 100 more Christian heads, teenaged or adult, male or female; blood shall be answered with blood, soul with soul, head with head."

Then in another incident a magazine editor escaped with his life and made it to a bridge where he had said he had seen 15 more corpses lying in the streets of the city. "Some of them had been beheaded, others had their body parts removed. I saw one boy holding a severed head with blood dripping from it."

Then there was another beheading of a Christian village leader. His severed head was found inside three plastic bags. The rest of his body was found elsewhere later. A handwritten note was found with his head that warned the authorities that they, "Will find 1,000 more heads."

**Thailand:** There were at least 15 cases where people have been beheaded in one year alone. In one of them, Islamic extremists slaughtered an entire family and beheaded a 9 year old boy because they would not submit to them.

**Tanzania:** A Christian Pastor was recently beheaded by Muslims. Pastor Mathayo Kachili was described as a devoted Christian and was butchered by Muslim men, "with multiple axe blows for refusing to convert to Islam."

**Chechnya:** Beheadings were done to captured soldiers and videos were circulated on the Internet. Then 4 Western telecommunication workers (Three Britons and one New Zealander) were beheaded and their heads were found on the side of the road.

**Saudi Arabia:** Saudi Arabian authorities also recently beheaded four men and the court ruled that the bodies of the four workers were to be crucified for public view as an example for others.

**Iraq:** Beheadings have been on the rise since 2003 and the brunt of the beheadings have been upon foreign civilians and military personnel. One video obtained by the Associated Press shows a young boy about 12 years old beheading a man.

**Nigeria:** About 40 men, women and children were beheaded recently when their village was attacked and burned to the ground.

**Malaysia:** The heads of many Christians who have been beheaded and dumped in plastic bags or displayed as trophies with warning notes that there will be many more such attacks.

**Somalia:** Recently three government soldiers were beheaded and four Christian aid workers who were helping with orphans were beheaded for refusing to renounce their faith in Christ. Then Muslims also beheaded two young boys because their Christian father refused to hand over information about a Church leader. "I watched my boys dragged away helplessly as my youngest boy was crying. I knew they were going to be slaughtered."

**One person stated:** *"I fear that if the international community does not immediately and successfully pressure the government to protect its Christian minorities with more than just lip service, that serious violence and civil war will erupt. A war with only one possible outcome:* **Increased persecution and the mass killings of Christians.** *"*[35]

Apparently, by beheading. Where have I heard that before? Once again, I don't know about you, but I'd say it's time we stop beating each other up as Christians and start getting along, how about you? The exact form of extermination that Jesus said would come in the Last Days is already here! I think we better get motivated.

### The Hitchhiker

*Woman<passenger>: Hi. Need a lift?*

*Hitchhiker: <shakes head yes>*

*Woman: <motions him to get in the car>*

*Driver: So what do you do?*

*Hitchhiker: What do I do. What do I do? Here I am hitchhiking in the middle of nowhere on a weekday afternoon, do you really think I have somewhere to be right now?*

*Driver: Hey, I didn't want to stereotype you.*

*Hitchhiker: No you did. You just didn't say it.*

*Driver: Look, the least I ask for is.... <interrupted by wife>*

*Wife: Look, honey, don't.*

*Husband: Don't? Let me finish. The least I ask for is just a little respect, alright? After all, we were nice enough to pick you up. I mean if it weren't for me you would still be stranded on the side of the road.*

*Hitchhiker: Yeah, right.*

*Husband: What?*

*Hitchhiker: I don't believe that for a second.*

*Husband: You don't know the first thing about me.*

*Hitchhiker: I think I'm pretty close. What did you say you do?*

*Husband: You didn't ask.*

*Hitchhiker: Well I'm asking now.*

*Husband: If you must know, I'm the pastor of one of the largest churches in the state.*

*Hitchhiker: Really. A pastor, huh?*

*Hitchhiker: STOP THE CAR!! STOP THE CAR!! PULL THE CAR OVER RIGHT NOW!!*

*<car swerving, wife screaming gets pulled over to side of road. Wife and husband get out with hitchhiker having them at gunpoint>*

*Hitchhiker: Your God is the reason I'm doing this, because I don't believe in your God and I've never found a Christian who truly believes in their faith. Turn around and get on your knees right now!*

*<Pastor complies. Hitchhiker puts gun to the back of husband's neck>*

*Wife: <still by car> NOOOOO!!*

*Hitchhiker: <turns around and points gun in her direction> SHUT UP!!! YOU STAY THERE AND BE QUIET AND DO NOT MOVE!!*

*Hitchhiker:* <turning back to husband> *Are you ready to find out what you're made of?*

*Pastor: Please no.*

*Hitchhiker: Now I'm going to ask you a very simple question with a very simple answer. Think carefully before you respond. You claim to be a Christian. Well let's see how important Christ is to you. HE TOOK NAILS ON THE CROSS FOR YOU. HE DIED FOR YOU, ARE YOU WILLING TO DIE FOR HIM?!? Now I'm gonna ask you this question and you have 10 seconds to respond. Your answer will determine whether you live or die. Your entire life comes down to this moment. Are you ready to die for your faith? Say the words, "I'm ready." and I'll pull the trigger. If not, then I'll let you leave, knowing that what you've devoted your entire life to-apparently means nothing.*

*Pastor: <sobbing>*

*Hitchhiker: So...are you ready...to die...for your faith?*
*10..9..8..7..6..5..4..3..2..ONE!!*

*Pastor: I'M NOT READY <crying> I'm not ready. I'm not ready. Not ready.*

Hitchhiker: *Actions speak louder than words*
*<then puts gun to his own head, staring at the pastor. Pastor says and does nothing. >*

*Hitchhiker: <pulls trigger, tear falls from hitchhiker's eye, then proceeds to show pastor that the gun was unloaded. Pastor stands there dumbfounded and ashamed>*

*Hitchhiker: I rest my case. Go. Just Go. <hitchhiker starts walking towards road then turns back around to pastor> If you were willing to die for Him then you would be willing to tell someone like me about Him.*
*But you're not the one. You're not the one. <walks away>*[36]

**V. The 5ᵗʰ way** we know we're headed for this **Global Persecution** of Christians is that **The Excuse is Already Here.**

I'm here to tell you that ultimate excuse is the Homosexual Movement. But don't take my word for it. Let's listen to God's.

**Romans 1:18-32** "The wrath of God is being revealed from heaven against all the godlessness and wickedness of men who suppress the truth by their wickedness, since what may be known about God is plain to them, because God has made it plain to them. For since the creation of the world God's invisible qualities – His eternal power and divine nature – have been clearly seen, being understood from what has been made, so that men are without excuse. For although they knew God, they neither glorified Him as God nor gave thanks to Him, but their thinking became futile and their foolish hearts were darkened. Although they claimed to be wise, they became fools and exchanged the glory of the immortal God for images made to look like mortal man and birds and animals and reptiles. Therefore God gave them over in the sinful desires of their hearts to sexual impurity for the degrading of their bodies with one another. They exchanged the truth of God for a lie, and worshiped and served created things rather than the Creator – Who is forever praised. Amen. Because of this, God gave them over to shameful lusts. Even their women exchanged natural relations for unnatural ones. In the same way the men also abandoned natural relations with women and were inflamed with lust for one another. Men committed indecent acts with other men, and received in themselves the due penalty for their perversion. Furthermore, since they did not think it worthwhile to retain the knowledge of God, he gave them over to a depraved mind, to do what ought not to be done. They have become filled with every kind of wickedness, evil, greed and depravity. They are full of envy, murder, strife, deceit and malice. They are gossips, slanderers, God-haters, insolent, arrogant and boastful; they invent ways of doing evil; they disobey their parents; they are senseless, faithless, heartless, ruthless. Although they know God's righteous decree that those who do such things deserve death, they not only continue to do these very things but also approve of those who practice them."

Now if you ever wanted to know why America is going down the tubes so fast, here it is. We're following the same path the Roman society did, and notice what it was. They first turned to an evolutionary mindset and said there was no God even though there was plenty of evidence of God's existence through His creation. This is called Intelligent Design and design in something implies a Designer, but you turned a blind eye to it with your supposed Wise Scientific Evolutionary Mindset and so God did what? He gave them over to what? *Sexual impurity* and they started to degrade themselves. And then because they refused to repent, turn around and acknowledge God, even after that judgment, they what? God gave them over again to *shameful lusts*. This time it was with homosexuality and lesbianism, right? It says it right there in the text and then what happened after that? They still refused to retain the knowledge of God, so now what? Now things got really dark. God gave them over to a *depraved mind* to do what ought not to be done. Evil, greed, slander, murder, strife, gossip, God-hating people who actually invented ways of doing evil and even approve of those who do such things! Does that sound familiar or what? That's America! Ever since 1960 that's what has happened to us. We've followed the same path and we're reaping the same destruction. We're under the wrath of God just like the Roman Society!

So here's the point with you and I today. Whether you realize it or not, this homosexual movement that has appeared on the scene in the last days after rejecting God through the lie of evolution in our schools and society is not only starting to be approved by people, just like the text said it would be in the last stage of total destruction of a society, BUT it's this movement and the "approval" of it that's become the ultimate excuse to get rid of Christians. And the excuse is now called a HATE CRIME. In other words, if you don't approve of their behavior you are saying you hate them and that is now being considered a crime that is not just punishable by fines, but jail time. And it's not only happening here in America but around the world. Let me show you what I mean.

### CWNews.org with George Thomas and Wendy Griffith

*Thomas: A new hate crimes law raises disturbing questions about freedom of speech and religion in the United States. Hello everyone. I'm George Thomas.*

*Griffith: And I'm Wendy Griffith. This week President Barack Obama signed hate crimes legislation into law. Later he hosted a reception at the White House for gay rights supporters.*

*Barack Obama: "We must stand against crimes that are meant not only to break bones but to break spirits. Not only to inflict harm but to instill fear."*

*Griffith: The new law expands Federal Hate Crimes legislation to include homosexuals. Gay activists have been pushing for this for nearly a decade and Democrats attached the measure to an unrelated defense spending bill. Opponents are afraid the new law threatens freedom of religion and speech.*

*Here's Jennifer Wishon from Washington.*

**Jennifer:** *Despite added language meant to strengthen free speech protections for Christians who preach biblically held beliefs against homosexuality, many Republicans fear it is not enough.*

**Rep. Mike Pence:** *Whatever language they added has an "escape hatch" and we know from experience at the State level and around the globe, that this represents a real infringement on the 1st Amendment-Freedom of Religion, freedom of expression of Americans.*

**Griffith:** *Many predict the new law could land Christians in jail.*

**Rep. Mike Pence:** *If you aid or abet or induce in the commission of a Federal crime, you're guilty of that crime. And so as the scenario goes, someone could preach a sermon out of Romans chapter one for instance, about sexual practices, and if someone was inspired by malevolent intent, in some way to go out and commit an act of violence-that pastor, that minister, that priest could be held liable under existing Federal law.* "[37]

Oh, and don't think it's going to stop with just the pastor…it's going to be ANY Christian, and that's because statistics say that, "Fewer and fewer in the U.S. see homosexuality as a sin." Gee I wonder why? Churches aren't preaching on it. In fact, churches are not only not preaching on it, they're "accepting it" and "condoning it" just like the text said they would. They're actually saying, "Homosexuality is a Gift, not a Sin," which reminds me of what A.W. Tozer said, *"This version of the Christian Religion is not transforming people; rather it is being transformed by the people. It is not raising the moral level of society; it is descending to the society's level and congratulating itself as if it scored a victory when society is actually smiling, accepting its surrender."* As well as destroying our nation like the text said it would. In fact, Rob Bell who we talked about before, not only denies hell, but he's now come out and said, "Those who oppose homosexual marriage are narrow Christians and need to repent" and if you don't "repent" you're going to have to. Right now churches in the UK are fearful they are going to be "forced" to have to perform "same sex marriages" and one man who has opposed it is facing losing his home. Another British Christian couple is being told they can't adopt because they oppose homosexuality and another preacher in England HAS been arrested for saying homosexuality is a sin. It's already begun. In fact, right now here in America there's a bill out there that is seeking to "deny the tax-exempt status" of any group that opposes gay marriage and a recent report came out that says, "Those who oppose gay marriage are now considered domestic hate groups."[38] You know, dangerous people who we need to get rid of. Again, just like the text said, once you go down this route you will not only destroy your nation, but things will progressively get worse and worse.

I'm telling you, this homosexual movement is not only being used right now to silence Christians and get rid of Christians, but it's going to open up the floodgates to all kinds of destructive behaviors like the text said that will further bring down our nation even faster!

"One Church Bishop warned that all this ongoing redefinition of marriage with same sex unions will soon include the idea of what's being called, "non-monogamy" or the concept of faithfulness between a man and a woman in marriage being outdated. The new concept will be the acceptance of "multiple partners" without the stigma of adultery. In fact, a court case has already been brought forth claiming that since same-sex marriage restrictions are being lifted, so should restrictions on multiple-partner marriages."

"One California Congresswoman right now wants to "federalize" a state law to prohibit counseling to change a person's sexual orientation, even if the person requests it. The bill says this would be "dangerous and harmful." Now the problem is, the language in the bill is so broad and vague that it could also include all forms of sexual orientation including pedophilia," and that "If pedophilia is a sexual orientation, then that means that discrimination laws also apply to pedophiles. Which means you cannot block a pedophile from being a preschool teacher or any other high-risk occupation."[39]

Gee, that doesn't sound good for our country! Do you see? Just like the text said, once you go down this route and approve of a behavior that God condemns, it destroys your society. Things progressively get worse. But it gets even worse than that! The IRONY of this hate crime law is that we true Christians are not advocating any "hate" or "violence" or "bodily harm" to anyone who is involved in homosexuality or lesbianism, and shame on anyone who says they're a born again Christian and they do! Knock it; off you're giving the rest of us a BAD NAME and you're making it easier for them to pass these laws! However, lest there be any doubt that the homosexual movement really isn't just about equality, but rather the removal of Christians and the rights to FREE SPEECH in America, let's take a look at what their real agenda is.

This is the Gay Manifesto by Michael Swift first published in Gay Community News February 15-21st in 1987. It is also reprinted in the Congressional Record. This is what it states:

*We shall sodomize your sons, emblems of your feeble masculinity, of your shallow dreams and vulgar lies. We shall seduce them in your schools, in your dormitories, in your gymnasiums, in your locker rooms, in your sports arenas, in your seminaries, in your youth groups, in your movie theater bathrooms, in your army bunkhouses, in your truck stops, in your all male clubs, in your houses of Congress, wherever men are with men together. Your sons shall become our minions and do our bidding. They will be recast in our image.*

*All laws banning homosexual activity will be revoked. Instead, legislation shall be passed which engenders love between men.*

*All homosexuals must stand together as brothers; we must be united artistically, philosophically, socially, politically and financially. We will triumph only when we present a common face to the vicious heterosexual enemy.*

*If you dare to cry faggot, fairy, queer, at us, we will stab you in your cowardly hearts and defile your dead, puny bodies.*

*We will unmask the powerful homosexuals who masquerade as heterosexuals. You will be shocked and frightened when you find that your presidents and their sons, your industrialists, your senators, your mayors, your generals, your athletes, your film stars, your television personalities, your civic leaders, your priests are not the safe, familiar, bourgeois, heterosexual figures you assumed them to be. We are everywhere; we have infiltrated your ranks. Be careful when you speak of homosexuals because we are always among you; we may be sitting across the desk from you; we may be sleeping in the same bed with you....All churches who condemn us will be closed. Our only gods are handsome young men...For us too much is not enough....All males who insist on remaining stupidly heterosexual will be tried in homosexual courts of justice and will become invisible men.*

*We shall rewrite history, history filled and debased with your heterosexual lies and distortions.*

*We shall be victorious because we are fueled with the ferocious bitterness of the*

*oppressed who have been forced to play seemingly bit parts in your dumb, heterosexual shows throughout the ages. We too are capable of firing guns and manning the barricades of the ultimate revolution.*
*Tremble, hetero swine, when we appear before you without our masks.*

HAVE YOU HEARD OR READ THIS ARTICLE BEFORE? WHY NOT?"[40]

I'll tell you why. Because then the REAL MOTIVE would be exposed. If ever there was a HATE CRIME that was it! I'm not advocating "hate" or "violence" or "bodily harm" to you, but by your own words, that's exactly what your agenda is to me & my family & to my Church & to my Country! Folks, we better wake up! This movement is not only bringing down our nation and incurring the wrath of God in the Last Days, but it's being used to silence the Church and get rid of Christians in the Last Days! And that's exactly what the Bible said would happen, when you are living in the Last Days! And it's happening now!

**VI. The 6th way** we know we're headed for a **Global Persecution of Christians** is that **The Execution is Already Here.**

Even here in America. Let's see what lies ahead, even for us. We're not safe.

**Revelation 7:9,13-14,16-17** "After this I looked and there before me was a great multitude that no one could count, from every nation, tribe, people and language, standing before the throne and in front of the Lamb. They were wearing white robes and were holding palm branches in their hands. Then one of the elders asked me, 'These in white robes – who are they, and where did they come from?' I answered, 'Sir, you know.' And he said, 'These are they who have come out of the great tribulation; they have washed their robes and made them white in the blood of the Lamb. Never again will they hunger; never again will they thirst. The sun will not beat upon them, nor any scorching heat. For the Lamb at the center of the throne will be their shepherd; he will lead them to springs of living water. And God will wipe away every tear from their eyes."

Now once again, the people spoken about here being martyred during the 7-year Tribulation and being given these white robes are the people who got saved *after* the Rapture, and again, the lesson is you should've got saved *before* the Rapture when the hammer came down! But once again, now you're going to pay with it for a price and that price is you're going to be martyred and killed. Again, notice the text. Where did these people come from? From just one part of the world? No! From every nation, tribe, people and language. A great multitude that no one could count, right? And logically, this would include America, right?

And so the question for us today is, "Do we see any signs of this global persecution of God's people even here in America where they actually want to kill us and martyr us?" Yeah, it's already begun! You put all these things together that we've been silent on, the propaganda, the plans, the excuse etc., and it's already happening here in America, much faster than I think we want to realize. Let's take a look at just how bad it's become right here in our own territory!

- In recent decades, the Bible, prayer, and Ten Commandments were taken out of the schools.
- The U.S. Supreme Court ordered the end of school sponsored religious activities, such as prayers during morning announcements.
- Lawyers are asking that the Bible be placed on the list of books considered dangerous for children.
- Requests have been made to do away with the Pledge of Allegiance because of its mention of God.
- The sharing of the gospel is now being equated as a form of "mental manipulation."
- The ACLU put pressure on a town to remove the fish symbol from its official logo calling it a "secret sign of Christianity."
- Tourists visiting Washington D.C. were ordered by police to stop praying in the rotunda of the U.S. Capitol.
- Arizona children were told they could not pray in front of the Supreme Court building.
- A minister was arrested for praying on the steps of the Supreme Court.
- A Texas Public School curriculum is teaching students to not only design a Socialist Flag but say that Christianity is a cult.
- Which explains why a professor in Florida recently made his students stomp on a piece of paper with the word Jesus written on it.
- A chaplain was fired for speaking the name of Jesus.
- Police Chaplains are being told to stop praying in the Name of Jesus.
- A North Carolina Pastor was fired as the honorary chaplain of the State House of Representatives after he closed the prayer in the Name of Jesus.
- A North Carolina court ruled that "Jesus prayers" can be banned.

- A North Carolina school ordered a child to remove God from their poem.
- A teacher is facing suspension for sharing a verse from the Bible.
- A graduate student in Georgia was given the choice to give up her Christian beliefs or be expelled from the graduate program.
- A New Mexico Court of appeals says states can require Christians to violate their faith.
- Vanderbilt University says that a Christian Club cannot require leaders to be devout Christians.
- Gideon Bibles are starting to be removed from hotels.
- A Texas woman was forced to cover up her t-shirt that said, "Vote the Bible."
- A Pastor was sentenced to two years in prison for teaching that parents should spank their children.
- A group called Military Bibles was declared a threat to national security.
- Senior Citizens are not allowed to pray for meals at a particular nursing home.
- A Christian was recently fined and sentenced to 60 days in jail for holding a Bible study in his home in Arizona.
- Another Pastor in California was jailed for exercising a peaceful, pro-life speech.
- Police were called to a Middle School in Lexington, Kentucky to stop 8th graders from praying during their lunch break for a student whose mother was tragically killed.
- A home school mom in New Hampshire was ordered to stop home schooling her daughter because the little girl "reflected too strongly" her mother's Christian faith.
- A Pastor in Kansas was convicted and fined for passing out Bibles by so-called "fellow Christians." *"The arresting officer said he was a Christian. The court judge said he was a Christian. The prosecutor said he was a Christian. The city attorney said he was a Christian and four of the six jurors said they were Christian. Yet they convicted me for handing out free Bibles."*
- As one person stated, "It is illegal in U.S. public schools to read the Bible, but many states require that a Bible is provided for every convict in jail. So if the children can't read the Bible in school, they'll be able to read it when they get to prison."

- Christians are not only being persecuted here in America, they are also being killed.
- Rev. Fred Winters was murdered while preaching in his pulpit in Maryville, Illinois.
- Pro-life activist Jim Pullion was murdered in front of his granddaughter's high school for showing the truth about abortion.
- Recently two street preachers were killed in the United States and a religious liberty group warned that, "Anti-Christian hostility is getting increasingly deadly" in the United States after two street preachers were shot and killed by a teenager who opposed their message. "The increasing demonization of Christians in our culture makes some feel it's open season on Christians." Gary Cass of the Christian Anti-Defamation Commission complained about a lack of interest in national media. "As of today, there are no national news organizations reporting this vicious murder of two innocent Christian men. Why? If two Muslims, or two feminists, or two homosexuals were murdered, wouldn't the media be all over it? These were two fine young men shot by another man for their Christian faith, yet the media does not seem to care."[41]

Gee, I wonder why? Maybe it's because you've got an agenda and that agenda is to get rid of Christians all over the world, even here in America, just like the Bible said. I don't know about you, but I'd say it's high time we stop beating each other up and start getting along and get motivated about what's really important because the hammer's about to come down!

But again, if you are a Christian, then don't be discouraged by these statistics! You should be motivated and excited! Why? Because Church History has shown that when persecution hits the Church it's a *good thing for the Church*! Why? Because number one, it teaches us, the Church, to never give up hope! As J. Vernon McGee says, "God is still on the throne! And as long as He is on the Throne, there is Hope!" Retreat is not an option! We just need to keep moving forward even against all odds like our Founding Fathers did. Let's see what they were up against!

- During the Revolutionary War, only 3 percent of the people actually fought against Great Britain. (REMEMBER 'ARNOLD' BY KENNETH ROBERTS)
- Only 10 percent of the citizens actively supported that 3 percent.
- Approximately 20 percent considered themselves to be on the side of the Revolution, but they did not actively participate.

- Toward the climatic end of the war, approximately 30 percent actually fought on the side of the British.
- The rest of the citizens had no disposition either way. They didn't care. They didn't want anything to do with what they deemed to simply be a political issue.[42]

But guess what? They still won! They whooped the biggest power on the planet! Why? Because the Founding Fathers had a motto they believed in and that was "No king but King Jesus." And they believed that God would honor that and He did! If our country is going to prosper again today then we've got to get that same motto back! "No king but King Jesus!" in America. We have to stop compromising with a globalist or flirt with a Mormon and stand on God's principles if we're ever going to see the same results! And yes, *it can still happen today*! Just ask the President of Uganda!

*"President Yoweri Museveni celebrated Uganda's 50th anniversary of independence from Britain at the National Jubilee Prayers event by publicly repenting of his personal sin and the sins of the nation. Here's what He said:*

*'I stand here today to close the evil past, and especially in the last 50 years of our national leadership history and at the threshold of a new dispensation in the life of this nation. I stand here on my own behalf and on behalf of my predecessors to repent. We ask for your forgiveness.*

*We confess these sins, which have greatly hampered our national cohesion and delayed our political, social and economic transformation. We confess sins of idolatry and witchcraft, which are rampant in our land. We confess sins of shedding innocent blood, sins of political hypocrisy, dishonesty, intrigue and betrayal.*

*Forgive us of sins of pride, tribalism and sectarianism; sins of laziness, indifference and irresponsibility; sins of corruption and bribery that have eroded our national resources; sins of sexual immorality, drunkenness and debauchery; sins of unforgiveness, bitterness, hatred and revenge; sins of injustice, oppression and exploitation; sins of rebellion, insubordination, strife and conflict.'*

*Next, the president dedicated Uganda to God saying, 'We want to dedicate this nation to you so that you will be our God and guide. We want Uganda to be known as a nation that fears God and as a nation whose foundations are firmly rooted in righteousness and justice to fulfill what the Bible says in Psalm 33:12: 'Blessed is the nation whose God is the Lord. A people You have chosen as Your own.'"*[43]

Don't ever give up hope! There's always hope! God is on the Throne! Never give up, never surrender and never quit! But that's not all. The second benefit that persecution has upon the Church is that it *Cleans Up the Church*, like these guys did.

*"A 2,000 member Baptist church was filled to overflowing one Sunday morning. And on this day, the preacher was just about ready to start the sermon when two men, dressed in long black coats and black hats entered thru the rear of the church.*

*Then one of the two men walked to the middle of the church while the other one stayed at the back. Then all of a sudden, both of them reached under their coats and pulled out automatic weapons.*

*And the one in the middle shouted, 'Everyone willing to take a bullet for Jesus stay in your seats!'*

*Well, naturally, the pews emptied fast, followed by the choir. Then all the deacons ran out followed by the choir director and even the assistant Pastor.*

*And in just a few moments, there were only about 20 people left sitting in the Church with the Pastor holding steady in the pulpit.*

*Then all of a sudden, the men put their weapons away and said, gently, to the preacher, 'Okay Pastor, all the hypocrites are gone. You can start the service now.'"*[44]

That's what persecution does. It cleans up the Church. It gets rid of all the fake, phony Christians who won't take a stand for Jesus, the goats and the tares that the Bible talks about. And when the fake ones go, it cleans up the Church, *strengthens* the Church, *purifies* the Church and then *amazing things* start to take place in the Church. Why? Because when a Church gets its heart right with God and when all the chaff gets removed, the Church starts to unite, believe and pray. And when a Church unites, believes and prays, even today, miracles abound, and that's when the captives are finally set free, like Alexander.

**Soviet Gulag:** *Alexander Ogorodnikov*

*The following is a true account of one man's struggle to survive imprisonment in the Soviet Gulag.*

*<showing man in arm and leg shackles being walked by two prison guards>*

*His crime....choosing to follow Jesus Christ.*

**Alexander Ogorodnikov:** *"The hunger continues. Not just for days, months, years. You cannot get rid of it. The other continual feeling is the constant cold. Terrible cold. Sometimes I felt as if my blood circulation was slowing down. I was personally amazed at the power of endurance, because by all accounts, I should have become seriously ill and died a long time ago."*

**Northern Siberia:**
*<re-enactment of Alexander being thrown in Siberian prison by KGB>*

**Alexander:** *"One night, I was thrown into a cell with a broken window. The KGB was determined to conduct an experiment and freeze me. Later they would say, 'He broke the window in the cell and died of cold.' I felt despair. I thought to myself, 'Has God really left me? Am I really forgotten and neglected? Have my years of suffering been in vain?' And in my despair I began to pray. I usually pray silently, but this time I started to appeal to God out loud. 'God, have you left me?' My cries were bursting from my heart literally in utter despair."*

**Woman:** *One night I had a dream. In my dream I was told to pray for Alexander. I had no idea who Alexander was but I told my church and we began to pray for him.*

**Alexander:** *"And right then, I suddenly felt a palpable physical warmth. Not the kind that comes from a heater, but like when a mother draws her freezing child to her breast and warms him with her tearful breath of compassion. It was a very living human warmth. It penetrates you, as if piercing you to the heart. And inside your heart, a spring opens up out of which flows peace. A wonderful, magnificent, soothing peace. I felt a very loving brotherly touch. Someone's* *caring hand touching my shoulder. I actually felt it and this gesture represented the words, 'You are not alone. You are not abandoned. We are with you. We are sharing your suffering'. This warmth was the energy God gave me to feel physically the heat of prayer with my own skin. My own being. As if the prayers converted the energy of love into the energy of warmth."*

*<door to prison opens and two guards enter>*

*Alexander: "In the morning, it was a shock to my executioners. They couldn't understand. I wasn't simply alive but my temperature was the same as that of a normal person. I heard the doctor explaining to my executioners in the corridor, 'This is impossible. We can't explain it.'"*

**Woman:** *"About six months later, we received a letter from Open Doors, to pray for Alexander. And we finally found out who this Alexander was. We had been praying for six months without knowing anything about him. Alexander had started a Christian movement that spread across the Soviet Union. For this crime against the State, he was imprisoned to a Labor Camp in Northern Siberia. The death sentence zone."*

**Alexander:** *It so happens that many people began praying for me and that's exactly when they released me.*

*Alexander was "unexpectedly" released with no explanation.*

**Alexander:** *"Prayer opened the prison doors and as the scripture confirms, 'Set the captives free.'"*

*Believe in the power of prayer. Believe and pray."*[45]

And believe it or not, even with all this amazing evidence pointing to the signs of Christ's soon return, some people are still living with a false sense of security by thinking that things will never get worse than they already are, like this guy:

"One day a man was having a pleasant day driving down the road when a police officer pulled him over. However, instead of a giving him a ticket, the officer informed him that, because he was wearing his seat belt, he had just won $5,000 in a safety competition. The man couldn't believe it! His day was getting better by the minute.

So the officer asked, "What are you going to do with the prize money?'

But the man responded before thinking about who it was he was talking to and blurted out, 'I guess I'll go to driving school and get my license.'

And just when things couldn't have gotten worse, the man's wife, who was seated next to him, chimed in, 'Officer, don't listen to him. He's always a smart aleck when he's drunk.'

Then as if that wasn't bad enough, this woke up the guy in the back seat, who, when he saw the cop, blurted out, 'I knew we wouldn't get far in this stolen car.'

And believe it or not, at that moment, there was a knock from the trunk and a voice asked 'Are we over the border yet?'"[46]

Now, that guy found out real fast that life can change dramatically for the worse in just a short amount of time, didn't he? But believe it or not, did you know that he's not alone? You see, many people today think that their lives are going to always remain the same and even get better through a *One World Religion.* They will even cry out that we are entering an era of unprecedented peace and safety. However, the Bible warns that this false security in a false religion will quickly turn into utter destruction by the coming of the Lord Jesus Himself.

**1 Thessalonians 5:1-3** "But as to the suitable times and the precise seasons and dates, brethren, you have no necessity for anything being written to you. For you yourselves know perfectly well that the day of the [return of the] Lord will come [as unexpectedly and suddenly] as a thief in the night.

When people are saying all is well and secure, and, there is peace and safety, then in a moment unforeseen destruction (ruin and death) will come upon them as suddenly as labor pains come upon a woman with child; and they shall by no means escape, for there will be no escape." (AMP)

People of God, I hope you're not one of those who have bought into this lie that man can somehow spawn his own utopia by creating A One World Religion. Why? Because you might wake up one day and discover that you've been left behind and do you know what? God doesn't want you to be left behind. Because He loves us, He has given us the warning sign of a One World Religion to show us that the Tribulation could be near and that Christ's 2nd Coming is rapidly approaching.

Like it or not folks, we are headed for *The Final Countdown*. We don't know the day or the hour. Only God knows. The point is, if you're a Christian, it's time to stop living for yourself and start living for our Savior! It's high time we Christians speak up and declare the good news of salvation to those who are dying all around us. But please, if you're not a Christian, give your life to Jesus today, because tomorrow may be too late! Just like the Bible said!

*Chapter Eight*

---

# One World Government

"One time this pastor decided to do a visual demonstration for his congregation to add some emphasis to his sermon. And so he placed four worms into four separate jars.

The first worm he put into a container of alcohol.
The second worm he put into a container of cigarette smoke.
The third worm was put into a container of chocolate syrup.
The fourth worm was put into a container that had good clean soil.

And so at the conclusion of the sermon, the Pastor reported the following results:

He said, "As you can see, the first worm in the alcohol…is Dead.
The second worm in cigarette smoke…is Dead.
Third worm in chocolate syrup…is Dead.
But the fourth worm in good clean soil…is Alive and Well!"

So the Pastor asked the congregation, 'Now what did you learn from this demonstration?'

And Kenny, sitting in the back row said, "Well apparently, as long as you drink, smoke and eat chocolate, you don't get worms!"[1]

How many of you would say that Kenny came to the ultimate *wrong conclusion* there? Believe it or not, did you know the Bible says one day the whole planet's going to come to an even worse conclusion than that one? You see, the Bible says the 7-year Tribulation starts off with a false peace and a false utopia of the Antichrist. But Antichrist comes and convinces people that they just entered the greatest time of their lives, when it's actually the worst time in the history of mankind. You talk about a horrible wrong conclusion! And that all begins at the Rapture of the Church!

The **#3** sign on *The Final Countdown* that God has given us to lovingly wake us up, is none other then **A One World Government**.

The Bible is clear. One day the whole planet really is going to be under the control or government of the Antichrist. But don't take my word for it. Let's listen to God's.

**Revelation 13:1-7** "And I saw a beast coming out of the sea. He had ten horns and seven heads, with ten crowns on his horns, and on each head a blasphemous name. The beast I saw resembled a leopard, but had feet like those of a bear and a mouth like that of a lion. The dragon gave the beast his power and his throne and great authority. One of the heads of the beast seemed to have had a fatal wound, but the fatal wound had been healed. The whole world was astonished and followed the beast. Men worshiped the dragon because he had given authority to the beast, and they also worshiped the beast and asked, Who is like the beast? Who can make war against him? The beast was given a mouth to utter proud words and blasphemies and to exercise his authority for forty-two months. He opened his mouth to blaspheme God, and to slander his name and his dwelling place and those who live in heaven. He was given power to make war against the saints and to conquer them. And he was given authority over every tribe, people, language and nation."

Now according to our text, the Bible is clear. There really is coming a day when all the inhabitants of the earth will be under the authority or government of who? The Antichrist, right? One day, the whole world will be unified into a *One World Government* that is actually *satanically inspired*. It says it right there in the text. But again, the question for you and I is, "Could that really happen?" Could the whole world really be deceived into creating a *One World Government* that's satanically inspired and is there any evidence that it's really going to take place just like the Bible said any time soon?" Yes! It's happening now!

**I. The 1ˢᵗ proof that we know we really are headed for a One World Government real soon is the Chronological Proof.**

What most people don't realize is that this One World Government is not only going to be put into place, because the Bible said it would, but what people don't realize is that it's been in the planning stages for a long time. Check out the progress for yourself:

- 1913: The League of Nations was formed
- 1919: The Council on Foreign Relations was formed
- 1922: The CFR endorses World Government
- 1945: The United Nations was formed
- 1948: The World Constitution is drafted providing a World Council to enforce World Law and calls upon nations to surrender their arms to a World Government
- 1959: The Diagram of World Government under the Constitution for the Federation of Earth is developed
- 1967: Richard Nixon calls for a New World Order
- 1968: Nelson Rockefeller pledges support of the New World Order
- 1970: Education and mass media begin to promote a New World Order
- 1972: The first draft completed of The Constitution for the Federation of Earth
- 1988: Mikhail Gorbachev speaks of a New World Order
- 1990: George Bush Sr. speaks of a New World Order
- 1992: The Earth Summit is held and produces the Biodiversity treaty and Agenda 21
- 1993: Bill Clinton speaks of a New World Order
- 1995: The term New World Order is replaced with Global Governance
- 1995: The State of the World Forums begin and continue yearly in San Francisco
- 1996: The World Food Summit is held
- 2000: The Millennium Assembly and Summit held at U.N. and studies how to implement Global Governance
- 2000: The Earth Charter is created (A New Universal Law)

- 2000: The State of the World Forum meets to advance Global Governance
- 2001: Tom Brokaw (popular US news anchor) announces the world now has formed into the New World Order.
- 2002: The Earth Charter is brought to the U.N.
- 2002: A World Criminal Court is ratified and begins
- 2002: The Earth Charter is expected to be endorsed at the next World Summit
- 2002: FDA approves VeriChip Microchip implant for humans
- 2003 – Russian President Putin says World Order needs to be formed
- 2003: UN discusses whether an international body such as the United Nations should be in charge of running the Internet
- 2004: Pope calls for a New International Order to Ensure Peace
- 2004: Bush Calls for New World Order
- 2004:CFR proposes the establishment by 2010 of a North American Union with a common currency called the amero
- 2005: Proposed that Europe lead the World
- 2005: Pope Invites Nations to Establish Ties
- 2005: China and Russia call for a New World Order
- 2005: Pope Calls for a New World Order
- 2006: Tony Blair calls for a New World Order
- 2006: Bush joins talks to create a North American Union
- 2007: Mexico's Fox openly calls for a North American Union
- 2007: Prior to taking office as British Prime Minister, Gordon Brown talks of a New World Order
- 2007: The European Union vows to shape globalization
- 2008: British Prime Minister Gordon Brown says it's time to build a "global society" and talks with other world leaders on far-reaching reform as part of a drive to create a "new world order."
- 2008: Blair announces he'll be president of Europe if given the power
- 2008: North American Army created between U.S. & Canada without Congressional approval
- 2008: The Vatican says that a New World Order is gaining ground
- 2009: British Prime Minister Gordon Brown said that a New World Order is emerging from the global financial crisis.
- 2009: Iran's President calls for a New World Order
- 2009: Henry Kissinger says that Obama is primed to create a New World Order.

**CNBC's "Squawk on the Street" Kissinger Interview from the NYSE**

***Erin Burnett:*** *What do you think is the most important thing for Barack Obama? Obviously you are here to talk about the anniversary for U.S./China diplomatic relations but if you had to say this is going to be the country, or the conflict or the place that would define the Obama administration, what would it be?*

***Kissinger:*** *But he can give new impetus to American foreign policy partly because the reception of him is so extraordinary around the world. I think his task will be to develop an overall strategy for America in this period when, really, a new world order can be created. It's a great opportunity, it isn't just a crisis."*

- 2009: Obama declares that, "All nations must come together to build a stronger, global regime."

***Barack Obama:*** *"North Korea broke the rules. Once again. By testing a rocket that could be used for long missiles. This provocation underscores the need for action, not just this afternoon at the U.N. Security Council, but in our determination to prevent the spread of these weapons. Rules must be binding. Violations must be punished. Words must mean something. The world must stand together to prevent the spread of these weapons. Now is the time for a strong international response and North Korea must know the path to security and respect will never come through threats and illegal weapons. All nations must come together to build a stronger global regime."*

- 2010: The International Monetary Fund says we are heading towards a New World Order.
- 2011: Iran's President again calls for a New World Order.
- 2012: Obama Signs an Executive Order that Pushes Us Closer To A North American Union And A One World Economic System.
- 2012: So-called "Experts" are calling for a One World Government.
- 2012: Vatican calls for a "World Political Authority" for the "common good."
- 2013: Vice President Joseph Biden called for the creation of a "new world order" with new financial institutions, updated global rules, and a prosperous China.

*Joe Biden New World Order:* *"The affirmative task we have now is uh, is to actually, um, create, uh, a New World Order because the global order is changing again and the institutions of rule that worked so well in the post World War II era for decades, they need to be strengthened. Some have to be changed. So we have to do what we do best. We have to lead."*

- 2013: Pope Francis met with leaders of non-Catholic religions, such as Orthodox, Anglicans, Lutherans and Methodists and others including Jews, Muslims, Buddhists, Hindus and even non-believers to "recognize their joint responsibility to our world to all of creation which we have to love and protect," and the United Nations Chief is now saying that Pope Francis is a "Global Spiritual Leader."[2]

Why is that important? Well, if you're going to have an Antichrist, you need a "Global Spiritual Leader" called "The False Prophet" in the Bible to help promote the Antichrist and his agenda for a One World Government. Not saying *he is* the False Prophet, but you can see all the pieces coming together, can't you? Now correct me if I'm wrong, but when you take a look at the timeline, I'd say somebody's pretty serious about forming this *One World Government*, how about you? I mean, it's almost like they're following some sort of a *Chronological Plan* and they're just about ready to pull the whole thing off, how about you? And that's exactly what the Bible said would happen, when you are living in the Last Days!

But you might be thinking, "Hey man, come on, there's no way America's going to go along with this! This is crazy! This is just some wacky conspiracy theory stuff! We are a Christian Nation! There's no way our leaders here in America would ever undermine our country's sovereignty and go along with a One World Government! That's insane! I mean, after all, our Declaration of Independence says, "We are endowed by our Creator (i.e. God) with these rights!" There's no way a faithful American would ever give up our sovereignty for a One World Government.

Well I hate to burst your bubble, but…

**II. The 2nd proof** that we know we really are headed for a One World Government is what I call the **Administration Proof.**

You see, we've already seen in our text that the Antichrist's government is going to be satanically inspired. Therefore, if America, yes even America, is going to go along with this One World Government, then at some point, logically, we're going to have to "snub" if you will, our total Christian heritage and foundation that our Founding Fathers set up on the principles of the Bible, *as well as*, turning away from God Himself, right? You *have to* if you're going to go along with a satanically inspired system. I don't recommend it, but logically, that's what you have to do. Well I hate to be the bearer of bad news, but believe it or not, that's what our previous administration was doing! Now, they're not alone, other administrations have done it too, but this one has actually gone down on record as being the most Anti-Christian administration in American History. But don't take my word for it, let's listen to the facts. Your first clue should have been when this speech was given in Washington D.C., 2006.

***Obama:*** *"Whatever we once were, we are no longer a Christian nation, at least not just. We are also a Jewish nation and a Muslim nation and a Buddhist nation and a Hindu nation and a nation of non-believers.*

*And even if we did have only Christians in our midst, if we expelled every non-Christian from the United States of America, whose Christianity would we teach in the schools? Would we go with James Dobson's, or Al Sharpton's? Which passages of Scripture should guide our public policy?*

*Should we go with Leviticus, which suggests slavery is ok and that eating shellfish is an abomination? How about Deuteronomy, which suggests stoning your child if he strays from the faith? Or should we just stick to the Sermon on the Mount - a passage that is so radical that it's doubtful that our own Defense Department would survive its application?"*

- September 2007 – For some reason, Obama chose not put his hand over his heart during the singing of the National Anthem.

Obama unpatriotic during "Star Spangled Banner":

***Rep. Jack Kingston:*** *The famous picture of him standing with Bill Richardson, Hillary Clinton who have their hand over their heart, saluting the flag during the pledge and Obama has his hands deliberately down. THAT is disturbing to me.*

***Bill Maher:*** *Deliberately down?*

*<shows video clip with "Star Spangled Banner" being sung with Barack Obama*

*being the only one just standing there with his hands down while Clinton and Richardson stand with their hands over their hearts>*

- April 2008 – Obama speaks disrespectfully of Christians, saying they "cling to guns or religion" and have an "antipathy to people who aren't like them."
- January 2009 – On his first day in office, Obama lifts restrictions on U.S. government funding for groups that provide abortion services abroad, forcing taxpayers to fund pro-abortion groups that either promote or perform abortions in other nations.
- February 2009 – Obama announces plans to revoke conscience protection for health workers who refuse to participate in medical activities that go against their beliefs, and fully implements the plan in February 2011.
- March 2009 – The Obama administration shut out pro-life groups from attending a White House-sponsored health care summit.
- March 2009 – Obama gave $50 million for the UNFPA, the UN population agency that promotes abortion and works closely with Chinese population control officials who use forced abortions and involuntary sterilizations.
- April 2009 – When speaking at Georgetown University, Obama orders that a monogram symbolizing Jesus' name be covered when he is making his speech.

**Bret Baier: Fox News on Obama visit to Georgetown U.**

*Baier: Obama's visit to Notre Dame is not the only Catholic institution raising eyebrows when it comes to President Obama. Officials at Georgetown University covered a monogram symbolizing the name of Jesus because it was inscribed on the stage where the President spoke Tuesday.*

*The monogram, IHS, which comes from the Greek for Jesus, was covered with a triangle of black painted plywood.*

*Catholic League President Bill Donahue says, "The cowardice of Georgetown to stand fast on principle tells us more than we need to know...But the bigger story is the audacity of the Obama Administration to ask a religious school to neuter itself before the president speaks there."*

- May 2009 – Obama declines to host services for the National Prayer Day event at the White House (a day established by federal law) but he does host White House Iftar dinners in honor of Ramadan.
- May 2009 – The White House budget eliminates all funding for abstinence-only education and replaces it with "comprehensive" sexual education, repeatedly proven to increase teen pregnancies and abortions.
- May 2009 – Obama officials assemble a terrorism dictionary calling pro-life advocates violent and charging that they use racism in their "criminal" activities.
- July 2009 – The Obama administration illegally extends federal benefits to same-sex partners of Foreign Service and Executive Branch employees in direct violation of the federal Defense of Marriage Act.
- September 2009 – The Obama administration appoints as EEOC Commissioner Chai Feldblum who asserts that society should "not tolerate" any "private beliefs," including religious beliefs, if they may negatively affect homosexual "equality."
- April 2010 – Christian leader Franklin Graham is disinvited from the Pentagon's National Day of Prayer Event because of complaints from the Muslim community.
- April 2010 – The Obama administration requires rewriting of government documents and a change in administration vocabulary to remove terms that are deemed offensive to Muslims, including jihad, jihadists, terrorists, radical Islamic, etc.
- July 2010 – The Obama administration uses federal funds in violation of federal law to get Kenya to change its constitution to include abortion.
- August 2010 – The Obama administration Cuts funding for 176 abstinence education programs.
- August 2010 – Obama speaks with great praise of Islam and condescendingly of Christianity.
- August 2010 – Obama went to great lengths to speak out on multiple occasions on behalf of building an Islamic mosque at Ground Zero, while at the same time he was silent about a Christian church being denied permission to rebuild at that location.
- October 2010 – Obama begins deliberately omitting the phrase about "the Creator" when quoting the Declaration of Independence – an omission he has made on no less than seven occasions.

**C-SPAN: Obama omission of God in the Declaration**

*Reporter: Robert, two questions. Twice in recent weeks the President has quoted from the Declaration of Independence and has omitted the Declaration's reference to rights "endowed by their Creator". Why did he omit this part of the Declaration?*

**Robert Gibbs:** *I, I, I haven't seen the comments Lester, but I can assure you that the President believes in the Declaration of Independence.*

- November 2010 – Obama misquotes the National Motto, saying it is "E pluribus unum" rather than "In God We Trust" as established by federal law.
- Throughout 2010 – While every White House traditionally issues hundreds of official proclamations and statements on numerous occasions, this White House avoided traditional Biblical holidays and events but regularly recognized major Muslim holidays, as evidenced by its 2010 statements on Ramadan, Eid-ul-Fitr, Hajj, and Eid-ul-Adha.
- January 2011 – After a federal law was passed to transfer a WWI Memorial in the Mojave Desert to private ownership, the U. S. Supreme Court ruled that the cross in the memorial could continue to stand but the Obama administration refused to allow the land to be transferred as required by law, and refused to allow the cross to be re-erected as ordered by the Court.
- February 2011 – Although he filled posts in the State Department, for more than two years, Obama did not fill the post of religious freedom ambassador, an official that works against religious persecution across the world; he filled it only after heavy pressure from the public and from Congress.
- February 2011 – Obama directs the Justice Department to stop defending the federal Defense of Marriage Act.
- March 2011 – The Obama administration refuses to investigate videos showing Planned Parenthood helping alleged sex traffickers get abortions for victimized underage girls.
- April 2011 – For the first time in American history, Obama urges passage of a non-discrimination law that does not contain hiring protections for religious groups, forcing religious organizations to hire according to federal mandates without regard to the dictates of their own faith, thus eliminating conscience protection in hiring.

- July 2011 – Obama allows homosexuals to serve openly in the military, reversing a policy originally instituted by George Washington in March 1778.
- August 2011 – The Obama administration releases its new health care rules that override religious conscience protections for medical workers in the areas of abortion and contraception.
- September 2011 – The Pentagon directs that military chaplains may perform same-sex marriages at military facilities in violation of the federal Defense of Marriage Act.
- November 2011 – Unlike previous presidents, Obama studiously avoided any religious references in his Thanksgiving speech.
- December 2011 – The Obama administration denigrates other countries' religious beliefs as an obstacle to radical homosexual rights.
- January 2012 – The Obama administration argues that the First Amendment provides no protection for churches and synagogues in hiring their pastors and rabbis.
- February 2012 – The Obama administration forgives student loans in exchange for public service, but announces it will no longer forgive student loans if the public service is related to religion.
- February 2012 – The U. S. Military Academy at West Point disinvites three star Army general and decorated war hero Lieutenant General William G. Boykin (retired) from speaking at an event because he is an outspoken Christian.
- February 2012 – The Obama administration makes effulgent apologies for Korans being burned by the U. S. military, but when Bibles were burned by the military, numerous reasons were offered why it was the right thing to do.
- April 2012 – A checklist for Air Force Inns will no longer include ensuring that a Bible is available in rooms for those who want to use them.
- May 2012 - The Obama administration opposes legislation to protect the rights of conscience for military chaplains who do not wish to perform same-sex marriages in violation of their strongly-held religious beliefs.
- June 2012 - Bibles for the American military have been printed in every conflict since the American Revolution, but the Obama Administration revokes the long-standing U. S. policy of allowing military service emblems to be placed on those military Bibles.

- January 2013 – Pastor Louie Giglio is pressured to remove himself from praying at the inauguration after it is discovered he once preached a sermon supporting the Biblical definition of marriage.
- January 2013 – Obama announces his opposition to a provision in the 2013 National Defense Authorization Act protecting the rights of conscience for military chaplains.
- February 2013 – The Obama Administration announces that the rights of religious conscience for individuals will not be protected under the Affordable Care Act.
- April 2013 – Officials briefing U.S. Army soldiers include "Evangelical Christianity" along with terrorist organizations Al-Qaeda, Muslim Brotherhood, and Hamas to show examples of "religious extremism."[3]

We're lumped right in there with them, as we saw previously! Correct me if I'm wrong, but it sure appears to me that our previous administration was not only snubbing their nose at God and mocking our Christian heritage, but it looks like they're heading down an Anti-Christian/Anti-God route that is precisely needed to prepare us for accepting an Antichrist government that is actually satanically inspired, like the Book of Revelation says is coming, right? Gee, it's almost like we're living in the Last Days or something and we need to get motivated! But that's still not all. Lest you think I'm playing party favorites and just picking on the Democrats, folks, you have to realize, it's both of them!

**III. The 3rd proof that we know we really are headed for a One World Government is the Quotation Proof.**

It doesn't matter what party you belong to anymore. This is the illusion. This is the lie! They have both become infiltrated by globalists who want a One World Government and a New World Order! Let me give you an analogy. It's like asking this question, "Who would you rather vote for? the Gambinos or the Corleones?" Okay, they're both in it together. But don't listen to my words, let's listen to theirs. You tell me if they don't want this One World Government and a New World Order…it's all over the world!

- **Henry Kissinger** "Today America would be outraged if U.N. troops entered Los Angeles to restore order. Tomorrow they will be grateful. When presented with this scenario, individual rights will be willingly relinquished for the guarantee of their well-being granted to them by the World Government."

- **Walter Cronkite** "It seems to many of us that if we are to avoid the eventual catastrophic world conflict we must strengthen the United Nations as a first step toward a World Government. To do that, of course, we Americans will have to yield up some of our sovereignty. That would be a bitter pill. It would take a lot of courage, a lot of faith in the new order. Pat Robertson has written in a book a few years ago that we should have a world government but only when the Messiah arrives. He wrote, literally, any attempt to achieve world order before that time must be the work of the devil. Well, join me. I'm glad to sit here at the right hand of satan."
- **Al Gore** "The climate bill will help bring about global governance. It is the awareness itself that will drive the change and one of the ways it will drive the change is through global governance and global agreements."
- **French President Chirac** said during a speech at The Hague that the UN's Kyoto Protocol represented, "The first component of an authentic global governance. For the first time, humanity is instituting a genuine instrument of global governance."
- **David Rockefeller** "We are grateful to the Washington Post, The New York Times, Time Magazine and other great publications whose directors have attended our meetings and respected their promises of discretion for almost forty years. It would have been impossible for us to develop our plan for the world if we had been subject to the bright lights of publicity during those years. But the work is now much more sophisticated and prepared to march towards a World Government."
- **Strobe Talbot** (Clinton's Deputy Secretary of State) "In the next century, nations as we know it will be obsolete; all states will recognize a single, global authority. National sovereignty wasn't such a great idea after all."
- **Richard Falk** "The existing order is breaking down at a rapid rate and the main uncertainty is whether mankind can exert a positive role in shaping a new world order...We believe a new order will be born no later than early in the next century..."
- **Mikhail Gorbachev** "Further global progress is now possible only through a quest for universal consensus in the movement towards a new world order."
- **Nelson Mandela** "The new world order that is in the making must focus on the creation of a world democracy, peace and prosperity for all."
- **George McGovern** "I would support a Presidential candidate who pledged to take the following steps...At the end of the war in the Persian

Gulf, press for a comprehensive Middle East settlement and for a new world order based not on Pax Americana but on peace through law with a stronger U.N. and World Court."

- **George Bush Sr.** "If we do not follow the dictates of our inner moral compass and stand up for human life, then his lawlessness will threaten the peace and democracy of the emerging new world order we now see, this long dreamed-of vision we've all worked toward for so long. Bush: We have before us the opportunity to forge for ourselves and future generations, a New World Order. A world where the rule of law, not law of the jungle governs the conduct of nations. When we are successful, and we will be, we will have a real chance at this New World Order. An order in which a credible United Nations can use its peacekeeping role to fulfill the promise and vision of the U.N.'s founders."
- **Madeleine Albright** "Today I say that no nation in the world need be left out of the global system we are constructing."
- **Mikhail Gorbachev** "The victims of the September 11th attacks will not have died in vain if world leaders use the crisis to create a new world order."
- **Robert Muller** (Former Assistant Attorney General of the U.N.) "We must move as quickly as possible to a one-world government; one-world religion; under a one-world leader."

**Assorted quotes of World Leaders and the New World Order:**

*Reporter: What sort of financial deal should Obama be seeking to strike when he travels to China next month.*

*George Soros: You know this would be the time because you really need to bring China into the creation of a New uh, uh, uh World Order. Financial World Order. Ah, they are kind of reluctant members of the IMF. They play along but they don't make much of a contribution so I think you need a New uh, World Order that uh China has to be part of the process of creating it. I think the makings of it are already there because the G20, in agreeing to peer reviews effectively is moving in that direction*

*Fox New reporting during House Hearing*

*Maxine Waters: What guarantees are you going to give this liberal about how that will reduce the cost of a gasoline at the pump if we let you drill where you say you want to drill.*

**John Hofmeister:** *I can guarantee to the American people because of the inaction of the United States Congress ever increasing prices unless the demand comes down and the $5 dollars will look like a very low price in the years to come if we are prohibited from finding new reserves, new opportunities to increase supplies.*

**Maxine Waters:** *And guess what this liberal will be all about. This liberal will be all about socializing uh umm will be about <hesitates> taking over and the government running all of your companies*

**RT Hon Gordon Brown MP:** *Our position was not that. Our position was to support action so that the will of the international community-that Saddam Hussein disclose and dispose of weapons-be reinforced. And at the back of my mind was this sense that, if the international community did not act here, then the international community would find it difficult to gain credibility for acting in other areas, and this New World Order that we were trying to create was being put at risk*

### The London Summit 2009

**Gordon Brown:** *I think a New World Order is emerging and with it the foundations of a new and progressive era of international cooperation.*

### Feb 25, 1972: President Nixon - Hangzhou, China

*You'll believe deeply in your system and we believe just as deeply in our system. It is not our common beliefs that have brought us together here but our common interests and our common hopes. The interests that each of us has to maintain our independence and the security of our peoples at the hope that each of us has to build a New World Order in which nations and peoples with different systems and different values can live together in peace.*

### 11/30/1989 Mikhail Gorbachev: Sheraton Chicago

*That does not describe why the world has changed so much and why the world has turned so much toward a New World Order and a new kind of civilization.*

### *11/16/91 George H.W. Bush: Speech to US Congress*

**Bush:** *Until now, the world we've known has been a world divided. A world of barbed wire and concrete block. Conflict. Cold War. Now we can see a new world coming into view. A world in which we have the very real prospect of a New World Order.*

*Oct 19, 1999 Hillary Clinton congratulates Walter Cronkite on receiving A Global Governance award from the World Federalist Association*

*We would like to bring you a message from the First Lady of the United States, Hillary Rodham Clinton.*

**Hillary Clinton:** *Good evening and congratulations, Walter on receiving the World Federalist Association's Global Governance award. For more than a generation in America it wasn't the news until Walter Cronkite told us it was the news.*

### *10/02/01 Tony Blair (Former Prime Minister of Great Britain) The Labour Party Annual Conference*

*This is a moment to seize. The kaleidoscope has been shaken. The pieces are in flux. Soon they will settle again. Before they do, let us reorder this world around us.*

### *BBC NEWS Fri. Oct. 12, 2001 UK Politics*

*Headline: Blair's push for new world order*

### *01/18/05 Henry Kissinger: Charlie Rose Interview*

**Kissinger:** *The United States is in a key position to shape this so that the problem of the Bush presidency will be the emergence of a new international order.*

**Rose:** *Within the next four years we will see the emergence of a new international order.*

**Kissinger:** *The beginning of a new international order.*

*The London Paper: March 12, 2007*

*Headline: 'NEW WORLD ORDER' TO SAVE THE EARTH*

*06/20/07 Gordon Brown:*

*The first decade of the 21st Century that out of what will be seen as the greatest restructuring of the global economy. Perhaps one even greater than at the time of the industrial revolution, a new world order was created."*[4]

What's that sound like? Sounds to me like somebody's taking this One World Government and New World Order thing pretty serious, how about you? And lest there be any misunderstanding where this One World Government and satanic Antichrist system is leading to, let's remind ourselves why the Bible calls it satanic. Here's what it's leading to. It ain't pretty. It's called total slavery!

**Revelation 13:16-17** "He also forced everyone, small and great, rich and poor, free and slave, to receive a mark on his right hand or on his forehead, so that no one could buy or sell unless he had the mark, which is the name of the beast or the number of his name."

The Bible clearly tells us that the Antichrist's system is not only going to be over the whole world, but he's also going to force the whole world to receive some sort of a Mark into their right hands or foreheads, in order to buy or sell, right? *Total slavery* to the Antichrist if you don't go along with his system, you're going to be shut out of the system! You won't buy or sell. And believe it or not, that too is already here. One man, Aaron Russo, exposed the whole thing a few years ago before he mysteriously died. Hmmm, I wonder why? Here's the actual conversation he had with one of these Globalists pushing for this One World Government and you tell me if they're not planning on this Mark of the Beast system, to control what you buy or sell.

*Aaron Russo:*

*This is Aaron Russo, a filmmaker and former politician. To his left is Nicholas Rockefeller of the infamous Rockefeller Banking and business dynasty. After maintaining a close friendship with Nicholas Rockefeller, Aaron eventually ended the relationship, appalled by what he had learned about the Rockefellers and their ambitions.*

*Aaron Russo: I got a call one day from a woman I knew, and she said, 'Would you like to meet one of the Rockefellers?'. I said, 'Sure, I'd love to'. And we became friends and he began to divulge a lot of things to me. So he says to me one night- [11 months before Sept. 11th 2001] There's going to be an event Aaron...we are going to go into Afghanistan so we can put in pipelines from the Caspian Sea. We are going to go into Iraq to take the oil and establish a base in the Middle East and we're going to go into Venezuela and then try and go in and get rid of Chavez. And the first two they've accomplished. Chavez they didn't accomplish. You're going to see guys going into caves looking for <laughs> looking for people that they're never gonna find-you know he was laughing about the fact that you have this "war" on "terror". There's no real enemy. He's talking about how by having this war on "terror", you can never win it...because it's an eternal war and so you can always keep taking people's liberties away.*

*I said how are you going to convince people that this war is real? He says by the media. The media can convince everybody that it's real. I mean you know you just keep talking about things. You keep saying it over and over and over and over again and eventually people believe it.*

*You know you create the Federal Reserve in 1913 through lies. You create 9/11 which is another lie. Through 9/11 you then are fighting a war on "terror" and also you go into Iraq, which was another lie. And now they're going to do Iran. So you know, one thing leading to another leading to another, leading to another.*

*So now what are you doing this for? What's the point of this thing? I mean you got all the money in the world you'll ever want. You got all the power, you know. I said you're hurting people, I said, it's not a good thing. And he would say why do you care about the people for. Take care of yourself and take care of your family.*

*And I said to him what are the ultimate goals here? He said the ultimate goal is to get everybody in this world chipped with an RFID chip and have all money be on those chips and everything on those chips and if anybody wants to protest what we do or violate what we want, we just turn off their chip.* "[5]

Wow! Revelation 13 right before our very eyes! So much for a wacky conspiracy theory! This is all happening right now, it's not make believe, it's real and we better get motivated. It's exactly what the Bible said would happen, when you are living in the Last Days! *It just happens to be happening now*! And here's the point. What more does God have to do? This is not a game! God doesn't want us going into the 7-year Tribulation and He certainly doesn't want us to go into HELL! And so that's why, out of love, He's given us these signs of a One World Government to show us that the 7-year Tribulation is near and that Christ's Coming is rapidly approaching.

Like it or not, we are headed for *The Final Countdown*. So the point is this. If you're a Christian it's time to get busy! We've got to lay aside our differences and start getting busy working together saving souls by the Spirit of God! That's the answer to the ills of our country! There's still hope! In fact, this guy says the same thing:

*"Since the recent election, we've seen same-sex couples lining up at courthouses in several states to receive their marriage licenses, and hundreds of people gathering in public places to light up marijuana cigarettes in the states where it has just been decriminalized.*

*This is only the tip of the iceberg. The moral decline we see on television programs – blatant immorality, senseless violence, media-friendly gay and lesbian behavior – is just a reflection of the moral corruption that has infected our entire nation. These are indeed dark days...but there is hope.*

*For far too long, as a nation we have neglected – and even rejected – the Word of God and His commands. Yet the Scriptures are mighty, able to penetrate even the most hardened and darkened hearts with convicting, life-giving power. This is the only cure for a sin-sickened country that is about to slip into a moral abyss, and it is why we must proclaim the Good News."*[6]

In other words, stop goofing off, stop beating each other up, and start getting busy working saving souls, sharing the Gospel. That's what'll turn our country around in the nick of time.

**IV. The 4th proof** that we know we really are headed for a One World Government is what I call the **Tactical Proof.**

Boy, is the enemy slick, or what? What most people don't realize is what we're seeing in world events, the tactics they're using to put this together behind the scenes, are the exact same tactics that the Bible said nearly 2,000 years ago that the Antichrist himself will use to set up his One World Government. But don't take my word for it. Let's listen to God's.

**2 Thessalonians 2:1-12** "Concerning the coming of our Lord Jesus Christ and our being gathered to Him, we ask you, brothers, not to become easily unsettled or alarmed by some prophecy, report or letter supposed to have come from us, saying that the day of the Lord has already come. Don't let anyone deceive you in any way, for that day will not come until the rebellion occurs and the man of lawlessness is revealed, the man doomed to destruction. He will oppose and will exalt himself over everything that is called God or is worshiped, so that he sets himself up in God's temple, proclaiming himself to be God. Don't you remember that when I was with you I used to tell you these things? And now you know what is holding him back, so that he may be revealed at the proper time. For the secret power of lawlessness is already at work; but the one who now holds it back will continue to do so till he is taken out of the way. And then the lawless one will be revealed, whom the Lord Jesus will overthrow with the breath of His mouth and destroy by the splendor of His coming. The coming of the lawless one will be in accordance with the work of satan displayed in all kinds of counterfeit miracles, signs and wonders, and in every sort of evil that deceives those who are perishing. They perish because they refused to love the truth and so be saved. For this reason God sends them a powerful delusion so that they will believe the lie and so that all will be condemned who have not believed the truth but have delighted in wickedness."

Now according to our text, the Bible clearly says whatever you do, don't reject God's truth, you better deal with the facts, right? Why? Because if you don't, you're going to be one of those people who are perishing, falling for the lies of the Antichrist; and notice what his tactics were to get people to fall for it. How does he get the job done? How does he dupe the whole world into not only following him but even to go along with this One World Government? Well apparently, it's *deceit*, right? His tactic is using a satanic lying counterfeit deceit. It's a pack of lies! And that shouldn't be a surprise because he's satanically inspired which means he's all about what satan's all about! Lies, deceit! Lies, deceit, right? That's satan! So is it any surprise that the Antichrist does the same thing to dupe people into going along with a One World Government? Of course not! It makes perfect sense.

But here's the point. I don't know about you, but I'm so glad we don't seen any signs whatsoever of people around the planet using satanic evil deceitful tactics to delude us into going along with a One World Government, any…time…soon…yeah, right! They're already using them in high gear, all over the planet! Okay? We're being duped!

**1. The 1st evil tactic they're using to get us to go along with a One World Government is the deceit of Fear & Manipulation.**

Once again, put yourself in the Antichrist's shoes. If you're going to deceive the whole world into creating a One World Government, then you first have to get everybody on the planet into a total state of fear, right? Why? Because then you can manipulate them. He's not dumb! He knows what he's doing! He knows historically people are more apt to surrender their freedoms in a time of fear than in a time of peace. So, if you create a crisis, you can manage the outcome. If you create a fearful event, you can manipulate the people to do whatever you want to have done, whether they realize it or not!

And if you've been paying attention, this is precisely what's been happening to our country for the last several years! For instance, in order to drum up fear, to manipulate us, we are being told that we have a "health-care crisis," a "child care crisis," an "economy crisis," a "constitutional crisis," a "terrorist crisis," and of course, that dreaded "environmental crisis."[7] We don't have problems anymore. No! Everything is a horrible crisis just waiting to explode! AHHH! And because of these "crises" that are seemingly out of control, we have been manipulated, whether we realize it or not, into a constant state of fear and we're starting to cry out for what they want us to cry out for. Some global entity, some external savior, some universal global government to fix all these global crisis that are seemingly out of control. We've been duped! Now you might think, "Come on, does this lying deceitful fear tactic really work on people, to get them to surrender their freedoms and go along with a One World Government?" You bet it does!

**A. The 1st thing this fear and manipulation tactic of the Antichrist is leading to is a Universal Congress.**

Again, put yourself in the Antichrist's shoes. If you're going to get the whole world to go along with a One World Government, then you first have to have some sort of Global Congress or Governing Body to oversee the whole operation, right? Well guess what the United Nations and countries around the world have been working on for decades? Right now, there is waiting for approval, or is already in place, the plans for *absolute total global control of the whole world*. Right now, there's a Universal Law of the land called the Earth

Charter, which is being proposed as a new universal law to unite all peoples of the world in order to save the planet…you know…the CRISIS thing! For those of you wondering what it's all about, here's the new universal law they're wanting all of us to follow.

*The Earth Charter is stated as being, "A declaration of fundamental principles for building a just, sustainable and peaceful global society in the 21st century." It was created by a commission from every corner of the globe, including world leaders such as Mikhail Gorbachev, Steven Rockefeller and the drafting effort involved more than 100,000 people in 51 countries.*

*So what exactly does it contain? "It clearly lays out the Constitution for a New Green Order." "The choice is ours, form a global partnership to care for Earth and one another or risk the destruction of ourselves and the diversity of life." But the real intent behind the Earth Charter, and the Global Green Agenda is to eliminate national sovereignty and place all humanity under the control of a single "Earth Government."*

*In fact, Mikhail Gorbachev said, "My hope is that this charter will be a kind of Ten Commandments, a 'Sermon on the Mount', that provides a guide for human behavior toward the environment in the next century." And Maurice Strong, a founding co-chairman of the Earth Charter and advisor to the U.N. said, "The real goal of the Earth Charter is that it will in fact become like the Ten Commandments."*

*In fact, speaking of the Ten Commandments, the Earth Charter has been placed into it's own "ark" called the "Ark of Hope," a total mockery of the Biblical Ark of the Covenant that housed the real Ten Commandments. It's carried around by "ark walkers" and the four sides have various artwork depicting the four directions (north, east, south and west), and also four elements (earth, water, fire and air). The top of the ark also features artwork that represents the fifth element: spirit, and around the edges of the top are a variety of religious and cultic symbols including the occult pentagram! Gee, that should tell you the source! In fact, here's a transcript of the video from its unveiling:*

*'Fundamental changes are needed; in our values, in our institutions and our way of living. The Earth Charter provides an ethical foundation for building a more sustainable world-respecting nature, universal human rights, economic justice and a culture of peace.*

*The creation of the Earth Charter was achieved through a decade long, worldwide, cross-cultural dialogue, commonly shared values. Beginning with the 1992 Earth Summit in Rio de Janeiro, Brazil. The Earth Charter drafting process continued gaining momentum at the 1995 Earth Charter International Workshop in the Hague, Netherlands.*

*These unique participatory and inclusive processes continued over the next 5 years through national and regional workshops worldwide. A new face began in the year 2000 with the official launching of the Earth Charter.*

*We make this gift of service to all our brothers and sisters in the human family; especially to the children, to those who suffer in poverty and under oppression and to future generations.*

*It is vital for humans and for nature that the Earth Charter movement continues to spread it's message of hope for a brighter future."*[8]

For a brighter future? Or for the ultimate excuse to create a One World Government? Sounds to me like the Antichrist is using an evil lie, a deceitful tactic in the Last Days to get us to go along with a One World Government.

But that's not all. If you're going to have a universal law of the land, then you need a Universal Governing Body to oversee this law, right? Well hey, that's why *right now* there's a document called *The Constitution for the Federation Earth*, with plans for a World Government, World Supreme Court, World Capitols and a World Police.[9] The only thing holding it up is ratification, which they're hoping is going to take place real soon.

But wait a minute. If you're going to have a universal governing body, then you need a *Universal Judicial System* to make sure people obey this new World Government, right? Well hey, that's why, right now, there's a *World Criminal Court* that went into effect July of 2002, thanks in part to the signing of the treaty by Bill Clinton on his last day in office. Thanks, Bill! Thanks for your help in forming a One World Government.

## International Criminal Court

*"Some of the worst crimes ever known have been committed during the 20th century. Millions of children, women and men have been victims of unimaginable atrocities that have deeply shocked the conscience of humanity.*

*Unfortunately, in the past, such crimes have often gone unpunished. Millions of people died during two World Wars and in fighting in Rwanda, Sierra Leone and in former Yugoslavia.*

*The International Criminal Court is the first criminal court with jurisdiction over the most serious crimes threatening the peace, security and well being of the world.*

*In 1998, during the Rome Diplomatic Conference on the International Criminal Court, 160 countries negotiated a treaty to design the world's first permanent international criminal court."*[10]

Yeah! Awesome! Now we have a court system to make us obey this World Government! But that's not all. If you're going to have a universal judicial system to enforce this universal law, then you need a *Universal Army* to punish those who don't obey this World Government and World law, right? That's why, right now, Tony Blair, the former British Prime Minister, has been calling for NATO to become the future "military arm of a new world order rather than strictly a defensive alliance."[11] If you think about it, we've already seen NATO exercise more and more military force over the sovereignty of nations, right? In our lifetime. I wonder who's next? But here's the point. Sounds to me if you put all this together, I'd say somebody's pretty serious about forming a One World Government, how about you? And the tactic they're using is fear and manipulation! And that's exactly what the Bible said the Antichrist would do, when you are living in the Last Days!

**B. The 2nd thing** this fear and manipulation tactic of the Antichrist is leading to is a **Universal Behavior.**

Yeah, they're going to dictate everything. Once again, put yourself in the Antichrist's shoes. If you're going to deceive the whole world into creating a One World Government then you have to provide a *Universal Standard of Behavior* so that you can dictate universal compliance, right? Well guess what? Again, this is what the United Nations has been working towards for decades, and again, they're using fear and manipulation to pull it off!

For instance, right now, in order to preserve our supposed endangered earth, thanks to the *World Heritage Protection* program, the UN has full authority over millions of acres of land right here in America.[12] Such areas include Yellowstone National Park, the Statue of Liberty, the Grand Canyon and the Yosemite Valley, just to name a few. Then, in order to preserve our supposed endangered food supply, right now the *World Food Summit* continues to meet to govern what crops we can grow, what livestock we can raise and even what we get to eat.[13]

But that's not all. In order to preserve our supposed endangered air, land and water supply, right now a program called *Agenda 21* has plans to dictate our total behavior. Things such as what job we can get, what housing we can have, what education and health care we get, what means of transport and even how many children we can have...just like China! Don't believe me? Here's what this program is promoting.

*"If you were to hear that in the very near future the United States will have no privately owned property, no air conditioning, no dams, no paved roads, no way to correct rivers for flood control, no golf courses, no pastureland used for grazing, would you believe it? These are all mandates of a United Nations program called Agenda 21. Here is a list of some of their "Unsustainable" Targets...*

- *Ski runs*
- *Grazing livestock*
- *Disturbing of soil surface/plowing of soil*
- *Building fences*
- *Commercial Agriculture/Modern farm production*
- *Chemical fertilizers*
- *The use of fossil fuels*
- *Any industrial activity*
- *Single family homes*
- *Paved and tarred roads*
- *Railroads*
- *Floor and wall tiles*
- *Technology*
- *Range lands, fish ponds, or plantations*
- *Harvesting timber*
- *Hunting*
- *Logging activities*
- *Dams and reservoirs, straightening of rivers, and power line construction*

- *In fact, they will not only control your birth, they will control your death,*
- *young and old alike. Here are the actual commercials.*

### Agenda 21 How will it affect you?

*We have only one earth. Our living planet that helps to sustain life. We are warned this life system is in crisis.*

*Fresh water. Clean Air. Good soil. The things we need to stay alive are being destroyed. Sustaining the environment is something we all have a vested interest in. After all, who wants to pollute the water or the land?*

*Let's look at the Chinese Communist government and its one child policy. Just like marriage in China, there are numerous hurdles you must overcome before permission is granted. For a Chinese couple to have a child, they have to get a birth license. In order for the couple to get a license, they have to go through a procedure that runs through local Communist Party functionaries. Without a birth license, no hospital or doctor can treat the mother or the child before, during or after the birth. The Chinese are required to inform the authorities of any illegal birth. In short, the Chinese government is in complete control.*

*Since China is one of the 5 permanent members of the U.N.'s Security Council, it has a great deal of influence on U.N. policy and how they view population control.*

*China's one child policy is now being considered as a viable solution towards Sustainable Development.*

*The P.C.S.D. shows their support in this very idea; and in their 1998 publication.*

*"We must move toward stabilization of the U.S. population and a reduced rate of population growth in the United States and the world." ---Sustainable America: America's Environment, Economy and Society in the 21st Century. <Forward by Al Gore>"*[14]

Yeah, you've lived a good life and don't you know according to Agenda 21 it's your patriotic duty to let them pull the plug on you, if you're old or have a deformity, to make room for the rest of us? People, this is sick! This is the kind of society the Antichrist is building using fear and manipulation. We've got to do this to save the planet!

But that's still not all. In order to preserve our supposed endangered animals, you know, because they're more important than humans nowadays. Right now they have something called the *Biodiversity Treaty* that's getting ready to dictate where you and I get to live and where the animals get to live, at least those they decide who get to live in the first place.[15] In fact, here is the actual map.

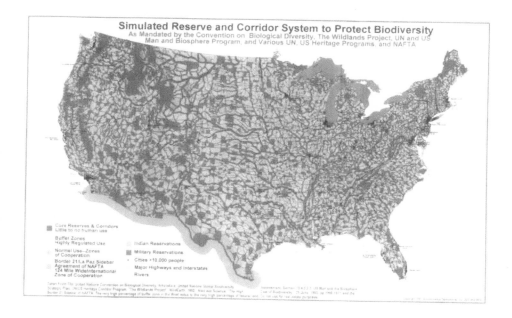

Simulated Reserve and Corridor System to Protect Biodiversity
As Mandated by the Convention on Biological Diversity, The Wildlands Project, UN and US Man and Biosphere Program, and Various UN, US Heritage Programs, and NAFTA

And what's strange about this map is not only how wild it is in the first place, but it starts to shed light to this passage of Scripture in the Book of Revelation.

**Revelation 6:8** "I looked, and there before me was a pale horse! Its rider was named Death, and Hades was following close behind him. They were given power over a fourth of the earth to kill by sword, famine and plague, and by the wild beasts of the earth."

So, let me get this straight. According to the Bible, 1/4th of the earth is going to die during the first half of the 7-year Tribulation by means of sword, famine, plague and wild beasts? Hmmm. I can see the sword thing, and famine, and plague, but who's concerned about wild beasts nowadays, right? I mean they're all in zoos and protected areas, right? Well not if these guys get their way. Put all this together. Thanks to the Earth Charter and thanks to Agenda 21 and the Biodiversity Treaty, we might very well see for the first time in mankind's history, a massive resurgence of wild animals all over the place, even in America! And once that famine in the text hits ....they're going to be hungry! I wonder what they're going to do. And the Bible says, one day, 1/4th of the planet is going to die by means of the sword, famine, plague, and wild beasts. Even *minute* passages like this are coming to life for the first time in our history! Isn't that wild?

**C. The 3rd thing** this fear and manipulation tactic of the Antichrist is leading to is a **Universal Border.**

**Revelation 17:9,12-13** "And now understand this. His ten horns are ten kings who have not yet risen to power; they will be appointed to their kingdoms for one brief moment to reign with the beast. They will all agree to give their power and authority to him."

Now according to the Bible, we see how the Antichrist's kingdom is going to be split up into ten different parts ruled by ten different kings or leaders, right? And then, at one point, they surrender their power and authority over to him, right? It says it right there! Wow, it's a good thing we see no signs of that happening...any time...soon. People splitting the planet...up...into different kingdoms...yeah, right! It's happening *now*! Again, the tactics they're using are fear and manipulation. You've heard the rhetoric, "Don't you want to ensure peace across the planet? Do you want to have another economic crisis like what we just came out of? Don't you want to guarantee the prosperity for the generations to come? Well hey, then join us in creating 10 World Regions to assure proper global control and everything will be just fine!" And folks, they're not just doing this, they're actually promoting exactly **10**! Not **5**, not **19**, not even **122**, but **10**! Check it out for yourself!

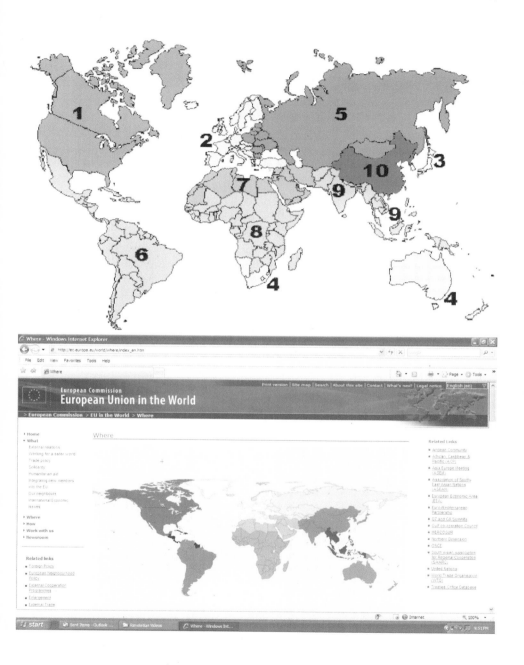

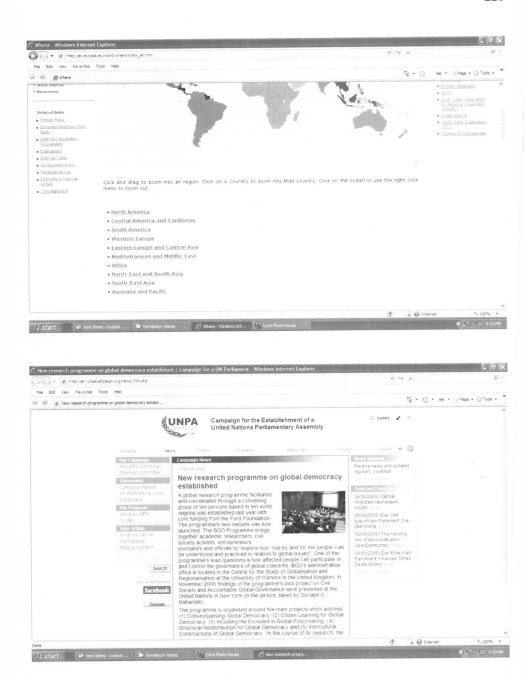

11 March 2009

## New research programme on global democracy established

A global research programme facilitated and coordinated through a convening group of ten persons based in ten world regions was established last year with core funding from the Ford Foundation. The programme's new website was now launched. The BGD Programme brings together academic researchers, civil society activists, entrepreneurs,

journalists and officials to "explore how 'rule by and for the people' can be understood and practiced in relation to global issues". One of the programme's lead questions is how affected people can participate in

16

I wish I was making this up, but this is really happening! In fact, if I didn't know better, I'd say the Antichrist is probably going to use the exact same type of Mark of the Beast technology that we saw before to not only control what people buy or sell, but I bet he'd probably use the same technology to control people's movements from one of these 10 kingdoms to another. But here's the point, we don't see any signs of that, do we? Well all I know is Mexican Officials are starting to do this with their border. Check it out.

### CNN Lou Dobbs Report:

*"Mexico is highly critical of U.S. Immigration policy, but it's taking extraordinary measure when it comes to its own immigration crisis. Mexico is taking drastic measures to control its illegal immigration across its Southern border. Now, Mexico will reportedly use an electronic chip to curb illegal immigration from Guatemala and Belize. The biochip implant will replace the so-called local pass currently being used to enter the country. In 2006, Mexico arrested 200,000 people trying to enter their country illegally."*[17]

Maybe there's something more behind this so-called "immigration crisis" than what they're telling us. Maybe they're using fear to manipulate us into getting one of these implants. But they wouldn't do that, would they? There's no way our government here in America would force us to get an implant to track our every move…or would they? Maybe we should've been paying attention to the congressional hearing for John Roberts when he was being grilled for the position of Chief Justice of the Supreme Court. You tell me if somebody's not planning on tracking our every move, even here in America!

### *John Roberts confirmation:*

*Joe Biden to then appointee John Roberts: And we'll be faced with equally consequential decisions in the 21st century.*

*Can a microscopic tag be implanted in a person's body to track his every movement. There's actual discussion about that. You will rule on that, mark my words, before your tenure is over. Can brain scans be used to determine whether a person is inclined toward criminality or violent behavior? You will rule on that.*

**Dr. Katherine Albrecht:** *I think the real concern that most people have, is that at some point, the government would say, "Line up and get your chip."*[18]

But hey, that'll never happen…"You will rule on that, mark my words." I don't know about you, but if congress is talking about implanting microscopic tags into people to track their every move, then my guess is they're probably going to implant microscopic tags into people to track their every move, how about you? And Biden was the Vice President and Roberts has been the Chief Justice for a while now. I wonder when he's going to rule on it…just like he did with the Health Care….we thought he'd never go along with that…Folks, we better wake up! This is all happening before our very eyes *right now*! God warned us 2,000 years ago! Jesus Christ is coming back and it might be a whole lot sooner than you think. The Antichrist's One World Government is being formed before our very eyes, he's using fear and manipulation to get it done, and you better be ready.

**V. The 5th proof that we know we really are headed for a One World Government is what I call the Control Proof.**

You see, the Bible is clear, we're not just headed towards an evil deceptive Antichrist's kingdom, but that kingdom is going to be one about absolute total control! I mean, everything! But don't take my word for it. Let's listen to God's.

**Revelation 13:11-18** "Then I saw another beast, coming out of the earth. He had two horns like a lamb, but he spoke like a dragon. He exercised all the authority of the first beast on his behalf, and made the earth and its inhabitants worship the first beast, whose fatal wound had been healed. And he performed great and miraculous signs, even causing fire to come down from heaven to earth in full view of men. Because of the signs he was given power to do on behalf of the first beast, he deceived the inhabitants of the earth. He ordered them to set up an image in honor of the beast who was wounded by the sword and yet lived. He was given power to give breath to the image of the first beast, so that it could speak and cause all who refused to worship the image to be killed. He also forced everyone, small and great, rich and poor, free and slave, to receive a mark on his right hand or on his forehead, so that no one could buy or sell unless he had the mark, which is the name of the beast or the number of his name. This calls for wisdom. If anyone has insight, let him calculate the number of the beast, for it is man's number. His number is 666."

Now according to our text, the Bible clearly says that the False Prophet in the Last Days is not only going to dupe the whole world into *worshiping* the Antichrist, or the beast, but he's what? He's going to *make* them do it, right? He *orders* them! In fact, so much so, if you don't worship the Antichrist, you're going to what? You're going to *die*! You're going to be killed, right? But he still goes on. He then says if you don't take this mark of the Antichrist, then what's going to happen to you? You're going to be *forced* into doing it, right? You won't be able to buy or sell anything, anywhere on the whole planet! How many of you would say, "Gee, that doesn't sound like a very good time?" Yeah, slightly! No wonder Jesus said in Matthew 24 it's going to be the worst time in the history of mankind!

But here's the point. The Bible clearly says this is all happening on a *global scale* which means in order for this to happen, for the Antichrist and the False Prophet to make and force and order people to do what they want them to do, you have to have some serious control over just about everything on the whole planet, right? Well believe it or not, that time is *now*! Little by little, while we've been asleep at the wheel, they've been grabbing total control of the planet to force us to go along with this!

**1. The 1st control mechanism** they've already put into place to FORCE US into going along with this One World Government is our **Food Supply.**

You might be thinking, "Well hey man, there's no way they're going to get me! I'm not going to go along with this One World Government! I'm just going to store up my own food supply and take care of my own basic needs and run and hide out in the hills! They can't get me! Ha! Ha! Ha! I'm free!" Really? Not if they control your *food supply*! And that's exactly what the Bible says the Antichrist is going to do in the Last Days!

**Revelation 6:5-6** "When the Lamb opened the third seal, I heard the third living creature say, 'Come!' I looked, and there before me was a black horse! Its rider was holding a pair of scales in his hand. Then I heard what sounded like a voice among the four living creatures, saying, 'A quart of wheat for a day's wages, and three quarts of barley for a day's wages, and do not damage the oil and the wine!'"

The last time we were here, if you recall, this text is dealing with the famine conditions during the first half of the 7-year Tribulation. And what it tells us is that the famine conditions are so bad at that time that the whole world is actually going to be on some sort of global food distribution program just to stay alive, right? What'd it say? One day's work you could get a quart of wheat for yourself, right? Or you could opt out of that for three quarts of barley, a less nutritional meal, literally animal feed as we saw before, to feed you and your family of two.

Now, here's the point. That's exactly what the same people who are pushing for this One World Government are saying we need to do *right now*! Get total control of our global food supply! In fact, they're already doing it! And once again, they're using fear and manipulation to get the job done to get us to go along with it! It's the same tactic we saw before! I mean, haven't you heard? We have a horrible *food crisis* on our hands! We've got salmonella outbreaks in spinach, tomatoes and even our peanut butter! No! Not the peanut butter! Yes, even the peanut butter! Think of the kids! What are they going to do? How will they survive? And then there's that E Coli thing, that mad cow disease and even that Hoof and Mouth disease! Oh no! What will we do? What will we do? Hey, I know, we just need some sort of global food entity, some global control system to control our global food supply to keep it safe for us and everything will be just fine….yeah right! And for those of you who don't think this is a manufactured crisis to grab control of our food supply, here's what all these fear tactics and scares are leading to.

The Obama administration created a "food safety" group to help "protect" the U.S. food supply. Mr. Obama said food-borne illness outbreaks have increased in recent years, including major salmonella outbreaks involving spinach, peppers, tomatoes and even peanuts. He said, "We are not just designing laws that will keep the American people safe, but enforcing them."

In fact, if you don't follow these new food laws, you might end up losing your property. And that's because there's a new House Resolution called the "Food Safety Modernization Act" that calls for the creation of a Food Safety Administration to "allow the government to regulate food production at all levels – and even mandates property seizure, fines of up to $1 million dollars per offense and criminal prosecution for those who fail to comply with regulations.

Another bill that has people worried is the Senate Bill 425 or "Food Safety and Tracking Improvement Act" that's backed by Monsanto, Archer Daniels Midland and Tyson. They say, "We must ensure that the federal government has the ability and authority to protect the public, given the global nature of the food supply." The bill calls for the establishment of a national database of our food supply with electronic records to identify "where the food was grown, prepared, handled, manufactured, processed, distributed, shipped, warehoused, imported and conveyed to ensure the safety of the food."

In fact, here's what one of the guys pushing this bill said, *"If the postal service can track a package from my office in Washington to my office in Cincinnati, we should be able to do the same for food products. Families that are struggling with the high cost of groceries should not also have to worry about the safety of their food. This legislation gives the government the resources it needs to protect the public."* Or to control the public and their food supply?

And lest you think it's not going to lead to that, a new law proposed by the European Commission would make it illegal to "grow, reproduce or trade" any vegetable seeds that have not been "tested, approved and accepted" by a new EU bureaucracy named the "EU Plant Variety Agency."

It's called the *Plant Reproductive Material Law*, and it attempts to put the government in charge of virtually all plants and seeds. Home gardeners who grow their own plants from non-regulated seeds would be considered criminals under this law. (Gee, looks like that Seed Vault by Bill Gates might "really" have an alternative motive after all…)

And then just in case you still tried to grow and produce your own food, *"Recently a SWAT team with semi-automatic rifles entered the private home of a food cooperative in LaGrange, Ohio, where they then herded the family onto the couches in the living room, and kept guns trained on parents, children, infants and toddlers, from approximately 11 AM to 8 PM. Agents then began rifling through all of the family's possessions, many items were taken, the family was not permitted a phone call and they were not told what crime they were being charged with. They were not read their rights. Over ten thousand dollars worth of food was taken, including the family's personal stock of food for the coming year. All of their computers and all of their cell phones were taken, as well as phone and contact records. The food cooperative was virtually shut down. There was no rational explanation, nor justification for this extreme violation of Constitutional rights."*[19]

Wow! Interesting. So much for storing up your own food supply! But that's not all. Just to make sure we go along with this total control of our food supply, we have another crisis on our hands. It's that dreaded obesity crisis! That's right, we have to let them control our food because there are people out there who can't control it! For the sake of themselves and the cost of the health care system, we have got to have somebody control our food! Don't believe me? Here's what it's leading to. Fat Report Cards!
A new forecast on obesity in America has health experts fearing a dramatic jump in health care costs if nothing is done to bring it under control. The projection recently released warns that 42% of Americans may end up obese by 2030 and that's why some schools are now giving out "fat" report cards to students to help "curb" this "bad" behavior.

**Child Obesity:**

*For some time now health officials in this country have been warning of a growing epidemic of childhood obesity. Many schools have responded, taking steps to promote exercise and healthier eating habits.*

*Well now in Denver they're going even farther, sending home a new kind of report card. Here's NBC's George Louis.*

**Louis:** *Ten year old Isabelle Martinez broke into tears when she read the notice placed in her backpack and intended for her parents. School health authorities have marked her down as overweight.*

**Flaurette Martinez:** *That was the first thing she saw, she said "Mom I'm* *overweight. I'm fat, Mom!" And it just broke my heart to hear her cry. She was just bawling.*

The way this information was delivered to the family was against any of the guidelines related to privacy and health information.

In fact, a bill has already been introduced in Congress that would put the federal and state governments in the business of tracking how fat or skinny American children are. In England, "food police" are secretly photographing schoolchildren's packed lunches to analyze the contents whereupon they then contact the parents and encourage them to "improve" their nutrition. Even here in America, new federal regulations are stipulating that the "new" electronic health records that Americans are supposed to have here real soon must record not only the traditional measures of height and weight, but also the Body Mass Index, or obesity rating.

The rationale for all this Big Brother type of behavior is not only for the well-being of the children, but for the future costs as well. They say, "If nothing is done, obesity is going to hinder efforts for health care cost containment. America could save $549.5 billion dollars if weight-related medical expenditures were controlled and this obesity problem is likely to get much worse without a major public health intervention."

And that's already begun. Believe it or not, salted popcorn may soon become a federal offense! Believe it or not, the FDA is planning an assault on salt by limiting the salt intake of Americans with the excuse that it's for the "protection" of the health of the public. The FDA would analyze the salt in spaghetti sauces, breads and thousands of other products that make up the $600 billion food and beverage market. The main culprit behind this effort to monitor our food supply is an outfit called the Center for Science in the Public Interest (CSPI) who is the leader among what's called, "the food police."

The head of CSPI is a guy named Michael Jacobson, who just happens to be a rabid vegetarian and who is horrified by nearly anything man chooses to eat. CSPI calls for taxes on foods with fat, sugar and sodium (called the "Twinkie Tax"). In fact, the state of New York is not only starting to "ban" certain food products under the fear of "damaging your health" but they are also calling for the implementation of an "obesity tax."

**Obesity Tax:**

*Reporter Steve Ference: If you do like drinking soda...*

*Mickey McMullin <customer>: It's crazy! Why would it be just a sugar soda?*

*Ference: Try this on for size. The Governor's proposed Obesity Tax, charging 18% sales tax for sodas on top of the 8% already collected.*

*Anitra Stinney <customer>: Of course it takes more money out of our pockets.*

*Ference: Here's the skinny on the plan. Any soda, except diet, would be taxed at the higher rate. Drinks containing less than 70% fruit juice could also be taxed.*

*Christian King <store owner>: But the biggest thing is us taking the brunt of the customer irritation or frustration with more tax. We get to see it.*

*John O'Leary <customer>: I don't drink it, so it doesn't bother me at all.*

*Ference: It's not only soda, the beer tax would more than double. Malt beverages would be taxed at the higher liquor rate.*

*King: There's a lot for convenient store customers not to like.*

*Ference: But many critics are wondering where the line is. Does it simply end with soda or does the taxing continue with things like cakes or even your favorite coffee?*

*James Calvin <NY Assoc of Convenience Store President> One of our concerns is not only about this particular proposal, but about what happens next. What's the next product that may contain sugar that would be taxed at an exorbitant level?*

All of that action, of course, serves only to drive up the cost of food while robbing Americans of a freedom to choose what they eat. In fact, CSPI has attacked nearly every food product on Earth, begging the question, "What's left to eat." Jacobsen suggests a sandwich of lettuce and bread - but be careful, because the bread has salt in it and the lettuce may have been sprayed with chemicals. In fact, he advises a near starvation diet of not much more than potatoes and carrots (don't over indulge in them). And he says, the American public cannot be trusted to make their own choices, "so he must do it for them." Gee, what's next? They gonna feed us "wheat" and "barley"? In fact, it's getting so bad that pretty soon you might even lose your job if you smoke or eat junk food!

**Smokers fired.**

*Katie Couric: How's this for an ultimatum at work; quit smoking or You're Fired! A year ago we told you about a Michigan medical benefits firm that canned four employees who refused to be tested for nicotine. Now a well know national company is threatening to do the same thing to workers who light up. Here's CNBC'S Diana Olick.*

*Diana Olick: On the smoke-free campus of Scott's Miracle Grow, the wellness center is packed with a lunchtime crowd.*

*James Hagedorn: We're trying to improve the wellness of our associates.*

*Olick: With a 5 million dollar gym, free health screening, free counseling and a promise to most of it's 5300 employees. You smoke. You're fired.*

*James Hagedorn: We gave them a year heads up, in stage four we have a choice, which is about sixty percent of our people. We'll give them pharmaceuticals. We'll give them counseling. We'll give them whatever they need.*

*Diana Olick: So what about states where this policy is illegal, like New Hampshire? Well one manufacturer there, Kimball Physics says, "If you even smell like smoke, you can't come into the building." In other words, these ladies couldn't go back to work."*

*Some companies, such as General Mills, are charging smoker's more for health care. And one medical benefits company itself is even going after smoker's spouses.*

*Woman on the street: So what's going to be next after that? People that overeat?*

*Olick: Perhaps, because it's corporate America, it chokes on the cost of healthcare, where there's smoke, there will be firing."*[20]

Now I don't know about you, but it sure looks to me like all these obesity and food fears are leading to a total control of our food supply, how about you? Looks to me like somebody's deceitful plan is working like a charm! Why, the next thing you know, we won't be able to buy or sell any kind of food unless we do what they say! Where have I heard that before? Oh yeah, that's right! That's the Antichrist's kingdom that's going to appear on the scene when you are living in the Last Days!

**2. The 2nd control mechanism** they've already put into place to FORCE US into going along with a One World Government is our **Water Supply.**

You might be thinking, "Well hey man, there's no way they're going to get me! Okay, so maybe they're going to control the food supply, but I'm going to store up food *right now* and then all I need is a good steady supply of water and I'm good to go! They can't get me! Ha! Ha! Ha! I'm free!" Really? Not if they control your *water supply*! And according to the Bible, that's going to become a huge issue during the 7-year Tribulation.

**Revelation 8:6,8-11** "Then the seven angels who had the seven trumpets prepared to sound them. The second angel sounded his trumpet, and something like a huge mountain, all ablaze, was thrown into the sea. A third of the sea turned into blood, a third of the living creatures in the sea died, and a third of the ships were destroyed. The third angel sounded his trumpet, and a great star, blazing like a torch, fell from the sky on a third of the rivers and on the springs of water, the name of the star is Wormwood. A third of the waters turned bitter, and many people died from the waters that had become bitter."

The Bible clearly says during the 7-year Tribulation that not only does the saltwater, the sea, get judged by God, but even the fresh water gets judged by God, right? It said the *springs*! And so what happened? Many people died as a result, right? And so this tells us whoever controls that water supply during the 7-year Tribulation gets to control a whole lot of people, right? So guess what? That's exactly what these same people who are pushing for this One World Government are saying we do *right now*! We've got to get a total control of our global water supply! WHY? Because haven't you heard? We've got a serious water crisis on our hands! There are chemicals being dumped into our streams, there are poisons that are leaching into our water table and there's those dreaded toxins being released into our municipal water plants. In fact, drugs are in our water supply. Don't believe me? Check it out for yourself!

**CNN Drugs in Drinking Water**

*Elizabeth Cohen (CNN Medical Correspondent): Well the Associated Press here spent 5 months investigating this and they looked at various municipal water supplies. Not all of them keep track of whether or not there are pharmaceuticals but the ones that do, they all had traces of various medicines. I am going to give you a list that will give you some idea of the kinds of things that they found.*

*For example, in Atlanta, where I am right now, they found that the water contained traces of Antibiotics, blood pressure drugs; and Cincinnati, cholesterol drugs and estrogen that women sometimes take for medicinal reasons. And New York City found traces of a seizure drug and an anti-anxiety drug. Now to give you sort of the "big picture", how many drugs did they find in the drinking water? In Philadelphia they found trace amounts of 56 different drugs. In New York City they found traces of 16 drugs and in Northern N.J. traces of 13 drugs.*

*So, of course the next question is what about bottled water? Well I hate to sound so pessimistic here, bottled water is often repackaged tap water and that doesn't help us much either, or even if sometimes it's spring water it could still possibly contain these trace amounts and those filters at home-they are not sensitive enough to get rid of the pharmaceuticals.*

Well there you have it! We've got a serious water problem. In fact, what's even more serious is how those drugs got in there in the first place. Many would say it's just from people taking these medications and then when they go to the bathroom they release it into the public water supply. But others would say maybe it's part of some other nefarious plan that's already been used by other nations on their populations for control purposes. Check this out.

According to an official Government report, one man testified, *"While a member of the Communist Party, 1 attended Communist underground training schools outside the City of New York. We discussed quite thoroughly the fluoridation of water supplies and how we were using it in Russia as a tranquilizer in the prison camps.*

*The leaders of our Communist school felt that if it could be induced into the American water supply, it would bring about a spirit of lethargy in the nation; where it would keep the general public docile during a steady encroachment of Communism.*

*We also discussed the fact that keeping a store of deadly fluoride near the water reservoir would be advantageous during the time of the revolution, as it would give us opportunity to dump this poison into the water supply and either kill off the populace or threaten them with liquidation, so that they would surrender to obtain fresh water. Both the Germans and the Russians added fluoride to the drinking water of prisoners of war to make them stupid and docile."*

But hey, that would never happen, would it? All I know is, all these manufactured crises over our water supply are leading to this. Total control. Believe it or not, right now it is "illegal" to collect rainwater in many states here in America. Don't believe me? Here's the actual report.

**Stealing Rainwater:**

*Who owns the rain? Turns out, not you. You're actually breaking the law if you try to capture rain falling onto your roof and pour it out on your flowerbed.*

*A prominent Utah car dealer found that out when he tried to do something good for the environment. John Oliver has the surprising story.*

**Oliver:** *Rebecca Nelson captures rain water in a barrel and she pours it on her plants.*

**Rebecca:** *We can fill up a barrel in one rainstorm so it seems a waste to let it just fall onto the gravel.*

**Oliver:** *Car dealer Mark Miller pretty much wanted to do the same thing on a bigger scale. He collects rainwater on the roof of his new building and stores it in a cistern and hopes to clean cars with it in a new water efficient car wash. But without a valid water right, state officials say you can't legally divert rainwater.*

**Miller:** *I was surprised. We thought it was our water.*

*Oliver: So, what about the little guy watering with rainwater at home what'll anybody do about that violation of the law?*

*If she really does do that then she ought to have a water right to do it.*

And lest you think this trend isn't going to go global, right now the U.N. is seeking to control the planet's drinking water. Right now they are pushing a program "The Blue Planet Project" and it's part of a global movement to promote the U.N.'s belief that "water is life" and that the world is now experiencing a global water crisis. More than 1 billion people do not have access to safe drinking water and more than 3.5 million people die each year from water-related diseases.

Therefore, they are proposing to control the planet's water supply. "We strive for water justice based on the principles that water is a human right, a public trust and part of the global commons." It's been called, "The Mother of All Power Grabs," but oddly enough, the news media has totally ignored what should be the biggest news story of the year."[21]

I don't know about you, but it sure looks to me like all these water fears are leading to a global control of our water supply. Looks to me like these fear tactics are working like a charm. I mean, the next thing you know, somebody's going to have the power to *force us* to do whatever they say…and where have I heard that before? Oh yeah, that's right! It's the Antichrist's kingdom that the Bible said would appear on the scene in the Last Days!

**3. The 3rd control mechanism** they've already put into place to FORCE US into going with a One World Government is our **Health Supply.**

Now you might be thinking, "Well hey man, there's no way they're going to get me! Okay, so maybe they're going to get control of the food supply and the water supply, but if I store up food now and a whole bunch of water somehow, someway, they can't get me! Ha! Ha! Ha! I'm still free!" Really? Not if they control your *health supply*! You see, according to the Book of Revelation, the 7-year Tribulation is going to cause a lot of injuries! You're going to need some serious health care! Check it out!

**Seal Judgments**

1st Seal - White Horse – Global False Peace
2nd Seal - Red Horse – Global War
3rd Seal - Black Horse – Global Famine
4th Seal - Pale Horse – Global Death – 1/4th of Mankind Killed by…
Sword
Famine
Plague
Wild Beasts
5th Seal - Altar of Souls – Global Persecution
6th Seal – Beginning of Great Tribulation which unleashes…
A Global Earthquake
Sun Turns Black
Moon Turns Red
Asteroids Fall to Earth
Sky Recedes
Mountains/Islands Removed from Places
Global Fear of God's Wrath

**Trumpet Judgments** – Opened by the Seventh Seal – Silence in Heaven
1st Trumpet - Hail/Fire - 1/3rd of Earth/Trees & All Green Grass Burned Up
2nd Trumpet - Huge Asteroid – 1/3rd of Sea Dies & 1/3rd Ships Destroyed
3rd Trumpet - Blazing Comet – 1/3rd of Rivers & Fresh Water Bitter – Many People Die
4th Trumpet - Solar Smiting - 1/3rd of Sun, Moon & Stars Struck – 1/3rd Day & Night without Light
5th Trumpet - Satan Releases Demon Horse of Locusts – People with Mark Tortured 5 Months
6th Trumpet - Four Angels Loosed from Euphrates – 1/3rd Mankind Killed

**Bowl Judgments**
1st Bowl – Ugly Painful Sores on Receivers of the Mark
2nd Bowl – All the Sea Turns to Blood – All Sea Creatures Die
3rd Bowl – All the Rivers & Fresh Water Turned to Blood
4th Bowl – Sun Scorches People with Fire – People Curse God
5th Bowl – Kingdom of Antichrist Plunged into Darkness
6th Bowl – Euphrates Dries Up
Prepares Way for Kings of East for Armageddon
Three Evil Frog-Like Spirits Deceive the World for Armageddon
Out of Mouth of Satan

Out of Mouth of Antichrist
Out of Mouth of False Prophet
7<sup>th</sup> Bowl – Final Pronouncement – IT IS DONE
Greatest of all Earthquakes
A New Look for Jerusalem - Split in Three
All Cities Collapse
A Cup of Wrath for Babylon
All Islands and Mountains Gone
A Massive Hailstorm – 100 lbs. each
Angel Harvest of the Righteous
Angel Harvest of the Unrighteous – Blood as High as Horse's Bridle (4 feet deep) for 1,600 Stadia (200 Miles)

Now maybe it's just me, but it appears you're going to need some serious health care during the 7-year Tribulation. My advice is don't go there in the first place! But as you can see, whoever controls the health care at that time, certainly controls a lot of people, right? But hey, good thing we see no signs of anyone getting control of our health care system to exert *power* and *control* over us…or do we? What in the world do you think just happened? Didn't you hear the debates? We don't have a health care problem, we have a health care *crisis*! We have to go along with this Universal Health Care system to make it right and fair and bring this crisis under control! But what they didn't tell you was that it was a ruse to grab control of your *life* and even your *death*. Don't believe me? Let's take a look what's in there!

What most people don't realize is that part of the new health care system that was passed also calls for the creation of a so-called "health care military" force. Here's the actual report.

**Obamacare Army:**

*Shepard Smith: Ah Health Care now-with the bill now a law, Fox News is asking what next? Today, a closer look at a little known provision of the overhaul. What you might not have heard, The Reform Law calls for the creation of a 6,000 person army, if you will. A sort of army of trained public healthcare professionals. With us now, Fox News Senior Judicial Analyst Judge Andrew Napolitano.*

*Napolitano: The language is intentionally vague and it's a little scary because of the military sounding words used in the creation of this group.*

*Smith:* Well they ought to change those words.

*Napolitano:* Well by referring to it as a reserve corp, the training is the same as the regular corp. It gives you the impression that the President has the power to take over the National Guard from State Governors in peace time. Now under the Constitution, he can't do that. But a fair reading of this legislation would let him do it. Another way to read the legislation is these are healthcare professionals but they're going to train with the military, meaning they're going to carry sidearms.

*Smith:* Oh really?!? They would carry sidearms?

*Napolitano:* Well if they're going to train with the military, that's what the military trains with. If you look on the debates on the floor of the Congress, there's nothing about this and many other clauses in this because members of Congress didn't have the time to read it.

*Smith:* Does it sound well intentioned to you?

*Napolitano:* No. No! No it doesn't! It doesn't sound well intentioned because of the military language. The government needs physicians and has the ability to hire them. But putting them under the direct command of the President, saying you will train with the military is what is scary. Why do we need military oriented physicians if the emergency is stateside.

Gee, why would you want a Health Care Military Force? Well maybe there's going to be some things in your new health care system that people are going to resist. And once you actually read that bill, that's exactly what's going to happen!

**Pgs.29,30,42:** It states that a government committee will decide what treatments you are allowed and what your overall benefits are. It mandates the rationing of health care as is being done in Canada and it gives the power of the Health Choices Commissioner to determine your health benefits. You will have no choice.

**Pgs.85,354:** It gives the government the right to ration everyone's healthcare, including Medicare recipients, basically rationing the care of every senior citizen in the United States as well as restricting the enrollment of special needs children and adults.

**Pg.167:** Any individual who is self-employed and does not have health insurance will be taxed 2.5% of income and forced to accept public health insurance. So paying for health care out of pocket will be banned from the face of the earth.

**Pgs.272,335-339:** It rations the care of cancer patients and limits the treatment choices made by patients with their doctors, based upon the patient's health and condition. This will result in the oldest, weakest and sickest patients being denied treatments simply because the statistics for success in their demographic category are poor!

**Pg.425:** It mandates "Advance Care Planning Consultation," to encourage seniors who are in poor health to be more accepting of death rather than fighting to stay alive with their loved ones, and then it provides an approved list of "end of life" resources to help "guide" seniors about the process of dying! In fact, every five years people in Medicare will have to have a required counseling session to tell them how to end their life sooner. It also recommends a method for death: "the use of artificially administered nutrition and hydration."

**Pgs.427,429:** It actually mandates a program for orders on the end of life, giving the government a say in how your life ends and gives an "Advance Care Planning Consultant" the power to order end of life plans for a patient.

**Pgs. 494-498:** It allows government to define "mental illnesses" and what services they will be allowed to be treated with.

**Pgs. 259,261,1006,1052** (Depends on which version of the Bill): It talks about, "The Secretary shall establish a national medical device registry (in this subsection referred to as the 'registry') to facilitate analysis of postmarket safety and outcomes data on each device that—"(A) is or has been used in or on a patient; and "(B) is a class III device; or a class II device that is implantable."

So the question is, "What is a class II medical implant device?" Well some say it's just strictly referring to implantable devices like pacemakers. However, it just so happens that a microchip implant is also considered a class II medical device. But don't take my word for it. Let's listen to the manufacturer. He admits it!

## Class II Medical Device:

*In medical news tonight, a chip, the size of a grain of rice could save your life. So we call on Dr. J Adler.*

**Adler:** *So what happens if you're in a bad accident and can't communicate with emergency workers and doctors? New microchip technology now makes it possible for the emergency room staff to find out about your medical history at the touch of the computer key. In the emergency room, a split second decision can make the difference between life and death.*

**John Halemka:** *So many emergency physicians have to operate blind. We have to make medical decisions not knowing what medicines you take or what allergies you have.*

*Hi I'm Dr. Halamka, we are going to check your scan today*

**Adler:** *Harvard doctor John Halamka says this Radio Frequency Identification chip may solve that problem. He had it implanted in his right upper arm. A scanner reads an identification number. Those 16 digits are then entered into a secure website where his medical history is stored. EMT worker Brian Orsatti says the chip could help emergency workers.*

**Orsatti:** *One of the big things, is if you ever have some type of trauma patient where they come in and are unable to give you their information and/or their medical history.*

**Adler:** *Anyone can get the chip and while some patients may be concerned about privacy issues, Dr. Halemka says the benefits are clear.*

**Dr. Halamka:** *I'm a rock climber and I believe if I fall off a cliff and you find me unconscious, the comfort of being able to scan me and figure out who I am outweighs my concern for privacy.*

**Adler:** *The procedure is done with anesthesia and is relatively pain free.*

**Halamka:** *It's like putting a knitting needle under your skin.*

**Adler:** *But in this case he says getting something  under your skin-is a good* *thing.*

**Scott Silverman CEO of VeriChip:** *And it is certainly critical to the evolution of information technology in healthcare, which we all know is archaic the way healthcare is done today in emergency rooms and physician's offices. You know VeriChip has been approved by the FDA as a class II medical device.*

Oh! So that's a class II medical device! Boy, have we been duped! And so if you put this together with **Pgs.58,59,195,** that states that government will have possession of all your health care records and history, including your finances, and you will have to have a National ID Health card and that they will be given direct access to your bank accounts and personal financial records to compel you to pay any out-of-pocket or premium costs "electronically"…

It just so happens that the microchip can do all of these things in one convenient implant. It can store your medical records, your personal information, including your finances, and it can even be used and is already being used around the world to make "electronic" payments tied into your bank account.

And this is why researchers are saying, "Could it be that we are seeing the structure being laid for America to become the first nation in the world that would require every U.S. citizen to receive an implanted microchip for the purpose of controlling medical care?" There are those that say the current legislation does not say this. But the current legislation and laws surrounding the Health Care Bill are still in the process of being written.

And one still has to wonder about the comments of Joseph Biden when asking Justice John Roberts at his Confirmation Hearing: *"Can a microscopic tag be implanted into a human body to track his every movement? You will rule on that, mark my words, before your tenure is over."*

And lest you think this won't go global, and I quote, "Obama Care Goes Global." Hillary Clinton announced at the United Nations International Conference on Population and Development, *"In addition to new funding, we've launched a new program that will be the centerpiece of our foreign policy, the Global Health Initiative, which commits us to spending $63 billion over six years to improve global health."*

One man states:

*"It's staggering to see the number of political leaders who profess to be Christians and yet who are the very same people who promoted this legislation that undermines their Christian belief system. The reason for this seeming contradiction is that the majority of so-called "Christian" politicians do not have a Biblical worldview. Their understanding of God's Word is superficial and often not genuine, which is a reflection of the lack of good Bible teaching in the pulpits of America.*

*We have entire denominations and churches who actually forbid the teaching of Bible prophecy and the Book of Revelation, which is the official policy of Communist China as well!"*[22]

Wow! Sounds to me like somebody doesn't want us to be in this study, how about you? I wonder who that might be? I don't know about you, but it sure looks to me like all these health care fears have led to the total control of our health supply. Looks like all those fear tactics worked like a charm. Why, if I didn't know better, I'd say pretty soon somebody's going to show up on the scene and say, "Take this chip…or you will *die!*" Where have I heard that before? Oh yeah, that's the Antichrist's kingdom that's going to appear on the scene when you are living in the Last Days!

**VI. The 6th proof that we know we really are headed for a One World Government is what I call the Monitor Proof.**

That's right, the Big Eye in the Sky! I'm talking about *Big Brother*. You see, the Bible's clear. We're not just headed towards an evil deceptive Antichrist Kingdom that exerts total control over the whole planet, but he's able to *ensure* control by developing a Big Brother system that monitors everything on the planet! And I mean everything! But don't take my word for it. Let's listen to God's.

**Revelation 13:11-18** "Then I saw another beast, coming out of the earth. He had two horns like a lamb, but he spoke like a dragon. He exercised all the authority of the first beast on his behalf, and made the earth and its inhabitants worship the first beast, whose fatal wound had been healed. And he performed great and miraculous signs, even causing fire to come down from heaven to earth in full view of men. Because of the signs he was given power to do on behalf of the first beast, he deceived the inhabitants of the earth. He ordered them to set up an image in honor of the beast who was wounded by the sword and yet lived. He was given power to give breath to the image of the first beast, so that it could speak and cause all who refused to worship the image to be killed. He also forced everyone, small and great, rich and poor, free and slave, to receive a mark on his right hand or on his forehead, so that no one could buy or sell unless he had the mark, which is the name of the beast or the number of his name. This calls for wisdom. If anyone has insight, let him calculate the number of the beast, for it is man's number. His number is 666."

We saw before how the Bible clearly says that the False Prophet in the Last Days is not only going to dupe the whole world into *worshiping* the Antichrist, but he's what? He's going to *make* them, he's going to *order* them, he's going to *cause* them, he going to *force* them to do whatever he says to do, otherwise they will what? They will *die*, right? And again I want to focus on the key words there, "make" "order" "cause" and "force." In the Greek they literally mean, "to carry out, to command, to direct or to execute." And so this implies that we have some serious enforcement going on here! In fact, it's *global* enforcement because again, that's the context. It's global. He forces the whole planet to do whatever in the world he wants them to do. So here's the point. In order to pull this off, think about it, you not only need some serious control over the whole planet, but you better have some serious ability to *monitor* everyone on the whole planet, right? Why? Because think about it! Trying to control the whole planet is a huge task for one guy! So here's the point. How are you going to find and enforce everyone on the planet to do your will? How are you going to micro-manage the whole planet, because that's what's going on here, into doing what you say? Because here's the facts. You know there's going to be a whole lot of resisters! Even if you grab control of the food, water and health care, as we saw before, people are still going to *resist*. They're still going to try to escape your system! So what do you do? How do you enforce those people to do what you say? Well, simple! You not only control the whole planet in what they get to eat and drink, but you develop a Big Brother system that monitors everything they think! You'll know who the resisters are! You're listening in! You'll make sure they can't leave your system! I'm here to tell you it's already here! They're already monitoring our every move! What we do, where we go, and what we think!

**1. The 1st type of Big Brother Surveillance System** they've already put into place to FORCE US to go along with this One World Government is the **Information System.**

You might be thinking, "Well hey man, there's no way they're going to get me! I'm not going to go along with this One World Government! I'm just going to unplug from this system and become an anonymous guy. That's right! I'm just going to disappear! They won't find me! Ha! Ha! Ha! I'm free!" Really? Not if they control your *information*! You see, whether you realize it or not, there are already in place massive amounts of databases to identify who you are. In fact, they're so big they're called mega-databases. For instance, just one, a U.S. company called Acxiom operates one of the world's largest databases on ninety-five percent of all American households. 24 hours a day they gather and store information on you and I from credit card transactions, magazine subscriptions, telephone numbers, real estate records, car registrations and even fishing licenses, to name a few, and because of all this information, they can provide a full profile of each one of us, right down to whether we own a dog or cat, enjoy camping or gourmet cooking, read the Bible or other books, what our occupation is, what car we drive, what videos we watch, how much gas and food we buy and even where our favorite vacations spots are. In fact, it's estimated that, *right now*, each adult in the developed world is **already located**, on average, in *three hundred different databases* with an average of 1,500 data points on you. That's a huge file! In other words, Big Brother is already here, yes, even in the U.S.!

But the question is, "Well, how in the world did these guys even get all this information from us in the first place?" Well believe it or not, there's a multitude of ways they've been getting it from us, in fact they've even tricked us into giving it up to them *voluntarily*!

## A. The 1st way they've done it is with "loyalty cards."

You know, those cards they give us at the stores that we shop at, or in the malls, or even the grocery stores. And the premise is, we're saving money in exchange for allowing them to create a massive database on virtually every single thing we buy! But when you look at the facts, we're being lied to! There are no savings! It's a bunch of baloney!

**Shopping discount card fraud:**

*Do you have a discount card?*

*No. What's that.*

***The Operational Plan.***

*Here's the plan. Find out what these big companies do with all that prying personal information in their possession after your loyal submission into their club card confederation.*

### The Targets.
*We target two loyalty programs because so many of you have these cards in your wallet.*

*With a no fee Shoppers Drug Mart Optimum card. Spend money, get points.*

### The Promise.
*Add up points to get free stuff. What do they get from you? Your name, birthdate, address and the ages of your children and all of your spending habits.*

*At Safeway, the free club card gets you special prices on select items. The promise-to save you money. What do they get from you? A look at the products you buy, connected with your name, address and phone number.*

*So who benefits from these cards, because consumers clearly think they do.*

**Katherine Albrect:** *Well we actually, in five years of doing this, have been unable to find a single consumer benefit from using these cards.*

*But hold on a second. We thought these cards were all about saving a dime. So we launched..*

### Project Grocery Bag
*We shopped at 4 different grocery stores including a Safeway. We buy the same 10 items in every store.*
*The tally at the Real Canadians Superstore $18.38.*
*Our corner market is almost $5 more at $23.15. IGA is just a few cents up at $23.59. But the big jump comes at Safeway where the total hits $28.10. That's almost $10 more than at Superstore but with the Safeway club card savings the total drops to $26.22, still more than the other 3 stores, but they tell us we've saved almost $2 dollars.*

**Albrect:** *What we advise people to do is find a store that doesn't have a card. Because we are essentially, with our shopping dollars, funding this whole monster. We are funding the system. We're funding the databases. We're paying* *the salaries of the people who are collecting this data on us. We are essentially paying to build our own data prisons here.*

Whoa! We've been snookered! So much for saving money! We're paying to fund our own database prison!

**B.** The second way they get us to offer up our information freely is through **Credit Rating Agencies**

Believe it or not, each Credit Rating Agency has files on over 200 million of us here in the U.S. and they not only know our credit history, but they also determine our credit future! They get to "determine" what you "buy" or "sell."...Where have I heard that before?

**C.** The third way they get us to offer up our personal information is through **Credit Card Companies**

That's right, there are currently 610 million credit cards in the U.S and of course, they not only know our credit histories, but they also know, "what we buy, when we buy, and when we're likely to default on our payments of what we buy!" And then they adjust our interest rate accordingly.

**D.** The fourth way they get our information is from **Search Engines**

That's right, all you computer users...you better beware! Listen to this! "Every search you perform on Google goes into Google's giant database, which it uses to keep a profile of your habits and interests. The search engine also tracks which links you click on during your search and *then* they use that information to place targeted ads into your browser." Did you ever wonder why when you were looking for tourist spots in Hawaii on your computer, that all of a sudden ads for airline tickets to Hawaii started popping up everywhere? It's not by chance! It's all interconnected! Then, believe it or not, they also use their Gmail service to monitor the content of your email and also place the same targeted advertising into your email account. So you get it at both ends! Then just to make sure they know everything about you, they also record your credit card information online, your personal account information and they even track which videos you watch, where you are planning to visit and what you plan on doing there. In fact, Google's co-founder, Sergey Brin, said their goal is to, *"Be like the mind of*

God." They want to know everything about you! And, *"It's a future that they're working feverishly to make a reality now."* Now if that wasn't creepy enough, Google also has a location-based map system that allows them to "know where people are in real time through the use of smart phones and other GPS-enabled devices." What? Can they really do that? Yeah, we'll get to that in a little bit!

**E.** The fifth way they get us to offer up our personal information for free is through **Social Media**

*You know, Facebook and Twitter! Aren't they great? Well, maybe you won't think so after this. Social Media, as we all know, has not only become one of the most important and popular forms of personal communication and personal information sharing all across the planet, but it's also become a gold mine for these database companies to build an entire massive database on every person on the planet! Don't believe me? Let's take a look at where Facebook came from anyway. Sounds suspicious to me!*

*"Do you have a Facebook? Have you thought about the privacy you put at risk. Facebook allows you to post your favorite music, movies, address, hometowns, phone numbers, email, clubs, jobs, education history, birth dates, sexual orientation, interests, daily schedules, exactly how they are related to friends, upload pictures of themselves and even political affiliations.*

*It's privacy policy even goes so far as to state it "also collects information about you from other sources, such as newspaper and instant messaging services. This information is gathered regardless of your use of the web site."*

*Have you seen Facebook's pulse feature? Pulse posts statistical trends among universities down to minute details such as percentage of females with conservative views, student body's top 10 movies and percentage of students who have read Catcher In The Rye.*

*The so called privacy policy goes on to say that they share your information with third parties, including responsible companies with which they have a relationship. Can you think of any marketing group that would pass on buying up such valid but so easily collected statistics such as these and others?*

*So maybe they're using us. But is there more? Funding came in the form of $12.7 million dollars from venture capital ACCEL partners. ACCEL's manager, James*

*Breyer was former chair of NVCA (National Venture Capital Assoc). Breyer served on the NVCA board with Gilman Louie, CEO of InQtell - a venture capitol firm established by the CIA in 1999. This firm works in various aspects of information technology in intelligence including most notably, data mining technologies. Breyer has also served on the board of BBN Technologies, a research and development firm known for spearheading the arpanet of what we now know today as the internet.*

*The IAO (Information Awareness Office) stated it's mission was to gather as much information as possible about everyone in a centralized location, for easy perusal by the United States government-including but not limited to-internet activity, credit card purchase history, airline ticket purchases, car rentals, medical records, educational transcripts, driver's licenses, utility bills, tax returns and any other available data. All of the above raises more questions than answers.* "[23]

Unless of course you know what the Bible says. That in the Last Days the Antichrist and False Prophet are going to build the exact same system! I don't know about you, but it sure looks to me like all this *information gathering* in the Last Days is leading to a total monitoring of our everyday lives, everywhere on the planet. Forget Facebook…let's call it what it is…TRACEBOOK! Again, think of the implications here! For the first time in the history of mankind, we can now literally know every single piece of information about every single person on the planet! I mean, what's next? Somebody's going to appear on the scene and use all this information against us to FORCE US into going along with whatever they want…us…to…do? Where have I heard that before? Oh yeah, that's right! That's the Antichrist's Big Brother Society and Control System that the Bible said would appear on the scene when you are living in the Last Days!

**2. The 2nd type of Big Brother Surveillance System** they've already put into place to FORCE US to go along with this One World Government is our **Communication System.**

So you might be thinking, "Well hey man, there's no way they're going to get me! Okay, so maybe they're going to grab control of all my personal information and build this huge massive database on me to try to pigeonhole me, but hey, I've still got my communication devices! I can just "secretly" communicate to people and stay hidden to avoid their radar! They can't get me! Ha! Ha! Ha! I'm free!" Really? Not if they control all *communication*! And the

Bible says during the 7-year Tribulation, communication might very well be a matter of life and death! I didn't say that, Jesus did!

**Matthew 24:3,7,9-10** "As Jesus was sitting on the Mount of Olives, the disciples came to him privately. 'Tell us,' they said, 'when will this happen, and what will be the sign of Your coming and of the end of the age?' Nation will rise against nation, and kingdom against kingdom. There will be famines and earthquakes in various places. Then you will be handed over to be persecuted and put to death, and you will be hated by all nations because of Me. At that time many will turn away from the faith and will betray and hate each other."

According to our text, Jesus clearly says there's not only going to be a massive rise of wars and rumors of wars, famines and earthquakes in the Last Days but He said what? He said, as we saw before, there's going to be a massive rise of persecution towards His followers; we dealt with that earlier, and as we saw, it's happening right now! But here's the point. What do they *do* to the followers of Jesus? They not only *hate* them and want to *kill* them, but they are going to *betray* them. Literally "turn them in" and that's exactly what the Greek word means! *Betray* is the Greek word "paradidomi" which means, "to give into the hands of, to give up to the custody of, for judgment, punishment and/or to be put to death." So the Bible says during the 7-year Tribulation, the followers of Jesus will be "turned in for death" or literally "betrayed" on a *global* scale.

So here's the question, "How is somebody going to do this, on a global scale, because that's the context? How are you going to know if somebody's a Christian anywhere on the planet and "turn them in" for death, "betray them" as long as they keep quiet in public and stay out of sight?" Well hey, there's no place to hide if you control the *communication*! All you have to do is make one little slip up and talk about Jesus and you're toast! It's already here! They're *already* monitoring every single conversation on the whole planet, for the first time in the history of mankind and they started with your *cell phone*! What? Yeah, that's right! It's so commonplace now that even old boyfriends are using it against their girlfriends!

**KGTV The News on 6**

*Cell phone spying*

*Cell phones are an essential lifeline for most of us, connecting us to work, family and friends.*

*But could they be used to spy on you? News 6 reporter Lori Fullbright has an investigation that will change the way you view your cell phone on tonight's 6 On Assignment.*

**Fullbright:** *Well Terry, I met a woman last fall who was being stalked by her ex-boyfriend. She was convinced he was using her cell phone to learn things about her that were private. Well it seemed pretty far fetched and police were stumped.*

*We started digging and started doing research and we actually did find a way to take control of someone else's phone. We can do all the things her ex was doing-listen to conversations, read text messages, even turn the phone into a microphone; and we can do it from anywhere and the victim would never know.*

*Carla Robinson's ex has stalked her for three years. Nobody could figure out how he was able to track her every move, her every conversation, especially when he was often out of state. We have discovered though how her ex could have turned her cell phone into a high tech snooping device. She allowed us to download the software we found onto her phone. We asked her and a friend to talk over coffee. She's not using the phone, it's just sitting nearby.*

**Carla:** *When we first started filing reports on this, the cops told us there was really nothing illegal about what he was doing because the laws were so far behind technology.*

**Fullbright:** *I'm a block away in my car listening to every word. I'm hearing it all through the microphone on her cell phone and she has no way of knowing. As long as they talk, I can hear them. I could be miles away doing this. Even out of state. I can also hear Carla's actual phone calls. We had her call her mom. Those nearby her can only hear Carla's side of the conversation, but me in my listening post, I can hear both sides.*

**Carla:** *Did you remember what you were going to ask me? Oh! You said you talked to Lonnie.*

*<Fullbright inside car listening> Carla's mom responding: Yeah, talked to Lonnie and um he didn't have a lot to say except he was going back to work and they've been busy with Brittney's baby and I got some pictures..."*

*Fullbright: And there's pretty much no way to know if someone's put this software on your phone. One red flag though, is your phone will light up periodically throughout the day with really no good reason.*

Okay, go ahead and check your phone, because I know you want to! Step on it if it has the red light! But seriously, is that creepy or what? This isn't make believe, it's happening now, even to the average Joe! But hey, maybe it's just those nasty old disgruntled boyfriends who do that. I'm sure our Government would never do something like that, would they? Unfortunately, yes! Right now there is a Global Monitoring Project called *Echelon* that is a cooperative effort among the United States, England, Canada, New Zealand and Australia. Under the guise of national security and terrorist threats, it simply monitors and intercepts all phone calls, all faxes, all data transfers, all radio transmissions and all emails. Don't believe me? Even the History Channel has been exposing it. It's like we either don't care or we've been conditioned to already accept it!

## U.S. eavesdropping:

*In the name of security, societies around the world are struggling to redraw the line between surveillance and privacy.*

*Bush: The bill before me will help law enforcement to identify, to dismantle, to disrupt and to punish terrorists before they strike.*

*Just months after the 9/11 attacks, President Bush secretly ordered the government to listen in on some American's phone calls without getting warrants. Technically, snooping on people's communications is not difficult. Almost every phone call, fax and email passes through a network of towers and satellites. This digital data can be intercepted with listening dishes or by using spy satellites. The U.S. alone has more than 30,000 eavesdroppers scattered around the world working with at least 100 spy satellites. Every three minutes they collect enough information to fill the Library of Congress. Governments tell us these technologies make us safer. But where is it all leading?*

I'll tell you! It's leading to the Antichrist's kingdom who's going to monitor everything on the planet! Where have I heard that before? But the question is, "So how does all this communication surveillance technology work?" Well, as you read, they simply monitor all transmissions via satellites and other means at the rate of two million per hour looking for key words like

"terrorize," or "assassination," or even the word "bomb." But you might say something in your conversation like, "That cheeseburger was the bomb!" But here's the problem. If you say "bomb" in your conversation or any other "key" words they're looking for, a hard copy as well as a recording of that conversation is sent to someone's desk to be analyzed. Now you might think, "Come on, this is just more of that wacko conspiracy stuff. This can't be true. There's no way they would allow this in the United States!" Well, don't take my word for it. Let's listen to Mike Frost who personally worked there for nineteen years, collecting information.

*"Communications know no borders. Somebody will pick it up somewhere, and it will end up on somebody's desk...I guarantee it.'*

*Case in point... 'a lady was on the phone talking to her friend about a school play that she'd been to the night before; her son was in a school play. She thought he'd done a lousy job and she said to her friend, 'Boy, he really bombed last night.'*

*That conversation was highlighted and ended up on an analyst's desk the next morning because the word 'bomb' was in there and all this lady was doing was talking about her son and his play the night before.*

*Now that conversation of that lady is held...indefinitely, so if two or three or four years later, she talks about somebody else bombing or something and the computer spits it out again as being the second or third hit on this person's name, you can graduate from being a possible terrorist to a probable terrorist. It's that easy.*

*If they say that you are a probable terrorist and pass that information on to those responsible for that sort of activity, just think about what could happen to your life, and you'd never know why.*

*All of a sudden, your MasterCard doesn't work anymore; all a sudden, your phone is down; all of a sudden, things are falling apart in your life; and you have no reason why, and nobody will ever tell you.*

*And he has a warning for anyone who says 'it can't happen to me.'*

*'If you don't want anybody to know about what you're saying, don't say it. Because if you do say it, somebody will be listening.'"*

Right now we have the technology to betray or turn people in anywhere on the planet, for the first time in the history of mankind! Maybe that's what they'll be doing during the 7-year Tribulation. They'll change the key word from "BOMB" to "JESUS" and you're a probable terrorist! But you might think, "Okay, well that's it! I'm just turning it off! They ain't going to get me! They're not listening to my conversations! I'm just turning my cell phone off right now!" Well, believe it or not, not even that works anymore!

**Fox News:**

**Smith:** *If you power down your cell phone there's no way the government could ever hear you. Certainly not the F.B.I. if it's turned off, right? Have we got news for you. Alright, here's that cell phone story you've been waiting for. Cell phone users beware. Big Brother may be listening. The Federal Bureau of Investigation can now hear everything you say-even when the cell phone is turned off. I know, it sounds kinda out there, but by using your phone's tracking device, authorities can now activate the microphone inside the dreaded thing-allowing them to eavesdrop on you and your conversations."[24]*

Wow! So much for personal privacy and private conversations! Aren't you glad everybody's been pushing for everyone on the planet to have cell phones, even kids, and if you can't afford one the Government will buy you one…for…free?" Hmmm, I wonder why? Great way to *monitor* everyone, isn't it? Correct me if I'm wrong, but it sure looks to me like all this *communication technology* is leading to a total monitoring of our everyday lives for the first time in the history of mankind. Anywhere on the planet! You can't hide! The next thing you know, somebody's going to appear on the scene and use all this communication technology against us to FORCE and/or BETRAY us into going along with a One World Government. Where have I heard that before? Oh yeah, that's right! That's the Antichrist's kingdom and Big Brother society that the Bible said would appear on the scene when you are living in the Last Days! But if you don't want to listen to God's warning, then maybe you should listen to the warning from the news! They're already admitting this is what's coming in the next few years!

**Biometrics in 2017:**

**Brian Williams:** *More now on our special coverage here tonight. Life in the U.S in ten years time. By that time, there may be all kinds of new ways to safeguard and identify all those things that make each of us unique; our faces, even our fingerprints, even our eyes. Here now with more on the future of technology, NBC's Tom Costello.*

**Costello:** *The year is 2017. You're rushed to a hospital, unconscious with no ID or medical history but thanks to a microchip under your skin, it's all there. Science fiction 20 years ago, but a biometric reality today.*

*Clark Nelson of Sagem-Morpho Biometrics: The technology is based on answering one simple question: Am I who I say I am?*

**Costello:** *Already, fingerprints and iris scans verify passenger identities at airports. Within 10 years, that technology may be even more widespread. Look for more complex facial recognition programs that scan a crowd of thousands looking for a single terrorist. Today's facial recognition software starts with eyes, then it maps out the contours of the face and compares that against a database of millions. A database that's growing by the day.*
*What's next? At the University of Bath, in England, researchers predict big changes for consumers.*

**Professor Don Monro:** *I think it is possible to free us completely of our wallets and keys by using biometric technology if that's what people want in 10 years time.*

**Costello:** *In fact, it's already here. The latest home security locks use fingerprints to control deadbolts. And at the Jewel-Osco grocery story in Chicago, some customers pay using their fingerprints. No paper or plastic.*

**Ayanna Grady:** *You don't really need anything other than your hand and you already got that with you.*

**Costello:** *So will future department stores scan our irises like in the movie Minority Report, then offer products catered to who we are?*

*<movie clip> Hello, Mr. Yokamoto! Welcome back to the Gap!*

*Costello: Experts say that technology is here now. The challenge is to safeguard our privacy in a brave new world. "*[25]

"You don't really need anything but your *hand* to buy or sell and you already got that with you." This is not make believe. This is happening right now. Right now we're already being conditioned to accept the Mark of the Beast in our hand and if you're not saved, you better get saved *now*.

Every single aspect of our lives is going to be monitored with a Big Brother Type of surveillance system to detect any resisters and *ensure* that we obey! In fact, with all this information and communications that he's gathering on us, they can even predict not only where we are, but even what "moods" we're in all across the United States! Remember what the Google Co-founder said, "We want to be like the mind of God?"

**Social Media & Smart Phones:**

**Reporter: Robert Lee Hotz**

*The smart phone in your pocket, multiplied by millions worldwide, is giving academic researchers a God's eye view of the world. Almost three quarters of the world's population has a mobile phone for conversation and internet access. Physicists, urban planners and social scientists are eagerly weaving millions of these electronic threads of data into patterns of people on the move. Through studies that, until now, were all but impossible. That dynamic ebb and flow of data reveals the invisible nervous system of our information age and the internet economy. Using these, a company called Sense Networks, founded by computer scientists at M.I.T. and Columbia University, used cell phone data to map trends in urban nightlife. They can follow the crowds around fashionable restaurants and trendy bars. This animation shows how people in San Francisco move from hot spot to hot spot over the course of an evening, and this animation shows 300 million posts via twitter in a day into a dynamic national mood map that shows how our collective emotions change during the day. Moving across the country like a weather front. The green is a measure of our good feeling. Red shows our unhappiness, and by this measure, Americans are happiest in the morning and late evening. It's one in a wave of ambitious social network experiments underway in the U.S. and Europe to track our movements, probe our relationships and ultimately affect the individual choices we all make. "*[26]

Looks like Google got their wish! We're like little ants on the ground as the Big Eye in the Sky watches our every move and even predicts our behavior! A mood map! Can you believe it? For the first time in the history of mankind, we can even predict people's moods on the planet just like watching a weather front on the weather channel!

**3. The 3rd type of Big Brother Surveillance System they've already put into place to FORCE US to go along with this One World Government is the Transportation System.**

Now you might be thinking, "Well, there's no way they're going to get me! Okay, so maybe they're going to control my personal information and build this huge massive database on me and pigeonhole me into doing what they say and maybe they're going to grab control of all my communication devices and listen to what I say, especially the word 'Jesus,' but hey, I'm out of here! I'm just going to hop in my car and check out of the system. They won't find me! Ha! Ha! Ha! I'm free!" Really? Not if they control your *transportation*! Believe it or not, the Bible is clear. Transportation is going to become a huge need during the 7-year Tribulation! You better hope you don't drive a Yugo! But don't take my word for it. Let's listen to God's.

**Matthew 24:15-22** "So when you see standing in the holy place the abomination that causes desolation, spoken of through the prophet Daniel – let the reader understand – then let those who are in Judea flee to the mountains. Let no one on the roof of his house go down to take anything out of the house. Let no one in the field go back to get his cloak. How dreadful it will be in those days for pregnant women and nursing mothers! Pray that your flight will not take place in winter or on the Sabbath. For then there will be great distress, unequaled from the beginning of the world until now –and never to be equaled again. If those days had not been cut short, no one would survive, but for the sake of the elect those days will be shortened."

Now according to our text, the Bible clearly says that during the 7-year Tribulation, after the Antichrist shows his true colors and goes into the rebuilt Jewish temple to declare himself to be god, the abomination of desolation that was spoken by the Prophet Daniel that Jesus is referring to here, that's what He's talking about, what's going to happen at that time? People are going to be *fleeing*, right? They're going to be trying to get out of there in *flight*, quick flight, right?

Why? Because other passages tell us that the Antichrist is going on a hunting spree at that time! He's going to be hunting people down and killing them! It's going to be a horrible slaughter literally, and that's what Zechariah says!

**Zechariah 13:8-9** "In the whole land, declares the LORD, two-thirds will be struck down and perish; yet one-third will be left in it. This third I will bring into the fire; I will refine them like silver and test them like gold. They will call on my name and I will answer them; I will say, They are my people, and they will say, The LORD is our God."

The Jewish people finally turn back to God at this point. But as you saw it comes at a horrible price! *Just the Jewish people alone,* 2/3rds of them are going to die at the hands of the Antichrist and only 1/3rd are going to be left. Other passages tell us that they are going to be sovereignly protected by God and we'll get to that later in the book. But the point is this. Notice why Jesus says it's going to be such a horrible time, in fact, worse than any other time. The slaughter is apparently going to be so great, that people there better high tail it out of there, right? ASAP! What'd He say? You better make flight, you better run, you better flee and you better do it fast! Don't go back into your house, don't go to your work place, don't get anything, just get out of there *now*, right?

Therefore, common sense tells us that at this time during the 7-year Tribulation a source of good reliable transportation is going to come in handy. Again, you better pray you don't own a Yugo! For those who say, "Well hey, they're not going to get me! I'm just going to hop in my car and flee like Jesus said! I'm out of here! They can't get me! Ha! Ha! Ha! I'm free!" Really? Well, all the Antichrist has to do is control your transportation and you ain't going nowhere! You can't flee! You can't run! And you can't even hide! You're going to stick around for the slaughter just like the Bible said. Can I tell you something? That's precisely what they're already doing! Total control of our Transportation!

**A. The 1st way they've already grabbed control of our Transportation System to prevent us from fleeing from a horrible situation, is Our Vehicles.**

Believe it or not, right now, Big Brother not only knows everything we do, everything we say, everything we think, but they've even developed a system that monitors everywhere we go. Our cell phones, as we saw, are already being used as tracking devices and just in case you don't have one, they can still know where you are at anytime anywhere on the planet with satellite technology. In fact, *right now*, Motorola has launched 66 low-orbiting satellites that can not only pick up signals from certain types of microchips (wouldn't that be handy if you implanted one) but now it's common knowledge that this kind of tracking system was *already used* to monitor the locations of military personnel in Iraq, boat traffic in Florida, and even garbage men in England are being watched right now from the sky on their jobs in order to make sure that they don't linger in one spot too long! But that's not all! Every square foot of farming land in Australian is now being watched via satellite to monitor food production and crop yields. Even here in America, satellites are being used by state governments to search for unreported improvements that might increase property taxes, to check for water-use permits and to find improper tree cutting. In fact, they're now also using satellites in England to measure the speed of motorists from space! You won't have a radar detector for that one!

That's still not all. Thanks to the backing by Bill Gates, we now have what's called *Internet In The Sky*. This is a system of 840 low-altitude satellites in twenty-one orbits with forty satellites in each orbit that creates a virtual electronic blanket around the whole planet, for the first time in the history of mankind! Now you can communicate and monitor any person anywhere on the planet from the top of the Himalayas to the bottom of the Dead Sea.[27]

Then, just in case you actually did try to hop in your car and flee away on the ground, they've got that covered too with satellites! Anybody hear of *OnStar*? Yeah! You know, that nifty convenient device they implant in your vehicle to give them the ability to make a call, or unlock our doors, or send somebody out in an ambulance if you get in a wreck? Isn't that great? In fact, what's really nifty is if someone steals your car, they can still *track your car* and catch those "bad guys" right? Isn't that great? Well, here's the problem. What if *you* became the "bad guy"? When push comes to shove, if you became a "suspected terrorist" Christian, would they use this technology against you? Would they actually turn you in to the authorities and stop your vehicle? Well, believe it or not, it's already being done!

**OnStar:**

*If you're a cable news watcher, there's a good chance that you caught one of the 30,000 car chases that take place in the U.S. each year. That amounts to nearly 3 high speed pursuits per hour. The risk is high for everyone involved, including innocent bystanders. On average, nearly 300 people are killed as a result of a car chase every year.*

*But OnStar, a company that offers 24 hour emergency roadside assistance says it has a solution. It's called Stolen Vehicle Slowdown Program.*

**Craig Loper** *<Mobile Deployment Systems> The key is to prevent the pursuit from becoming a high speed chase.*

*It lets law enforcement take remote control of a stolen vehicle using satellite technology.*

**OnStar President Chet Huber:** *The way that Stolen Vehicle Slowdown works is our subscriber will report their vehicle stolen. We'll contact the police and we'll actually get the location of the vehicle using the OnStar system and the GPS capabilities that's built into the current technology. When the law enforcement officers have the vehicle in sight and when they determine it's safe to slow the vehicle down, we'll send a data message wirelessly into the vehicle. It will actually depower the vehicle in it's engine control module and take away control of the accelerator from the felon.*

*<OnStar> Attention driver, this vehicle is being slowed at the request of a law enforcement agency.*

Attention driver! This vehicle is being slowed down because you're a suspected terrorist Christian and you're trying to flee the Antichrist system! We already have the technology *right now* to *flip a switch* and stop your vehicle wherever you are! So much for "fleeing the scene!" No wonder it's going to be a blood bath when the Antichrist shows his true colors!

But that's not all. You might be thinking, "Well hey, that's it! I'm not going to get that system installed on my vehicle! No siree! I'm just going to skip the whole thing and they still can't get me! Ha! Ha! Ha!" Well, you're assuming you're going to have a choice! You see, believe it or not, right now, the Government is working on, "mandating black boxes in all new cars and this will allow them to "have constant real-time tracking, eavesdropping and surveillance" on any car wherever you go. Don't believe me? Here's just one news report sharing it.

**Black Boxes for Cars:**

*These days, as you may know, cars have a lot of features that the owners of the Model T back in the day could never have imagined, seat warmers, dvd players,*

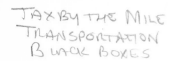

*rear-view video cameras, even Wi-Fi. Soon, though, there may be a controversial and mandatory new feature-the ability to spy on your every move.*

*ABC's Mark Greenblatt is on the story. Mark, good morning.*

**Mark:** *Well good morning to you. Some call this plan sneaky, others say it will improve safety. But now the government wants to make it mandatory for your car to get one of those so-called black boxes, like they have in airplanes that can tell all if you get into a crash.*

*You're probably used to hearing about black boxes helping investigators solve airplane crashes. But car manufacturers have quietly placed similar devices in more and more vehicles, turning our own cars into snitches, and now the Federal Government wants to require every small vehicle made from now on to get one of those black boxes saying this proposal will give us the critical insight and information we need to save more lives.*

Really? Or maybe *track* more lives. Did you notice how car manufacturers are already putting them in there and you may not even know? Did you catch that part? In fact, these new "mandatory" black boxes will also enable them to do another thing they've been proposing to do for a while now. Get this. "A tax-by-the-mile system." That's right! They want to "tax" you for every mile you drive, because after all, it's good for the environment! You should ride a bike, you know! In fact, speaking of the environment, IBM has a patent out now for a device called the "Intelligent Stop Light" that enables them to turn off your car at a stoplight to "conserve fuel." Isn't that nice! Very environmentally friendly! And there's even a new proposed law out there that would put video cameras in your car to "film the occupants in the vehicle or the vehicle's surroundings and transmit those images back to a central office for inspection," just in case you get into an accident, you know. In fact, in San Francisco, they've already installed "real time video cameras" on a majority of their buses, and other cities are doing the same thing *and* they're even "adding microphones to record passenger conversations."[28] Why didn't they tell us they were doing that?

But here's the point. Correct me if I'm wrong, but it sure looks to me like all this new transportation technology is leading to a total monitoring of our everyday lives, for the first time in the history of mankind. The next thing you know, somebody's going to appear on the scene and start hunting people down and yet unfortunately nobody's going to be able flee and it's going to be a horrible bloodbath. Where have I heard that before? Oh yeah, that's right! That's the Antichrist's kingdom and Big Brother Society that the Bible said would appear on the scene when you are living in the Last Days!

**B.** The 2ⁿᵈ **way** they've already grabbed control of our Transportation System to prevent us from being able to flee from a horrible situation is **Our Cameras.**

So you might be thinking, "Well, there's no way they're going to get me! Okay, so maybe they're going to control my personal information and build this huge massive database on me, maybe they're going to be able to monitor all my conversations, maybe they're going to track and control my vehicle wherever I go, but hey, I'll just stay on foot! That's right! I'm just going to ride a bike or walk around, I don't need a car! Ha! Ha! Ha! I'm still free!" Really? Not if they put *cameras* wherever you go! And believe it or not, that too is *already* happening! Thanks in part to Executive Orders, under the guise of "terrorism" and other "bad guy" reasons, the government now has full authority to utilize all kinds of new surveillance technology on us! That's right! Us! Not a foreign entity…us! And one of the biggest ways they're doing that is by installing cameras literally wherever we go! In fact, it's so commonplace now that even USA Today put out an article on it!

*"Whether as motorists or pedestrians; as visitors to convenience stores, banks, ATMs or the post office; as shoppers with credit cards or telephone users; even at leisure, in parks, playgrounds and golf courses, we're constantly on candid camera. Full-time surveillance is a reality of modern life."*

Yes, even here in America! All in the name of supposedly reducing crime, or terrorism, or traffic concerns, or a whole list of other supposed excuses, millions of cameras *right now* are not only going up right here in America, but all over the world! And *they're all tied together.* Let me demonstrate. *Right now* you can go to tons of websites to "monitor" traffic & "monitor" people, "just for fun" not only here in America but around the planet. Which means for the first time in history we can monitor someone anywhere on the planet! Now if you don't believe me, try it out for yourself! Just do a web search for "online traffic cameras" or "live cams" or something like that and start monitoring people anywhere. Recently I was on a website called "Earth Cam" and I was watching live footage from Moscow and then hopped over to a resort in Hawaii and began watching people walk by "live" and I was wondering, "Gee, I wonder if those people in Hawaii have any idea that a Pastor from Las Vegas is watching them in his office!"

And here's the point. Well surely this is all just for fun, right? I mean, surely they would never use this technology for them to keep an eye on us for control purposes, would they?" Well, you tell me if that's not where we're headed! *Right now* in England, there are over *4 million* cameras in the government and private sector and it's been dubbed a virtual "surveillance canopy," and believe it or not, it's all pretty much common knowledge to the average Britain and one person said this about just how dense this surveillance really is:

*"So dense is the network that in many urban areas people may be monitored from the moment they step out of their front door and be kept under observation on their way to work, in the office and even in a restaurant if they choose to dine out. Over the course of a day they could be filmed by 300 cameras. The latest figures show that, in cities, people are captured on film at least once every five minutes."*

Are you serious? Don't take my word for it. Check it out for yourself!

**CCTV in London**

*We're all being watched. On streets. In subways. Even in our own homes. Invisible eyes are searching for criminals and terrorists. New technologies track them before they strike. Intricate surveillance networks. Advanced facial recognition.*

*"See if he matches anyone in our database."*

*Even tracking devices implanted inside the body. Technologies that can make the invisible-visible. Electronic trails that reveal who we are and where we've been. Go behind the security doors and discover the secret in the often disturbing world of surveillance.*

*Morning rush hour in the most heavily surveiled city in the world. Over half a million cameras keep watch over Britian's capitol. Mechanical eyes loom from every corner. The average Londoner is filmed from over 300 cameras during the course of their day. A ring of cameras surrounds the center of London. Within seconds, every plate number is fed into a computer that tracks the comings and goings of each vehicle. This is just one small piece of a massive video surveillance system stretching across the city.*

*The current figure is roughly 4 million surveillance cameras throughout the U.K. If you're in London, Westminster's director, Robert McCallister, can follow nearly every move you make.*

**McCallister:** *When you come out of your house in the morning and you get on some form of transport, there's probably a CCTV camera. If you walk down a pedestrian street. If you go into a store. Anywhere that you are if you are within the city of London, you're probably at some stage going to be captured on CCTV.*

*The all-seeing thousand eyes of Big Brother.*

Well that's kind of creepy! But maybe that's just England. That would never happen in the U.S., would it? Actually, it's already here! Not only do we have the same kind of surveillance in virtually every major city in the U.S. *right now* but the most watched city in the U.S. right now is Chicago. It's called "Operation Virtual Shield."

## Chicago: Surveillance State

*Over the last decade the U.S. government has expanded it's domestic surveillance network to unprecedented levels. From rows of street cameras to airport pat downs, many say our civil liberties and privacy are at stake. Here's the story from U.S.'s most monitored city.*

*Welcome to Chicago- the most watched city in the U.S. From old school blue light cameras to state of the art technical capabilities- watchful lenses fill the streets.*

*In what has been dubbed Operation Virtual Shield, thousands of public and privately owned security cameras have been put in place and linked together, creating a capsule of surveillance over the entire city, more extensive than anywhere else in the United States.*

*Officials say it's worth the price, but privacy concerns are at a peak.*

*Over 1,200 security cameras located throughout the city are said to be powerful enough to be able to zoom into a text of a book or even a text message. To journalist, Salim Muwakkil, the concept of privacy in the U.S. is long gone.*

***Muwakkil:*** *You become immune to the surveillance attitude that law enforcement has taken.*

*Salim says Chicago increasingly resembles the chilling anti-utopia described in George Orwell's legendary novel 1984, where every word, action and even thought was monitored by Big Brother.*

***Muwakkil:*** *Surveillance State. The only thing that's missing are the microphones advising us on how to live our lives.*

Unfortunately, they already have that as well and we'll cover that in a bit. Believe it or not, that's still just the tip of the iceberg. Total monitoring of our lives! Believe it or not, they're even installing cameras in forests!

*"US Forest service admits **putting surveillance cameras on public lands**.*

*Last month, Herman Jacob took his daughter and her friend camping in the forest and while poking around for some firewood, Jacob noticed a wire. He pulled on it and followed it to a video camera and antenna.*

*The camera didn't have any markings identifying its owner, so Jacob took it home and called law enforcement agencies to find out if it was theirs.*

*All the while wondering why someone would station a video camera in an isolated clearing in the woods. He eventually received a call from the U.S. Forest Service and was ordered to take it back.*

*Jacob returned the camera but still felt uneasy and said this, "Why would the Forest Service have secret cameras in a relatively remote camping area, and what do they do with photos of bystanders and how many hidden cameras are they using, and for what purposes?"*

Yeah, I agree! Why do you have to put cameras in the forest? But that's still not all. It's a *global* movement! *Right now* Japan has also followed suit with tons of its own cameras and they've even gone so far as to do what that guy said was the only piece missing in George Orwell's 1984. They've installed *intercoms* on their cameras to warn people of inappropriate behavior. "Hey! Stop that! We see you! That is not right! Knock it off!" But hey, that's just in Japan, right? We wouldn't do that here, would we? Again, unfortunately, we already are! *Right now* they've already installed hidden microphones on utility poles and rooftops in Los Angeles to monitor "strange noises" of course and they've even launched a new program here in the U.S. called "Intelli-streets" where our light posts do much more now than just emit light!

## Intellistreets

*Diana Lewis: Some critics say this is nothing more than the watchful eye of Big Brother keeping track of your every moment. 7 Action News reporter, Julie Bonovich gives us a closer look at this high tech system from Farmington Hills.*

*"Your attention please."*

*Julie Bonovich: That voice you just heard came from this street light.*

*"Please stand by for a public safety announcement."*

*Ron Harwood (Inventor): In each lighting fixture or in each lighting pole there's a processor, very much like an I-Phone and it takes inputs and outputs, it talks back and forth and the poles actually talk to each other.*

*Bonovich: LED screens and cameras add to the wireless infrastructure that is remotely controlled. It can provide entertainment, save energy, make announcements.*

*"This is a security alert."*

*Bonovich: And it even counts people for police. The system is also capable of recording conversations and by spring of next year, there's a good chance you can see them popping up in your city.*

*"This is a security alert. A security alert!"*

Can you believe that? George Orwell eat your heart out! I wonder if they'll have a security alert for Christians one day? "Security Alert! Have you seen this person? We heard them mention the Name of Jesus! Security alert!" Not science fiction anymore, is it? But that's still not all. Just to make sure you get monitored no matter where you go, even if you were to somehow find some spot where they didn't actually have a camera or light post, they can still monitor you with something called *smart dust*! And what smart dust is, is it's a tiny little surveillance device so small, it's literally the size of a piece of dust and it can float in the air just like dust and be suspended by air currents for hours sensing and communicating information on you. Don't believe me? Here's a new report on it.

***Lori Matsukawa:*** *A project first dreamed up by the military to get information from the battlefield.*

***Dennis Bounds:*** *They call it Smart Dust and the new technology may soon make it possible to keep track of anything, anywhere, including you.*

*Every square inch of every city will be alive with intelligence because every street and every building will have a network of microcomputers built right into them. Dr. Kristofer Pister calls it smart dust.*

***Dr. Pister:*** *Smart Dust particle or mote is a wireless sensor with sensing, computation, communication and power in one package.*

*Tiny specs of computer smart dust will form a vast invisible network that can help manage the infrastructure of even the largest city. Smart Cities in the future will take this low power, inexpensive small technology and basically distribute it everywhere. These tiny computers record information about their surroundings. Information they can send to other computers. Smart dust will also allow buildings and streets to recognize you and respond accordingly.*

***Guida Jouret (of Emerging Markets Tech Cisco):*** *Increasingly the environment will respond to who we are and adapt in consequence.*

***Dr. Pister:*** *The city will know who you are, where you are if you want it to.*

*Your workplace will know you. Smart Dust at the entrance will boot up your computer. Smart Dust embedded in the elevator doors will automatically ring your floor.*

*Smart Dust is going to sense the environment and allow us to improve the way we live our lives.*

*Smart Dust is a very, very small particle, that's nano sized, that has a specific function. Smart Dust may already be in our atmosphere. This looks like, if you look at certain times of the day-and you see dust but its not dust- it's like an iridescent glitter, there's a specific difference between regular household dust.*

*I got one of those 10 million watts of spotlights-if you go out at night and point it up to the sky and you can't believe what's floating in the air. It's really disgusting.*

*Like if you're seeing this iridescence-it looks just like glitter-that's a smart dust type material versus regular household dust that does not reflect back."*[29]

Sure hope you don't breathe that in! So much for being able to hide or flee! Looks to me like all this new camera technology is leading to a total monitoring of our everyday lives for the first time in the history of mankind. I mean, the next thing you know, somebody's going to appear on the scene and start hunting people down and nobody's going to be able to flee because even the *dust* will give you away! No wonder it's going to be a bloodbath!

What more does God have to do? This is not a game! This is real! God doesn't want us going into the Antichrist's kingdom and He certainly doesn't want us to go into HELL! So that's why, out of love, He's given us these signs of a *One World Government* and a *Big Brother Society* to show us that the 7-year Tribulation is near and that Christ's Coming is rapidly approaching. And that's why Jesus Himself said:

**Luke 21:28** "When these things begin to take place, stand up and lift up your heads, because your redemption is drawing near."

Like it or not, we are headed for *The Final Countdown*. So the point is this. If you're a Christian, it's time to get busy! We've got to lay aside our differences and start getting busy working together saving souls by the Spirit of God!

But if you're not a Christian, then I beg you, please, heed the signs…heed the warnings…give your life to Jesus today…because the last place you ever want to be is in the Antichrist's kingdom and he's going to monitor everything! And I mean everything, like this guy found out!

# Pizza Palace

*<Phone Rings>*

**Mary:** *Pizza Palace where you have it in 30 minutes or its free. This is Mary. Can I take your order?*

**Customer:** *Hi, uh Mary, yes I'd like to order.*

**Mary:** *Is this Mr. Kelly?*

**Customer:** *Uh, Yes.*

**Mary:** *Thank you for calling again sir. I see your national identification number is 610204998-45-54610 is that correct?*

**Customer:** *Uh, yes?*

**Mary:** *Thank you, Mr. Kelly. I see you live at 736 Montrose Court but you're calling from your cell phone. Are you home?*

**Mr. Kelly:** *I'm just leaving work but I'm..<interupted>*

**Mary:** *OH! But we can deliver to Bob's Auto Supply! That's at 175 Lincoln Avenue, yes?*

**Mr. Kelly:** *NO! I'm on my way home. How do you know all this stuff?*

**Mary:** *We just got wired into The System, sir.*

**Mr. Kelly:** *Oh...well...I'd like to order a couple of your Double Meat Special pizzas.*

**Mary:** *Sure thing. There will be a new $20 charge for those, sir.*

**Mr. Kelly:** *What do you mean?*

**Mary:** *Sir, The System shows your medical records indicate that you have high blood pressure and extremely high cholesterol. Luckily we have a new agreement* *with your national health care provider that allows us to sell you Double Meat Pies as long as you agree to waive all future claims of liability.*

**Mr. Kelly:** *What!?*

**Mary:** *Do you agree, sir? You can sign the form when we deliver but there is a charge for processing. The total is $67 even.*

**Mr. Kelly:** *$67?!*

**Mary:** *That includes the delivery surcharge of $15 to cover the added risk to our driver traveling through an orange zone.*

**Mr. Kelly:** *I live in an orange zone?*

**Mary:** *Now you do. Looks like there was another robbery on Montrose yesterday. Hmmm. You could save $48 dollars if you ordered our special Sprout Submarine Combo and pick it up yourself. Comes with tofu sticks, they're very tasty sir. Good value too.*

**Mr. Kelly:** *But I want double meat.*

**Mary:** *Well I'm sure you can afford the $67 then. You just bought those tickets to Hawaii-they weren't cheap, eh? Ohhhh, I see you checked out the Budget Beach Bum at the Library last week. Hmmmm. Up to you sir.*

**Mr. Kelly:** *Alright, alright. I'll get the Sprout Subs.*

**Mary:** *Good choice, sir! Gotta watch that waist if you're hitting the beach, eh? 42" inch waist, wow. I'd say tofu and sprouts is like required.*

**Mr.Kelly:** *That's HOW MUCH?*

**Mary:** *Just between you and me-there's a $3 dollar off coupon in this month's Total Men's Fitness magazine. Your wife Betty subscribes to that, right? Anyhow, clip that and it's $19.99 even. WHOA! Looks like you maxed out on all your credit cards.* "[30]

But wait a second. Do they really have secret databases on us? Yes! Maxine Waters spilled the beans:

**TV One's Washington Watch**

*Maxine Waters on Obama's database*

**Roland Martin:** *Look, the inauguration represented the beginning of his 2nd term.*

**Maxine Waters:** *Yes.*

**Martin:** *But it also represented the countdown of the end of his presidency.*

**Waters:** *That's right.*

**Martin:** *And the reality is, like anything else, you better get what you can while Obama's there because look, come 2016, that's it.*

**Waters:** *Well you know, I don't know. And I think some people are missing something here. The President has put in place an organization that contains the kind of database that no one has ever seen before in life. That's going to be very, very powerful. That database will have information about everything on every individual in ways that it's never been done before.*"[31]

You secretly put in a huge database on everyone that's bigger than anything we've ever seen! Why didn't you tell us about that? But that's not all! They not only monitor our *Information System* as you just saw, but our *Communication System* and earlier we saw how they even monitor our *Transportation System* and our *Camera System*. You're not going to be able to run, or flee, or do anything like Jesus said because they're not only monitoring your vehicle anywhere on the planet, but they've got cameras watching you anywhere on the planet! You're not going to be able to hide!

**4. The 4th type of Big Brother Surveillance System** they've already put into place to FORCE US to go along with this One World Government is the **Location System.**

Now you might be thinking, "Well, there's no way they're going to get me! Okay, so maybe they're going to control my personal information and build this huge massive database on me and pigeonhole me into doing what they say and maybe they're going to grab control of all my communication devices and listen to what I say, especially that word 'Jesus.' Maybe they're going to track and control my vehicle wherever I go and if I try to escape on foot they'll still see me with one of these cameras they've got installed everywhere. A light post could give me away! But hey, forget that! I'm just going to stay in my house. Yeah, that's right! I mean, after all, a man's castle is his own domain, right? Safe and secure! They won't get me! Ha! Ha! Ha! I'm free!" Really? Not if they control your *location*! Believe it or not, the Bible warns us that *not even your home* is going to be a safe place during the 7-year Tribulation! But don't take my word for it. Let's listen to God's.

**Matthew 24:15-22** "So when you see standing in the holy place the abomination that causes desolation, spoken of through the prophet Daniel – let the reader understand – then let those who are in Judea flee to the mountains. Let no one on the roof of his house go down to take anything out of the house. Let no one in the field go back to get his cloak. How dreadful it will be in those days for pregnant women and nursing mothers! Pray that your flight will not take place in winter or on the Sabbath. For then there will be great distress, unequaled from the beginning of the world until now –and never to be equaled again. If those days had not been cut short, no one would survive, but for the sake of the elect those days will be shortened."

Now as we saw before, in this passage, the Bible clearly says that during the 7-year Tribulation, after the Antichrist shows his true colors and goes into the rebuilt Jewish temple to declare himself to be god, that's the abomination of desolation spoken of by the Prophet Daniel that Jesus is referring to here, people are going to be fleeing, right? Jesus says you need to get out of there now in quick flight, right? Why? Because again, as we saw before, Zechariah says that it's going to be a time of horrible slaughter. Just the Jewish people alone, 2/3rds of them are going to be annihilated! That's why Jesus says "Get out of there and FLEE!"

But that's not all. What did He say you *shouldn't* do? He said the last thing you want to do is "FLEE" to your *house*, right? In fact, I'd say *any* dwelling because the Greek word here for "house" is "oikia" and it means, "yes, a house, but it also means "an inhabited edifice or dwelling." So maybe the reason why Jesus says specifically to "get out of town" and "flee to the mountains" is because maybe any building whatsoever won't be safe at this time! Which means, not just your house, but your workplace, your favorite pad, or even your Church Sanctuary, no inhabited edifice or dwelling is going to be safe! You just need to get out of there! Run, flee and head to the hills, like Jesus said! Why? Because has it ever occurred to you that not even your "home" is going to escape Big Brother's Eye? And for those who think this is still science fiction, believe it or not, they're already doing it! Believe it or not, these same people who are pushing for a One World Government are already grabbing control of our private locations!

## A. The 1st way they're doing that is Through Our Computers.

That's right! Believe it or not, for those of you who think that you're just going to stay safe and out of sight in your home or work when the hammer comes down, after the Antichrist shows his true colors and goes on that manhunt, you're wrong! He's going to use your *computer* to keep an eye on you! Believe it or not, they right now not only have radar guns that can peer through concrete walls and see you if you try to hide in any building, including your home, but they even have satellites in orbit with the same capability on the way.[32] Government officials right now can actually aim an antenna at your computer monitor screen and from the radiation emitted from it, they can reconstruct the images on their screen…and monitor you! In fact, it's so commonplace now you don't even need one of these devices! Anyone can tap into somebody else's computer and spy on them literally through their webcam! Check it out…they're called *Ratters*!

**Yahoo News/Upgrade Your Life:**

***Becky Worley:*** *There's a new type of computer spying on the rise and its, ugh, really creepy. It's called "ratting" using remote access tools for rats to gain control of a victim's computer. Once a hacker has access, they can completely control the device. What's on the rise is an online community of voyeurs, who turn on the web cams of these ratted computers. They record these videos and some even post them in forums or on YouTube to share with others. When a computer is controlled, it is called a slave. Ratters like to scare slaves by displaying graphic image files on their computers or opening the DVD drive remotely. They can even make the computer read aloud using text to speech applications just to startle or annoy victims."*[33]

You are my slave, the Antichrist owns your machine! Not that far away, is it? But hey, maybe that's just those computer geeks or those disgruntled boyfriends we saw on the cell phones, but I'm sure that's as far as it'll ever go. Well, actually, believe it or not, it's going much farther than that! Believe it or not, there's already an international movement going on right now for the governments around the world to grab total control of your computer and take anything they want from it under the guise of copyright violations. It's called ACTA or the *Anti-Counterfeiting Trade Agreement.*

## RT News: Not so private computers

*Personal computers may soon be not so private with the U.S. and some European nations working on laws allowing them access to search the contents held on a person's hard drive. President Obama's administration is keeping unusually tight lipped about the details which was raising concerns among computer users and liberty activists.*

*Almost everyone owns a music player and a laptop. But what if the government decided to allow itself to get into these personal devices for no specific reason whatsoever. Amid extreme secrecy from the public, the United States is hammering out an international copyright treaty with several other countries and the European Union. Under the Anti Counterfeiting Trade Agreement or ACTA, governments will get sweeping new powers to search and seize material thought to be in breach of copyright. But why all the secrecy? But what it will do on a larger scale is let Big Brother watch you, however this time on a completely different level.*

*Leaks from the text suggest that border guards will get unprecedented powers to search travelers without warning. They will be able to go through, copy and confiscate any digital material a person has on their laptop.* "[34]

Create a crisis and you can manage the outcome. We have a copyright crisis! Let us control your computer and keep everything safe. Any government around the world can have access to my computer and take anything they want, under the guise of copyright! Well, that's convenient!

And for those of you who think that's not fair, believe it or not, you may have already given them the permission to do so. How many of you remember that program "Cash for Clunkers?" You know, they came out with it right after the Economy crashed to get us to buy cars? Wasn't that a great program? Wasn't that wonderful? Well, you may not think so after this! Believe it or not, what they didn't tell you was that once you signed up to that program you just gave all your rights of your computer up to the government!

**Beck:** *This is frightening*

**Guest:** *It really is. People shouldn't go on it right now. While you're doing this.*

**Beck:** *Do not do this at home. Trust me you'll understand why. Okay, can you take a shot of this right here Oscar? Um, here's www.cars.gov. Let's say you go in-if I understand this right-I go in and I say, 'I want to turn in my clunker'. The dealer goes to cars.gov and then they hit submit transaction. Here it says privacy act and security statement. And your like, 'oh its a privacy act from '74, oh whatever, I agree' Let me show you what it DOES say when you pull it up. Can you pull up the full screen on what it says? A warning box comes up and it says:*

*"This application provides access to the DOT CARS system. When logged on to the CARS system, your computer is considered a Federal computer system and is the property of the U.S. Government. Any or all uses of this system and all files on this system may be intercepted, monitored, recorded, copied, audited, inspected and disclosed to authorized CARS, DOT and law enforcement personnel, as well as authorized officials of other agencies, both domestic and foreign."* [35]

Wow! What a lie! So much for personal privacy in your own home! Looks to me like we've been snookered and it also looks to me like for the first time in man's history, put all this together, even if we try to stay at home during some horrible time frame instead of fleeing, it looks like our *computer* will turn us in! They'll know exactly where we are and what we're doing! No wonder it's going to be a bloodbath!

**B. The 2nd way they've already grabbed control of our Private Locations so we can't flee from a horrible situation is Through Our TV's.**

Ahhh. Are you serious? Yeah, they've already thought of everything! You see, you might be thinking that when this time of calamity hits in the 7-year Tribulation and the Antichrist goes on his hunting spree, that you're just *still* going to try to stay home and keep safe, but you won't have any of these "new fangled" computers! No siree! You're just going to stick to your good ol' fashioned Television Set! They can't monitor me with that! Really? Well, you're assuming that with all these "new fangled" TV's that they keep getting us to buy every single year, that they don't have some sort of special capability. You know, being able to watch you back! But that would never happen, would it? Well, all I have to say is George Orwell 1984, eat your heart out!

*Laura Warren: Big screens, flat screens but there's no screen --it's kinda like going to the movies--like this screen.*

*April Ramos: There's like Netflix on it, you can Skype, I think you can play some games on it.*

*When you think of the mac daddy of television, Samsung's Smart TV is it.*

*Ramos: It has all kinds of cool things. You can download APPS like you would on an I-Phone.*

*Warren: April Ramos bought the Samsung Smart TV last summer and so far it's lived up to it's expectations. From Skype, to Netflix, banking to social media, the TV does it all. But with the good...*

*Samsung has said they are aware of the problem and that they are going to fix it.*

*Warren: ...comes some bad.*

*If it's connected to the internet, including your phone, there's the possibility of a security breach.*

*Warren: Just last month a security firm demonstrated in this video how they were able to hack into the Samsung Smart TV. The "hole" in the Smart TV could potentially allow hackers to gain access to sensitive information through your TV. And perhaps the scariest possibility-the new TVs have built in cameras, which means your TV could be watching your every move.*

*And they can pretty much view the camera 24/7 if they wanted to.* "[36]

Sounds like these new fangled "Smart TV's" really should be called "Big Brother TV's, how about you? Is there anything left on George Orwell's vision of

1984 that's not already in place? Correct me if I'm wrong but it sure looks to me like if we try to stay home during some horrible time frame instead of fleeing like Jesus said, our TV's are going to turn us in! We're not going to make it, they'll be watching our every step! No wonder it's going to be a bloodbath!

**C. The 3rd way** they've already grabbed control of our Private Locations is **Through Our Weapons.**

What? Are you serious? Yeah folks, it's getting pretty crazy! You see, you might be thinking, "Well alright, when this time of calamity hits in the 7-year Tribulation and the Antichrist goes on his hunting spree, I'm still just going to stay home but I'm going to get rid of all my computers and all my TV's and I'm going to stockpile weapons just in case they try to barge in my home!" Really? You don't think they've thought of that too? What do you think is behind all the news lately and this push for a ban on all our weapons? You really think that's by chance? This is precisely why our Founding Fathers put the Second Amendment in the Constitution....*to protect from evil dictatorships.* They knew if a Government went evil, the people had to have the right to bear arms to protect themselves! Why? Because gun control is the first step to True Tyranny! Just ask these guys!

37

This is why the Founding Fathers put the 2nd Amendment in there. We need to have the right to "bear arms" to protect ourselves! But not anymore! They've convinced us to give up this right with all these school crises, these shootings and other shootings in public, to let them control our weapons. Yet in reality when you look at the facts, weapons are actually safer than doctors.[38]

## Doctor Related Deaths Per Year

| | |
|---|---|
| Surgery-Related | 32,000 |
| Unnecessary Procedures | 37,136 |
| Infection | 88,000 |
| Medical Error | 98,000 |
| Malnutrition | 108,800 |
| Bedsores | 115,000 |
| Outpatients | 199,000 |
| Adverse Drug Reactions | 322,000 |
| TOTAL: | 999,936 |

## Weapons Related Deaths Per Year

| | |
|---|---|
| TOTAL Weapons Deaths | 13,636 |

Now maybe it's just me, maybe I'm not the best at math, but I'm kind of thinking we need to start a ban on doctors, how about you? Isn't that the same logic? Isn't that the greater need? But that's not all. I'm telling you, they've thought of everything! Even if these laws don't ever get passed on gun control, they're actually working on a way to keep you from being able to fire your gun in the first place! Believe it or not, they're working right now on a new technology that restricts your ability to even fire a gun, unless of course you had a chip in your hand!

## CNN report: Smart Guns

*All eyes on Washington this week as your political leaders are working on a gun control bill to expand background checks. Behind the scenes, inventors and entrepreneurs are coming up with their own solutions to try and curb gun violence. They're called "Smart Guns". Makers say they're childproof and could prevent future tragedies.*

*What if your gun could only be fired by your hand? The New Jersey Institute of Technology has spent the last 13 years developing a gun that analyzes a person's grip and only fires for it's owner. The goal here is using science technology to make sure that someone who's not supposed to fire this gun does not fire this gun. A child. A criminal. Someone who's taken the gun and tries to use it against you.*

**Michael Reece** *(Assoc .Professor, NJIT) Right, or stolen the gun or actually had someone else buy it*

*ArmaTix, a German company, takes a different approach. It's guns are activated by a watch and a unique pin number.*

*It says it's good. You're now able to shoot. Ready to fire.*

*Ready only if you're wearing the watch. If at any point an unauthorized user takes the gun and tries to shoot, it will not fire.*

*TriggerSmart uses similar wireless technology like what's in electronic toll readers to unlock it's guns.*

> **Robert McNamara** *<Founder, TriggerSmart>Now I'll introduce the RFID tag and now the gun is ready to fire. The chip can be worn in the form of a ring on your finger or a bracelet. Now they're starting to imbed chips in humans in the fatty part of the hand.*"[39]

So now I won't be able to fire my gun unless I have a microchip in my hand. Smart guns, smart TV's, smart phones, smart computers, doesn't sound too smart to me. Sounds pretty dumb! Sounds like for the first time in mankind's history, if you try to hide out in your house during some horrible time frame and even try to defend yourself, *you're toast*! It ain't going to happen! No wonder Jesus said get out of there and flee, it's going to be a blood bath.

**D. The 4ᵗʰ way** they've already grabbed control of our Private Locations so we can't flee a horrible situation is **Through Our Drones.**

That's right, you talk about the ultimate Big Eye in the Sky! We've got them! They're called Drones and for the first time in the history of mankind we now have *armed machines* that can not only fly in the sky monitoring anyone, anywhere on the planet, but they can take you out as well! They're called UAV's or Unmanned Aerial Vehicles. And they're not only being used to monitor and "take out targets" from the air around the globe, but for the first time in our history, they're being used on American Citizens.

## RT Game of Drones

*Liz Wahl: Well we begin this afternoon with signs of the U.S. maybe moving in the direction of becoming a police state. Now we've heard about drones being used in the Middle East. Most recently Iran seized a U.S. drone accused of spying on the country. But now are reports that Predator Drones are being used on American citizens on U.S. soil. This next video transcript pretty much sums it all up.*

*Nelson County North Dakota sheriff, Kelly Janke, was looking for 6 missing cows on the Broussart family farm. But three armed Broussart brothers chased them away. Janke called the Highway Patrol, the SWAT Team, the Bomb Squad and a Predator Drone operated by U.S. Customs and Border Protection. The Drone was used to surveil the property until the Broussart brothers were observed to be unarmed. Then the S.W.A.T. Team moved in to make the arrests.*

*Liz Wahl: Yep, that really happened. An unmanned multi-million dollar drone was reportedly used to help local police to track down stolen cows and their owners. So what is happening here in the U.S., and is this a sign of things to come?* "[40]

Unfortunately, I think it is. But let's back up a little bit. Granted, stealing someone's cows is a serious offense, I totally agree, but come on! Using a Predator Drone on an American Citizen period, let alone just for stealing cows? What else is being done that we don't know about with these drones? I thought they were just for those terrorist people in foreign countries? Again, what if we the Christian became a terrorist? Will they use it on us? Oh and by the way, this was kind of creepy. How many of you realize that at the last U.S. Census Bureau they did, when they came to your *house*, do you know what else they were recording on us? They used machines to take our precise *GPS location* of our house![41] Hmmm. I wonder why? GPS coordinates come in handy for a Drone Strike! But hey, that's just crazy thinking....but I wish I could just stop there. What's even crazier is how this Drone technology is advancing so fast that they've also come out with what's now called MAV's or Micro Aerial Vehicles. And what these things are, are miniature tiny drones that look like a *fly* or a *bird*, but it's not! It's a drone that can not only monitor you, but take you out! Don't believe me? Take a look.

## Micro Air Vehicles

*Micro Air Vehicles, or M.A.V.'s will play an important role in future warfare. The urban battlefield calls for tools to increase the war fighter's situational awareness. The capacity to engage rapidly, precisely and with minimal collateral damage. M.A.V.'s will be integrated in the future Air Force layered sensing systems. These systems may be airdropped or hand launched, depending on the mission requirements.*

*The small size of MAVs allows them to be hidden in plain sight. Once in place, an MAV can enter a low powered, extended surveillance mode for missions lasting days or weeks. This may require the MAV to harvest energy from environmental sources, such as sunlight and wind, or from man made sources such as power lines or vibrating machinery. It will blend in with its surroundings and operate undetected. MAVs will use microsensors and microprocessor technology to navigate and track targets through complicated terrain such as urban areas.*

*Small size and agile flight will enable MAVs to covertly enter locations inaccessible by traditional means of aerial surveillance. MAVs will use new forms of navigation such as a vision based technique called 'opticflow'. This system remains robust when traditional methods such as GPS are unavailable.*

*Individual MAVs may perform direct attack missions, and can be equipped with incapacitating chemicals, combustible payloads or even explosives for precision targeting capability."[42]*

Can you believe that? This isn't make believe, this is reality now! The Antichrist has got it worked out that there's no safe place to hide! You better run like Jesus said! But the Bible is clear. Even with all this technology, God is the One Who's in Charge, not the Antichrist! He demonstrates that by sovereignly protecting 1/3rd of the Jewish people! 1/3rd are going to make it out alive as we saw before.

**Zechariah 13:8** "In the whole land, declares the LORD, two-thirds will be struck down and perish; yet one-third will be left in it."

And John tells us where they go for safety.

**Revelation 12:6,14,17** "The woman fled into the desert to a place prepared for her by God, where she might be taken care of for 1,260 days. The woman was given the two wings of a great eagle, so that she might fly to the place prepared for her in the desert, where she would be taken care of for a time, times and half a time, out of the serpent's reach. Then the dragon was enraged at the woman and went off to make war against the rest of her offspring – those who obey God's commandments and hold to the testimony of Jesus."

So we see here that Israel is sovereignly protected during the back half of the 7-year Tribulation. The Antichrist can't get to them like he did with the other 2/3rds so he gets mad and turns on the rest of the people who follow God. Many researchers believe that the place mentioned here in the desert that the Jewish people flee to for safety is none other than Petra and there's several reasons why. How many of you remember that cool looking carved rock place in the Indiana Jones movie where the buildings were carved out of the side of the mountains, with that reddish look there? That's a real place called Petra and researchers believe that Petra is the perfect place to flee at this time for the Jewish people.

*First of all* because it's *accessible* in a short amount of time. Petra is only 120 miles southeast of Jerusalem and you could feasibly get there in a quick amount of time if you were fleeing some horrible situation in Jerusalem, and that's why Jesus said pray that it's not on the Sabbath or you're pregnant, nursing with kids, you just gotta get there quick...and you can!

*Secondly*, it also fits their description geographically. In Matthew 24 Jesus said to "flee to the mountains" and here we saw in Revelation they "fled into the desert." So, is it a contradiction? Of course not! Petra has both! It's a mountainous desert area! In fact, the highest mountains in Jordan are in the Petra area. And Petra would also be a difficult place for the Antichrist to reach them because the only way to get into the city is through a long narrow passageway that's about 6000 feet long.

*Third*, Petra has the right availability to house the amount of Jews who will need to take refuge there. 1/3rd are going to make it out alive and so you have to house about a couple million people. So guess what? Petra's got that ability too. Tourists today only see about 5% of the city and yet it covers a total of 20 square miles, not to mention the massive network of caves and cave dwellings to house all the people. AND, not only does Petra have a water supply for most of the year, but for some unknown reason, whether they realize what they were doing or not, one researcher shared with me, recently the U.N. installed a "continuous water supply to Petra." Hmmm. So now you've got plenty of *water* when you hide out!

But that's still not all. Why does the Antichrist give up in his pursuit of the Jewish people? How does God make provision for that? Well, the same researcher stated this, *"As I thought about scripture, and looked at what was happening, I wondered why it would be safe in Petra for the Jews. Why couldn't the enemy just fly over and bomb them? (You know a drone?) But I learned from another source that the reason this could not happen was because planes could not fly over Petra, in that, for some reason, the electronics on the aircraft would not work if they fly over the area. Could this be God's provision, for the Jewish remnant?"* And they concluded with this, *"All of this has caused me to keep an eye on what is happening in the Holy Land today and to also remember that our God is always in control, no matter what anyone says."*[43] In other words, the Antichrist is the BIG LOSER, we're the BIG WINNERS!

So here's the point. What more does God have to do? Put all this together. This is not a game! This is real! This is all happening right now! All the pieces are coming together and the Scripture is being fulfilled like never before! This is why, out of love, God has given us these signs of a *One World Government* and a *Big Brother Society* to show us that the 7-year Tribulation is near and that Christ's Coming is rapidly approaching. And that's why Jesus Himself said:

**Luke 21:28** "When these things begin to take place, stand up and lift up your heads, because your redemption is drawing near."

People, like it or not, we are headed for *The Final Countdown*. So the point is this. If you're a Christian, it's time to get busy! What more does God have to do to get OUR attention? We've got to lay aside our differences and start getting busy working together saving souls by the Spirit of God and if ever there was a time to STAND UP for freedom, it is now, like this guy warns!

*Martin Niemoeller was a Lutheran minister who lived in Hitler's Germany during the 1930s and 1940s. His words echo down to us over succeeding decades:*

"In Germany they came first for the Communists, and I didn't speak up because I wasn't a Communist. Then they came for the Jews, and I didn't speak up because I wasn't a Jew. Then they came for the trade unionists, and I didn't speak up because I wasn't a trade unionist. Then they came for the Catholics, and I didn't speak up because I was a Protestant. Then they came for me, and by that time no one was left to speak up."[44]

We better speak up now or we're fooling ourselves into thinking history won't repeat itself. The Antichrist is going to make what Hitler did look like chump change!

But if you're NOT a Christian, then I beg you, please, heed the signs…heed the warnings…give your life to Jesus now because the last place you ever want to be is in the Antichrist's kingdom. One day he's going to force you into taking his mark, the Mark of the Beast and you will have nowhere to run and nowhere to hide! Jesus is the ONLY WAY OUT of this MESS!

Believe it or not, even with all this amazing evidence pointing to the signs of Christ's soon return, some people still have no clue as to what's causing all the pain in the world, like this lady:

*"One day a lady was throwing a party for her granddaughter and she had gone all out. She hired a caterer, a band and even a clown. But just before the party started, two bums showed up looking for a handout and so feeling sorry for them, the woman told them that she would give them a meal if they will help chop some wood for her. They gratefully agreed and headed to the rear of the house where the wood was.*

*Meanwhile the guests arrived and all was going well with the children having a wonderful time. But there was one problem. The clown hadn't shown up. Then after a half an hour, the clown finally called to report that he was stuck in traffic and would probably not make the party at all.*

*At this the woman was very disappointed and unsuccessfully tried to entertain the children herself. Just when she was about to give up hope, she happened to look out the window and saw one of the bums doing cartwheels across the lawn. In fact, she continued to watch in awe as he swung from tree branches, did midair flips and leaped high in the air.*

*So the lady spoke to the other bum and said, 'What your friend is doing is absolutely marvelous. I have never seen such a thing. Do you think your friend would consider repeating this performance for the children at the party? In fact, I would pay him $50!'*

*So the other bum says, 'Well, I dunno. Let me ask him. HEY WILLIE! FOR $50, WOULD YOU CHOP OFF ANOTHER TOE?'"*[45]

Now, that lady was totally clueless about that guy's pain, wasn't she? She had no idea about what was really taking place. But you know what? She's not alone. You see, many people today think that their lives are going to become pain free and a virtual paradise through a *One World Government*. They think they can once and for all get rid of God's authority and rule themselves. Yet they are totally clueless about what's really taking place. The Bible says that God is not only laughing at them, but that He will also soon rebuke those who reject His authority over their lives.

**Psalm 2:1-5** "Why do the nations rage? Why do the people waste their time with futile plans? The kings of the earth prepare for battle; the rulers plot together against the LORD and against his anointed one. 'Let us break their chains,' they cry, 'and free ourselves from this slavery.' But the one who rules in heaven laughs. The Lord scoffs at them. Then in anger he rebukes them, terrifying them with his fierce fury."

People of God, I hope you're not one of those who have bought into this lie that man can somehow provide his own paradise by creating a *One World Government*. Why? Because you might wake up one day and discover that you've been left behind. Please, I beg you, get right with God *now* before it's too late! Whatever you do, don't be like one of those people who say something like this. "Okay, I'm not going to accept Jesus right now, but if I see you Christians disappear in this Rapture thing, I'll know it was true and I'll get saved then." Are you kidding me? Don't you realize that if you wait until the Tribulation to get saved it will cost you your head *literally*! I didn't say that. God did!

**Revelation 20:4** "And I saw the souls of those who had been beheaded because of their testimony for Jesus and because of the word of God. They had not worshiped the beast or his image and had not received his mark on their foreheads or their hands."

People, stop kidding yourself. If you won't get saved now when it's still relatively easy to be a Christian, you mean to tell me you will when you're literally threatened with getting your head chopped off? Stop lying to yourself! Wouldn't it make much more sense to get saved now and avoid the Wrath to come? Please, I beg you, get right with God now! And here's the great news. God doesn't want you left behind. Because He loves us, He has given us the warning sign of a *One World Government* to show us that the Tribulation could be near and that Christ's 2^nd Coming is rapidly approaching. Jesus Himself said this:

**Luke 21:28** "When these things begin to take place, stand up and lift up your heads, because your redemption is drawing near."

Like it or not, we are headed for *The Final Countdown*. We don't know the day or the hour. Only God knows. The point is, if you're a Christian, it's time to get up off our blessed assurance and get bold for Almighty God! It's high time we Christians speak up and declare the good news of salvation to those who are dying all around us. But please, if you're not a Christian, give your life to Jesus today, because tomorrow may be too late! Just like the Bible said!

*Chapter Nine*

---

# One World Economy

"Once there was this young married lady who was leaving a convenience store with her espresso in hand and she noticed a most unusual funeral procession.

What she saw was a black hearse that was followed by a second black hearse about 50 feet behind the first one and behind the second hearse there was a solitary old woman walking a dog on a leash. Then behind her, a short distance back, were about 200 women walking in single file.

So the young woman couldn't stand it anymore and she goes up to the old lady walking the dog and respectfully asked her, "Excuse me, Maam, I'm sorry for your loss and maybe this is a bad time to disturb you, but I've never seen a funeral like this before. Whose funeral is it?"

The old lady responded, "It's my husband's."

The young woman said, "Oh. And what happened to him?"

The old woman responded, "He yelled at me and my dog attacked and killed him."

So the young lady, she was a little startled at this, but she inquired further and asked again, "Okay, but who's in the second hearse there?"

The old woman responded, "That's my mother-in-law. She was trying to help my husband when the dog turned on her and killed her too."

And in a very touching magical moment that only two women can share, the young woman whispered the to old lady, "Can I borrow the dog?"

And the old lady responded, "Get in line."[1]

Seriously, believe it or not, as messed up as that joke is, did you know those 200 ladies aren't the only ones "getting in line" for a funeral! Yeah, that's right! Believe it or not, the Bible says one day the whole planet is going to be getting in line for a funeral during the 7-year Tribulation. And this one's not going to be caused by a mangy ol' dog but from the Hand of Almighty God! He's going to pour out His wrath on this wicked and rebellious planet and most of the population is going to their own funeral! You don't want to "get in line" for that one, and that all of course begins at the Rapture of the Church! The reason why it's going to be such a horrible time is because for those who refuse to accept Jesus Christ as their Personal Lord and Savior, they'll be catapulted into the 7-year Tribulation and its not a joke! It really is an outpouring of God's wrath on a wicked & rebellious planet. In fact Jesus said in Matthew 24 it's going to be a "time of greater horror than anything the world has ever seen or will ever see again and that "unless that time of calamity is shortened, the entire human race would be destroyed." But praise God, God's not only a God of wrath, He's a God of love as well and *because He loves us*, He's given us many warning signs to show us when the Tribulation is near and when Jesus Christ's 2nd Coming is rapidly approaching.

The **#2** sign on *The Final Countdown* that God has given to us to lovingly wake us up is none other then a **One World Economy**.

That's right, the Bible is clear. One day the whole planet is not only going to be under the authority of the Antichrist with this One World Government, but it's also going to be under his Economy as well. He's not only going to *monitor you*, but he's going to *control all the money*! Now he's really got you! But don't take my word for it. Let's listen to God's.

**Revelation 13:11-17** "Then I saw another beast, coming out of the earth. He had two horns like a lamb, but he spoke like a dragon. He exercised all the authority of the first beast on his behalf, and made the earth and its inhabitants worship the first beast, whose fatal wound had been healed. And he performed great and miraculous signs, even causing fire to come down from heaven to earth in full view of men. Because of the signs he was given power to do on behalf of the first beast, he deceived the inhabitants of the earth. He ordered them to set up an image in honor of the beast who was wounded by the sword and yet lived. He was given power to give breath to the image of the first beast, so that it could speak and cause all who refused to worship the image to be killed. He also forced everyone, small and great, rich and poor, free and slave, to receive a mark on his right hand or on his forehead, so that no one could buy or sell unless he had the mark, which is the name of the beast or the number of his name."

Now according to our text, the Bible says there really is coming a day when all the inhabitants of the earth will not only be under the authority of the Antichrist, but even his what? His economy or monetary system, right? You can't buy or sell, you can't do anything with money without his permission and so here's the point. The Bible clearly says, one day, believe it or not, the whole world will be unified into a *One World Economy* that is actually *satanically inspired*. But again, as always, the question is, "Could that really happen?" Could the whole world really be deceived into creating a *One World Economy* for the Antichrist to, at one point, hijack and take over for his purposes? Is there any evidence that this is really going to take place just like the Bible said? Uh, yeah! In fact, it's happening now!

**I. The 1st proof** that we know we really are headed for a One World Economy is the **Chronological Proof.**

What most people don't realize is that this One World Economy of the Antichrist is not only going to be put into place, because the Bible said it would, but what people don't realize is that it's been in the planning stages for a long time and they're just about ready to pull it off! See for yourself:

- 1913: The Federal Reserve created: It is neither federal nor a reserve and is owned by banks. It was planned at a secret meeting in 1910 on Jekyll Island, Georgia by a group of bankers and politicians. This transferred the power to create money from the American government to a private group of bankers and thus violates Article I of the Constitution, which states, "Congress shall have the power to coin money and regulate the value thereof." (NOT BANKS!)

- 1944: The World Bank was formed (world's foremost lender)
- 1944: (IMF) International Monetary Fund formed (world's overseer of international financial system)
- 1944: (GATT) General Agreement on Tariffs and Trade (liberalized world trade)
- 1968: Club of Rome formed (group of economic elite world advisers)
- 1973: Trilateral commissioned formed by banker David Rockefeller to develop a worldwide economic power
- 1973: (SWIFT) Society for Worldwide Interbank Finance Transactions created (universal electronic banking organization that transfers monetary transactions between countries and corporations)
- 1975: Declaration of Interdependence signed which declares that our economy should be regulated by international authorities.
- 1979: Smart card developed
- 1993: Mondex International formed
- 1994: (NAFTA) North American Free Trade Agreement (free trade between Canada, U.S., and Mexico)
- 1995: (WTO) World Trade Organization formed (develops and enforces worldwide trade rules)
- 1999: The Euro is born (new universal currency of several European countries)
- 2002: The first Euro coins and banknotes go into circulation
- 2002: Call for a Global Tax to be paid to the United Nations at World Conference held in Monterrey, Mexico
- 2002: Fast Track Bill approved that prevents congress from changing or even having an extended debate on any trade agreement negotiated by the President
- 2003: Proposal appears for credit card implants
- 2003: Proposal to keep children safe with a microchip

**Roger Ebert:** *Right now my mind is telling my body to talk and it's supplying my mouth with words that I'm giving to you. And the mind could also learn to say to the chip-go to a certain webpage and download some information and supply it to the inside of my eyeballs.*

**Bill O'Reilly:** *You believe that you can actually be able to tell your mind through a chip to provide you with information that you can then speak. So on this program it would be great for me to put a little chip in there and if I didn't know* *something I could say to the chip-I would have to say it out loud or just think it?*

**Ebert:** *Either way.*

**O'Reilly:** *I could just think it-gives me an answer.*

**Ebert:** *Right now, we're loaded up with bionic stuff already. I'm wearing glasses. I have fillings in my teeth. This is a wristwatch. I'm wearing clothing which allows me to adjust to the climate as I go outside. So obviously it's only a matter of time until convergence allows us to match the number one tool of the next century and that would be the computer chip. Clothes are tools, glasses are tools.*

**O'Reilly:** *Sure, but all these are external but the computer chip would be in you and that's what frightens me.*

**Ebert:** *Well, it could be in you or it could be wherever you wanted it to be. And it would allow you to make telephone calls without having a cell phone. It would allow you to surf the web without having a monitor.*

**O'Reilly:** *Well show me how…so if I had a chip imbedded in my head I can make a telephone call by just start talking? "Call Mom"?*

**Ebert:** *Um, yeah.*

**O'Reilly:** *And Mom- I would be able to talk to her?*

**Ebert:** *You would just say "Hello Mom"*

**O'Reilly:** *But I wouldn't have a phone or anything.*

**Ebert:** *No. And so you would have to have some body language so people would know what you were doing. Let's say that you're standing at the American Airlines terminal*

**O'Reilly:** *Yeah.*

**Ebert:** *And you're calling the Advantage desk and saying I've missed my flight. Do you have any seats at 10 o'clock? Ok, if you're standing there saying that, someone's going to look at you like you're one of these crazies.*

**O'Reilly:** *Not if everyone had the chip; they'd all know what was going on.*

**Ebert:** *Well, then you would do this <puts hand to side of head in a phone symbol> This means, I'm not just talking to myself. I'm talking on the phone.*

**O'Reilly:** *This sounds so..*

**Ebert:** *If you're reading the web on the inside of your eyeballs.*

**O'Reilly:** *Yeah.*

**Ebert:** *It would look rude to people. It would look like I'm staring straight through you. Well I'm not staring straight through you, I'm looking at the FOX NEWS webpage, right. So how do I want people to know that? I would just go like this <make an L gesture with hand>.*

**O'Reilly:** *This sounds so unbelievable.*

**Ebert:** *If I'm downloading information <makes hand gesture next to head, like a Martian antennae>.*

**O'Reilly:** *<laughing> But it's true. It could happen.*

**Ebert:** *Things are converging so quickly and computers are already such an amazing tool.*

**O'Reilly:** *But we checked it out a little further than your article and the scientists tell us that it is absolutely true and absolutely possible for a human being to have a chip imbedded in their system and to have many, many things appear in their mind upon command. So you would say I need to know the name of the 18th President. BING!*

**Ebert:** *Not only that, I meet you and call up your credit report while we're talking and eventually, the time will come when a child is implanted with a little chip back here and we'll learn to control the chip in the same way you learn to control your bodily functions and your voice and your movement.*

- 2004: Biometric payments expanding to grocery and convenience stores

- 2004: Bank card crimes fuel rush to biometric systems
- 2004: Microchip and global satellite firms reach agreement
- 2004: Chirac calls for a global tax
- 2005: House approves electronic ID cards
- 2005: The Bank for International Settlements calls for global currency
- 2005: (FTAA) Free Trade Agreement of the Americas is proposed to provide free trade in the whole Western Hemisphere
- 2005: Proposal for a Digital Birth ID
- 2005: Chief of Police who received VeriChip advocates forced government chipping to buy and sell
- 2006: VeriChip sells first Baby Protection System and in talks with Military
- 2006: The International Monetary Fund wins new powers to "police" the global economy
- 2006: Rise of people voluntarily receiving microchips implants
- 2006: Couples receive implants as a sign of love for each other

**Good Morning America**
**Under My Skin-A New Kind of Love Connection**

*Charles Gibson: This next story we have for you is kind of wild. You might call it microchip commitment. A young man by the name of Emil Gastra and Jennifer Tomlin-they are dating-have total access to each other's homes, cars and computers. And they have that access by way of matching electronic microchips that are implanted under their skin. They're joining us this morning to make you understand. Try to make me understand all of it. They're joining us from Vancouver, Canada and I appreciate your being with us. Before we get to this, what this chip actually looks like, Emil, I want you to give me some demonstration. We have some videotape here of what you can do with this. For instance, I understand you can unlock you're car door and open your car door without ever putting a key in it.*

*Emil: Yeah, actually I can just walk up to the car and present my hand to the sensor which is in the windshield of the car. It reads the chip ID and says, 'okay this is Emil' and unlocks the car and disarms the alarm.*

*Gibson: And you can do the same thing with your front door.*

*Emil: Uh, yeah, I then come right in and there's a little sensor on the door, and place my hand up next to it. It reads my ID and unlocks the deadbolt.*

**Gibson:** *And you can also, I understand you folks are sitting in front of a computer, you can also uh, turn on your computer this way?*

**Emil:** *Uh yeah, I can log in as it indicates me.*

**Gibson:** *So you meet this guy, Jennifer, and you start dating and he tells you what he's done and he suggests that maybe you do the same thing.*

**Jennifer:** *Uh, he wrote his book and after about a year, seeing all the cool projects, I decided to do it myself.*

**Gibson:** *And what are the future applications of this. I presume it will be able to do more things than just open your car door, your front door or log onto your computer.*

**Emil:** *Yeah, uh, the common theme is access control. But there are some people that are matching profiles to it so you get in your front door but then your home automation system knows that it's you and sets lighting and music and that kind of preference.*

**Gibson:** *And it's inserted under your skin with a needle.*

**Emil:** *Uh, yeah but left hand was done with a scalpel actually and it was placed under by a cosmetic surgeon. Right hand was done with the same needle injector that's used on pets actually.*

**Gibson:** *So this is something for the future, I can say, you know, how does a couple commit to one another? Well 'I will put you on my front door in my microchip.' I suppose there will be a lot of future applications. Maybe we'll all have one of these under our skin in time.*

- 2006: Young shoppers want to pay with chip in skin
- 2007: Proposal for animal tags for people
- 2007: Russia launches final satellites for its own GPS
- 2007: Secret new plan for EU Super State unveiled
- 2008: Seven year plan aligns U.S. with Europe's economy
- 2008: Hospitals tagging babies with electronic chips

- 2008: The World Economic Forum meets again in Switzerland
- 2008: Experts say the Global Economy is at Maximum Danger
- 2008: The International Monetary Fund says that the world's economies must work together to keep the global markets from being destroyed
- 2008: The Gulf Cooperation Council approved a proposal to create a monetary union and move toward a single currency
- 2009: Russia says the World needs a New Currency
- 2009: China begins to discuss a New World Currency
- 2009: Gordon Brown says a New World Order is Emerging from the current Global Economic crisis
- 2009: Protestors in Europe begin chanting "Abolish Money"
- 2009: The U.N. calls for a New Global Currency
- 2010: Russia's President pledges to help spur on a New Economic Order
- 2010: The International Monetary System begins talks on a global currency
- 2010: Debit Card Spending overtakes Cash Spending
- 2010: The International Monetary Fund predicts a New World Order and strives to become the new global financial authority
- 2011: The Vatican Calls for Oversight of the World's Finances

## CNN: Vatican: New World Economic Order

*Blitzer: Some are calling them radical ideas by the Catholic Church to fix the global economic crisis. Our Lisa Sylvester reports.*

*Sylvester: The division between the haves and have nots is long central to the Catholic Church. Now the Vatican is picking up on the momentum and speaking out on what it calls the idolatry of the market. For the first time, the Vatican has outlined what it sees as a moral fix for the problem of poverty. A proposal to create a new financial authority including a Global Central Bank and a new tax on global financial transactions.*

*Rev. Thomas Reese: Globalization has made us all in the same boat and we're gonna either sink together or we're gonna prosper. But we're only gonna do that if we work together as a wealth community to deal with these issues.*

- 2011: The head of the International Monetary Fund warns that unless the World Economies band together we risk "losing a whole decade" of financial recovery
- 2012: U.S. said to be Headed Over a Fiscal Cliff
- 2012: Google launches a new "Wallet" application that provides the convenience of a "single tap" on one's phone to buy products and services
- 2013: China shows signs of rapidly becoming the new world's economic superpower
- 2013 The U.S. and the European Union launched talks to create a new free trade alliance that would be the most ambitious ever, encompassing half the world's economic output and a third of the global trade[2]

So we're almost there, having true global trade abilities, as well as linking all our Economies together. But here's the point. Correct me if I'm wrong but when you take a look at the timeline, I'd say somebody's not only pretty serious about forming this *One World Economy*, but by the looks of it, they're just about ready to pull the whole thing off, how about you? And that's exactly what the Bible said would happen, when you are living in the Last Days!

But you might be thinking, "Hey man, come on, there's no way America's going to go along with this! This is crazy! This is just some wacky conspiracy theory stuff! There's no way our leaders here in America would ever undermine our country's monetary system and go along with a One World Economy! That's insane! It not only goes against the sovereignty of our nation, but it'll totally destroy us!"

**II. The 2nd proof** that we know we really are headed for a One World Economy is what I call the **Fear & Manipulation Proof.**

Believe it or not, they're using the same tactic we saw with a One World Government to get the job done for a One World Economy! It's called fear and manipulation. Again, put yourself in the Antichrist's shoes. If you're going to deceive the whole world into creating not only a One World Government but now with a One World Economy...then you first have to get everybody on the planet into a total state of fear, right? Why? Because as we saw before, once you get people into a state of fear you can manipulate them. The Antichrist is not dumb! He knows what he's doing! He knows historically people are more apt to surrender their freedoms in a time of fear than in a time of peace. So, if you create a crisis, *even an economic one*, globally, you can manage the global outcome. You can manipulate people into doing whatever you want them to do whether they realize it or not!

And this is precisely what's been happening to our country, if you've been paying attention, for the last several years economically! We not only have a "health-care crisis," a "child care crisis," a "food crisis," a "water crisis," a "terrorist crisis," an "environmental crisis" but we also have that dreaded never-ending ongoing "economic crisis," right? Everything is a horrible crisis including the economy just waiting to explode and because of these "economic crises" that are seemingly out of control, all over the world, we have been manipulated, whether we realize it or not, into a constant state of fear and we're starting to cry out for what they want us to cry out for. Some global entity, some global savior, some Global Universal Monetary System that'll fix all these global economic problems so we can get our prosperity back! We've been duped! Now you might think, "Come on, does this lying deceitful fear tactic really work on people, to get them to surrender their freedoms and go along with a One World Economy?" Uh, you bet it does! In fact, these guys admit we have been deliberately pushed over the edge, on purpose, to get us to this point of no return, to create a One World Economy.

*Ok Roger, you're special subject tonight is the economies of the European community. Your time starts now. Best of luck.*

**Roger:** *Ok.*

*How much does Greece owe, Roger?*

**Roger:** *Uh, 367 Billion dollars.*

*Correct. Now who do they owe it to?*

**Roger:** *Mostly to the other European economies.*

*Correct. How much does Ireland owe?*

**Roger:** *865 Billion.*

*Correct. And who do they owe it to?*

**Roger:** *Other European economies, mostly.*

*Correct. How much does Spain and Italy owe?*

**Roger:** *One trillion dollars each.*

*Correct. Who to?*

**Roger:** *Mainly France, Britain and Germany.*

*Correct. And how are Germany, France and Britain going, Roger?*

**Roger:** *Well they're struggling a bit, aren't they.*

*Correct. Why?*

**Roger:** *Because they've lent all these vast amounts of money to other European economies that can't possibly pay them back.*

*Correct. So what are they going to do?*

**Roger:** *They're going to have to bail them out.*

*Correct. Where are they getting the money to do that, Roger?*

**Roger:** *<chuckles> That's a good question. I don't know the answer to that one!*

*How much does Portugal owe?*

**Roger:** *Now hang on a minute. What was the answer to that earlier question.*

*Just keep answering the questions, Roger. Where is Portugal going to get the money it owes to Germany, if Germany can't get back the money it lent to Italy.*

**Roger:** *Just a minute. What was the answer to the previous question. The question was-how can broke economies lend money to other broke economies that haven't got any money because they can't pay back the money the broke economy lent to the other broke economy and shouldn't have lent it to them in the first place because the broke economy can't pay it back!*

*You're wasting very valuable time, Roger. How much does Spain owe Italy?*

*Roger: 41 Billion dollars, but where are they going to get it?*

*Correct. What does Italy owe to Spain?*

*Roger: 27 Billion. But they haven't got it, they're broke.*

*Correct. How can they pay each other if neither of them has any money.*

*Roger: They're gonna get a bail out, aren't they?*

*Correct. And where's the money coming from for bailout?*

*Roger: THAT'S WHAT I'M ASKING YOU!"*[3]

Now that would be funny, if it weren't so true! But here's the point. Sure doesn't sound like we're going to come out of this one, does it? I'm telling you, that's precisely what they want! This thing has been created! Why? Because again, they know us. People are more apt to surrender their freedoms in times of fear than in times of peace. Therefore, if you create a crisis, even an economic one, you can manage the economy of the whole planet. In other words, you get to create your One World Economy with fear and manipulation! It's working like a charm! And for those of you who don't believe me, it's already led to a *Universal Bank.* Again, put yourself into the Antichrist's shoes. He's not dumb! He knows if you're going to get the whole world to go along with a One World Economy, then you first have to have some sort of *Global Banking System* to oversee the whole operation, right? Well what do you think the United Nations and countries around the world have been working on for decades and have put in place over this last Economic Crisis? *Right now,* there is already in place the plans for absolute total economic control of the whole world. Right now, there's *already* a Universal Bank as we saw in the timeline called the *World Bank* which is the world's leading lender of money to the nations around the planet.

But wait a minute. If you're going to have a universal bank then you need a *Universal Lending Institution* to oversee the dispersion of loans, right? Well what do you think is the function of the *International Monetary Fund* which oversees the whole world's financial system and even fixes the exchange rates.

But wait a minute. If you're going to have a universal lending institution then you need a *Universal Money Exchanger* to funnel all this money to all the different countries, right? Well, guess what? Right now there's a Universal Electronic Banking System called *SWIFT*, which automatically makes sure that all the different money transactions in the world match all the different currencies.

But wait a minute. If you're going to have a universal money exchanger then you need to have a *Universal Strong Arm* to punish those who don't obey this World Banking System, right? That's why, *right now*, there's the *World Trade Organization* which not only sets the trading rules for the world, but they punish all countries who do not obey with billion dollar fines.[4]

So again, correct me if I'm wrong, but it sure sounds to me like if you put all this together, I'd say somebody's not only pretty serious about forming a *One World Economy*, but it sure looks like they're just about ready to pull it off and they're using fear and manipulation, to get us to go along with it!

### III. The 3rd proof that we know we really are headed for a One World Economy is the Quotation Proof.

Lest you think I'm making this whole thing up and I downloaded this from "wackyconspiracyguy.org" you tell me if this is not their plans! If you don't think the world leaders are really using this latest Economic Crisis to create a One World Economy, then don't take my word for it, listen to theirs! Ever since that crash, world leaders immediately began using that event as an excuse to say, "We've got to come together to form a *Global Economy* to prevent this from ever happening again!"

**Prime Minister Gordon Brown:** "The international financial crisis has given world leaders a unique opportunity to create a truly global society. Britain, the United States and Europe are key to forging a New World Order. Uniquely in this global age, it is now in our power to come together so that 2008 is remembered not just for the failure of a financial crash that engulfed the world. We can together seize this moment of change in our world to create a truly global society."

**President George W. Bush:** "It is essential that we work together because we are in this crisis together. Together we will work to modernize and strengthen our nations' financial systems so we can help ensure this crisis doesn't happen again."

**European Commission President Manuel Barroso:** "We need a new global financial order."

**German Chancellor Angela Merkel:** "It is time to rethink the world's financial system and prevent any repetition of the current crisis."

**Morgan Stanley Chief Executive John Mack:** "We need a new global body to oversee the financial crisis", warning that it is like "nothing he's ever seen before."

**Timothy Geithner president of the Federal Reserve:** "We need a new global monetary authority, a de-facto global financial dictatorship, operating across borders and forcing nations and corporations to register and adhere to strict monitoring and regulations."

**China:** They are calling for a new global currency controlled by the International Monetary Fund, stepping up pressure to global leaders, for changes to the financial system.

**Russia:** Is calling for a new international currency system and wants to overhaul the entire global financial order and even introduce a new supra-national currency to avoid future global financial crises.

**United Nations:** They are proposing the biggest overhaul of the world's monetary system since WWII by calling for a new global currency.

**Banks:** The Institute of International Finance, a group that represents 420 of the world's largest banks and finance houses, has issued yet another call for a one-world global currency. They are encouraging a return to a commitment to utilize International Monetary Fund special drawing rights to create an international one-world currency.

**Single Global Currency Association:** Are calling for the world to embrace a Single Global Currency to be managed by a Global Central Bank within a Global Monetary Union. If the European Monetary Union can successfully provide stable currency to countries, why not a Global Monetary Union for all countries? "We shall achieve this goal through education and persuasion."[5]

Or as Revelation 13 puts it "We're going to force, order and make you do it!" But here's the point. They admit it! They're using this latest Global Crisis to create a *One World Economy* and a *One World Currency*. In fact, they're not only calling for a One World Economy and a One World Currency, but they're even calling for a **Global Tax** on all the countries on the whole planet! Just when you thought you paid enough, you ain't seen nothing yet!

**UN wants Global Tax**

*Neil Cavuto: Have ya heard about this doozy, because before Iran apparently blows up the world, the United Nations wants to hit up the world with a tax, actually lots of taxes. To cover everything from fighting climate change to fighting poverty. There's talk of a billionaires tax, a global carbon emissions tax, even plans for a world bank transaction tax. I have no idea what that one's for. But the fact that the White House apparently isn't saying BOO about it-any of it makes some wonder whether we, in the United States, should be worried about it. Former U.K. parliament member John Brown says we should. He's with me now. This is weird but can the U.N. actually do this?*

*John Brown: Well only if it's supported by the members and of course it's a most open, surprisingly open and aggressive bid for world government. But of course it fits exactly with Obama's strategy which he openly declares his redistribution of wealth from the successful to the less successful from within the United States. But this goes on a whole long step further. This is redistribution of American and European wealth to the Third World. I mean it's nasty enough to pay taxes for a huge government that you think interferes with your life. But to pay and throw it around the whole world?*

*Cavuto: But, then there will be no place to escape*

*Brown: Absolutely! And that's what they want. World Government. No place to escape.*

As well as an economy that will force you into it. And believe it or not, you may not even hear the news of this taking place before it's too late. One man states:

*"The jury is still out on which way the United States will go on the issue of global economic control by the UN. Most Americans will never know the issue is on the table until after the decisions are made. The media is not likely to address*

*the issue, nor is it likely to be a topic of congressional debate. These events are taking place in other parts of the world with decisions being made by officials who are not elected by anyone. No elected official in the United States has any authority to alter or veto these decisions. The world is moving swiftly toward global governance.* "[6]

AND a Global Economy. Where have I heard that before? Oh yeah, that's right! That's what the Bible said would happen when you are living in the Last Days! And lest there be any misunderstanding that this One World Economy is truly generated by the Antichrist and his satanic buddies, let's remind ourselves where it's all heading and why the Bible calls it satanic. It's not just about forming a One World Economy, but a Cashless Economic System that leads to total economic slavery!

**Revelation 13:16-17** "He also forced everyone, small and great, rich and poor, free and slave, to receive a mark on his right hand or on his forehead, so that no one could buy or sell unless he had the mark, which is the name of the beast or the number of his name."

The Bible clearly tells us that the Antichrist's economic system is not only going to be over the whole world, but in order to be a part of that system you have to have some sort of a Mark into your right hand or forehead, to buy or sell, right? But hey, good thing we don't see any signs of people taking a Mark into their bodies to make payments for anything…they…buy…or…sell…right? Yeah, right! It's already here! For the first time in the history of mankind, we not only have the technology to pull of this Mark of the Beast or Antichrist system, but we even have people who are *already doing it*! This is how close we are! How are these night clubbers in Europe making payments? How do they buy and sell? Let's take a look!

**Baja Beach Club**

*At the Baja Beach Club in Rotterdam, Holland, this may look like a regular party but it's no normal club. The Baja has an elite group of special VIP's who are different from other clients. They need no identification and no cash to buy drinks or food. To enter the club all they have to do is offer up an arm to a scanner and tonight, 21 year old Ryoni Schoutin is joining the "in" crowd. He's getting an electronic chip implanted in his arm. It's called Radio Frequency Identification. An RFID chip is a small device that transmits a radio signal that's read by a scanner. In 2003, the Attorney General of Mexico and some of his staff received RFID implants inside their bodies to allow them access to sensitive areas.*

*Each tiny chip has a number. A scanner connected to a database can instantly reveal who the person is and much more. Technically, there's no limit to the information the database can hold.*

*The chip itself is a little larger than a grain of rice. It will remain inside Ryoni's body for the rest of his life. The chip is implanted just millimeters below the skin. If it goes in too close to the muscle, the muscle could be damaged and Ryoni will feel the chip when he moves. If all goes well, he won't even know it's there. The procedure is over in seconds and now it's time to party. Although others have to pay cash at the entrance, when Ryoni arrives, his name and number instantly identify him as a member of the club. He makes his way to the VIP deck and uses his implant to buy a drink. The Baja is a glimpse of a not so distant future. Already, some people have chips with critical health information. Something that soon everyone will have that will identify them and allow a new form of surveillence."*[7]

And total economic slavery! You won't be able to buy or sell without it! Is that Revelation 13 before our very eyes or what? So much for a wacky conspiracy theory! This is all happening right now, it's not make believe, it's real and we better get motivated. It's exactly what the Bible said would happen, when you are living in the Last Days! *It just happens to be happening now*!

**IV. The 4ᵗʰ proof that we know we really are headed for a One World Economy is what I call the Union Proof.**

That's right, I'm not talking about the teamsters, believe it or not it's something way worse than that! I'm talking about Economic Unions that the Bible said would come in the Last Days! But don't take my word for it. Let's listen to God's.

**Revelation 17:5-13** "This calls for a mind with wisdom. The seven heads are seven hills on which the woman sits. They are also seven kings. Five have fallen, one is, the other has not yet come; but when he does come, he must remain for a little while. The beast who once was, and now is not, is an eighth king. He belongs to the seven and is going to his destruction. The ten horns you saw are ten kings who have not yet received a kingdom, but who for one hour will receive authority as kings along with the beast. They have one purpose and will give their power and authority to the beast."

Now according to the Bible, we see how the Antichrist's kingdom is going to be split up into ten different parts ruled by ten different kings or leaders, right? Then, at one point, they surrender their power and authority over to him, right? It says it right there. Use your mind of wisdom! But here's the point. It's a good thing we see no signs of that happening today! The planet being split up into…10 different…kingdoms… Yeah, right! It's happening *right now*! We already saw they're already creating 10 World Regions to ensure proper Economic control of the whole world and it's not just 5, not 19, not even 122, but exactly *10*! Where have I heard that before?

I'm telling you, we have been slowly and methodically prepared for this. For instance, in our lifetime we saw the birth of the European Union, one of the 10 chunks, right? And what is that? Isn't that a *region* of countries coming together economically with their own currency called the Euro? That seemed to be the kick-off event because we now have the formation of the African Union which is a *region* of countries coming together in Africa economically with their own currency. Then there's even plans for a South American Union, an Asian Union, a Mediterranean Union, a Central Asian Union, a Pacific Union and even a North American Union between Canada, United States and Mexico and we'll get to that in a little bit.[8] But here's the point. If I didn't know better, I'd say the world's being split up into different economic regions *right now* right before our very eyes and I'm thinking they're going to end up with…**ten**, how about you?

Then if that wasn't scary enough, we not only see the world being split up into 10 different economic unions that the Bible said would happen in the Last Days, but we even have the birth of the Revived Roman Empire that the prophet Daniel said would come in the Last Days! It happened with the signing of the Lisbon Treaty that hardly anybody has even heard of! This recently happened!

### Jimmy DeYoung on the Revived Roman Empire

*Mrs. Clinton, when she met with Katherine Ashton, said that this was unbelievable what had happened. It was historic. You know most people in America never even heard what was going on in the European Union, with the Lisbon Treaty being ratified on November the 3rd. And on the 19th of November. These two elected leaders taking charge of the European Union. In fact, Mrs. Clinton made this statement, "That decades from now we'll look back on this historic event" the treaty being ratified, the election of the leaders.*

*She called it a major milestone in the world's history and I think it is. I remember back when the treaty was finally ratified, we made the statement-Watch in January. Things are going to move quickly- And that's where the E.U. is going. It's going together as Europe as a single unified country instead of 27 nation states. It is, I believe, a major milestone and we're starting to see it open before our eyes. The nationalities of the individual countries are disappearing. The sovereignty-they're giving up sovereign rights over their citizens. So what you have is a move from 27 states of the world that is sort of like a Federation, although it's not a true Federation. Moving to a single country, which now encompasses land area almost all of the former Roman Empire. And if we add the neighborhood policy relationships if you will, between the E.U. and the Mediterranean states, we are starting to see a Roman Empire forming.*

*Daniel chapter 7:7 talks about 10 horns on the awesome beast known as the Roman Empire. Those 10 horns according to Daniel 7:24 will be the revived Roman Empire who will come to power soon after the Rapture of the church. The revived Roman Empire will play a key role in the geo-political communities of this world. But the Bible says prophetically in Daniel 2:44, in the days of these kings and the dates of the revival of the old Roman Empire, look up, Jesus Christ is about to come and set up His Kingdom that will be for a thousand years and then into eternity future. I believe we are living in that time period. But before the revived Roman Empire can come back on the scene, the Rapture of the Church must take place and I think that that could happen at any time-even today! Hope you're ready to see Jesus Christ face to face at the Rapture of the Church.'"*[9]

And I hope you're not left behind! This is all happening, it's not make believe, it's all happening right before our very eyes for the first time in 2,000 years! A Revived Roman Empire is being put into place *right now*, just like the Bible said would happen in the Last Days! In fact, speaking of a Revived Roman Empire, we are now also seeing how Europe is wanting to elect a President to oversee all this Revived Roman Empire and it's not just any President but listen, a "New *Super* President" that would be the overall powerful leader of Europe, with responsibility over Europe's economic matters, all foreign policy and any European military operation. You know, *absolute total control* of a newly Revived Roman Empire! That's what they want right now! But that's still not all. You talk about being *ripe* for the Antichrist who's going to take charge of this Revived Roman Empire, as we just saw, but we are also seeing the planet readily admitting that they are totally willing to follow an actual Antichrist even if he's the devil in disguise!

*"This chilling quote is from Paul-Henri Spaak, former Belgian Prime Minister and the President of the Consultative Assembly of the Council of Europe. Here's what he said:*

*'We do not want another committee. We have too many already. What we want is a man of sufficient stature to hold the allegiance of all people and to lift us out of the economic morass in which we are sinking. Send us such a man and be he God or the devil, we will receive him.'"*[10]

You put all this together, it sure looks to me like the planet is being split up into ten different economic kingdoms, there's a Revived Roman Empire coming and people *right now* across the planet are ready to follow some man, any man, who will lead this empire just as long as he brings peace and prosperity, *even if he's the devil in disguise…*where have I heard that before? Oh yeah, that's what the Bible said would happen when you're living in the Last Days.

**V. The 5th proof** that we know we really are headed for a One World Economy is what I call the **American Proof.**

You see, what many people do unfortunately is they assume that America "should" be in Bible prophecy because after all, we're one of the world's leading powers today, right? I mean, we've got to be in there, right? Not necessarily. In fact, I'd say no, not in a positive sense anyway and we'll get to that in a second. But what people unfortunately do is they try to "squeeze" America into several Prophecy texts, when in reality it has nothing to do with us. Let me show you what I mean.

**1. The 1st passage** they try to squeeze America into is **Isaiah 18** and the **Tall Smooth Skinned People.**

**Isaiah 18:7** "At that time gifts will be brought to the LORD Almighty from a people tall and smooth-skinned, from a people feared far and wide, an aggressive nation of strange speech, whose land is divided by rivers – the gifts will be brought to Mount Zion, the place of the Name of the LORD Almighty."

Well there you have it! Isaiah 18 is clearly talking about a tall and smooth people who are feared far and wide that live in a nation that is divided by a river. It's got to be America! We're separated by the Mississippi River and we're powerful and we're filled with people who are tall, so this has got to be speaking of us, right? I know that's what people want it to mean, I know that's what they hope it means, but that's not at all what the context means! First of all, the context is talking about the land of Cush, which if you do your homework is modern-day Ethiopia, which means the river dividing this nation is the river Nile. So no, as much as you'd like to think so, it has nothing to do with America.

**2. The 2ⁿᵈ passage they try to squeeze America into is Ezekiel 38 and the Village of Tarshish.**

**Ezekiel 38:13** "Sheba and Dedan and the merchants of Tarshish and all her villages will say to you, 'Have you come to plunder? Have you gathered your hordes to loot, to carry off silver and gold, to take away livestock and goods and to seize much plunder?'"

Well there you have it! Some people would actually say, this passage here in the context about the Gog and Magog Battle, is talking about the United States of America. I mean, Tarshish they say has got to be England and the villages mentioned here must be speaking of England's colonies, you know, like the United States, right? It's got to be us! That's what people want it to mean, but that's not at all what the context means! First of all, the people in Ezekiel's time considered Tarshish to be Spain and so that would make the villages or colonies spoken here the nations of South and Central America, even if you wanted to look at it that way. So either way, no, as much as you'd like to think so, it has nothing to do with America.

**3. The 3ʳᵈ passage they try to squeeze America into is Revelation 12 and the Great Eagle.**

**Revelation 12:13-14** "When the dragon saw that he had been hurled to the earth, he pursued the woman who had given birth to the male child. The woman was given the two wings of a great eagle, so that she might fly to the place prepared for her in the desert, where she would be taken care of for a time, times and half a time, out of the serpent's reach."

Well there you have it! Revelation 12 and the Great Eagle, it's got to be America! I mean, after all, one of our prominent national symbols is the Eagle…it's got to be us who rescues Israel, right? That's what people want it to mean, but that's not at all what the context means! First of all, all you have to do is do your homework and go back to Exodus 19 where it says, "*God* carried Israel on 'eagles' wings," which means *God* rescued them in the first Exodus, so He's going to do it again in this next one. So no, as much as you'd like to think so, the Great Eagle has nothing to do with America.

**4. The 4ᵗʰ passage they try to squeeze America into is Revelation 17 and the Great Prostitute.**

**Revelation 17:1-2** "One of the seven angels who had the seven bowls came and said to me, 'Come, I will show you the punishment of the great prostitute, who sits on many waters. With her the kings of the earth committed adultery and the inhabitants of the earth were intoxicated with the wine of her adulteries.'"

So there you have it! The Great Prostitute spoken here is clearly speaking of America. I mean after all, we rule over many waters and we export all kinds of rotten adulterous material to the whole world, right? It's got to be us! Yes, we do, do that unfortunately, but that's not what this passage is talking about. First of all, the context is speaking of Babylon the Great, the one-world *religious* harlot system that comes against Israel and is also in conjunction with the political system of the Antichrist and yes, maybe America has unfortunately been showing signs of turning their backs on Israel and we'll get to that in a second, but we're not the Antichrist's empire that controls the entire world. As we just saw earlier, it's clear the Antichrist does NOT rise out of the United States. He comes out of the Revived Roman Empire, which is being formed right before our very eyes in *Europe*, not here. So no, as much as you'd like to think so, Revelation 17 has nothing to do with America.[11]

So the question is, "Does America appear in Bible Prophecy at all?" I would say maybe, only in judgment. If you look at Isaiah 34, he declares that *all the nations* that come against Israel in the Last Days will be judged. So if we fall anywhere in Bible prophecy, I'd say it's this. Unfortunately one day, the United States will no longer be a *friend* to Israel and will actually become an *enemy* instead and will be judged by God for this behavior! But hey, good thing we see no signs…of…that…happening…any…time soon. Yeah right! What was the Obama administration doing? They turned their back on Israel like never before!

We're in a heap o' trouble! But, speaking of judgment, I not only see America heading towards unfortunate destruction like Isaiah 34 warns, but I also see us disappearing from Bible Prophecy through a process of *integration.* In other words, we're going to be "swallowed up" or "integrated" into one of the 10 Economic Unions that Revelation 17 talks about and for those of you who don't believe me, I've got proof.

**A. The 1st proof** we know America is going to be swallowed up by an Economic Union is the **Currency Proof.**

Believe it or not, *right now* there have been talks and plans for many years now for the United States to be merged into what's called the North American Union. This proposed "union" would be made up of the United States, Canada and Mexico and have a new currency called the *Amero.* Believe it or not, it was leaked out several years ago on a financial news broadcast. You tell me if somebody's not serious about this.

**CNBC interview on the Amero**

*Steve, we also just heard from Paul Chuck, although he does expect the dollar to weaken into Christmas against the Euro. Do you think that momentum will impact any other asset classes?*

***Steve Previs:*** *Well, I'll tell you, take a look at the precious metals that have taken off on the upside, on the back of this dollar drop. We're coming into an encyclical bottom for gold and it rises going into December/January. So that might be the reverse of the dollar fall. Apart from that, I think people who are dollar based need to focus on the Amero. That's the one thing that nobody is talking about but I think it is going to have a big impact on everybody's life in Canada, the U.S. and Mexico. If you Google it, you will find out all about it.*

*Well you can tell us a bit more about it right now.*

***Previs:*** *You always hear it on CNBC. <laughing> The Amero is the proposed new currency for the North American community which is being developed right now between Canada, U.S. and Mexico to make a borderless community much like the E.U. and the dollar-the Canadian dollar, the U.S. dollar and the Mexican peso replaced by the Amero.*

*Do you really think that will get any leeway?*

**Previs:** *Ah, you may want to visit a couple websites and see how far along it is. The Canadians are pretty upset about it, where as the Americans apart from the Texans who know anything about it, the rest of the public is really with their head in the sand on this one."*[12]

Hmmm. You mean to tell me that the United States, Canada and Mexico are going to have a new currency called the *Amero*, and we're going to be pushed into an Economic Union the Bible said would come in the Last Days? But come on! That's just some wacky conspiracy stuff! Really? Makes you start to wonder why the two main languages taught in schools for many years have been either French (you know Canadian) and Spanish (for Mexico). Maybe they've been working on this for a long time.

**B. The 2nd proof** we know we're headed for an Economic Union in the Last Days is the **Highway Proof.**

You see, right after that video came out on the Amero, there were tons of people scoffing about it saying this is all just a bunch of baloney, this is some wacky conspiracy theory stuff and that guy just happened to make a mistake, *live TV* and just got caught up in the hype on the Internet that you can't trust in the first place. Really? Well, it's one thing to scoff at a news broadcast talking about the Amero, but what do you do with all the other news broadcasts that talk about a new highway that connects all three countries? How do you explain that one?

**NAFTA Lou Dobbs**

**Lou Dobbs:** *Open border advocates are refusing to acknowledge rising evidence of a NAFTA Superhighway. Many in the Mainstream Media absolutely refuse to acknowledge the reality. The plans could be a major step towards that North American Union of the United States, Canada and Mexico. President Bush said that opponents of a NAFTA Superhighway in his view are laying out a conspiracy. Senator Obama says he sees no evidence of a North American Union. Even some news organizations are criticizing me for raising the issue. Time Magazine journals Joe Klein accused me of quote "spewing false and inflammatory nonsense." So we asked Bill Tucker to report on the issue. He found that there's plenty of evidence for plans for new transportation links between Mexico and Canada and only in my opinion, a fool would refuse to see* *those links.*

**Bill Tucker:** *There is no NAFTA Superhighway. Not officially. Some even call it the invention of the far right wing. But some politicians find the denials almost laughable.*

**Rep. Ted Poe:** *The folks in Washington are in denial about the NAFTA Superhighway or whatever you want to call it. It's the concept that there will be a highway-freetrade-from Mexico through the central part of the United States, all the way to Canada.*

**Tucker:** *In Texas, planning and development is underway for what are officially called "Transportation Corridors". The Trans Texas Corridor. I-69, a combination of railines, utility lines, car and truck lanes, plan to be as wide as three football fields laid end to end. It will be financed by a private foreign company, most likely Spain Centra, who will then own the lease on the road and the revenue generated by the tolls. Texas may use Eminent Domain to lay claim to some of the land needed to build it. For an imaginary road, there is a lot of money and effort involved and some very real opposition.*

*Large group of protesters marching and shouting: WE DON'T WANT THIS CORRIDOR!"*[13]

But we all know those people are marching against something totally non-existent and is nothing but a wacky conspiracy…theory…yeah, right! Did you notice a company in Europe, in Spain will control the whole thing?

## C. The 3rd proof we know America is headed for an Economic Union in the Last Days is the Political Proof.

You see, believe it or not, I know it might be a tough cookie to swallow, but we've got to deal with the facts. There is treason in high places in our country today! And for those of you who still want to scoff at this Amero talk and NAFTA Super Highway and combining all three countries into a North American Union, all you need to do is look at the *political proof.* If they weren't serious about doing this, then why have all of the Presidents from all three different countries been meeting together for years and talking about it? I mean, if you're not serious about it, why do you keep meeting together making plans for it, as far back as the *Bush administration!*[14] But hey, maybe that was just the

Bush administration. I mean, after all, the media clearly thought he was kind of loopy anyway. I'm sure the President of Mexico had no plans for this...really? You might want to check this out. Mexamericanada.

## MexAmeriCanada

*Beck: Now four years ago, I bet I was a lot like you. I started paying attention to the border crisis and I thought to myself-why is this happening? I mean it doesn't even make sense. I thought we thought about security. Well since I couldn't apply logic in understanding what was happening on the border, I started looking for alternative theories and it took me down lanes I didn't want to go. But honestly, I mean who's watching the border? Who would benefit from these things screwed up. I hate to break it to you but after 2 years of denying it and saying this can't be, it's the only reason I have found that explains everything that's going on in our country with the border. Our country has been sold out in the name of global profits and votes at the ballot box. This is where the Security and Prosperity Partnership of North America or SPP comes in. This little agreement, international agreement, cooked up by President Bush, the former President of Mexico and the Prime Minister of Canada. Their mission is to blur or completely erase the borders between Canada, U.S. and Mexico to get goods and services freely flowing between all three countries in the dream of one big happy MexAmeriCanada and that would finally become a reality. Sound great? Not so much.*

*On Larry King live, where everybody like you, like me who've been saying now wait a minute I don't want to believe this, but it looks like it's happening. We've all been called crazy. This is what Vicente Fox said on Larry King live. Roll the tape.*

*Vicente Fox: What we propose together, President Bush and myself, it's ALCA which is trade union for all of the Americans.*

*Larry King: You mean like the Euro dollar?*

*Fox: Well that would be long, long term. I think that the process is to go first step in trading agreement. And then further on, a new vision like we're trying to do with NAFTA.*

*Beck: He says in this interview that he's asked, "So it would be like the Euro dollar?" "Well long, long term". I was with one of the country's leading economists, having dinner the other night and I said what point do you start-and this guy's an optimist- I said at what point do you start worrying about the dollar. And he said, "Glenn, about six months ago" He said its "almost like we're intentionally destroying the dollar."*[15]

Hmmm. Maybe because we're being prepared to receive a new currency combined with all three countries. But hey, maybe that's just Mexico and the United States. I'm sure Canada would never go along…with…this…really? Well actually, their leadership is saying "surrendering your National Sovereignty is the right thing to do to secure a new future!"

## Global Governance Ottawa: Prime Minister Paul Martin

***Paul Martin:*** *Let me close with just one more thing on this question of sovereignty. It's very difficult for a large country to accept that somebody is going to come in, like the United States or like the Europeans, and is basically going to come in and say, "You're not doing your regulation in a proper way." Fair game. But what's going to happen when China and India are economies as powerful as the United States or Europe. And what's going to happen when there's a mortgage meltdown in India. What's going to happen when a Chinese hedge fund goes under and the results of that tsunami don't stop at the Chinese or Indian border. But that in fact you find them in Idaho or Iowa and California. Who's going to deal with that? Unless we're prepared to understand that in fact we're all going to have to give up a little bit of our sovereignty in order to make the world work."*[16]

In order to form a New Economic Union between Canada, United States and Mexico that will be one of the 10 Economic Unions the Bible said would come in the Last Days. Okay, but maybe that was just the Bush administration and era. I mean, our former President promised all kinds of *change* but I'm sure this is not the kind of change he was talking about…is he?

## North American Union

***Lou Dobbs:*** *Well another announcement today by President-elect Obama, giving new life to the North America Union. A plan by business and political elites to tear down the trade barriers among the United States, Canada and Mexico and to create a NAFTA Superhighway. All of which to be done without the approval* *of Congress or the American people. President-elect Obama named a diehard free trader and a NAFTA supporter to be his U.S Trade Representative. Bill Tucker has our report.*

**Bill Tucker:** *Ron Kirk is President-elect Obama's pick to be frontman on trade. Kirk made his name in politics serving as Mayor in Dallas where he was known as a staunch supporter of free trade agreements, NAFTA in particular. He was a big proponent of a trade corridor from Mexico up through Texas. A road he once referred to as a NAFTA freeway.*
*His nomination was welcomed by the U.S Chamber of Commerce and the National Association of Manufacturers. Advocates for a change in trade policy are not so happy.*

*Now the apparent contradiction in Obama's words and actions has activists on another front worried. Last February, Obama pledged that he would resume the Security and Prosperity Partnership talks between Mexico and Canada that President Bush initiated. He also said that the talks will be 'transparent'. Those opposed to the North American Union say that now whether he will or will not deliver on that promise becomes something they doubt, Lou.*

**Dobbs:** *Well this is, this is..early on, the President-elect is starting to look like when it comes to trade, as Lori Wallach, a public citizen pointed out, Global Trade Watch, I mean the old boss is starting to look a lot like the new boss."*[17]

In other words, it doesn't matter what President we have or what party gets elected, they're all in it together and they're all working at destroying our great country, The United States of America. It's not only treasonous, but it's fulfilling Bible Prophecy before our very eyes. It's allowing us to be swallowed up into one of these 10 Economic Unions that the Bible said would appear on the scene when you're living in the Last Days! No wonder we're not found in Bible Prophecy, other than judgment! We got integrated! This is all happening right now before our very eyes.

**VI. The 6th proof** that we know we really are headed for a One World Economy is the **Currency Proof.**

That's right, I'm talking about a *Cashless Society* and believe it or not, that's exactly what the Antichrist is going to need to pull off his Last Days

Society and Mark of the Beast! But don't take my word for it. Let's listen to God's.

**Revelation 13:11-17** "Then I saw another beast, coming out of the earth. He had two horns like a lamb, but he spoke like a dragon. He exercised all the authority of the first beast on his behalf, and made the earth and its inhabitants worship the first beast, whose fatal wound had been healed. And he performed great and miraculous signs, even causing fire to come down from heaven to earth in full view of men. Because of the signs he was given power to do on behalf of the first beast, he deceived the inhabitants of the earth. He ordered them to set up an image in honor of the beast who was wounded by the sword and yet lived. He was given power to give breath to the image of the first beast, so that it could speak and cause all who refused to worship the image to be killed. He also forced everyone, small and great, rich and poor, free and slave, to receive a mark on his right hand or on his forehead, so that no one could buy or sell unless he had the mark, which is the name of the beast or the number of his name."

Now as we saw before, according to our text, there really is coming a day when all the inhabitants of the earth will be under the *Universal Economy* or monetary system of the Antichrist himself, right? He's literally going to control all the buying and selling. One day, believe it or not, the whole world will be unified into a *One World Economy* that is actually *satanically inspired* and as we saw previously, that's exactly what's happening *right now* before our very eyes! BUT, that's not the only thing he's going to need to do to pull off this One World Economy and Mark of the Beast System. If you're paying attention there, if you think about it, he's not only going to have to combine all economies into one, but he has to combine all the *currencies* into one, right? In other words, he has to, at some point, make the money around the world electronic or *cashless*, right? Why? Because as we saw, he controls all the buying and selling with a what? A Mark in the right hand or forehead, right? So this tells us it *has to be* some form of "electronic" payment. It's common sense. I mean, you don't tape a dollar bill to your hand to make a payment here in this passage, or slap 20 bucks on your forehead to pay for your groceries. Obviously you've got to have some sort of electronic capability to make a financial transaction with the Mark of the Beast system either in your right hand or forehead, right? It's common sense! It's right there! So, here's the point. I don't know about you, but I am so glad we see no signs whatsoever of us ever going to some form of Cashless Society around the world that enables us to make electronic payments, even with our body parts, uh, yeah, the sarcasm reveals the truth! It's already here!

In fact if you think about it, we have slowly but surely been conditioned to move towards a coming cashless society that the Bible predicted would come in the Last Days. Let me give you some examples. *In the last century alone* we have gone from paper currency to electronic cash. It's happening very fast! For instance, if we didn't have any money on us, don't worry, just write a check. Then if we didn't have the money to write a check, don't worry, just charge it to a credit card. But if we didn't want to pay the interest on a credit card, don't worry, just take it out of your checking account with a debit card. As we already saw, it's so popular now that as of 2010, Debit Card spending overtook Cash as spending. We already LOVE this electronic transaction stuff! In fact, so much so that all these features have now been combined into one called a *smart card*. So what in the world is a smart card? Well, a smart card is about the size of a regular credit card only this one has a tiny microchip in it that can store and receive information and make financial transactions as well. And because of this feature, you can use them for all kinds of things.

- Personal ATM
- Purchases (at stores, restaurants, vending machines, gas, toll roads, etc.)
- Telephone calls
- Access to cable and satellite programs
- Internet purchases
- Vehicle and building access
- Personal computer access (replace all passwords)
- Loyalty programs (airlines, grocery stores, etc.)
- Rapid Check-in (hotels, airlines, etc.)
- Personal Identification Holder (Soc. Security, Driver's License, Student ID, Health and Insurance ID, voting information, picture, and fingerprints)[14]

All of that on one card? Isn't that nifty! That's not all. These kind of smart cards are already being called the "new digital cash" or "electronic purse" and they're expected to become the world's first truly universal currency. Why? Because it's all electronic! It's cashless! Who cares what country you come from or what currency you have, right? It can all now be interchanged electronically anywhere in the world. You can buy and sell anywhere on the planet for the first time in mankind's history with just one form of payment, an electronic one. Isn't that swell? In fact, believe it or not, pretty soon, you may have to use this card to pay for EVERYTHING! The Government's going to like this thing.

**Tax card**

*Man bolts upright in his bed as an alarm clock beeps annoyingly loud. Alarm shuts off only after man swipes his "tax card". Immediately clock displays "Tax PAID."*

*Man hops in his shower, but water won't turn on. Swipes the tax card and the water begins to come out of the showerhead.*

*Man is now in his kitchen and puts bread into the toaster, swipes the card again to allow him to toast his bread.*

*Man, dressed for work, heads to his car in the garage and swipes the tax card to allow him entry to his vehicle.*

*Man arrives at the Fuel and Tax Collection Station and swipes his Tax Card to get gas. Parks on street and swipes card for the parking meter, flashing "Tax Paid."*

*Gets to his cubical at work and tosses the Newspaper down with top story "New Window Tax". Flips open his laptop and swipes the tax card. Window opens up and says TAX PAID, Have a nice Day!*

*Man is running to the restroom and fumbles for the card again unlocking the stall door."*[19]

Now I don't know about you, but we're not too far from that already! I mean, won't it be great when we all convert to this Cashless Society? The government's going to love it! They'll tax us into oblivion. It's going to be a new form of *Economic Slavery*, or as the Bible puts it, you won't be able to buy or sell anything as you saw, without it. As weird as all this new technology sounds, these kind of cards are not only the rage in making payments, but *billions* of these cards are being issued *right now* and have been for many years! In fact, in Europe, *right now*, smart cards are not only commonplace but will soon become a necessity. England is expecting to have all governmental services online and will issue citizens with smart cards to access the system. You *have* to have one, just like we saw! And even here in the U.S. in light of the terrorist attacks, the Pentagon made smart cards *mandatory* for *millions* of troops and civilians for opening secure doors, getting cash, buying food and checking out weapons. Isn't that convenient![20]

But that's not all. They're not only using so-called convenience as a selling point, but *security* as well. I mean, can't you imagine if we would just get rid of all paper currency? Why, you talk about security! Think about it! We could reduce fear and get rid of all sorts of crimes!

*"The immediate benefits would be profound and fundamental. Theft of cash would become impossible. Bank robberies and cash-register robberies would simply cease to occur.*

*Attacks on shopkeepers, taxi drivers and cashiers would all end...Urban streets would become safer...Security costs and insurance rates would fall.*

*Property values would rise...Sales of illegal drugs, along with the violent crimes that follow, should diminish.*

*Hospital emergency rooms would become less crowded...A change from cash to recorded electronic money would be accompanied by a flow of previously unpaid income-tax revenues running in the tens of billions of dollars.*

*As a result, income-tax rates could be lowered or the national debt reduced."*[21]

Wow! Don't you feel safer already? We've got to do this! But that's still not all. A cashless society, they say, would not only provide a whole new sense of so-called convenience and security, but they say it'll provide a whole new sense of *flexibility*. Now who doesn't need more flexibility in these crazy fast times? You see this electronic cash can be used not just in a smart card, but even in your *cell phone*. Right now, cell phones are doubling as mobile cash machines to make purchases anywhere in the world from street vendors to pizza delivery and now, with the wave of your phone, which you know, you hold in your *hand*, you can buy just about anything from a boat to a burger. Another article states this:

*"Grabbing a burger is getting easier. Soon you will just have to wave your cell phone as you pass McDonald's drive-through. Immediate gratification is always the best marketing tool.*

*There is no dialing, no ATM, no fumbling for a wallet or dropped coins – only radio-frequency burgers.* "²²

Wow! Wouldn't that be awesome? Just to be able to wave my phone in my *hand* and make a payment for what I buy or sell. But you might be thinking, "Come on, people aren't really going to do that are they?" Well actually, it's become the latest craze!

**Point and Pay**

*Larry Bell: Well cell phones, as you know have evolved into tools used for more than simple phone calls.*

*Cheryl Jennings: Yeah, but don't you know you can use the cell phone to pick up a check at a restaurant or pay for a purchase at a store?*

*Larry Bell: That's incredible what they're doing now. 7 On Your Side's Michael Finney is here to show us how that's done exactly.*

*Michael Finney: Yeah, I think we can all agree cell phones don't do enough.*

*Bell: Yeah, take pictures, whatever.*

*Finney: Today's cell phone, you can check email, play games, take pictures and of course actually talk on one. But soon, they will also let you point and pay for things you want to buy.*

*Cell phones are intended to help you stay connected. Now they can help you breeze through the checkout line too.*

*Dave Archabald: It's great. It's very convenient.*

*Finney: Bill Archibald is using his cell phone to buy lunch. He simply puts his phone at a special receiver, hits pay and his bill is charged to his credit card.*

*Archabald: It saved me time and I think it made everybody else in line behind me happy.*

*Finney: All you have to do is call your credit card company to activate the program. They'll download your personal info right into a special chip that's already in your phone.*

***Greg McBride (Bankrate.com):*** *This chip contains the same type of information that the magnetic strip on the back of your credit card does.*

***Finney:*** *George Fernandez is with VioTech, a company developing this technology. He says it's not just your credit cards you'll be able to leave at home.*

***Fernandez:*** *It can be credit, debit or prepaid or any sort of card.*

***Finney:*** *Though it's convenient, experts say there may be a downside.*

***McBride:*** *Well the big risk is in the age of identity theft that if you lose your phone it's tantamount to losing your credit card or debit card."*[23]

Oooh! That wouldn't be good. Sounds like there's a security flaw in it. We'll get to that in just a second. But you might be thinking, "Well, come on! This is just some wacky conspiracy theory! There's no way people today are serious about going to a cashless society across the whole world, this will never catch on! Maybe some isolated places, but not the whole world!" Really? Well believe it or not, for the first time in mankind's history, we're not only seeing individuals jumping on the bandwagon to go to a cashless society, be it a card or a cell phone, but we even have *whole countries* who are promoting it and converting to it *right now!* Starting with Sweden.

**Sweden's cashless society**

***Linda Nyberg:*** *Karin Linder stocks up on supplies at the supermarket, but Karin, like most people here in Sweden, won't be paying with cash when she gets to the checkout.*

***Karin:*** *I personally never use cash. As you see here I'm shopping. I use my scanner. When I check out I'll use my credit card. And my banking, I do on my I-Phone. So that's it. I don't need any cash.*

***Nyberg:*** *And in Sweden, only about 3% of all transactions are now made with cash. The Swedes have always adapted quickly to new technology. They've been using internet banking for about 20 years. And mobile phone use is among the* *highest in the world. Sweden was the first country to use these: bank notes. But every year, less of these are being printed. And it seems like Sweden is on a journey to be completely cashless.*

**Nyberg:** *Most public transport is prepaid using a phone or a credit card. And big businesses are adapted to these services. By October, this bank in central Stockholm will be entirely cash free.*

**Daniel Wahlstroem (Danske Bank):** *It's most definitely consumer driven. We're seeing for quite some time that the need for cash based services has reduced and you look for 2009 to 2012, we actually reduced the number of teller transactions by 40%*

**Nyberg:** *Sweden's drive to be cashless marches on. And others in Europe are likely to follow.*

In other words, the whole world will eventually switch to it. Correct me if I'm wrong, but I'd say people, even whole countries are converting to a cashless society, how about you? Sweden's not the only one. I'm telling you, other countries are starting to go down the same route *right now*! Including Japan, Nigeria, Australia, and other countries in Europe are saying we too want to convert to a Cashless Society![24]

But that's still not all. Not to be left out, banks are also jumping on the bandwagon. Right now Credit Card companies are turning their cards into smart cards, which means, you may already have one and not even know it. That's not the only sneaky thing they're doing. Listen to this. Believe it, they're desperately trying to hide from you the fact that these Smart Cards are *not secure*! In fact, they're easy to rip off electronically!

**Skimming**

**Reporter:** *Sneaky crimes. Stealing credit cards and private information by a process called skimming. California just recently passed a law making it a crime. But for someone willing to break the law, these high tech cards have a privacy loophole that can make you an easy target. Jason Martinez, live in Hollywood to explain that one. Jason..*

**Martinez:** *First let me show you how these new credit cards work. They use the same technology as some of your work I.D. cards, where you hold it up to the* *reader and it scans and its got the information for the computer to read. But imagine this is the credit card, that's the cash register. It's supposed to make life easier for you and more convenient but doesn't it make life easier for identity thieves too?*

**Commercial:** *Now there's a simpler way to pay...*

**Martinez:** *The credit card companies love this new technology called radio frequency identification-also known as R.F.I.D. Instead of swiping your card, all you have to do is hold it up to a scanner and you're out the door. Sounds easy and it may be, but could it also make the crime of stealing your identity easy?*

**Walt Augustinowitz:** *The idea is that it's a lot quicker.*

**Martinez:** *Businessman, Walt Augustinowitz, shows us just how simple it could be for a thief to use this new technology to steal some of your personal information.*

**Augustinowitz:** *I bought a credit card reader for $9 on Ebay. Had it shipped to me, hooked it up to my laptop. Waved my credit card in front of it and there was all my information onscreen.*

**Martinez:** *You don't even have to have your credit card out to have your identity stolen. It could be in your wallet, in your back pocket and all it takes is for somebody with a reader to walk by and scan it. <gets scanned by person walking by> He just got my credit card number.*

*And it's not just your credit card number in jeopardy. Some driver's licenses, passports and I.D. cards also have R.F.I.D. technology.*

**Augustinowitz:** *Master Card and Visa want you to be using these new cards.*

**Martinez:** *We put together a group of about ten business people who volunteered to test their vulnerability.*

**Augustinowitz:** *What I'm trying to show is, someone with no technological experience can buy something like this off of Ebay, hook it up with a laptop and go out and do this in public.*

*Martinez: Watch what happened when the very first volunteer walked up to see if any of her cards could be detected. With a $9 reader that anyone can buy off the internet, the credit card number was scanned and after the beep, a computer screen showed her card number and expiration date. And she didn't even know her card had the new technology.*

*Sapna Sood <volunteer>: This is totally really scary. Yeah, this is really scary. I realize I have these cards in my wallet all this time.*

*Martinez: Credit card companies say many consumers feel more secure with PayPass because they never have to turn the card over to a cashier and it never leaves their hand."*[25]

Hmmm. Once again, there's that *hand* thing. But again, as you can see, this new technology is *not at all secure!* So you might be thinking, "Well hey, this is crazy! This is nuts! Somebody needs to alert the public about this! They not only gave us these new Smart Cards and we might not even know, but they're not tamper proof! We've got to let people know!" Well, believe it or not, The Mythbusters, of all people, *tried* to expose this security flaw, but the Credit Card companies immediately shut that down and forbade them from airing their program.

## Mythbusters censored

*Audience member: The one I wish you would revisit more is R.F.I.D. Now I know that...does Kerry still have that tag in her arm?*

*Adam Savage: Dude. The R.F.I.D. thing <shakes head, laughing> I'm sorry. It's just not going to happen.*

*Audience member: Alright.*

*Adam Savage: Here's what happened. I'm not sure how much of the story I'm allowed to tell but I'll tell you what I know.*

*<audience laughing claps and cheers>*

*Adam Savage: We were going to do R.F.I.D. and on several levels-you know-how hackable, how reliable, how trackable, etc., etc. and we, uh, one of our researchers called up Texas Instruments and they arranged a conference call between, I think, Tori and the head producer over there for the other team, Linda Wolkovitch and one of the technicians at Texas Instruments. We were supposed to have a conference call to talk about the technology on like Tuesday at 10 am, Linda and Tori get on the phone and they.. uh.. Texas Instruments comes on, along with the chief legal council for American Express, Visa, Discover and everybody else. I got chills just as I described it. They were way, way out-gunned and they absolutely made it really clear to Discovery they were not going to air this episode talking about how hackable this stuff was and Discovery backed way down, being a large corporation who depends upon the revenue of the advertisers. Uh, and now it's on Discovery's radar and they won't let us go near it. So I'm sorry. It's just one of those things, but man, that was.. Tory still gets a little white when he describes that phone conversation."*[26]

Hmmm. Talk about a conspiracy. This leads me to the nagging question, "Well, why? Why would you knowingly release to the public a Cashless Electronic Payment System that's *not secure at all?*" Well hey, maybe if you create a crisis, you can manage the outcome! First, let everybody get used to this new payment system, but then later, as you saw, the Smart Card system has a fatal flaw where you can not only lose the card itself or your cell phone, but it can be skimmed by somebody ripping you off of your cash. So maybe you appear on the scene with a *new solution.* You know, wouldn't it be great if you had your smart card or cell phone technology not just on the outside of you, but on the inside of you? I mean, if you did that, you'd not only never lose it, it would be much more secure. But we aren't falling for that, are we? Well believe it or not, just to make sure, IBM has already started the propaganda for it!

## I.B.M. COMMERCIAL

*A man dressed in black and a long trenchcoat walks abruptly into a grocery store, looks around and walks right past a security guard who looks and observes him from a distance suspiciously.*

*Man in trenchcoat walks past a magazine rack. Grabs one and stuffs it into his trenchcoat. He continues to walk briskly down the aisles and grabs random stuff off the shelf and puts it in his trenchcoat. Walks past the meat and grabs two steaks and stuffs them into his coat as a butcher chops meat and looks at him. Security camera is seen and we view from the security screen man continuing to stuff his coat with things from the shelf.*

*Man walks past several more people that are staring at him. He turns down the frozen food isle with two elderly people on scooters passing him as he stuffs frozen goods in his trenchcoat. He shuts the freezer door and gives them a smirk.*

*We see the security guard walking down an isle in the store towards the man. Man grabs a newspaper and walks toward the door, after passing though a large scanner. Security guard calls out to him, "Excuse me sir!" Trenchcoat man slowly turns around. Security guard, "You forgot your receipt!" Trenchcoat man snatches receipt, smirks and walks out.*

*Woman's voice: Checkout lines. Who needs them.*

*Security guard: Have a nice day.*

*Woman's voice: This is the future of e-business.*

*IBM.* "[27]

This is the future of the planet. You won't be able to buy or sell unless you have this form of internal payment. But that's not all. MasterCard purchased 51% of a smart card company called MONDEX and MONDEX just happens to be *the only electronic cash system in the world* that allows for multiple currencies on one card. MONDEX was so excited about this backing from MasterCard that they said:
*"This is the final stage in becoming a global reality. With MasterCard's backing, there's nothing to stop MONDEX now from becoming the global standard."*

Then, if that wasn't weird enough, the President of Visa has hinted at taking the tiny microchips in their smart cards and putting them into much "handier things" like a watch or even a ring.[28] I mean, come on, what's next? Some sort of smart card tattoo or body implant? Exactly, that's where all this is leading to! In fact, we already have people lining up to get this new form of implant to buy and sell!

## Wrist implant

*Is it the wave of the future or is it just another fad. It seems that some people are considering throwing away keys to the house and car in favor of a computer chip implanted in the wrist. A wave of the hand and the door opens right before their eyes. But as Jennifer Kirby reports, this apparent trend has its critics.*

***Jennifer Kirby:*** *Keith Kennedy has always hated fumbling with his keys. Now, he only uses one thing for all the doors he needs to unlock. It's an electronic chip implanted in his wrist.*

***Keith Kennedy:*** *Basically, it's just convenient but I'm a little bit more comfortable having more security to my house, my car and my business.*

***Kirby:*** *His business is a body piercing shop, but his passion is this new chip. He worked with a computer expert to develop the software. The chips work like swipe cards. Electronic readers identify people by their codes. Larissa Kraft got a chip to get into her house.*

***Larissa Kraft:*** *I've had to spend 5-10 minutes going through my bag to find my keys. That's no longer an issue.*

***Kirby:*** *Right now this kind of technology is used for tracking cattle and identifying lost pets. Retailers also use it for tracking packages through the system. As for chipping people, a night club in Spain is doing it so patrons don't have to carry membership cards. And a few people in the United States have chips for quick access to their medical records.*"[29]

Or, payment accepted! Thank you for using the Antichrist Mark of the Beast System! And as freaky as that is folks, that's still not all. Listen to this. You see, what most people don't realize is that MONDEX, the world's first possible global standard that is being backed by MasterCard, as we saw, it stands for Monetary Dexter. And if you'll look for yourself in the dictionary you will see that monetary means "pertaining to money" and dexter means "right hand." Hey, wait a second. Money in the right hand? Where have I heard that before? Maybe it's just me, but it sure looks to me like we're headed for a time where we're not only going to have a *One World Economy* across the planet, but we're going to see people using some form of cashless payment possibly inside their bodies, for buying and selling on the planet. Where have I heard that before? We better wake up! It's high time we get motivated and start living for Jesus Christ because there's not a lot of time left!

**VII.** The **7**th **proof** that we know we really are headed for a One World Economy is what I call the **Technology Proof.**

That's right, I'm talking about the new technology out there that's called **R.F.I.D.** or Radio Frequency Identification and it just happens to be not only new, but it's the exact kind of technology the Antichrist needs for his Mark of the Beast system. For the first time in man's history, we not only have a One World Economy and a One World Electronic Currency, but we even have the *technology* to pull it all off. But don't take my word for it. Let's listen to God's.

**Revelation 14:1-11** "Then I looked, and there before me was the Lamb, standing on Mount Zion, and with Him 144,000 who had His name and His Father's name written on their foreheads. And I heard a sound from heaven like the roar of rushing waters and like a loud peal of thunder. The sound I heard was like that of harpists playing their harps. And they sang a new song before the throne and before the four living creatures and the elders. No one could learn the song except the 144,000 who had been redeemed from the earth. These are those who did not defile themselves with women, for they kept themselves pure. They follow the Lamb wherever He goes. They were purchased from among men and offered as firstfruits to God and the Lamb. No lie was found in their mouths; they are blameless. Then I saw another angel flying in midair, and he had the eternal gospel to proclaim to those who live on the earth – to every nation, tribe, language and people. He said in a loud voice, 'Fear God and give Him glory, because the hour of His judgment has come. Worship Him who made the heavens, the earth, the sea and the springs of water.' A second angel followed and said, 'Fallen! Fallen is Babylon the Great, which made all the nations drink the maddening wine of her adulteries.' A third angel followed them and said in a loud voice: 'If anyone worships the beast and his image and receives his mark on the forehead or on the hand, he too, will drink of the wine of God's fury, which has been poured full strength into the cup of his wrath. He will be tormented with burning sulfur in the presence of the holy angels and of the Lamb. And the smoke of their torment rises for ever and ever. There is no rest day or night for those who worship the beast and his image, or for anyone who receives the mark of his name.'"

Whoa! Now maybe it's just me, but I'm kind of thinking that if you're ever going to put some sort of Mark on your head, you might want to make sure it came from God, how about you? Wow! What was going on there? If you weren't Marked by God during the 7-year Tribulation and instead received the

Mark from the Antichrist, uh, things weren't looking up, were they? Not at all! Words like, God's fury, His wrath, tormented with burning sulfur in the presence of the holy angels and of the Lamb forever and ever, kind of give it away for me anyway! So here's the point. For the first time in mankind's history, we can see how this text is about ready to come to pass. We not only see a trend where our society is starting to choose between God and the devil, but we are also seeing how the technology for the Antichrist to mark the whole planet is already here. It's called. *R.F.I.D.* or *Radio Frequency Identification.* So before we get into the next and final topic of our study, The Mark of the Beast, I want to get you equipped with this new and emerging technology that I believe is going to be used to pull off the Mark of the Beast. When I refer to R.F.I.D., I want you to know what it is. And once you look at this technology, I think it will give you some definite concern, like it does with me.

**1. The 1ˢᵗ concern I have with RFID is What This Technology Can Do.**

Let's take a look at, "Just What Is R.F.I.D."
First of all, RFID stands for Radio Frequency Identification and it's a new technology that uses tiny microchips on or in things called RFID tags to store information about things as well as track them from a distance. It's able to do this because it uses radio waves to communicate this information over distances to a computing device through a built in antenna, and since an RFID tag uses radio waves to beam its information, it also means that just like a radio wave it can do so right through wood, windows, walls, wallets, purses, clothing, backpacks etc.

The device that scans or picks up the information off the RFID tag is called a scanner. It can be likened to the radio in your home or car that picks up radio waves from a music station enabling you to listen to the broadcasted music being played. These readers come in a wide variety of sizes with some mounted stationary beside a conveyor belt in a factory or in the dock doors of a warehouse, or even made portable as in a handheld device, or even in an entryway or exit way like at Wal-Mart. In fact, some RFID tags can send a signal up to a mile or more, and in some cases they can even transmit their information all they way to low orbiting satellites.

One of the amazing attributes of RFID tags is not just the storing of information, but in their tiny size. For instance, one of the smallest tags made by Hitachi is called the "mu chip" and is only half the size of a single grain of sand! In fact, here's video transcript showing just how small and just how fast they can produce these tiny little monitoring devices called RFID.

**Alien Tech -Roboblocks**

*Robot: "Welcome to Alien Technology. Center for the development and exploitation of fluidic self assembly."*

*Jeff Jacobsen (CEO-Alien Technology USA): In here, are thousands of 350 micron nanoblocks. They are the approximate size of the nanoblocks we're designing for R.F.I.D. application.*

*What you're looking at here is serial #1 of the world's first fluidic self-assembly machine. This machine has the ability to assemble 2 million nanoblocks per hour. This 55,000 square foot facility when fully facilitized, which will only take 2 or 3 more years, will be capable of producing 80 billion R.F.I.D. tags per year.*

*Peter Gawley <VP Sales-RAFSEC UK>: Today, transponders are produced at a rate of thousands or tens of thousands per hour. We need to move to a level of where we're producing or capable of producing millions and billions per hour.*

Now I don't know about you, but those things are not only tiny, but they sure can crank them out! Oh, but that's not all. Because of the tiny size of RFID tags, they can not only be placed on the outside of an object, but on the inside, totally out of sight, hard to detect. But it's with these unique abilities to store and/or receive information and beam it over distances, that companies are literally planning on placing RFID tags on all products worldwide to provide an instant and continuous monitoring of product location, tracking of inventory and management of the entire global consumer supply chain.

They're already being used for thousands of applications such as preventing theft of automobiles, collecting tolls without stopping, managing traffic, gaining entrance to buildings, automating parking, controlling access to gated communities, corporate campuses and airports, dispensing goods, providing ski lift access, tracking library books, buying hamburgers and even automated instant store checkouts replacing the need for a cashier, just to name a few.

In fact, whole areas can be scanned for RFID tags including the people who are wearing or carrying them. Keep in mind this can all be done without your knowledge or consent and it can be done by anybody with the right kind of reader device giving them a kind of x-ray vision to spy on you by the things you're wearing and carrying, to track you wherever you go.

Remember, because RFID tags are so tiny, they can be hidden and sewn into the seams of clothes, sandwiched between layers of cardboard, molded into plastic or rubber and integrated into consumer packaging, making it extremely hard to find them. In fact, this technology is evolving so fast and has become so sophisticated that right now, RFID tags can even be printed, meaning that the dot on a printed letter "i" could be used to track you. Right now many huge corporations and government agencies are actually envisioning a day when every single item, product and person on the face of the planet is being tracked with RFID!

But you might be thinking, "Come on! Surely these people aren't serious about identifying and tracking each and every item anywhere on the globe, are they? I mean that's the craziest thing I've ever heard!" Well, crazy or not, listen to these people for yourself.

## Auto ID

*Kevin Ashton <Auto ID Center>: It's very, very exciting to take something that was apparently impossible and make it possible.*

*What I find extremely exciting about this is that it's a revolution which comes very silently.*

*Our goal is to connect computers to the real physical world, to the mechanical world.*

*Ashton: The fundamental capability of having your machines sense the world around them opens the door on a whole new world of possibility.*

*Dick Cantwell: The whole ID Center is to have one common set of standards that are based on end user needs that can be applied ubiquitously all around the world.*

*Prof Peter Cole: The key contribution of the M.I.T. Auto ID Center is the realization that everything can be labeled with tiny small bits of data on the label.*

*Ashton: It's the beginning of a new journey. A journey to understand what comes next after the barcode.*

*The electronic barcode is a numbering system. It's kind of like an internet protocol, IP address on your computer. Except here, we're trying to number, not just computers but inanimate objects.*

*Helen Duce: Something like P & G who sell products in Asia and Europe, America, South America. So, for them, it's really important that there's one single system that they can use everywhere in the world.*

*Cantwell: This technology is no longer in the discussion stage or the far out stage. This is something that will be happening and will be happening in the relatively near future.*

*This is not a question of "if". This is a question of "when".*

*There's no doubt in our mind, Auto I.D. will become a reality, and probably faster than anyone really believes.*

*It's a big dream that there will be an R.F.I.D. reader on every shelf of the universe.*

> *Our mission is very simple. We want to create a single global technology that will enable computers to identify any object, any where automatically.* "[30]

This is not science fiction of the future. It's present day reality and present day technology. It's a fact! I don't know about you but it sure does appear to me that this new technology called RFID really does not only have the ability to monitor and control products all over the world, but to even monitor and control the people who buy those products all over the world, how about you?

**2. The 2nd concern I have with RFID and that's What These Corporations Will Do.**

You see, as you just saw, these corporations not only admit that this is precisely what they want to do, track all people and products around the world, but the moment you try to confront them with this, they come back with an onslaught of lame excuses as to why there's nothing to fear, no need to be afraid, it's not as bad as people are trying to make it. Really? Well let's take a look at some of their lame excuses and you tell me if there's nothing to be concerned about.

## A. The 1st Lame Excuse they give is We Will Disarm the Tags.

This is probably one of the biggest comebacks the industry uses to qualm people's privacy fears concerning RFID tags. They say, "Hey, don't worry. We can always have the tags disarmed after you purchase the products with RFID tags on them." Really? First of all, some RFID tags have what's called a "dormant state" that can be set to "appear" as if they have been deactivated only to be reactivated at a later time. Very sneaky! And that's not only sneaky, but others in the industry are sounding the alarm that they are in fact leaving these tags on anyway, as you'll see next.

*David Haffenreffer: Barcodes have been with us for such a long time now that it's hard to imagine a world without them. But a new generation of inventory technology is being rolled out now that can soon make barcodes a thing of the past. The technology is called Radio Frequency Identification or R.F.I.D. It uses implanted microchips and tiny antennas to keep track of products with pinpoint accuracy. But opponents say the search for greater efficiency and profits will compromise our privacy. Katherine, you think these little chips implanted in everything from, oh I don't know, Gillette Razors to other products, may wind up being an invasion of our privacy.*

*Katherine Albrect: Well actually, David, the problem really has to do with the ways these chips are different and the system of tracking inventory is different from the barcode. There's really three fundamental ways that it differs. The first is that this system, unlike the barcode where you have the same number on a can of Coke. This system would actually create unique individual numbers for every single item manufactured on the planet. So imagine that you're walking through a doorway and now everything in your pocket, everything in your wallet, everything in your backpack or your suitcase could be identified by someone who has hidden a scanner device in there without your knowledge or permission. All the way down to what you're wearing under your clothes and I think that's really the concern here is that this technology is silent and it enables physical items to be identified at a distance.*

*Haffenreffer: What about the idea that people can have the tags neutralized on the way out of the store if they choose.*

*Albrecht: As far as turning off the tags, the concern that we have is that already these items equipped with these devices are being sold in stores today. There have been numerous trials around the country and indeed around the world, where without consumers knowledge they have picked up items equipped with these tags and which we call spy tags and actually have been surveilled through hidden cameras in the stores, tracked as they moved around with these items, photographed as they pick the items up and then took the items home without the tags being killed. So our concern here is that to our knowledge, there have been no trials of all the many items that have been sold with R.F.I.D. where the tags have actually been turned off at the point of checkout so while it makes a nice story, it's not happening in reality. And Benetton, the Italian clothing manufacturer had proposed in March, with which they were actually going to be embedding these tags in the actual sewn in label of women's clothing. That particular line was a line of women's underwear. So they would be walking around with tracking devices sewn into their bra. You know that is obviously a terrible idea."*[31]

Sounds to me like we're being lied to! But that's not all.

## B. The 2nd Lame Excuse they give is We Can Be Trusted.

As if what you've heard so far isn't bad enough, believe it or not, many people in the industry also come back with this next unbelievable response, "Hey, don't worry. You can trust us. You see, we're only using RFID to better serve you the customer and we only have your best interests at heart." Really? Well all you have to do is not only look at their words but even their *behavior* and it tells a different story.

For instance, this dishonest behavior in using RFID technology to track people was recently demonstrated by Gillette. In its RFID pilot program, they conducted what was called a "smart shelf" test at the Tesco Supermarket in Cambridge England and believe it or not, they automatically and secretly photographed shoppers taking RFID-tagged Gillette razors off the shelf to see if the technology could be used to deter shoplifting.

Then in another study, uncovered by the Chicago Sun Times, shelves in a Wal-Mart in Broken Arrow, Oklahoma were equipped with readers to not only track the Max Factor Lipfinity lipstick containers stacked on them, but they then watched the shoppers in action using webcams on the shelves and viewed their behavior 750 miles away by Procter & Gamble researchers in Cincinnati, Ohio so they could tell when lipsticks were removed from the shelves and they did this over a four-month period!

But that's still not all! This dishonest tracking behavior became even more fueled when a public relations document was accidentally exposed called the "Auto-ID Consortium Public Relations Campaign." It was put out to "neutralize opposition" stating how corporations would get consumers to "resign themselves to the inevitability of it" while merely pretending to address their privacy concerns.[32] And we're supposed to trust these guys? They have our best interests at heart? I don't think so! Repeat after me...LIAR, LIAR, PANTS ON FIRE!

### C. The 3rd Lame Excuse they give is We Have No Tracking Plans.

As if what you've seen thus far isn't shady enough, no amount of media "spin" could hide their true intentions when you simply look at the RFID patents they've already filed. It clearly shows they aren't just planning on tracking products, but shocker, even people as well. Let's take a look at just a few of those patents.

First of all, Bank of America has a patent out for what's called the "System and Method for Interactive Advertising" combined with a "Crowd Identification Device" that's designed to scan RFID tags on the things that people are wearing and carrying. It's designed to scan RFID tags on the things that people are wearing and carrying in order to pinpoint and identify them. Believe it or not, this patent goes on to describe a system very much like in the movie *Minority Report* in which people who come near a kiosk or other advertising venues are immediately recognized by the RFID tags they're wearing or carrying things like key fobs, cards or other RFID enabled items on them. Then the system captures video images of the consumers recording physical characteristics, face, iris and retinal characteristics to be processed by the Crowd Evaluation Device. So why in the world would they want a device that can do that? Why to get you to give them more of your hard earned money! Believe it or not, the whole stated purpose of this patent is to personally identify you so they can bombard you with personal ads targeted to your personal interests, preferences or demographics wherever you go, just like in the movie *Minority Report*.

But that's not all! Who could forget Proctor & Gamble's "Systems and Methods for Tracking Consumers in a Store Environment" where RFID readers would be placed in store ceilings, floors, shelving and displays reading RFID tags on both carts and individual items. Then the system would measure where a shopper travels in the store, for how long, what he or she picks up and whether a purchase results. In fact, they squarely admitted this goal when they said that this device will enable them to get a "detailed analysis of what consumers experience in stores where they go, how long they stay there and what influences the paths they choose." And why would they want to do this? Why, to bilk you of even more of your cash! They state, "Actual tracking of consumers in the store environment generates much more substantial information that can be used to effectively direct consumers to higher profit margin items."

And not to be outdone is NCR's "Automated Monitoring of Activity of Shoppers in a Market" where the plan is to watch a shopper's every move in the store aisle, recording their activities on a moment-by-moment basis and making a record of everything they do – down to the split second and this is accomplished by having RFID tags on every item in the store and reader devices hidden in every shelf and every shopping cart so that several inferences could be made. For instance, if a shopper places an expensive item in the cart then the system could suggest an expensive item to go along with it. Or if a customer puts a cake mix into the cart, then the system could assume they need eggs and suggest accordingly.

In fact, IBM has plans for catering to the rich. They have another tracking system called "Margaret" named after the developer's wealthy mother-in-law and it places RFID readers in doorways to identify people as they enter banks and other financial institutions. They then pick out the wealthy clients in order to give them preferential treatment. Don't believe me? Here's what they said: "An RFID tag fitted into the customer's bank card or passbook could be used to signal their arrival at a branch. As they pass through the doors, the card would alert a customer information system. Bank staff could personally greet high-net-wealth customers, or customers could be greeted by name by tellers who already have their account information on-screen when they arrive at the counter." And it's even been suggested that this type of doorway reader could be used "in upscale restaurants or retail boutiques, where a high-degree of personal service is important."

But that's not all. IBM also has another patent out called "Person Tracking Unit" that scans the RFID tags on unwitting members of the public as they move through retail stores, airports, train stations, elevators, libraries, theaters and even public restrooms, and if all that wasn't bad enough, they even go on to say that the government could use this device to track suspicious people in public places using the RFID tags in the things people are wearing and carrying."[33]

Now I don't know about you, but it really does appear to me that the industry really is planning on using RFID technology not just to track us, but to get even more cash from us, how about you?

### D. The 4th Lame Excuse they give is We Never Said Such a Thing.

Believe it or not, not only do these corporations' true tracking intentions get revealed in their patent applications, but it's even more revealing in their personal quotations. Here are just a few of them. You tell me if we're not headed for a time when we're all tagged and tracked like a product at the store.

- Paul Saffo research Director of the Institute for the Future – "At the end of the day, we're going to feel like tagged bears."
- A marketer at an Auto-ID Center meeting – "Won't it be great when we know every time the consumer takes the lid off the toothpaste in their own bathroom?"
- Helen Duce of Auto-ID Center – "The Auto-ID Center has a clear vision – to create a world where every object – from jumbo jets to sewing needles – is linked to the Internet. Success will be nothing less than global adoption."
- Mark Roberti from the Auto-ID Center – "The Auto-ID Center's vision is a world in which low-cost RFID tags are put on every manufactured item and tracked using a single, global network as they move from one company to another and one country to another. Indeed, we envision individual items – cans of Coke, pairs of jeans and car tires – being tracked from the moment they are made until the time they are recycled."
- IBM Patent 20020116274 – "The widespread use of RFID tags on merchandise such as clothing would make it possible for locations of people, animals and objects to be tracked on a global scale."
- Steve Halliday of AIM Global – "If I talk to companies and ask them if they want to replace the bar code with these tags, the answer can't be anything but yes. It's like giving them an opportunity to rule the world."

- Scott Silverman the CEO of Applied Digital Solutions – "The same scanner in a Wal-Mart that is used to bar-code your goods can be used to identify you."
- Scott McNealy CEO of Sun Microsystems "They're going to slap that baby's bottom, then slip an ID chip in their neck or between their shoulders so you can keep track of your kid."
- Kevin Ashton Executive Director of Auto-ID Center – "People might balk at the thought of police using RFID to scan the contents of a car's trunk without needing to open it." And then in another statement he said that in order for RFID to be accepted into society that, "We will have to die. Our generation will never fully embrace a world where everything can be tagged and tracked. It's just too new. But the next generation will."

It's precisely because these corporations and companies are so serious about these claims that many privacy advocates have said this:

- Charlie Schmidt – "If you let them, companies like Gillette will monitor personal use of their products in your home. Throw one of their razors in the trash, and another one would be on its way."
- The Guardian – "RFID tags can still work long after the product has been bought. If the tags become as ubiquitous as the manufacturers would like, people could be bristling with the chips in clothes and possessions. Anyone from police to potential thieves could work out exactly what they carry."
- Food Production Daily – "A major concern is that the RFID chip could result in every product on earth having its own unique ID. The use of unique ID numbers could lead to the creation of a global item registration system in which every physical object is identified and linked to its purchaser or owner at the point of sale or transfer."
- The Privacy Bulletin – "After a relatively short period of tracking a vehicle, it may be possible to predict when someone is or is not at home; where they work, spend leisure time, go to Church services and shop; what schools their children attend; where friends and associates live; whether they have been to see a doctor; and whether they attend political rallies."
- Katherine Albrecht of CASPIAN – "What motivates me is an absolute resistance against the idea that we would all just be reduced to being numbers and tagged and tracked like cattle. When I see RFID and I think

about a world in which the powers that be – be they corporate or government – can essentially watch, surveil, track, manipulate and control the people, that's what motivates me: a desire to see that not happen to my generation, to my children, to my grandchildren. History is going to judge us based on how we respond to this threat now."

If these corporations really aren't planning on making this global tracking of items, animals and even people a reality, and if these various privacy advocates are just blowing things out of proportion, then why are there, right now, state lawmakers in different states writing bills addressing privacy concerns and in some cases proposing the outlawing of RFID technology being used to monitor citizens? And why do some of these bills even make it a felony to implant human beings with a "spy chip" without their consent? And for goodness sake, why in the world would State Senator Debra Bowen say, "How would you like it if, for instance, one day you realized your underwear was reporting on your whereabouts?"[34]

Now I don't know about you, but I *wouldn't* like it if my underwear was reporting my whereabouts, how about you? Hey! There's no need to fear, no need to be afraid, privacy advocates are just blowing things out of proportion when they clearly have plans to use RFID to monitor and control all the products and people around the world. I'd say that's a little bit of a *concern* to me, how about you? In fact, I'd also say it's the obvious first step in implementing The Mark of the Beast the Bible predicted would come when you are living in the Last Days! RFID is not only going to cover every single sector of society from a shoe to me and you, but it will enable, *for the first time in man's history*, a truly global monitoring system of both people and products right down to whether or not they will be able to buy or sell. It's all here, A *One World Economy,* a *One World Electronic Currency,* and now a *One World Technology* to pull the whole thing off! Looks to me like we're being corralled into a decision making time where we're going to have to decide whether we're going to receive some sort of mark into our bodies or remain faithful to God and be shut out of the system. Where have I heard that before? Oh, yeah! That was our opening text!

### 3. The 3rd concern I have with RFID is What Its Deployment Will Do.

Once this RFID stuff goes into full force in our society, it will not only become the biggest prison planet this world has ever seen, but the Bible says it's a sign you're headed for the wrath of God! But don't take my word for it. Let's listen to God's.

**Revelation 16:1-7** "Then I heard a loud voice from the temple saying to the seven angels, 'Go, pour out the seven bowls of God's wrath on the earth.' The first angel went and poured out his bowl on the land, and ugly and painful sores broke out on the people who had the mark of the beast and worshiped his image. The second angel poured out his bowl on the sea, and it turned into blood like that of a dead man, and every living thing in the sea died. The third angel poured out his bowl on the rivers and springs of water, and they became blood. Then I heard the angel in charge of the waters say: 'You are just in these judgments, you Who are and Who were, the Holy One, because You have so judged; for they have shed the blood of your saints and prophets, and you have given them blood to drink as they deserve.' And I heard the altar respond: 'Yes, Lord God Almighty, true and just are your judgments.'"

In other words, it is perfectly right for God to dish out His wrath on the people's behavior and notice what that behavior was. They not only killed His prophets and His people, but what was the very first thing mentioned there? These people not only had the audacity to reject Jesus Christ and His offer of salvation, but then they had the audacity to turn around and worship the actual Antichrist instead AND receive "his" mark of ownership! That's not only audacious, it invites God's *judgment*! What'd He do? He Judged them with painful and ugly sores that broke out on them and He turned all the water into blood. Blood they shed, blood they get, you reap what you sow!

So here's the point. Once again, if you unfortunately find yourself in the 7-year Tribulation and if you unfortunately made a foolish mistake of rejecting Jesus Christ as your Lord and Savior, that the last thing you ever want to do during this time frame is receive the Mark of the Beast, right? You talk about going from bad to worse, *real fast*! Here's the point. Once again, whether people realize it or not, for the first time in man's history we can see how this text is really about ready to come to pass and that's because, once again, this technology we've seen called **R.F.I.D.** is not only the exact same kind of technology the Antichrist needs to pull off the Mark of the Beast, to Mark all the people on the whole planet, but as we saw, it's already being *deployed right now* on the planet!

**A. The 1st deployment** they're putting this technology into is **The Retail Industry.**

Let's take a look at this Antichrist world they're creating for us, this Prison Planet system, with this Mark of the Beast Technology, starting with The Retail Industry. That's where it's going into first and you tell me if it's not leading to a total monitoring society of our worst nightmare! Once again, IBM helps us to envision our future.

## IBM COMMERCIAL: LOST DRIVER

*<Tractor trailer slams brakes to stop from hitting a woman at a desk in the middle of the road in the middle of nowhere>*

**Truck driver:** *<opens door> Can you kindly tell me what you're doing in the road?*

**Woman:** *I'm with the Help Desk. You're lost. You're headed to Fresno.*

**Truck driver:** *Fresno. Right.*

**Woman:** *This is the road to Albuquerque.*

**Truck driver:** *How did you know we were lost?*

**Woman:** *The boxes told me.*

**Truck driver:** *The boxes?*

**Woman:** *RFID radio tags on the cargo. Helps track shipments.*

**Truck driver to other driver:** *The boxes knew we were lost.*

**Other driver:** *Maybe the boxes should drive.*

**Truck driver:** *Very funny.*

*INVENTORY OFF TRACK? IBM CAN HELP*[35]

Yes, IBM can help, help us envision the future where every box on the planet can be tracked with RFID. Believe it or not, this is what they are planning on doing in the Retail Industry. Every box in the entire global supply chain can be found and tracked, right? "The boxes told me," right? They're being tracked anywhere with RFID and as we saw before, that's not where they're stopping. Their ultimate goal is to not only embed these RFID tags into boxes for tracking purposes in the Retail Industry, but even in people and animals for the same tracking purposes. I really believe it's the beginning of the Mark of the Beast System. As wild as that is, the way they're getting us to buy into this nightmarish scenario is a step by step plan to slowly but surely convince us that this really is for our overall good.

### a. The 1st justification they use is Hey It's Good for the Companies!

These companies say that if a product is returned or exchanged with an RFID tag on it, it's for our good because the employees who do the restocking could be told exactly where to place the item. I mean, don't you just hate it when you find things in the wrong spot? Oh, there's so much good written all over that! Then they say, since RFID can track and trace anything they're put on, theft rates would drop dramatically and automatically alert management when an item has not been paid for so that should reduce the cost for us…yeah, right…it goes in their pockets as, by the way, people are being scanned as they leave the store. Then, believe it or not, they even say that RFID in retail could be used to track employees to improve their performance. Yay! Isn't…that…good! They admit that store management could verify through an automated system with RFID, whether or not an employee was at the appropriate station at the start of the shift or end of a break allowing them to know if an employee spends excessive time in the break room or is goofing off in a corner somewhere and they are automatically generating a report of this inappropriate behavior.[36] *Total monitoring in the workplace*! Gee, I don't know about you, but that doesn't sound good to me! So much for freedom! Sounds like the beginning of a prison planet system no matter how much you try to justify it!

### b. The 2nd justification they use to try to get us to go along with this RFID system in Retail is they say that, Hey It's Good for the Consumer!

Once again, repeat after me…LIAR, LIAR, PANTS ON FIRE! For instance, they say that if RFID is used in the retail industry this will enable shelves to automatically be monitored to ensure they remain stocked at appropriate levels so that you the customer never miss a sale! Then they say that if fitting rooms were equipped with RFID readers to identify the merchandise that's brought in, shoppers could see a video in the fitting room describing the features of that item and could see a person modeling it and even suggest accessories to go along with it. Wouldn't that be great? You wouldn't even have to try it on anymore! Or, for those of you who like to be more personal with your clothes, they say the system could also scan the shopper or use pictures of the shopper stored in a database that they recognize once you came into the store so that you yourself can see what you personally look like in the outfit without changing your clothes! Isn't that convenient! But that's not all. They also say if we just go along with system, it will usher in an era of consumer convenience beyond our wildest dreams, it will be paradise in the store and all of life, like this article shares. Let me visualize what this article says is going to be our soon coming future with RFID!

*"It's the near future. You're watching your favorite morning news show to see what's happening in the crazy world of technology but the show is interrupted by commercials. So you think this is a good time for a cup of coffee, when suddenly the face of your girlfriend shows up on the screen telling you to buy the latest model of mp3 player with a miniature hard disk of 1.5 TB and a weight of only 20 grams (suitable for any occasion), offered by Wal-Mart.*

*But you don't have time to think about that because the next commercial shows your best friend recommending to you the latest car model that's personalized according to the exact wishes you described to a car dealer just a couple days ago.*

*But now you're getting annoyed so you turn off the TV set, but you forget to disconnect from the Internet so now you hear your girlfriend's voice on the speakers of the stereo reminding you that only the best roses can be purchased at Roses.com for her upcoming birthday next week.*

*But this is interrupted by the doorbell as your friends arrive to take you to a baseball game at the local stadium in which you don't worry about a ticket because they're no longer needed. You just show up and walk in where your presence is automatically recognized by an RFID reader and the cost is automatically debited from your account.*

*But there's a small crowd at the game, so you decide to move down to the more expensive seats. As you do, none of the people who paid good money for those better seats are concerned about your behavior because they know what you apparently forgot. The more expensive seat automatically senses your presence too and it promptly sends a signal to the ticket office which in turn debits your bank account for the difference in price.*

*So after the game you head home when suddenly the muffler on your car announces, 'I have a leak,' and suggests an appointment with a local mechanic the next day to which you agree.*

*And since you're hungry you stop off at a convenience store to get a hotdog whereupon a screen pops up on the computer in front of the attendant at the counter that tells him to 'Ask the customer if he would like extra nacho cheesy potato chips.' So the attendant does, to which you of course say yes because they're your favorite kind.*

*So after you drop your buddies off, you head home and upon entering the door your home computer asks you if you'd like to order a pizza in three hours, which happens to be the normal time you eat every night. Since you know you'll be hungry again by then, you say 'yes' and then proceed to take out your garbage.*

*But as soon as you put the garbage in the garbage can, the can sends you an audible alert telling you that you just put a recyclable item in the wrong bin which you immediately correct to avoid yet another fine from the waste management company.*

*But then you decide to wash some clothes before the pizza arrives so you throw your laundry into the machine but an alarm goes off there too as the washing machine informs you to not put your white dress shirt in with your red T-shirt, and just in case you don't comply, it deactivates itself until you do.*

*So later that night, after you finished the pizza that arrived right on time, you go to the refrigerator to get a drink of water when it informs you that you're out of milk and then asks you if you want to order more from the grocery store to which you yawn and say yes and then promptly head off to bed.*

*Are you hallucinating? Is this a bad scenario of a poor science fiction movie? No! Welcome to the wonderful world of RFID where we know everything about how to serve our favorite customer.*"[37]

Isn't that good for us! I don't know about you, but that RFID envisioned future is just a little too creepy for me. Talk about a total monitoring control society! But it gets even worse! No matter how they try to justify it, it's going to lead to a whole bunch of privacy problems!

**a.** The **1ˢᵗ privacy problem** it's going to lead to is **Personalized Pricing.**

As wacky as you've seen it so far, these guys are actually planning on implementing what's called a *personalized pricing system* that's designed to monitor our "income" and "spending habits" just to squeeze out even more of our cash! And they're blunt about it! They even call it, "the "Personalized Pricing Tool." In the RFID enabled system, they will classify us whether or not we're a "Barnacle" or a "bottom feeder" where they admit, "If we're not dropping big money in their stores, they don't want us around and we will be *financially penalized*. In other words, we get a *higher price* to get us out of their store! Don't believe me? Listen to how Marty Abrams, he's a policy advisor for Hunton & Williams law firm, listen to how he describes how marketers are planning on doing just that with RFID.

He says, *"You know that awful feeling you get when you sit next to a guy who paid $100 for the same flight that cost you $600 to board? Soon you could have the same experience with food, clothing and even children's toys every time you shop.*

*Imagine approaching a shelf and seeing the price tag change before your very eyes, flashing you a personalized price tailored to your shopping history and profitability to the store.*

*It's called 'Customer Specific Pricing' and RFID could make it a reality."*

Talk about discrimination! Believe it or not, they're already working on these "electronic price tags" that change before our very eyes!

**Future Store:**

*A virtual tour of the Future Store. Shows a touch screen LCD TV on the shopping cart displaying personal shopping list, position on where you are located in the store and where exactly you have to go to find your item on the shelf.*

*Store displays prices of items via Electronic Shelf Labeling then flashes a special offer displaying a now lower price in "real time". Future check out involves pushing cart to the walk-through scanner where goods and prices are registered automatically and all at once; thereby checkout takes only seconds without having to unload your cart."*[38]

Isn't that convenient? All automatic, all electronic, no money transacted, in order to buy or sell. The "electronic smart shelf" automatically changes the price as it is approached. Now some people's price will go down because they're not a "bottom feeder" like the rest of us and they want them to stay in the store! That's not only discriminatory, it's freaky and it's a privacy problem!

**b. The 2nd privacy problem is it's going to lead to is Personalized Tracking.**

These guys really are planning, including the government, "To track us as we move through retail stores, airports, train stations, elevators, libraries, theaters and even public restrooms." It's literally everywhere and that includes your *home*! They actually plan on putting what's called RFID Sniffers in your house so that no matter where you are, they'll know everything about you, that's right, their favorite customer! Don't believe me? Check out the patents they've already filed for!

There's an actual patent out called the "Inventory & Location System" that describes how RFID readers could be installed in your home's doorways, floors, closets and even your car to inventory all your RFID retail items and report their findings on a minute-by-minute basis back to the marketers.

Don't believe me? Listen to the patent for yourself. *"As a customer enters the door of his residence, a sniffer placed on the floor near the doorway detects the new RFID tagged purchase. This wireless sniffer automatically and continuously emits a signal that searches for an RFID label which it has never seen before. The user's house may contain many sniffers which all wirelessly communicate with a personal computer. A mobile sniffer could even be installed in the user's car and would be able to report new purchases as the car enters the driveway or garage so retailers and suppliers can analyze their sales and marketing strategies."*

Now wait a second. How could they do that unless the RFID tags were still left on or were somehow still readable after the point of sale?

Oh, but that's not all. The 2nd way they plan on personally tracking us is with "Sniffers" in the Trash. Believe it or not, companies are also planning on using RFID in retail to continually track, monitor and market us by the contents of our trash from vehicles equipped with RFID readers that scan for tags as they drive by!

For instance, BellSouth has a patent out for a device called, "System and Method for Utilizing RF Tags to Collect Data Concerning Post-Consumer Products" whereupon they can collect, sort, process and sell the data contained in our trash with RFID tags on them. They say, *"By combining captured pre-consumer information with post-consumption information the entire life cycle of an item may be tracked. This information may be useful to any number of entities, including retailers, manufacturers, distributors and the like. Grocery stores, pharmacies and retailers may find it useful to know how long it takes a particular item to go from being stocked on the shelf to being placed in a waste or recycling receptacle."*

Now wait a second. How could they track an item from the store to the trash unless of course the RFID tags were still left on or were still somehow readable after the point of sale?

Oh but that's still not all! The 3rd way they plan on tracking us is with "Sniffers" everywhere! Companies are also planning on using RFID in retail to continually track, monitor and market us by turning the whole world into one giant RFID enabled shopping mall that they call the "Real-World Showroom."

**Real World Showroom**

*Imagine if the entire world was your personal showroom. Where you see products in use and you can buy them right there, right away. With the advent of inexpensive radio frequency identification or RFID tags and the ubiquity of mobile devices, the gap between where we use products and where we buy them begins to disappear.*

***Joe Tobolski:*** *Accenture, our research has developed a prototype called Real*

*World Showroom. Using a wireless PDA, equipped with an RFID reader, I can query everyday objects around me such as a tie my friend is wearing.*

*Information about the product, such as pricing, availability and delivery options is retrieved from a variety of online sources. Click a few options and the tie is yours.*

***Tobolski:*** *As these ties become pervasive, products will advertise themselves and their product owners will become sales channels. For instance, if I buy a friend's tie, he can receive a sales commission for that sale.*

*But real world showroom is more than a shopping tool. It's a way to find out everything about a product. By scanning a data tag on a used car, for instance, you can see if it's been involved in an accident, how many times it's been sold, or get a certified odometer reading. Scan a stereo and you can see it's supply chain history to make sure it's not a grey market item.*

***Tobolski:*** *Real World Showroom is an example of what we at Accenture like to call silent commerce. In the future, more and more commerce will be conducted between people in real time and in real world situations, not just at the store or on the web. "*[39]

In other words, the whole world becomes a giant shopping mall. Isn't that awesome! Again, how could they do that unless the RFID tags were left on after the point of sale of all products in the Retail Industry? Oh yeah! That's right! Repeat after me.. LIAR, LIAR, PANTS ON FIRE! It's precisely because of these privacy issues that "privacy advocates" are warning us that we are headed for one of the worst invasions of privacy in the history of mankind, if we allow this to continue.

**High Tech Tracking**

Now to the latest front in the invasion of privacy.

We take the debate to the edge of the newest technology.

***Ann Cavoukian:*** *<Ontario Privacy Commission> The inter-telecommunications technology, cell phones, all these technologies have the capability of tracking your activities, your whereabouts, your movements and placing you at certain* *places at certain times so surveillance is expanding dramatically.*

*We all know we are watched pretty much everywhere we go. Maybe it's worth it for a safer city. But is it worth it for more convenient shopping? Because in this digital age, every time money changes hands, we already leave a little piece of our digital DNA. Numbers that tell a story of who we are, what we are like. But what's the next step? And now we're in a world where everything we buy-the clothes on your back, to a bottle of cough syrup can be tracked wherever it goes. Well, imagine no more because that technology is already here. In the near future, this chip will be imbedded in every product you buy, storing product information and locating it at an exact time and place. From manufacturing, to distribution, to the retail store.*

**Paul Heino:** *<CEO of Sundix> It's a chip that replaces barcodes. You put a chip on an item and then you go about your normal business. Loading it onto trucks or passing it onto your shelves and every time it moves past an antenna it gets scanned regardless of orientation.*

*The information control benefit is obvious, real-time updates on what's selling, what isn't. That's why these executives from around the world are so excited.*

**Heino:** *Through the old supply chain, you're going to see a 20% savings in labor. You're going to see an 80% reduction in theft.*

*But here's the potential problem. When you bring it home, because the chip doesn't ever really stop transmitting information.*

**Cavoukian:** *The ability to track an individual consumer, with the variety of products that they've purchased and you really aggregate that information and you build profiles on the kind of purchases that individual has made, it grows exponentially.*

*RFID is now being adopted by Wal-Mart.*

**Cavoukian:** *You go into a lingerie store, you go into an economy store, you can paint a picture and then link that to the kind of position I might have as a public official or a school teacher or there could be enormous abuses of that information.*

*Of course, there is another side to this story.*

**Heino:** *Think about tagging pets and getting your dog back even though there's no collar. Think about lost children.*

*Your child's movements can be tracked minute by minute in a world where scanners are everywhere. Perhaps that's privacy worth giving up.* "[40]

I don't think so! But did you catch that? That's convenient! First you can use it on products and then apparently it's a natural slide to put these *in what*? You're *pets* and your *children* to track us wherever we go. Where have I heard that? Oh yeah! That's right! That's the Mark of the Beast technology that the Bible said would come when you are living in the Last Days...*it's already here being implemented!*

The Bible is clear. Once we accept this stuff in full force, RFID, we are headed, literally, for a bloodbath! But don't take my word for it. Let's listen to God's.

**Revelation 19:11-21** "I saw heaven standing open and there before me was a white horse, whose rider is called Faithful and True. With justice He judges and makes war. His eyes are like blazing fire, and on His head are many crowns. He has a name written on Him that no one knows but He Himself. He is dressed in a robe dipped in blood, and His name is the Word of God. The armies of heaven were following Him, riding on white horses and dressed in fine linen, white and clean. Out of His mouth comes a sharp sword with which to strike down the nations. 'He will rule them with an iron scepter.' He treads the winepress of the fury of the wrath of God Almighty. On His robe and on His thigh He has this name written: KING OF KINGS AND LORD OF LORDS. And I saw an angel standing in the sun, who cried in a loud voice to all the birds flying in midair, 'Come, gather together for the great supper of God, so that you may eat the flesh of kings, generals, and mighty men, of horses and their riders, and the flesh of all people, free and slave, small and great.' Then I saw the beast and the kings of the earth and their armies gathered together to make war against the rider on the horse and His army. But the beast was captured, and with him the false prophet who had performed the miraculous signs on his behalf. With these signs he had deluded those who had received the mark of the beast and worshiped his image. The two of them were thrown alive into the fiery lake of burning sulfur. The rest of them were killed with the sword that came out of the mouth of the rider on the horse, and all the birds gorged themselves on their flesh."

Now that's a passage you don't hear preached very often, but it's coming! Now other than the obvious point that we're dealing with another intense text, how many of you would say that the last mistake you'd ever want to make, if you made the first unfortunate mistake of rejecting Jesus Christ as your Lord and Savior and were thus thrust into the 7-year Tribulation, how many of you would say the last mistake you'd ever want to do is join the two Biggest Losers of all time, the Antichrist and False Prophet and allow them to delude you into taking the Mark of the Beast, right? Don't do that! Whatever you do, don't do that! I mean, that's going from bad to worse! Why? Because words like "blazing fire," "iron scepter," "thrown alive into the fiery lake of burning sulfur," and "birds gorging themselves on your flesh all over the planet," kind of give it away! It's a bad time!

So once again, here's the point. Whether people realize it or not, this Mark of the Beast technology that we see in the text is *already* being unleashed on the planet with RFID. It's not 50 years down the road, it's being implemented right now and people right now are being deluded into accepting it.

**B. The 2nd deployment** that they're putting this RFID technology into is in **The Food Industry.**

I'm telling you, they're covering all the bases and I truly believe it's a power issue. They know that we don't just buy "products" but "food" and food just happens to be what we need to sustain everyday life. Once again, IBM is out there helping us envision our new RFID future, including controlling our food supply!

**IBM COMMERCIAL**

*<Group of people surrounded by sheep in a field with a woman sitting at a business desk>*

**Man:** *Is this the help desk?*

**Woman:** *Yes, it is.*

**Man:** *We need help.*

*Woman: With what?*

*<Group of people all talking at the same time>*

*Woman: I understand.*

*<Group all starts talking at same time again>*

*Woman: <Points at each person> Farmer, Designer, Weaver, Buyer, Shipper Seller.*

*Group: <in unison> Yeah*

*Woman: You need a customized real-time web portal.*

*Group: <in unison> A what?!*

*Woman: To get you on the same page.*

*Group: <in unison>:Perfect!*

*PARTNERS NOT CONNECTED? IBM CAN HELP "*[41]

Everything on the planet not connected yet? IBM can help! What'd they say? We're going to connect everything on the planet from the farmer, to the designer, to the weaver, to the buyer, to the shipper and to the seller, right? Everything you "buy and sell" *including your food*! And as wild as that is, this really is their goal! Every product, every pet, every piece of food you eat is going to be tracked with RFID. In fact, the industry has a term for it. It's called from the *Farm to the Fork*." In other words, they're going to be able to track every single piece of food item on the planet from the farm, all the way to your fork on your dinner table in your home and that's exactly what they're planning on doing. They not only want to track you and your products in the store, but they want to keep on tracking you, even in the home! And that includes your food!

The reason why they're doing this is because they're not dumb. They know you can live without certain products, but not food! They know we don't have to have that nifty electric can opener that sings the star spangled banner every time we use it. In fact, speaking of which, I heard they even invented a toilet seat that played the star spangled banner when you sat down on it. But the problem was, every time somebody sat down to use the restroom, they had to stand back up as soon as the music started playing! It's the Star Spangled Banner, you're supposed to stand up! But seriously, they know we can live without those nifty colored socks that Jon wears all the time that fit into each individual toe with those rainbow striped colors on them.

But here's the point, when it comes to food, they know we can't live very long without that, can we? I believe it's a power play. If somebody wanted to *force* you into doing something you didn't particularly want to do, like the Mark of the Beast, then just control the food supply, right? Down to where every little piece of food you could get on the whole planet is at all times, and hold that over your head! This is what they mean by the term, Farm to the Fork. This really is their goal with RFID and I really believe it's part of the overall Mark of the Beast System in the Last Days and once again, as wild as this is, the way that they're getting us to go along with this nightmare scenario is a step by step plan to slowly but surely convince us that this is for our overall good.

## The 1st justification they use is Hey It'll Keep Your Food Fresh!

These companies say that if all food products on the whole planet are tracked and monitored with RFID, then this will ensure that all our food is always fresh, at all times and always readily available. That's because RFID tags can not only track all food items on the whole planet, but they can *sniff* food and tell if it's gone bad. That's because RFID tags can not only store and receive information, but monitor things like chemical smells in food to see if they are spoiled and they say if we put these things on every single piece of food item around the whole planet, why, we'll never have to deal with rotten fruit again! Isn't that awesome! In fact, they even say this "sniffing" ability could ensure the safety of our planet!

**Sensing technology**

*Nearly 30 years ago, the first barcode machine was born. Now decades later, the technology we usually associate with scanning our groceries is doing everything from stocking shelves to keeping our Homeland secure.*

**John Bruno:** *<Sr VP, Symbol> RFID is the natural evolution to where barcodes were.*

*We're talking about Radio Frequency Identification or R.F.I.D.*

***Bill Nuti:*** *<Pres/CEO Symbol> RFID has been around for a very long time. In fact, today, when you travel through a toll booth and you have an easy pass, that's an R.F.I.D. technology.*

*Now companies like SYMBOL are providing RFID technologies to revolutionize the way we live once again. Like at the supermarket, creating a 24 hour virtual stock boy or gal.*

***Bruno:*** *The shelf was empty and the proximity reader knew that the shelf was empty. It sent a signal to the stocking rotation folks to take something from the back room and put it on the shelf.*

*From stocking shelves to taking stock at the airport, where RFID is improving baggage tracking and security.*

***Bruno:*** *What RFID has done is now taken the technology to the next level. Previously, you would actually have to manually pull a trigger or point a laser or point an image or add a barcode to read it. Now, as it passes within a proximity RFID reader, the information that would normally be in a barcode is now transmitted.*

*And experts say, one of the biggest benefits of the technology is cutting down on human error and while improving productivity and lowering operating expenses. What else is in the future for RFID? How about something called sensing technology which can do everything from sniffing out rotten fruits and veggies at the grocery store, to sniffing out potential terrorist threats.*

***Nuti:*** *Sensing technologies would have the ability to sense chemical, radiological and biological weapons in a cargo container. They would also be able to sense the freshness of produce in an aisle in retail.*

*Now that's smart technology."*

Did you hear that? We've got to do this! This "smart" technology will not only sense our food for us so it'll never go rotten, but it'll even protect our planet from potential terrorists! We've got to do it now! I don't know about you, but no matter how they try to justify it and try to get us to go along with it, I truly believe when this goes into place it's going to open up Pandora's box. For instance, what if a particular food product was deemed unhealthy by the government for consumption and if you're paying attention, we already saw earlier, they're already doing just that! So here's the point. With all these new "tracking" and "sniffing" abilities with RFID on our food supply, you now have a "practical way" to really ensure and monitor people's food *for their own good* and if you don't think they're really planning on doing that, then look at this promotional piece from NCR Corporation. It's called, "50 Ideas for Revolutionizing the Store through RFID." One of their ideas states:

*"If food were tagged with RFID that could provide ingredients and materials composing the item, shoppers could be warned about items to which they or their family member were allergic when those items were placed in their shopping carts. A smart system could then suggest alternatives that did not contain the problematic component and tell the shopper where to find them."*

In other words, if you put something *wrong* that they deem is "unhealthy" for you, in your cart, then you have to *put it back*! Now you might be thinking, "Well hey, that's not too bad. Being told whether or not a food item will trigger an allergy and suggest an alternative with RFID, that's kind of convenient." But the only problem is, what if one day it switches from being voluntary to mandatory and by the way, it's already started, like this person shares.

*"Imagine what would happen if health insurers, public health officials and even employers could also peer over your shoulder at your food choices and set their own restrictions on what food products you could or couldn't buy.*

*Already, police departments have fired officers for smoking cigarettes in their off duty hours claiming that smoking raises health insurance costs for others. Employees in King County, Washington (the Seattle area), will be charged an extra one thousand dollars in annual healthcare fees if they don't participate in a snoopy 'health incentives' program that monitors their lifestyle choices.*

*Why wouldn't these same tactics someday be deployed at the supermarket?*

*The grocery cart that watches your spychipped food choices would make it possible for employers and health insurance companies to impose similar conditions on people's grocery store purchases.*

> *Why stop at tobacco? Cops could lose their jobs for buying red meat or beer. Giving computers the power to prevent shoppers from buying certain products sounds like a Big Brother increment just waiting to happen."*[42]

And I'd say, it's Stage One of the Mark of the Beast System about ready to happen. You can't "buy or sell" or eat "any food item" you "buy or sell" without some form of governmental approval. Where have I heard that before? That's the Mark of the Beast system! I don't care how much you justify it! It's not good!

The **2nd justification** they use to try to get us to go along with this RFID system in the Food Industry is they say that **Hey It'll Keep Your Food Safe!**

Once again, please repeat after me…LIAR, LIAR, PANTS ON FIRE! You see, they know no normal person is going to roll over and let these companies or governmental institutions control and monitor our food supply. That's crazy! That's nuts! Who would let them do that? So therefore, they've resorted to that tried and true tactic, that's worked every time, to get us to go along with it anyway. It's called *fear and manipulation*! In other words, if you create a crisis, you can manage the outcome and in my opinion, this is exactly what they're doing to get us to surrender to a global monitoring of our food supply with RFID. I mean, haven't you heard? We don't just have a food problem, we've got a *food crisis*! There's mercury in our fish, there's E-Coli in our meat products, there's chronic wasting disease in our deer, there's that mad cow disease and that avian bird flu thing? What will we do!!! Right? And with all these global food fears they've created like Mad Cow Disease and all the others I just mentioned, they are being used, in my opinion, to create a crisis that will then create a manufactured public outcry, the one they *want us to cry out for* where people will want to know and demand exactly what's in their food supply, where it came from, what's being done to it, all the way from the Farm to the Fork. Hey! Where have I heard that before? They appear on the scene and announce, "Hey, we just happen to have a reliable tracking system to ensure the safety of our food all the way from the Farm to the Fork. Its called RFID and if we implement it on every item on the whole planet, we'll all be safe!" In fact, they're already conditioning us to think this food tracking and labeling is a good thing.

**Foodprint**

*<grocery store meat counter>*

*Customer: May I have 3 of these steaks please?*

*Butcher: Three sirloin?*

*Customer: Yes*

*Butcher: Certainly you can. Three sirloin steaks coming up.*

*Customer: What's Foodprint?*

*Butcher: Foodprint? Well, to cut a long story short, it means you can now find out exactly where your beef came from and all the information that's contained in your number, your unique Foodprint number, is on the sticker.*

*Customer: So if I buy prepacked pork for the chill cabinet <fridge> I know it's fully traceable and now if I buy beef over the counter, from the butcher, you can trace it back too.*

*Butcher: Exactly. So not only do you get all the usual information on weight, price, date and so on; you will be able to find out where it came from too. With Foodprint, you're 100% assured of it's traceability. For customers like yourself, it's another guarantee of super value quality. Enjoy that!*

*Customer: I'm feeling I will.*

*Butcher: Foodprint is the start of a massive and unique traceability system. It is an excellent incentive and well worth alerting customers to.*

Yeah, and I'll alert you too! It's the beginning of the Mark of the Beast system on your food supply. You see what they're not telling you is that in order to pull off this "Farm to the Fork" vision of our food supply is that right now it's being implemented *voluntarily*. But here real soon, it's going to become *mandatory*! You're not going to have a choice in this anymore. They're going to monitor all your food. It's a program called NAIS or *National Animal Identification System*. It states that, "Every single livestock animal in the United States will be identified, tagged, tracked, logged and reported to the government. It was started under the guise to help meat producers deal with all these food crises, these disease scares, and here's the problem. All animals, and I mean *all* animals. Not just the big corporate factory farm animals, like you think, but all animals. This includes the half-dozen chickens at grandma's house, where, believe it or not, her "premises" and each chicken must be registered with the government as the program now stands. In fact, a pet parakeet in a cage on the 20th floor of a condo in Miami Beach must also be registered, along with the premises and there are no exceptions. Every small independent farmer, pet owners and homesteaders, everyone will have to tag and track every single animal they have and there are *no exceptions*. Lest you think this won't cover our whole food supply, the stated goal of the RFID industry was to have 900 billion food items and 824 million livestock all tagged, all tracked, all monitored with RFID by 2015.

So the question is, "Why? Why are they pushing this?" Well, I don't think you get the answer until you understand Bible Prophecy. You see, I think it's STAGE ONE of an even bigger plan that the Bible talks about. You see, put yourself in the Antichrist's shoes. I mean, here you are with the ultimate goal of tracking and tagging every single person on the whole planet and controlling what they "buy and sell." So how are you going to get people used to the idea of receiving an implant themselves? Well hey! Wouldn't it make sense to implement a kind of Phase One, if you will, and try it out on animals first? First get all the animals on the planet tagged and then once people accept that and get conditioned to that, then mandate it for those that resist, then maybe Phase Two would kick into gear where people would be more willing to be treated like cattle themselves and get their own implant too, for their safety of course! In fact, maybe you could manufacture another disease crisis, this time with humans, to get you to go along with it and lest you think that's really not the plan, listen to this interview with Digital Angel's CEO Kevin McGrath. Digital Angel by the way, is a former maker of RFID implants for animals AND humans, and you tell me if he not only admits to the existence of both phases, he assures us that their full implementation is coming very soon!

**Digital Angel Animal tracking**

*Tara Murphy <Senior anchor, Forbes.com Video Network: RFID technology, to*

track everything from pets to humans. We'll have more from the CEO of Digital Angel when Forbes.com returns.

**Murphy:** Welcome back, I'm Tara Murphy. Chips that contain RFID technology allow you to track everything from humans to pets to airplanes. Digital Angel is one of the companies that manufactures such chips. Joining me now is Kevin McGrath. Mr. McGrath is the President and CEO of Digital Angel. Kevin, thanks for being here.

**McGrath:** Sure. It's my pleasure.

**Murphy:** So, why don't you start by telling me how these chips exactly work.

**McGrath:** Well it's an RFID chip, and everybody knows about RFID. You think about it in terms of Wal-Mart and pallets and boxes moving around. We have developed an expertise in using RFID in animals and humans. So, we have probably chipped more animals in the world than all the other companies combined. We've chipped cats and dogs in the United States and Europe and Japan. We've chipped, believe it or not, salmon in the upper Northwest. We chip livestock. We put RFID chip into ear tags that go on the side of livestock. In fact, we are the 2nd largest livestock tagging company in the United States. We're the oldest livestock tagging company in the United States. The applications are numerous.

**Murphy:** So we see so many great uses of RFID technology. When do you think we're going to start to see a greater penetration.

**McGrath:** Well, on a number of different fronts. First of all our companion pet front, we do a million-we chip a million pets a year in the United States, 2 million pets a year in Europe. So..so that's big. It's going to get much bigger. With regard to livestock; people have heard about the National ID program, the mad cow scare. Making sure all the animals, all the livestock are tagged. I would guess you would start to see major increases in the amount of RFID tags. Our business' are tripling in that area but can go up by a factor of 10. With regard to humans, humans is an area that is moving the slowest in many respects, simply because it's the area obviously from a privacy perspective we all have the most concerns about. But right now, as we speak, we are in clinical implementation in 9 hospitals in the Northeast corridor. Our goal is 25 hospitals by the end of the year. Our goal is every single major trauma center in the United States."[43]

Your goal is every major Trauma Center in the United States will have the RFID implant technology ready to go. Wow! Aren't you glad the government took over our health care system and makes it *mandatory* for us to have…But hey, I'm sure they'll never make it mandatory for us to get an RFID implant, will they? They're doing it with animals and that guy admitted their business has tripled. Don't think that we're not next. The Bible says we are! But that's right! Once again, just to make sure you and I go along with this Mark of the Beast system, Hollywood and the Media are right there encouraging us to do just that. I mean, come on! It's okay, nothing to be afraid of, everybody's doing it! I mean, even ABC is promoting the Mark of the Beast!

## ABC News: Brave New World

***Peter Jennings:*** *Technology on the cutting edge. We were interested to hear that more than 100 law enforcement officials in Mexico are having microchips implanted in their arms. The chips allow someone to be scanned, sort of like a cereal box at the supermarket checkout. In Mexico, this will be one more tool in the fight against crime. Here's ABC's John McKenzie*

***McKenzie:*** *You've seen it before, right out of Hollywood. A microchip inside the body. A hidden high tech identification tag. Now Mexico's Attorney General, and 160 of his deputies, have had microchips implanted in their arms to control access to the country's new Criminal Investigation Center.*

***Rafael Macedo de la Concha -Attorney General:*** *<translated> It is to provide access of the Attorney General to the right people in exclusive areas, where there is valuable, sensitive information.*

***McKenzie:*** *The microchip, the size of a grain of rice, is injected under the skin and gives off a low frequency radio wave. A scanner reads each chip's identification number to verify the official's security clearance. The chip, developed by Applied Digital Solutions is similar to those used in the U.S. to identify and return runaway dogs. In humans, it can have several uses. The chips can also be programmed to carry medical information. The one in this patient details his blood type, allergies and the fact that he has Alzheimers disease. Some researchers are developing microchips for use in the home so that one can turn on lights and open doors hands free. The next step, say researchers, is developing an implantable chip with a global positioning system to track people* *miles away, whether kidnapped or lost just as cars can be tracked--a kind of lo-jack for the body."*[44]

In other words, you can be tracked and tagged like an animal anywhere on the planet! You see, many people today think that their lives are going to be filled with untold riches and absolute security through a *One World Economy*. They think that they have all the time in the world to respond to the gospel after they first go and make all their riches. But the Bible says that God isn't going to keep repeating His message of salvation over and over again. The offer won't be there forever. He simply says that if you hear His voice calling you, you need to respond today.

**Hebrews 3:7-8,10-11** "That is why the Holy Spirit says, 'Today you must listen to his voice. Don't harden your hearts against him as Israel did when they rebelled, when they tested God's patience in the wilderness. There your ancestors tried my patience, even though they saw my miracles for forty years. So I was angry with them, and I said, Their hearts always turn away from me. They refuse to do what I tell them. So in my anger I made a vow: They will never enter my place of rest.'"

People of God, I hope you're not one of those who have bought into this lie that man can somehow manifest his own heaven on earth by creating a *One World Economy*. Why? Because you might wake up one day and discover that you've been left behind and do you know what? God doesn't want you left behind. Because He loves us, He has given us the warning sign of a *One World Economy* to show us that the Tribulation could be near and that Christ's 2nd Coming is rapidly approaching.

Like it or not, we are headed for *The Final Countdown*. We don't know the day or the hour. Only God knows. The point is, if you're a Christian and you haven't noticed; there are no U-hauls behind a hearse. Therefore, let's stop pampering our lusts and let's start praying for the lost! It's high time we Christians speak up and declare the good news of salvation to those who are dying all around us. But please, if you're not a Christian, give your life to Jesus today, because tomorrow may be too late! Just like the Bible said!

*Chapter Ten*

---

# The Mark of the Beast

"A man was sitting at home one evening, when the doorbell rang. When he answered the door, a 6-foot tall cockroach was standing there. But before the man could do anything, the cockroach immediately punched him between the eyes and scampered off.

Well, the next evening, the man was sitting at home when the doorbell rang again. When he answered the door, there was the cockroach again. This time it punched him, kicked him, karate chopped him and then scampered away.

Once again, the third evening came and the man was sitting at home when the doorbell rang. That's right, when he answered the door the cockroach was there yet again.

This time it leapt at him and stabbed him several times before scampering off. At this the gravely injured man managed to crawl to the telephone and summoned for an ambulance. Soon he was rushed to intensive care where they were barely able to save his life.

So the next morning, the doctor was doing his rounds and he asked the man what happened. So the man explained about the surprising nightly attacks of the 6-foot cockroach which culminated in the near fatal stabbing.

But not at all surprised himself, the doctor simply informed the man, 'Yes, there's a nasty bug going around.'"[1]

Now, that doctor wasn't at all surprised about what happened to that man, was he? And it's all because he was well informed about the danger that was out there, right? But unfortunately, many people aren't very well informed about another danger that's out there. And that's the danger of God's wrath which is one day coming upon this wicked and rebellious planet, and because people refuse to get right with God through Jesus and get saved, they are sadly running the risk of being left behind and will be catapulted into the seven-year Tribulation that is coming upon the whole world, and the reason why it's going to be such a horrible time is because for those who refuse to accept Jesus Christ as their Personal Lord and Savior, they'll be catapulted into the 7-year Tribulation and it's not a joke! Again, it's an outpouring of God's wrath on a wicked & rebellious planet! In fact Jesus said in Matthew 24 it's going to be a "time of greater horror than anything the world has ever seen or will ever see again. And that "unless that time of calamity is shortened, the entire human race wiould be destroyed." But praise God, God's not only a God of wrath, He's a God of love as well and because He loves us, He's given us many warning signs to show us when the Tribulation was near and when Jesus Christ's 2$^{nd}$ Coming was rapidly approaching.

The **#1** sign on *The Final Countdown* that God has given to us to lovingly wake us up is none other than **The Mark of the Beast**.

That's right, the Bible is clear. One day the whole planet is not only going to be under the authority of the Antichrist and economy of the Antichrist, but it's also going to be under his Identity or Mark as well and that is going to be his seal of ownership on them and it will seal their eternal destruction! But don't take my word for it. Let's listen to God's.

**Revelation 13:11-18** "Then I saw another beast, coming out of the earth. He had two horns like a lamb, but he spoke like a dragon. He exercised all the authority of the first beast on his behalf, and made the earth and its inhabitants worship the first beast, whose fatal wound had been healed. And he performed great and miraculous signs, even causing fire to come down from heaven to earth in full view of men. Because of the signs he was given power to do on behalf of the first beast, he deceived the inhabitants of the earth. He ordered them to set up an image in honor of the beast who was wounded by the sword and yet lived. He was given power to give breath to the image of the first beast, so that it could speak and cause all who refused to worship the image to be killed. He also forced everyone, small and great, rich and poor, free and slave, to receive a mark on his right hand or on his forehead, so that no one could buy or sell unless he had the mark, which is the name of the beast or the number of his name. This calls for wisdom. If anyone has insight, let him calculate the number of the beast, for it is man's number. His number is 666."

Now according to our text, the Bible clearly says there really is coming a day when all the inhabitants of the earth will not only be under the authority of the Antichrist and economy of the Antichrist, but what? They're going to receive the *Mark* of the Antichrist. They will actually be deceived into receiving some sort of mark on their bodies, either in the right hand or forehead, to connect themselves to the Antichrist system so they can "buy and sell" and escape the threat of death! But again, as always, the question is, "Could this really happen? Could the whole world really be deceived into receiving *The Mark of the Beast* and is there any evidence that it's really going to take place just like the Bible said? Yes! In fact, it's happening now!

### I. The 1st way that we know we really are headed for this Mark of the Beast system is the **Conditioning Proof.**

You see, what most people don't realize is that this Mark of the Beast system of the Antichrist is not only going to be put into place, because the Bible said it would, but what people don't realize is that it's been in the planning stages for a long time AND they've been working real hard, double time, in conditioning us to accept it, *right now*.

### 1. The 1st way they're conditioning us to receive the Mark of the Beast is the **Media Proof.**

Even as far back as former President Calvin Coolidge (20's) he admitted: *"Advertising in the media is the most potent influence in adapting and changing the habits and modes of life affecting what we eat, what we wear and the work and play of a whole nation."*[2]

In other words, he admitted the media and advertisements they use, the power of it, can convince us to buy things we don't need, to impress people we don't know, who in the end don't even care, AND it shapes our belief systems. In other words, it *gets us to do things we normally wouldn't do*, say like accepting the Mark of the Beast, and if you don't believe they're using the media and modern day advertising to get us to do just that, then let's take a look at the historical proof.

1973: As far back as 1973, Senior Scholastics introduced school age children to the concept of buying and selling using numbers inserted in their forehead. In the September 20, 1973 feature 'Who Is Watching You?' the secular high school journal speculated: 'All buying and selling in the program will be done by computer. No currency, no change, no checks. In the program, people would receive a number that had been assigned them tattooed in their wrist or forehead. The number is put on by laser beam and cannot be felt. The number in the body is not seen with the naked eye and is as permanent as your fingerprints. All items of consumer goods will be marked with a computer mark. The computer outlet in the store which picks up the number on the items at the checkstand will also pick up the number in the person's body and automatically total the price and deduct the amount from the person's 'Special Drawing Rights' account.'

1974: In the article 'The Specter of Eugenics,' Charles Frankel pointed out that Linus Pauling (a Nobel Prize winner) suggested that a mark be tattooed on the foot or forehead of every young person.

1980: The U.S. News and World Report warned out that the Federal Government was contemplating 'National Identity Cards,' without which nobody could work or conduct business.

1981: The Denver Post Sun reported that chip implants could someday replace I.D. cards and the June 21, 1981 story read in part, 'The chip is placed in a needle which is affixed to a simple syringe containing an anti-bacterial solution. The needle is capped and ready to forever identify something – or somebody.'

1996: The May 7, 1996 Chicago Tribune questioned the technology, wondering aloud if we could trust Big Brother under our skin?

1997: Applications for patents of subcutaneous implant devices for 'a person or an animal' were applied for.

1998: Time Magazine ran the story, 'The Big Bank Theory And What It Says About The Future of Money,' that stated, 'Your daughter can store the money any way she wants – on her laptop, on a debit card, even (in the not too distant future) on a chip implanted under her skin.'

1998: BBC covered the first known human microchip implantation.

1998: Sunday Portland Oregonian warned that proposed medical identifiers might erode privacy rights by tracking individuals through alphanumeric health identifier technologies. The feature depicted humans with barcodes in their foreheads.

2002: FDA approves VeriChip Microchip implant for humans.

**CBS 4 News:**

*Reporter: Science fiction became reality today. The Food and Drug Administration approved a computer chip that's implanted into people. The chip would contain a person's medical records. The microchip has already been used to identify lost pets and as Lisa Kieva shows us, they have a lot of potential in people.*

*Every second counts when you need help. But you're unconscious and doctors need critical information.*

*Dr. Ray Gessinger: We want to know what medications you're on. We want to know what you're allergic to. We want to know what your health problems are.*

*Kieva: This tiny chip can lead to a wealth of information about you. If you had been implanted with a device, a doctor would scan your upper arm and then...*

*Doctor: A number would come up when you get scanned.*

*Kieva: That number is then entered into a computer database and your medical records appear. Engineers at Digital Angel in St. Paul developed the groundbreaking chip. The company already sells a million ID chips for dogs and cats. That research helped the company develop something safe for humans.*

*Jim Santelli: We, over the years, developed a plastic sheath, the tissue adheres to it and it doesn't move.*

*Kieva: It stays put in your upper arm after doctors use a syringe to implant it there. It will be marketed to people with health problems that may cause them to become unconscious. There are other uses. The military is considering the chip to replace dog tags. Workplaces with tight security concerns might ditch card entry systems and ask you to implant a chip instead.*

2003: Proposals appear for credit card implants
2003: Proposals appear to keep children safe with a microchip
2003: EU wants to use a chip to monitor visitors
2004: Biometric payments expanding to grocery and convenience stores
2004: Bankcard crimes fuel rush to biometric systems
2004: Baja Beach Club in Barcelona Spain launches microchip implantation for VIP members
2004: Microchip and global satellite firms reach agreement
2004: Mexico attorney general gets microchip implant
2004: Japan school kids to be tagged with RFID chips
2004: Proposal for chip implanted in police officer's hands to allow only officers to fire guns
2005: California school requires radio ID tags for students
2005: Proposal for a Digital Birth ID
2005: Chief of Police who received VeriChip advocates forced government chipping to buy and sell
2005: Scientist calls for world DNA database
2006: Employees get microchip implants
2006: VeriChip sells first Baby Protection System and in talks with Military
2006: Proposals for Britons to be microchipped like dogs in a decade
2006: Rise of people voluntarily receiving microchip implants
2006: Young shoppers want to pay with chip in skin
2007: Invisible RFID Ink available for cattle and people
2007: Proposals calling for animal tags for people
2007: FBI aims for world's largest biometrics database
2007: Alzheimer's Patients lining up for microchips
2008: Hospitals start tagging babies with electronic chips
2008: Prisoners are to be chipped like dogs
2008: Microsoft patents a system that could link workers to their computers to read their 'heart rate, galvanic skin response, EMG, brain signals, respiration rate, body temperature, movement, facial movements, facial expressions and blood pressure.' The system could also alert employers to changes in the worker's mental or physical health.
2009: VeriChip, begins working with another company to develop under-the-skin devices to detect "bio-threats."
2009: Stimulus Bill is passed in U.S. that now tracks each individual's health records electronically and assigns an electronic ID to every person to maintain their health records.
2010: Biometric cash machines start to appear in Europe

2010: Obama Administration begins plans to require all American workers to obtain a national biometric identification card.

2010: Germany rolls out National Identity Cards embedded with RFID.

2010: One in four Germans polled want a microchip under their skin.

2011: Obama Administration begins plans to create an Internet ID for All Americans.

2012: A new microchip is developed that now knows your location within centimeters.

2012: Google produces the new Google Wallet cashless system that will provide the convenience of buying products and services without cash. The product will also provide I.D. verification so people can check in for a flight, download virtual boarding passes and keep their driver's license and their credit cards all in one location.

**Google Wallet:**

*This is your wallet. It tells a story. What you buy. Who you love. What you keep close. But what if your wallet was engineered rather than sewn? What if you were struck by a better idea? What if your wallet was a Google Wallet? It would start with your cards-credit and debit. Visa, MasterCard, American Express and Discover-all stored securely in the "cloud". All your cards, all together in a virtual wallet that goes anywhere. Use it on your phone and tap to pay for a double shot macchiato at your favorite cafe, or a taxi ride to the club, or gummy bears at the movie theatre. And when you go online, your wallet goes with you. So it's easier than ever to order everything you need for your next vacation. And that new song from your favorite band is just a single click away. Whether you're shopping in the store or online, your wallet keeps all your payment info safe and secure. It's everything you love all in one wallet.*

2012: FBI launches $1 Billion face recognition project

2012: 2013: Verizon latest commercial for its Droid DNA phone prepares people for being chipped by showing a man being implanted with various smartphone parts to merge his body and his phone.

2013: A new "biostamp tattoo" is developed that attaches to the wearer's skin and will allow them to replace ALL passwords and ALL other forms of Identification.

*"A team of scientists, led by University of Illinois professor John Rogers has created a new, less intrusive way of gathering data from the human body. Unlike*

*conventional equipment that hardwires patients to a stationary machine; epidermal electronics, as they're called, attach to the skin in the same way you'd attach a temporary tattoo.*

**John Rogers:** *Our thought was that if you could convert the electronics from the rigid boxy form that exists today into a format that looks like the skin in terms of mechanical properties, shape, stretchability, toughness, then you could almost make like a second skin that would laminate on the surface of the biological skin in a completely seamless integrated fashion that would be essentially invisible to the user but able to deliver all this kind of new functionality through the skin. The kind of functioning systems that we demonstrated in this paper involve devices that come out of the brain function, so they laminate on the forehead where they can monitor brainwaves and determine certain aspects of brain activity.*

*If you cover it with a temporary tattoo, first of all, other people cannot see it. It is very easy to wear and since we are using a wireless system, the patient can go do normal life without any restriction."*

2013: Officials are calling for a national registration of each person's DNA at the time of birth.[3]

You can have a normal life without restriction, you know, you can still "buy" and "sell." Did you notice that thing was already being put on the hand and the forehead? And it's not some unsightly, ugly looking thing, it can actually be embedded in a tattoo that even kids would like and it also answers some of the skeptics out there that say it's logistically impossible to Mark everybody on the planet at the same time. It would just take too much time they say. Really? Not if everybody gets one of those in the mail, you could do it all in one shot!

But correct me if I'm wrong, when you take a look at the timeline, I'd say somebody's not only pretty serious about implementing this Mark of the Beast, but by the looks of it, they're just about ready to pull the whole thing off, how about you? Apparently, the media and the advertising is working like a charm! For the first time in man's history, it's here! And that's exactly what the Bible said would happen, when you are living in the Last Days!

**2.** The **2ⁿᵈ way** they're conditioning us to receive the Mark of the Beast is what I call the **Matrix Proof.**

Whether you realize it or not, a matrix is being created *right now* that connects everything on the planet that's needed to pull off this Mark of the Beast system. It's called the *Internet* and if you'll notice, all information, all finances, all knowledge and all forms of media, all are being connected and merged with this new invention called the Internet and the key word there I believe is...*net*, the net is closing in on us! It's not just in existence *right now*, but we've already, in just a few short years, been conditioned to accept it and to rely upon it for almost all our needs, including financial needs. You can buy online, you can sell online, you can bank online, you can do all your studying and research online, you can shop online, you can watch TV online, you can register online, you can make your appointments online. You can do just about anything and everything online! Everything is going online, have you noticed?

Now here's the point. It's a giant matrix system that's starting to control everything we do, including our finances and buying and selling and that's what's needed for the Mark of the Beast system! This is why I've said I truly believe that this term in the Bible "buying and selling," is a loaded term. When you're shut out of the Antichrist's system, this matrix he's creating, buying and selling is just the tip of the iceberg. If you think of the Internet, it's everything! Again, here's the problem. *Right now* we can access it with a certain amount of freedom, but what if one day somebody hijacked this matrix system that controls everything on the planet, then what would we do? You talk about a power play, right? Well I'm here to tell you, that's not just a theory, it's reality *now*! Right now we are seeing signs of the Internet, that connects everything on the planet, including finances, to become limited. The freedom to access the Internet is being taken away, and the net is closing in on us. Let's take look.

- China turned its back on Internet censorship promises and moves forward with a sort of "digital" Great Wall.
- Former President of Italy, Silvio Berlusconi, pushes for an "international" agreement to "regulate the Internet."
- Thailand's Government begins blocking 1,000's of websites.
- The UK is promoting a "Digital Economy Bill" to block whatever websites it wishes.
- The U.S. Department of Defense begins banning employees and soldiers from certain websites.
- Australia is working on implementing a mandatory Internet filter modeled on the Communist Chinese government system that will allow the government to block any website it desires, including "Christian" sites.

- The World Economic Forum is calling for the Internet to be policed by means of "licenses" similar to driver's licenses. "We need a kind of World Health Organization for the Internet. If you want to drive a car you have to have a license to say that you are capable of driving a car, the car has to pass a test to say it is fit to drive and you have to have insurance." The same system they say should be used for the Internet and we will need to have government permission to use the web. Or another method they're proposing is to use mandatory fingerprint scanners like the ones that are starting to be included on new computers. "You would have to register your fingerprint at a central government data center and then scan each time you want to access the Internet. Misbehave online and your access will be denied."

- And during his presidency, President Obama signed an Executive Order that quietly gave himself power to seize the Internet, in the event of a national crisis, of course.

- And if you think that's bad, the United Nations is seeking to control the whole Internet around the whole world. They're calling it the International Telecommunication Union, or ITU; here's the logo.

Their plan is to create a new set of international laws to structure the way the Internet works as well as give them global censoring capabilities. Even though one man stated, "It'll be the biggest power grab in the U.N.'s history," the U.N. assures us that it's just a, "Chance to create a global roadmap to connect the unconnected."[4]

You make sure everybody's connected to this matrix system, but make sure we control it. Now if you don't think that's what they're planning on doing, let's remind ourselves of what Google's co-founder, Sergey Brin, said. Their goal is to, "Be like the mind of God," where they, "want to know everything about you!" and, "It's a future that they're working feverishly to make a reality now." Well, how are they doing that? How are you going to connect everybody to this matrix system at all times? They've recently come out with what's called Google Glass. And what they are is these glasses that you put on your head, so you can communicate to the Internet and Google, at anytime, anywhere, no matter where you go, even without a computer or cell phone.

**Google Glass:**

*Here are the basics of how to use glass.*

*This is your touch pad.*
*It runs from your temple to your ear.*

*Tap the touch pad to wake up Glass.*

*You should see the display above your line of sight.*
*Adjust it to see everything.*

*Home screen shows a clock.*
*This is your timeline.*

*The row of cards.*
*Things to the left are happening now, are coming up.*
*Like the weather, an upcoming flight, or an event in your calendar.*

*You can tap on any card to see more.*
*Click down anywhere to go back to the timeline.*

*"Ok Glass, record video."*

*Switches to scene with dancer*

*"This is it. We are on in 2 minutes."*

*Switched to guy flying personal airplane*

*"Ok Glass, hangout with the flying club."*

*Switched to scene of guy with ice sculpture.*

*"Google photos of tiger heads."*

*Switches to scene of dog playing with toy.*

*"You ready, you ready?"*

*Switches to scene of kids playing with bubbles.*

*"Ok Glass, take a picture."*

*Switches to scene of girl running in circles at park,*

*"laughing"*

*Switches to scene of girl ice skating*

*Switches to man with pet snake on arms*

*"Wow, look at that snake."*

*Switches to family on Roller coaster*

*"Ok glass, record a video."*

*Switches to scene of bicyclist riding thru traffic.*

*Switches to scene of passenger in car driving thru traffic on Golden Gate Bridge. "after this bridge first exit."*

*Switches to scene of skiers skiing down hill.*

*Switches to scene of airplane doing tricks.*

*Switches to scene of girl jumping off indoor trampoline into foam pit.*

*Switches to man ice sculpting a tiger.*

*Switches to scene of couple running thru airport in a hurry to catch their flight.*

*Switches to scene of model walking down the runway.*

*Switches to scene of girl blowing out her birthday candles*

*Switches to scene of man eating Thai food on his canoe*

*"Google, say delicious in Thai."*

*Switches to jelly fish at aquarium.*

*"Google, jellyfish."*

*Switches to scene from the hot air balloons*

*"It's beautiful..."*[5]

It's beautiful! I can be connected to the Internet with a pair of glasses on my head at anytime. I can send photos, ask questions, talk to people, request a map, take a video, post online and use Social Networking. It's beautiful. Then if I use Google Wallet, maybe I can even pay my bills and shop online with Google Glasses on my head! But that's just step one of what they have admitted is their ultimate goal. Listen to this:

"Soon Google hopes to have the ubiquitous presence of a personal assistant that never stops working, capable of conversing naturally in any language. Ultimately, as Page and co-founder Sergey Brin have asserted, the goal is to *insert a chip inside your head* for the most effortless search engine imaginable."

Because as we all know, glasses could slip off your head or you can lose them...but not if you've got a Google Chip in your head...

***The first stage** of this new level of intimacy is **Google Glass**."*[6]

They admit it and I would say, it's the first step of "being the mind of god" and the Mark of the Beast system that the Bible said would happen when you're living in the Last Days!

**3. The 3rd way they're conditioning us to receive the Mark of the Beast is the Quotation Proof.**

If you really think they're not really working hard at getting us conditioned to receive the Mark of the Beast system the Bible said would come in the Last Days, all you gotta do is listen to their quotes! They admit it! And not just Google, but all kinds of people! In fact, they're totally blunt about it! But again, don't take my word for it. Let's listen to theirs.

- Digital Angel Spokesman said, "We've changed our thinking since September 11. Now there's more of a need to monitor evil activities."
- The British Ministry of Justice is investigating the use of satellite and radio-wave technology to monitor criminals. Instead of being contained in bracelets worn around the ankle, the tiny chips would be surgically inserted under the skin of offenders in the community, to help enforce home curfews. "All options are on the table, and this is one we would like to pursue."
- Dr. Peter Zhou chief scientist of Digital Angel said, "A few years ago there may have been resistance, but not anymore. People are getting used to having implants. New century, new trend…this will be very, very popular. Fifty years ago the thought of a cell phone, where you could walk around talking on the phone, was unimaginable. Now they are everywhere." Just like the cell phone, Digital Angel "will be a connection from yourself to the electronic world. It will be your guardian, protector. It will bring good things to you. We will be a hybrid of electronic intelligence and our own soul."
- Andy Rooney said on 60 Minutes, "Something has to change though. They have to find a better way to identify the bad guys or the rest of us are going to stay home and watch the rest of the world go by on television. But we need some system for permanently identifying 'safe' people. Most of us are never going to blow anything up. And there's got to be something better than one of these photo IDs. A tattoo somewhere maybe. The Saudi's used an American device to scan the eyes of travelers. I wouldn't mind having something implanted permanently in my arm that would identify me."
- John Walsh of America's Most Wanted said about implants, "It's a brilliant idea. I wish someone would develop it because, number one, time is crucial when a child is missing and you could locate them by the chip. And even if

you weren't lucky enough to locate them, finding the body is crucial for two things: the ending of the search of the parents and helping with the prosecution of the case. So I hope that somebody develops that in my lifetime."

- Scott Silverman President of Digital Angel said, "It's a shame that recent tragedies seem to have prompted this increased attention, but the only way to assist in the prevention of future tragedies is for parents, law enforcement and others to become aware of available technologies. Although our technologies have a variety of other applications, we believe VeriChip, Digital Angel and the forthcoming PLD have the potential to help safeguard children and provide greater peace-of-mind to parents."
- While interviewing Scott Silverman, Sean Hannity said he "loved this idea of putting microchips in kids to keep track of them."

**Sean Hannity – The Mark**

*Hannity:* *"Digital solutions could track human beings by satellite. Alright, we got the Vandams, we got Elizabeth Smart, we got this girl in Pennsylvania, we got Samantha Runion, one... We got this other little girl. One after another after another after another after another, and we got parents around America saying we can't even allow our kids to play in the front yard. Is there anything technologically speaking that they can do, that can help in the situation of a kidnapping. Is there for example, a microchip, a watch, a tracking device that we could use for our kids?"*

*Scott Silverman:* *"We are working on a product that we call internally a PLD. PLD stands for Personal Locating Device which is an implantable GPS, for which our company owns the patent, and can be implanted surgically in the clavicle area of a child, or someone you are interested in tracking. It is the first implantable microchip for humans. It has multiple security, financial and healthcare applications."*

*Hannity:* *"The one thing I would just suggest, and I'm just an outside soon to be investor, I love this idea by the way Scott. I think it's great..."*

- Author Mac Slavo wrote, "With more Americans than ever before being dependent on government redistribution of wealth and services to get by, acceptance by most people of this technology is not such a far off proposition, especially with the threat of cutting off access to those services which people have become so dependent upon for survival. Those who refuse the chip, of course, would soon be labeled unpatriotic domestic terrorists, added to no fly lists (because if you're not chipped, you're probably hiding something and are obviously dangerous), and we'd soon see FBI/DHS bulletins distributed to doctors, retailers and government bureaucrats about how to identify potentially threatening activities of non-chippers. If you see an unchipped, say something. It's your duty."

- And just in case you don't want to listen to him, even the previous Pope is saying being chipped and tracked is okay! In fact, he recently implemented it for his staff.

*"Pope Benedict the 16th and his security detail will reportedly start using RFID technology to begin tracking Priests and employees at the Vatican. The move to use the tracking technology comes as the Pope's butler stole sensitive documents from his apartment last year and gave them to the news media."*

*Switches to scene at San Antonio, Texas high school*

*"The North side school district welcomes the support."*

*Craig Wood – School District Attorney "It is nice to know, that one of the major religions of the world who have had the opportunity to study the Bible and take into account its application in the real world doesn't believe that RFID has anything to do with Revelation".* [7]

Wow! Well apparently, if the Pope says it's okay, then it must be okay, right? Talk about shades of the False Prophet who "dupes the whole world into receiving the Mark of the Beast!" But hey, that's just those Catholic people. I mean hey, we're Protestants! I mean, it's good news to know that our leaders, our Pastors would never do that to us, or would they? Check out what one so-called Protestant Pastor said about the Mark.

Mark Jackson – Church of England Minister *"I'm assistant Minister of Grace Church Elage. Ya, I wouldn't have a problem probably buying or selling or using money in this way. I personally don't have a problem with this idea of having a microchip put in your arm as a sort of credit card that you can buy and sell in clubs or go down to Sams Breez and buy your food. No, I would not have a problem with that as a Christian. I think you can worship Jesus Christ at the same time having the mark in your arm, Yes..."* [8]

Can you believe that? We live in a day and age where so-called Christian Pastors, Protestants, are saying that you can receive the Mark and somehow still be a Christian! Excuse me? That's not what the Bible says!

**Revelation 14:9-11** "A third angel followed them and said in a loud voice: 'If anyone worships the beast and his image and receives his mark on the forehead or on the hand, he, too, will drink of the wine of God's fury, which has been poured full strength into the cup of his wrath. He will be tormented with burning sulfur in the presence of the holy angels and of the Lamb. And the smoke of their torment rises for ever and ever. There is no rest day or night for those who worship the beast and his image, or for anyone who receives the mark of his name.'"

In other words, you're going to *hell* if you receive the Mark of the Beast! You wonder why I'm teaching on Bible Prophecy? We have a so-called Christian Pastor saying it's perfectly fine. People are being led astray in the Church because they're ignorant of Scripture and Bible Prophecy. But here's the point. It sure looks to me like somebody's taking this *Mark of the Beast* thing kind of seriously, how about you?...*in our lifetime!* Everybody's promoting it! Even to the highest levels of society, even the Pope, even some Pastors, if you can believe that. And that's exactly like the Bible said would happen, when you are living in the Last Days!

**4. The 4<sup>th</sup> way** they're conditioning us to receive the Mark of the Beast is the **Biometric Proof.**

The Bible is clear. You not only have to be connected to this Global Matrix System in the Last Days that the Bible calls the Mark of the Beast, but you have to be connected to it, with your *body*. But don't take my word for it. Let's listen to God's.

**Revelation 20:1-6** "And I saw an angel coming down out of heaven, having the key to the Abyss and holding in his hand a great chain. He seized the dragon, that ancient serpent, who is the devil, or satan, and bound him for a thousand years. He threw him into the Abyss, and locked and sealed it over him, to keep him from deceiving the nations anymore until the thousand years were ended. After that, he must be set free for a short time. I saw thrones on which were seated those who had been given authority to judge. And I saw the souls of those who had been beheaded because of their testimony for Jesus and because of the word of God. They had not worshiped the beast or his image and had not received his mark on their foreheads or their hands. They came to life and reigned with Christ a thousand years. (The rest of the dead did not come to life until the thousand years were ended.) This is the first resurrection. Blessed and holy are those who have part in the first resurrection. The second death has no power over them, but they will be priests of God and of Christ and will reign with Him for a thousand years."

Now maybe it's just me, but I think it's pretty obvious there's a *great* payoff for those who refuse to receive the Mark of the Beast, right? It says they're *blessed*, how? They get to rule and reign with Jesus Christ, personally, for 1,000 years and they will actually become priests of God! How many of you would say that's *much better* than the alternative there? The second death, that's mentioned there by the way, is referring to the act of being chucked into the Lake of Fire forever and ever and forever being tormented for all eternity, years without end! It's a horrible scenario. I didn't say that, God did!

**Revelation 20:14-15** "Then death and Hades were thrown into the lake of fire. The lake of fire is the second death. If anyone's name was not found written in the book of life, he was thrown into the lake of fire."

In other words, here's your destiny if you continue to reject Jesus. You go from hell, to the Great White Throne Judgment to the Lake of Fire! That's the second death! It just got worse for you *forever*! You thought hell was bad? You ain't seen nothing yet! So here's the point. How many of you would say, that's a pretty rotten future, you know what I'm saying? And so the question is, "Well then, how does the Antichrist get people to risk this horrible destiny by receiving his mark? How does he do it?" Well, notice where the Mark is. The Bible says it's on their *foreheads* or their *hands*, right? And so this tells us, that the Antichrist, at some point, has to condition the world into not only being linked to this Global Matrix System that controls all the buying and selling on the planet, but he has to get them used to being linked to this system using a body part, right? Specifically, the right hand, or the forehead, right? It says it right there. Now I don't know about you but man it's a good thing we see no signs of that ever happening any time soon, people using a body part to make payment for something! Yeah, right! It's already here! In fact, it's got a name. It's called *Biometrics*. Whether people realize it or not, for the first time in man's history, we now have the ability to biometrically identify people anywhere on the planet and link them to a global matrix system that controls all of our buying and selling. It's here now! That's how close we are to the actual Mark of the Beast.

**A. The 1ˢᵗ way that Modern Biometrics are conditioning us to receive the actual Mark of the Beast is the Database Proof.**

You see once again, put yourself in the Antichrist's shoes. If you're going to monitor and control the whole planet with this Mark of the Beast system, you not only need to track people wherever they go, but you have to have some sort of database to identify who they are and what they're buying and selling in the first place, right? It's common sense! And we saw earlier in our study, that they've already got those kind of databases. They're called mega-databases and as we saw, just one company in the U.S. called Acxiom operates one of the world's largest databases on ninety-five percent of all American households. 24 hours a day, they gather and store information on you and I from credit card transactions, magazine subscriptions, telephone numbers, real estate records, car registrations and even fishing licenses, to name a few and because of all this information, they can provide a full profile of each one of us, right down to whether we own a dog or a cat, enjoy camping or gourmet cooking, read the Bible or other books, what our occupation is, what car we drive, what videos we watch, where our favorite vacation spots are and even how much food and gas we buy. They know what we buy and sell! In fact, it's estimated that, right now, each adult in the developed world is already located, on average, in three hundred different databases with an average of 1,500 data points on you.[9] That's a huge file! In other words, for the first time in mankind's history, the ability for the Antichrist to know everything about everyone on the whole planet, including who you are, where you are, what you buy and sell, is already here! So here's the point. Databases are just step one. We know, Biblically speaking, at some point, we have to be linked to these databases *biometrically*, or with our body parts, right? That's what the Bible says. So guess what? That too is already here! Not just databases, but a push for biometric databases. Don't believe me? Let's take a look at the new trend!

- The FBI is embarking on a $1 billion effort to build the world's largest computer database of peoples' physical characteristics, a project that would give the government unprecedented abilities to identify individuals in the United States and abroad biometrically. In the coming years, law enforcement authorities around the world will be able to rely on iris patterns, face-shape data, scars and perhaps even the unique ways people walk and talk, to solve crimes and identify criminals and terrorists. "It's going to be an essential component of tracking," said Barry Steinhardt. "It's enabling the Always On Surveillance Society."

### CNN: FBI Billion dollar database

*Alina Cho: The government is taking a big new step looking to build a huge database of people's physical characteristics. The FBI's taking on a billion dollar project to gather their fingerprints, palm patterns, even digital pictures of faces. Eventually, it could expand to include iris patterns, face shape patterns, scars, even information on how you walk and talk. It's called biometrics and it could change the face of law enforcement. But it is also causing a lot of controversy. American Morning Legal Contributor Sunny Hostin is joining us now. So we're talking about some incredible stuff like tracking the shape of your earlobes? So what is the FBI's goal in doing all of this?*

*Sunny Hostin: Well the goal is to have a comprehensive database to track terrorist suspects, criminals, that sort of thing.*

*Cho: For those of us who aren't on terror watch lists, like the two of us. I mean do we need to be concerned about this kind of thing?*

*Hostin: I think so. I really think so. You know, the ACLU and other groups are saying Big Brother is watching but you do have to be careful. And it's interesting because a lot of this information is already in a database. I'm already in a database having been a Federal prosecutor and having security clearance. I'm already in that database. What the FBI wants to do is take that information and KEEP it and THAT'S the problem.*

*Cho: Sunny, thanks.*

*And hope that you're not on that terror watch list <laughs>*

- The Next Generation database is intended to "fuse" fingerprint, face, iris and palm matching capabilities by this year. "The long-term goal: 'ubiquitous use' of biometrics. A traveler may walk down an airport corridor and allow his face and iris images to be captured without ever stepping up to a kiosk and looking into a camera." Intelligence agents could exchange biometric information worldwide. The FBI is building its system according to standards shared by Britain, Canada, Australia and New Zealand. "People's bodies will become de facto national identification cards."

- The Obama Administration began plans to require all American workers to obtain a national biometric identification card.

- Biometric Database of all adult Americans is hidden in the Immigration Reform Bill. The immigration reform measure the Senate began debating would create a national biometric database of virtually every adult in the U.S., in what privacy groups fear could be the first step to a ubiquitous national identification system. Buried in the more than 800 pages of legislation is language mandating the creation of a massive federal database administered by the Department of Homeland Security and containing names, ages, Social Security numbers and photographs of everyone in the country with a driver's license or other state-issued photo ID. Employers would be obliged to look up every new hire in the database to verify that they match their photo. Privacy advocates fear this will lead to the proof of self being required at polling places, to rent a house, buy a gun, open a bank account, acquire credit, board a plane or even attend a sporting event or log on to the internet. "It starts to change the relationship between the citizen and state; you do have to get permission to do things," said Chris Calabrese. "It could be the start of keeping a record of all things." Another man stated, "The most worrying aspect is that this creates a principle of permission to do certain activities and it can be used to restrict activities. It's like a national ID system without the card."

- President Obama wanted a National DNA Database.

*RT News: Now Barack Obama's proposing a new plan to create a National DNA database. It will be created by taking the DNA of every single person that is arrested, even if they're not necessarily convicted of a crime.*

- Australian officials are calling for a national DNA database taken at the time of birth.

*The New South Wales government and Police have begun a major push to have all Australians entered on the National DNA Register as a way to fight crime. They want everyone's DNA to be recorded at birth.*

*Robert Ovadia: Murders, rapes, armed robberies, assaults, kidnappings. There are 60,000 outstanding cases on the New South Wales crime scene database. And the Police Force's chief scientist says if they could match DNA they've recovered to a name...*

**Dr. Tony Raymond:** *<Chief Police Scientist> Probably half of those would be solved immediately.*

**Ovadia:** *Immediately?*

**Raymond:** *Well, you would have a profile and you'd have a profile of the person it'd match.*

*The proposal is for a DNA database of all Australians from birth.*

**Ovadia:** *It would be a matter of gamechanger you think?*

*Oh it would be a massive gamechanger.*

- Israel launches a new Biometric Database tracking project. Despite protests by privacy groups, Israel will begin amassing biometric data on its citizens.
- Scientists are calling for a World DNA database.[10]

What? Why would you want to do that? Well, then you could accuse anyone around the world of committing a crime, and then do away with them. This is the kind of society we're headed for. Sure looks to me like every single person on the planet can be accurately and specifically identified, tracked and linked to a database using their biometrics, how about you? A body part is linking them to a database for the first time in man's history and I don't know about you, but I'd say that's exactly what the Antichrist needs to pull off the Mark of the Beast System!

**B. The 2nd way Modern Day Biometrics is conditioning us to receive the actual Mark of the Beast is the Head Proof.**

According to the Bible, if you're going to control and monitor the whole planet with *The Mark of the Beast*, then you not only need some sort of general biometric database to identify who people are and to link them to the system, but at some point, it has to get specific with the body parts. Let's remind ourselves of what those parts are.

**Revelation 14:9-10** "If anyone worships the beast and his image and receives his mark on the forehead or on the hand, he, too, will drink of the wine of God's fury, which has been poured full strength into the cup of His wrath."

In other words, don't do it! But the point is, what was the first body part mentioned there? The *head*, right? And once again, I'm so glad we see no signs of people using their head specifically to buy and sell stuff, how about you? Yeah right! That too is already here. Let's take a look.

- Eyeball-Scanning is now a reality. Scientists have developed iris-scanning technology to be deployed at schools, airports and banks. "Imagine a world where you're no longer reliant on user names and passwords. If we're going through a turnstile and you have authorization to go beyond that, it'll open the turnstile for you, if you embed it into a tablet or PC, it will unlock your phone or your tablet or it will log you into your email account." The system is being rolled out at some schools this fall. Kids will simply look into the binocular-shaped scanner and it will "beep if they're on the right bus and honk if they're on the wrong one." As one person said, "Apparently, this is cheaper and easier than having teachers tell kids where to go." It also syncs with a mobile app to keep parents apprised of their kid's every move. "Every time a child boards or exits the bus, his parent gets an email or text with the child's photograph, a Google map where they boarded or exited the bus, as well as the time and date." So basically, it's now impossible for kids to peace-out and skip school undetected instead of getting on the bus. The technology could soon be available at banks — "you can gain access to an ATM in a blink" — and airports — "the system will analyze your iris as you pass through security, identifying and welcoming you by name." As one person stated, "If this means shorter lines at customs, we're all for it." And they've even developed the technology where you don't have to be right up next to it. The new eye scanners can look deep inside your eye from 15 feet away and can scan 50 people per minute and can see through contact lenses and glasses. In fact, Iris scanning it set to secure a whole city in Mexico and then the world. The million-plus citizens of Leon, Mexico are set to become the first example of a city secured through the power of biometric identification. Iris and face scanning technologies will allow people to use their eyes to prove their identity, withdraw money from an ATM, get help at a hospital and even ride the bus.

## Iris Scanner and Facial Recognition

*Man:* *<waving arms> THIS WAY FOR YOUR ID*

*Welcome to the college orientation of the future. First, get your ID card. Then get your eyeball scanned.*

*Woman to student: Look into this mirror, tell me if you can see your eyes.*

*Entering buildings using your eyes. Sound like science fiction?*

*<flashback to scene from Minority Report where character of Tom Cruise walks into a Gap and gets IDed by an eye scanner>*

*Biometric security. It's a growing trend. Iris scanning is catching on in colleges and even some elementary schools. Since Newtown, some elementary schools are experimenting with using iris scans to ID kids getting on and off the school bus and several companies are competing for the business.*

*This scanner is for airports. <voice of scanner as each man passes through: welcome Jerry. Welcome Luciano. Welcome David>*

*Man in car pulls up to eye scanner at gated apartment building to be let out.*

*Employee at a company stands in front of eye scanner to unlock a door.*

*Smartphone starts speaking: I am your BioLock security. Please choose your authentication method. Owner of phone: See you can drag the lock to where it says scan face or scan eyes. So let's do a facial scan..*

*Smartphone: "Stand By while I attempt to authenticate" <miniature monitor displaying owner's face in real time comes up in display. Phone scans face> "Authentication process complete. Access granted."*

- Every other means of access (license, credit card, keys, etc) has the potential of being augmented or replaced by iris and face scanning. Get on a bus, pass security on the way into work, pay for a meal, order packages online – all without using anything besides your eye.

- The Homeland Security Department plans to test futuristic iris scan technology that stores digital images of people's eyes in a database and is considered a quicker alternative to fingerprints at a Border Patrol station in Texas where they will be used on illegal immigrants.
- There are billions of facial images already in databases throughout the world.
- State police have linked surveillance cameras to facial recognition software and are using them to instantly recognize and match "wanted people" to image databases. Researchers are working on capturing images of faces from as far away as 200 yards.
- Computers can now tell what you are thinking just by looking at your face. Researchers at MIT are developing software that can read the feelings behind facial expressions. They call it the Mood Meter that senses the general mood of crowds. Here it is in action.

*MIT Mood Meter. Clip showing college students seeing themselves on a display with either green happy faces or yellow indifferent face covering over their own faces as the camera senses mood by the expression on a persons face. If you were smiling, it covered your face with a green happy face. Video transitions to what looks like an airport area with the same results, cameras reading and interpreting the mood of individual people, including one red unhappy face popping up on the monitor.*

- Billboards and TV's can now detect your face. Next time you are looking up at a billboard, there's a chance it may be looking back down at you. Immersive Labs has developed software for digital billboards which can measure the age range, gender and attention-level of a passer-by and quantify the effectiveness of an outdoor marketing campaign. Beyond just bringing metrics to the outdoor advertisements, facial detection technology can tailor ads to people based on their features. Plan UK, a children's charity group, ran a bus-stop advertisement as part of their "Because I Am A Girl" campaign where women passing by would see a full 40-second clip, while if man saw the ad, it would only display a message directing him to their website. The next generation of systems could take this data collection much farther - an algorithm could judge whether you look happy, sad, sick, healthy, comfortable or nervous and direct personalized advertisements to you. Today, these types of sensors may be part of the television when you purchase it. Already in the last year alone, Sony, Samsung, Lenovo and Toshiba have each introduced "Smart TVs" with facial recognition technology built-in. Intel is reportedly making this technology a centerpiece of its new push into the commercial TV sector, using it as leverage to bring reluctant media companies on board to their platform. At this rate, it won't be long before your TV is watching you as well.

- Facebook recently hit the headlines when it bought face.com, an Israeli firm that pioneered the use of face recognition technology online. The social networking giant uses the software to recognize people in uploaded pictures, allowing it to accurately spot friends. The system then learns what a user looks like as more pictures are approved. This data is then used to identify you in the real world.
- Google also recognizes the potential of facial recognition. They just acquired a facial recognition company to allow them to do what Facebook is doing and even much more. There are talks how they will incorporate this with Google Goggles that enables people to identify people by their face with their smart phones and some wonder if they will not also incorporate this in their Google Glass headsets.
- Shoppers could soon be automatically recognized when they walk into a shop using Facedeals. This is a camera that uses photos uploaded to Facebook to recognize people as they walk in and gives them specials to buy drinks with. Here's a transcript of the video.

*Facedeals: We ask ourselves. Why have the Facebook check-ins gone mainstream. Check-ins provide a powerful mechanism for business. Businesses deliver discounts to loyal customers. But few businesses and even fewer customers are taking advantage of this. So we set out to evolve the check-in process by creating a seamless method of checking in and getting deals. Facedeals is an automated check in system using passive facial recognition to notify you of deals customized just for you. Cameras have been developed to identify Facedeals participants in a matter of seconds. When a face is patently recognized, the deal is set into action. It's that simple.*

- Ecuador has now implemented the world's first Countrywide Facial and Voice Recognition System.
- The FBI has just launched a $1 billion face recognition project.

Hmmm. Why would you want to do that? Surely they wouldn't take this nationwide, would they? But you might be thinking, "Well hey, that's just using your eye or face or head to link yourself to a database. That's not buying and selling. The Bible says you have to use your head to specifically buy and sell and make financial transactions. So that's not happening yet." Really? I'm telling you, it's a step by step process! First get the databases, then get the biometrics, then get specific with the head to link to this database and then use that head to make a payment. *It's already here!*

**Uniqul:**

*Imagine coming to a store and your wallet is already there. You pick up your things and approach the check out. Give a meaningful nod. And that's it.*

*Imagine you're late to your plane. There was a huge que, but you instantly check in while running to the border control.*

*Imagine you drive to the Petrol station. You casually fuel your tank and your payment is done simultaneously. You just had to click okay.*

*Imagine the shop where all those magic things came to life. People coming with friends just to show it off. Well this is not fiction anymore. They all got a Uniqul calendar. Now whereever they go, I recognize them. Processing takes under a second. They sign in as soon as I see them. All they had to do was click okay.*

*Hi! I'm your new friend. UNIQUL."* [11]

Hi! I'm you're new friend, Antichrist! All you have to do is click "OK" and make a payment with your head. Gee, where have I heard that before? Looks to me like we're seeing for the first time in man's history people are starting to make payments with their *head*, how about you? I mean, what's next? Some sort of chip in your head, to do the same thing? This is how close we are to the actual implementation of the *Mark of the Beast* in the Last Days! It's not fifty years down the road, it's happening right now.

**3. The 3rd way Modern Day Biometrics is conditioning us to receive the actual Mark of the Beast is the second option there, the Hand Proof.**

**Revelation 13:16-17** "He also forced everyone, small and great, rich and poor, free and slave, to receive a mark on his right hand or on his forehead, so that no one could buy or sell unless he had the mark."

And so here we see again the second option for the Mark of the Beast System, is to not only use your head, but what was the second choice there? Your *hand*, right? Again, I'm so glad we see no signs of people using their hand to buy and sell stuff in a biometric way. Yeah right! That too is already here. Let's take a look.

- Fingerprint scans are now being used in America to access computers.
- Fingerprints are now required to enter certain parks in the United States. "City officials said the new security measure will allow law enforcement to determine who was at the park if something were to happen there and help stop vandalism, drug use and break ins.
- A new company called IDair has developed a system that can scan and identify a fingerprint from nearly 20 feet away. IDair's 20-foot-range machine is currently in development and is described as functioning similar to satellite imagery. Coupled with other biometrics, it could soon allow security systems to grant or deny access from a distance without requiring users to stop and scan a fingerprint, swipe an ID card, or otherwise lose a moment dealing with technology. IDair's founder says that at some point his technology could enable purchases to be made biometrically using fingerprints and irises as unique identifiers rather than credit card numbers and data embedded in magnetic strips or RFID chips and the technology can be used in both in-store and online settings as well as to gain access to services.
- Hand scanners are being used by businesses and airports to automatically identify travelers.
- Hospitals are implementing Palm Scans. "Imagine going to the hospital and having your doctor or nurse retrieve your vital medical records simply by scanning the palm of your hand. It is happening now at a local medical center. Employees at Salem Community Hospital said they are the first in Ohio to have the new 'Patient Secure' system."

Wow! Don't you feel so much more secure? But you might be thinking, "Well, wait a minute. That's just using your finger or hand to link yourself to a database. So what? Nobody's going to be using their hand any time soon to buy and sell stuff." Really? I'm telling you, once again, it's a step by step process! First get the database, then get the biometrics, then get specific with the head and now with the hand to make a payment. *It's already here*! Both options are here!

**Scene starts on Action News showing clip of minority Report movie.**

*"You have seen science fiction in movies using unique biological characteristics instead of keys. A facial or iris scan to unlock doors and accounts. An electronic*

*paperless society. Come summer that kind of technology will leap off the big screen and one metro grocery store will make your identity available right at your fingertips. Its sci-fi technology that is about to enter the checkout lane all in the name of speed and convenience. You will be able to buy anything from bread to beer if you agree to give the store your ultimate identity."*

**Grocery store Manager:** *"Walk in with just your fingers."*

**Grocery store customer:** *"It's much easier to swipe your fingers than to go thru all the cards."*

**Fox news Host:** *"A new form of technology has made its way to the register. Ready for this? Payment by fingertip. In Florida coast to coast convenient stores have become the first to use such technology. It's nothing more than converting your debit or your checking account to apply to your finger tip."*

**CBS news host:** *"The LA unified school district is pushing a program to finger print some kids before they can get their lunch. Digitizing lunch scans district-wide has stirred a bit of controversy. LASD is the second largest school district in the school system across the country. There's over ½ million meals served every day. Students at Oshay Learning Center are expected to be the first in the district that use a finger print like scanner to biometrically identify them for meals in the lunch room. Officials say the system poses no security or privacy risks to children or their families and would help bring district cafeterias into the 21st century."*

**ABC news host:** *"It looks and sounds like something out of the future, but a new palm scanner device will help schools keep track of what children are eating there. The electronic device will be implemented at all Bosha Parish schools. Workers are currently being trained on how to use it. A small infrared camera is used to scan the child's hand. And because palm and finger prints are unique the system can keep track of everything to the tee and even what they are not supposed to eat. Food allergies can also be listed as well as items you don't want your children eating. If a student picks one of those items the system won't let them buy it..... THE SYSTEM WONT LET THEM BUY IT...."*

**Concerned Christian:** *"You know, today it's the fingerprint, tomorrow the microchip. Maybe that ushers in the Mark of the Beast."*[12]

Yeah, I agree. At least that guy gets it. Sure looks to me like we're seeing for the first time in man's history how people are starting to make payments using their *hand*, how about you? Did you notice it was specifically the right hand? What's next? Some sort of chip implant in your hand to do the same thing? Lest you think this won't ever catch on worldwide, listen to this.

"Biometic ATM machines are starting to appear in Europe and there are now tens of thousands of them in Japan being used by millions of people. In fact, the machines are also dotted around parts of Asia, Latin America, the Middle East and even parts of Africa, where, according to banking analysts, they are preferred by rural workers living in remote areas who are not accustomed to carrying bank cards.

Out of 900 consumers recently involved in a pilot scheme, 94% said that they were ready to use finger print based technology when purchasing goods and services." In other words, I want to buy with my hand!

And for the first time in mankind's history, we even have a new Global Biometric Payment System already in place. It's called, *World Pay* and it's, "The world's first biometric payment system."[13]

You can use your hand or head to make payment anywhere in the world. This is how close we are, and as always, the point is this. What more does God have to do to get our attention? This is not a game! This is real!

**5. The 5th way we're being conditioned right now to receive the actual Mark of the Beast is the Convenience Proof.**

You see, the Bible is clear. You can expect to see in the Last Days not only a "push" for the Mark of the Beast, with this biometric stuff, your body parts, but you can expect that people are going to somehow be "conditioned" to think that this is an awesome thing to do and one of the biggest ways they're doing that, is by selling this Mark of the Beast Systems as a *convenience*. And hey, who doesn't want a little convenience in their life, right? The problem is, it's one thing to fall for this tactic, but it's another thing to not understand its significance. You see, we just can't seem to interpret this as an obvious sign from God, that we're living in the Last Days. But don't worry, this same attitude happened at Jesus' First Coming. But don't take my word for it. Let's listen to His.

**Luke 12:54-56** "He said to the crowd: 'When you see a cloud rising in the west, immediately you say, 'It's going to rain,' and it does. And when the south wind blows, you say, 'It's going to be hot,' and it is. Hypocrites! You know how to interpret the appearance of the earth and the sky. How is it that you don't know how to interpret this present time?'"

In other words, Jesus is saying here, "I am standing right in the midst of you and I've already done all these miracles right in front of you guys, I've demonstrated that I really am God in the flesh and I've fulfilled tons of Old Testament prophecies showing I really am the Messiah and you still don't get it? Then you have the audacity to say you need more proof? What?" What does Jesus say about these people and their skeptical attitude towards His First Coming? "You hypocrites," right? He says, "You don't need that much information to make a decision about the weather." In fact, He says, "With just a minimal amount of evidence, one simple fact, you make confident conclusions about the *weather*. You do it all the time. You don't require a lot of information to make that prediction. You don't need a TV weather guy. You don't need a Doppler radar. You don't need the Internet. You don't even need satellites. You just look over here and you see a dark cloud coming off the sea and you say, 'Hey, it's going to rain.' And you know what? You're right. That's how it works. It turns out that way." In other words, with only a minimal amount of evidence you draw a confident conclusion about the weather, but when the actual evidence of the Messiah's actual coming is staring you right in the face, you still don't get it and that tells us their real problem was not a *lack* of information, it's just they didn't *want* to get it! So Jesus calls them hypocrites! In fact, this isn't the first time Jesus used this word hypocrite. He used it repeatedly over and over again in Matthew 23, which is right before Matthew 24, the classic passage dealing with His Second Coming.

**Matthew 23:13** "Woe to you, teachers of the law and Pharisees, you hypocrites! You shut the kingdom of heaven in men's faces. You yourselves do not enter, nor will you let those enter who are trying to."

**Matthew 23:14** "Woe to you, scribes and Pharisees, hypocrites, because you devour widows' houses, and for a pretense you make long prayers; therefore you will receive greater condemnation."

**Matthew 23:15** "Woe to you, teachers of the law and Pharisees, you hypocrites! You travel over land and sea to win a single convert, and when he becomes one, you make him twice as much a son of hell as you are."

**Matthew 23:16-17** "Woe to you, blind guides! You say, 'If anyone swears by the temple, it means nothing; but if anyone swears by the gold of the temple, he is bound by his oath.' You blind fools! Which is greater: the gold, or the temple that makes the gold sacred?"

**Matthew 23:23-24** "Woe to you, teachers of the law and Pharisees, you hypocrites! You give a tenth of your spices – mint, dill and cummin. But you have neglected the more important matters of the law – justice, mercy and faithfulness. You should have practiced the latter, without neglecting the former. You blind guides! You strain out a gnat but swallow a camel."

**Matthew 23:25-26** "Woe to you, teachers of the law and Pharisees, you hypocrites! You clean the outside of the cup and dish, but inside they are full of greed and self-indulgence. Blind Pharisee! First clean the inside of the cup and dish, and then the outside also will be clean."

**Matthew 23:27-28** "Woe to you, teachers of the law and Pharisees, you hypocrites! You are like whitewashed tombs, which look beautiful on the outside but on the inside are full of dead men's bones and everything unclean. In the same way, on the outside you appear to people as righteous but on the inside you are full of hypocrisy and wickedness."

**Matthew 23:29-34** "Woe to you, teachers of the law and Pharisees, you hypocrites! You build tombs for the prophets and decorate the graves of the righteous. And you say, 'If we had lived in the days of our forefathers, we would not have taken part with them in shedding the blood of the prophets.' So you testify against yourselves that you are the descendants of those who murdered the prophets. Fill up, then, the measure of the sin of your forefathers! You snakes! You brood of vipers! How will you escape being condemned to hell? Therefore I am sending you prophets and wise men and teachers. Some of them you will kill and crucify; others you will flog in your synagogues and pursue from town to town."

In other words, Jesus says, "You didn't want to hear the truth of His First Coming and when I send you in the future, faithful Prophets to proclaim My

Second Coming, you're not going to hear it either! In fact, just like the First Time, you're going to kill and try to shut up the messenger the Second Time!" And it is my contention that this same hypocrisy demonstrated by the people of Jesus' day during His First Coming is the *exact same thing* we're seeing *today* with His Second Coming! People are trying to kill the messenger! Shut him up! Don't confuse me with the facts! I don't want to hear this! And yet Jesus would say, "You hypocrites!" You can interpret the weather with a tiny little bit of information and yet, out of love, I send faithful men to you to give you a ton of information about My next coming, which you should be *excited* about, so you won't be caught off guard and you either assassinate them or hide behind the accusation that you don't have enough proof. Excuse me? How much more proof do we need? What *more* does God have to do to get our attention today? How much more information does He have to give us to show us we're living in the Last Days? Jesus Christ is about ready to come back! His Second Coming is approaching! Especially with this sign here of the Mark of the Beast! We've already seen, again, how they're pushing it with the Media, the Matrix, the Quotations, the Biometrics and if that wasn't enough, they're packaging it all up right now and selling it to us under the guise of convenience so we'll hurry up and accept it now? It's that close! But don't take my word for it, let's look at the proof!

**A. The 1st way** we know we're being conditioned to receive the actual Mark of the Beast under the guise of convenience is the **Pampered Proof.**

Haven't you heard? Who wouldn't want to get a chip, right? I mean, that would be convenient. If you would just get one, *right now*, your very own biometric implant, you would bring such great comforts to your life, beyond your wildest dreams! What's a biometric implant you ask? A biometric implant is a tiny little chip about the size of a grain of rice that is implanted just beneath your skin and its benefits are that it can't be stolen and you can't lose it because it's implanted inside your body which means it's with you wherever you go. Isn't that great? Isn't that convenient?

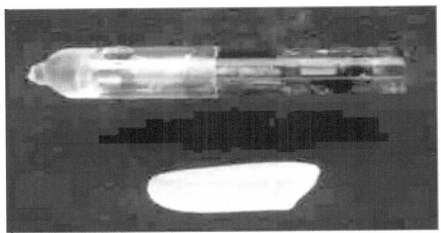

## VeriChip Human RFID Implant compared to long-grain rice

That's right, for those of you who still might be a little bit squeamish, don't worry. It's already been approved by the FDA back in 2002 and we all know we can trust the government with our lives. Yeah right! But that's right, don't listen to me, let's look at the facts. Let's see just how much our lives will become pampered if we'd only receive the biometric implant!

### IMPLANTS WILL MAKE US MORE PAMPERED

- You can have tiny cell phones implanted into your bikinis.
- You can have T-shirts implanted with Internet links.
- You can have an implant in your clothes that will tell you what clothes (shirt, tie, blouse, etc.) goes with what.
- You can have an implant in your makeup to see what you'd look like before you put it on when you look in the mirror.
- You can have implants that act like "intelligent shopping agents" who will know everything about you from personal quirks to shoe size and will search instantly anywhere in the world via the Internet to find you the best deal.
- You can have implants in your house to customize anything from the temperature to even background music.
- You can have an implant in your jacket to allow you to switch on the TV, check your phone messages, or even tell the oven to start cooking a meal.

- You can have an implant in your refrigerator to tell you when you're out of food and automatically order it for you from the store!
- Or for those of you who still want to go to the store, if you get an implant, you could breeze through the store and check out lane without ever having to pull out a wallet, especially when those unexpected guests come over!

*"Grandma" is sitting in her rocker knitting. Phone rings. Grandma picks up the phone.*

**Grandma:** *Hello?*

**Grandchild:** *Hi Grandma! We're gonna come over for dinner <laughs> Right now!*

*Grandma panics as she looks at a picture of her huge family. Grandma jumps out of her rocking chair.*

*Grandma is now seen running up and down the aisle of the grocery store throwing various food items into her shopping cart. She is next seen standing with a fully loaded cart near the check out. She observes a pretty young woman walk through a scanner without unloading her cart. Grandma looks to the left and smiles at an elderly man in the "old style" check out line.*

*"Grandpa" smiles back. They both continue to give several flirty smiles back and forth as Grandma, without moving, proceeds to push her cart away from her and her entire cart of food gets scanned all at once.*

*Grandma looks back at the elderly man and shrugs, walks over, grabs her receipt and leaves the store. Grandpa looks down in sadness as he is still standing in line waiting with his one item.*

*Grandma is back home and plops back in her rocker and kicks her feet up.*

- And even kids can get in on the action. You can have an implant in your candy bar to win free money.
- Or for those of you who want to be more health conscious and stay away from those candy bars, you can have an implant in your food to help you control and monitor your food intake and lose weight. It's called the smart plate!

*Another part of this system is our Smart Plate. A plate that reads our food and works as an invisible diet management system. When a cupcake is placed on a plate, it is scanned by an RFID reader inside. The reader is programmed to monitor every product that is eaten from the plate. An LED light hidden under the veneer lights up to give a brief visual correspondent. Besides nutrition information like calories or fat, the user can also learn more about his food, about it's food miles or it's trading history. A Sushi roll could tell us about it's heritage and it's ingredients. For people with food allergies the Smart Plate can send hazard alerts about dangerous ingredients and stop us from eating things that may harm us.*

*This system aims to become the future medium between food intake and knowledge. It extracts data directly from food and creates a new perception of what we're going to eat.*

- And for those of you who do not have a strong enough will to listen to your Smart Plate, you can also use this with another feature called, "The Permanent Companion." This computer interface will not only control your shopping list at home but even on the road. "It can act as a real body coach which helps consumers keep a healthy diet and lose weight by keeping an eye on your weight and calories, suggesting recipes for suitable meals and sending you an alert whether or not you can eat a little more or should start exercising."
- You can have implants in your car to access the Internet and/or pay for toll charges, gas, or even food at the Drive Thru, that is, if your Perfect Companion says it's okay!
- You can have an implant in your carrying bag to track you and help you avoid pedestrian traffic jams.
- You can have implants in your umbrellas to track your every move and let marketers know how well their advertising is doing.
- You can have tiny implants in your magazines so that publishers not only know how many people actually read their magazine, but even how long they spent reading the pages, if they skipped reading some of the pages, if they skipped some of the articles, whether or not they read it from front to back or back to front, and of course, if they looked at the advertisements in the magazine.
- You can have implants in television sets that eject artificial scents when different advertisements or scenes are viewed. (I told you watching TV smells!)

- You can have an implant in your fingertip that will transfer all your vital personal information with a handshake. (A digital authentication law has already been passed through Congress giving these "electronic signatures" the same legal status as writing your name on a document.)
- You can have an implant in your hand that will unlock your car, start your car, open up doors, log on to your computer and so much more, like this guy!

*Amal Graafstra: I wanted a more convenient way that made more sense to me to get into my office.*

*IT professional Amal Graafstra, describes himself as an implant hobbyist. A do-it-yourself microchipper. He had a Radio Frequency Identification device, or RFID inserted into his hands. It's technology commonly used to identify dogs and cats.*

*Everyday after work, with the groceries in hand, I use it every day to get into the back door and it's better than fumbling around for keys.*

*Does it seem like a dramatic thing to undertake just to be able to get into the house?*

*Graafstra: For some, probably. But for me, when looking at it, you know I said, "Well it's just really moving that RFID card from my pant's pocket to a skin pocket."*

*It's not as far fetched as it sounds. Given that people are already willing to insert microchips into their hands.*

If you'd just get a skin pocket implant, your life would be filled with such great comfort. I mean, wouldn't it be cool to have a microchip implant? Wouldn't that be convenient? That's precisely what they want you to think! Getting you ready for the Mark of the Beast *right now* like this article shares:

*"How'd you like to avoid waiting in lines for the rest of your life? Breeze through everywhere like you owned the place. Watch lights snap on, doors open automatically, money pop out of ATMs as you approach.*

*Never have to show an ID, buy a ticket, carry keys, remember a password. You'd leave stores loaded with packages and waltz right past the cashiers. You wouldn't have to carry a wallet. Ever. Family and friends could find you instantly in any crowd.*

*These latest injectable devices have taken things a step further. What next? I approach my car, which knows who I am. The door swings open and the driver seat and steering wheel adjust to my usual settings, the radio starts to play my favorite station and a speech unit offers to navigate me to Heathrow.*

*As I board the plane, a sensor in the aircraft door activates the chip which tells the on-board flight system who I am. 'Welcome...seat 4a is ready for you. This flight is worth 450 air-miles.'*

*I arrive in New York and hire a car, which also recognizes me and adjusts accordingly. The hotel room unlocks and bills me as I enter. Room service arrives to stock the fridge with favorite items plus the extras I usually order.*

*None of this is science fiction. All of this is possible using today's tools. It is just a question of connecting them together."*[14]

And the so-called "good news" is they already have! What are you waiting for?

**B.** The 2nd **way** we know we're being conditioned right now to receive the actual Mark of the Beast under the guise of convenience is the **Productive Proof.**

You see, if only you'd get an implant, it'd make your life so much more productive. Why, we would get a lot more done and who wouldn't want to save more time? Let's take a look at that.

### IMPLANTS WILL MAKE US MORE PRODUCTIVE

- You can have implants in your clothes that will talk with your washer so you don't have to. Simply load the clothes into the washer and the tag will do the rest of the work by telling the washer how it should be laundered.
- You can have implants on all manufactured items to create a self-managing intelligent supply chain all around the world! That really is their goal, to tag the whole world!

*Matrics:*

*Piyush Sodha, CEO: Matrics is founded four years ago
to revolutionize the RFID business.*

*Founders- Dr. William Bandy and Michael Arneson*

**Sodha:** *The acronym stands for Radio Frequency Identification. In our judgment,
RFID will be the single most significant enabling technology to impact the supply
chain institution in the 21st century.*

## Tag the World:

**Arneson:** *The idea being that each product has a serial number, ID and
therefore, each item can then be uniquely identified. What we've done is
essentially program a chip with a 112 bits of ID and Error Correction code,
giving you 2 to the 96th power unique ID's (79,228 trillion trillion unique ID's)
That will sequentially and uniquely ID every single product in the world.*

- You can have an implant in your trash and trash bin to force people to recycle
  and fine them if they don't and tax them based on how much garbage is thrown
  away.
- You can have an implant in your shoes to help you win a marathon.
- You can have implants for your employees to monitor their location, who
  they're with, their timekeeping, efficiency and productivity.
- You can have another implant for your restaurant employees so that when they
  use the restroom it activates another implant in the wash basin to monitor
  whether or not they washed their hands and alert you if there's a need for
  disciplinary action.
- You can have an implant in your child's diaper to track their urinary health. It's
  called the "Smart Diaper."
- You can have an implant to connect you directly to your computer. But just be
  careful not to get a virus like this guy did.

## Sky News

*He is a real life cyber-man. The scientist with the implanted computer chip. A
tiny lump is all that gives it away. A wave of his digitally enhanced hand and
security doors magically open. Only he can operate his phone and only if he*

*holds it in the hand fitted with the chip. But now, Dr. Mark Gasson is suffering a very 21st century malady. The first human to be infected with a computer virus.*

**Dr. Gasson:** *When the systems read my tags, the computer virus has actually appeared throughout the whole database. So it's actually replicated itself and copied it throughout the database. So any of these people that are using their swipe cards to access the building, the actual virus will be copied onto their card.*

*The cybernetics experts at the University of Reading have the chip implanted in a minor operation. In the future, your medical records could be stored like this. But the chips are vulnerable. Already many implanted devices like pacemakers have on board computers that communicate with doctors. If they're corrupted by a virus, the consequences for patients could be fatal. In the future, chips will be used even more widely. Perhaps even as memory upgrades for the brain. They too could be scrambled by malicious computer code. Our bodies have been fighting biological viruses but as man and machine merge, so computer viruses could prove a new threat to human health.*

- You can have implants that sense brain wave patterns and convert them into signals used to operate electrical appliances.
- You can have an implant to act as an internal alarm clock that determines how much sleep you can get.
- You can have an implant to constantly monitor your body functions such as pulse, heart rate, sugar levels and even make sure you always take your pills!

*For the 20 million Americans who live with diabetes, daily finger pricks are a painful part of life. Getting the proper glucose reading is critical in controlling your diabetes. There is now a group of biotech companies that say they can change the way diabetics can monitor their blood sugars with an implantable microchip like this one.*

*The chip is placed in the tissue and comes in contact with fluids in the body and the sensors react to the presence of particular compounds in these fluids, detect them and then send the information to the outside.*

------------

*The FDA has approved of a kind of attachment for all types of pills. It's a tiny harmless transmitter that will electronically register if you've taken your pill or not. It mixes with stomach acids and sends out a signal that you've indeed taken the pill. Its creators-its inventors hope it might be used for seniors who often forget to take their meds.*

- You can have an implant to send an electrode to your brain to activate a former paralyzed muscle or limb.
- You can have an implant connected to the eye to provide sight for the blind.
- You can have an implant to extend human intelligence or memory.
- You can have an implant to save your life.

## CNN Welcome to the Future

*Now imagine a device that could tell them all they need to know about any medical condition you have in a matter of minutes at any hospital, anywhere in the world. Sound far fetched? It's closer than you think.*

**Dr Feldman:** *On a typical day patients come in with heart attacks, strokes, major trauma, cancer patients and septic shock. You name it. We have it.*

*What might improve the odds for some of those patients at New Jersey's Hackensack University Medical Center is this..*

*That tiny chip that Dr. Joseph Feldman, head of the hospital's Trauma Unit, holds in his hand. It's a Radio Frequency Identification or RFID tag. The same technology to tag animals to help reunite a pet with its owner. RFID has now won Food & Drug Administration approval for use in humans.*

**Dr. Feldman:** *RFID technology is very attractive to emergency departments. It enables people to quickly identify not only who the person is, but what their medical history is and what would normally take hours sometimes takes only a matter of minutes.*

*How does it work? With a wave of a wand. The Doctor reads a unique ID number that logs on to a central database to quickly access your medical history, surgical history, any medications you take, your allergies and blood type. Even an emergency contact. Sixty five American hospitals have agreed to implement the technology. And the company that makes the chip expects that number to grow to 200 soon.*

*You know, if I have the chip I can travel all over the world. That would give me the freedom of living the life without bounds."*[15]

Did you hear that? Your life could become so much more productive if you'd just get the implant! I mean, come on, wouldn't it be constructive to get one now? Again, that's exactly what they want you to think! They're preparing us to receive the actual Mark of the Beast *right now!*

**C. The 3rd way we know we're being conditioned right now to receive the actual Mark of the Beast under the guise of convenience is the Protected Proof.**

You see, if only we'd get an implant, our lives will become so well protected that we'll never have to worry about anything ever again! Let's take a look at that so-called awesome possibility!

### IMPLANTS WILL MAKE US MORE PROTECTED

- You can have an implant to track your car wherever you go, for theft purposes and allow authorities to find unregistered vehicles.
- You can have an implant in your casino chips to make sure people don't cheat!
- You can have an implant in your towels so people can't steal them in hotels.
- You can have an implant in your luggage to ensure it's exact whereabouts.
- In fact, speaking of safety in airports, even passengers could get an implant on a bracelet that'll shock them "when they get out of line."

**Fox News**

*Megan Kelley: Imagine showing up for your next flight at the airport and being handed a device, a little bracelet, that would serve as your boarding pass. It would track your lost luggage and it would also shock you with the same power as a taser if you get out of line. Well a top official at the Department of Homeland Security has expressed interest in these so-called safety bracelets. So is this really the future of air travel. And will passengers accept it?*

------

*EMD Technology*
*Electro-Muscular Disruption*

*The bracelets will allow a crew member, using Radio Frequency transmitters, to quickly and effectively subdue hijackers. The Electro-Muscular Disruption signal overrides the attacker's central nervous system and will render the most elite and aggressive terrorists completely immobile for several minutes. This will allow the crew to subdue and handcuff that individual.*

-------

**Kelley:** *Is it possible, Neil, could we get to the point in air travel, where we have to put on a bracelet where the stewardess can shock us if we get out of line?*

**Neil:** *Yes, they did express an interest in this and apparently had a meeting with this one individual who has this one device. But if they ultimately ever do this, it's going to be quite different than what we're talking about today and we may actually see these kinds of devices put on felons in order to get parole. People that are pedophiles so that it sets off an alarm if they get too close to a school. We may see all sorts of applications of this down the road.*

- Speaking of applications, maybe they're going to be working towards something more secure, and they are. You see, the only problem with these "security" bracelets is that you could lose them. So how about a more permanent solution like a chip? I mean, if it's good for the airport workers, it's good for us, right?

## KENS 5 News
## Airport Employees

*Metal detectors, liquid bans, random bag checks, as passengers we've come to expect tight security measures associated with flying. Soon, those measures will extend beyond those taking off to include those who never leave the airport. San Antonio International officials tell KENS 5 that Congress is putting into motion measures that will ensure airport employees are subject to stricter security checks.*

**Selena Hernandez:** *Chris, right now, all airport employees must pass a Police and F.B.I. background check. Soon, those checks may include something a little more intrusive. Members of Congress are currently debating how to keep closer tabs on those who have access to secure areas. Meaning everyone from restaurant employees to airline mechanics could soon be subjected to more rigorous background checks. Under discussion- a check of an employee's credit history. A search of their bags and property before entering secured areas and* *perhaps the most extreme measure-the use of biometric readers for fingerprints and eyes, even possibly a chip implant.*

- You can have an implant in your computer so no one can steal it.
- You can have an implant in your uniforms to help eliminate shortages and ensure you get back every garment you turn in.
- You can have an implant in your socks so you'll never lose them.
- You can have an implant in all library books to ensure penalties are paid and reduce theft.
- You can have implants in your skis to monitor your performance and manage safety.
- You can have an implant in your bike so that traffic lights could warn other motorists of your whereabouts.
- You can have an implant in trees to ensure their safety and prevent unlawful cutting and hold data about its location, size and who cut it down.
- You can have an implant in your cactus so people won't steal them.
- You can have an implant in your pet to make sure it never gets lost.
- You can have an implant in your body to instantly find people involved in airplane crashes or other natural disasters.
- You can have an implant to instantly alert you if someone's body temperature has changed like from falling in water or in a fire.
- You can have an implant put on nuclear devices, machines, or dams to give advance notice of impending danger.
- You can have an implant put in businesses to instantly alert you of break-ins or tampering.
- You can have an implant to monitor and pinpoint missing livestock.
- You can have an implant to automatically monitor parolees and save money on prison costs.
- You can have an implant to find out if an Alzheimer patient has wandered off.
- You can have an implant to instantly locate a lost or abducted child. In fact, you might have to get one real soon, the moment you're born.

**More RFID**

*Heidi, the miniature Schnauzer, was found months after it disappeared because of an implanted microchip. With the Food and Drug Administration's blessings, hospitals prepare to implant the information-filled VeriChip, under patient's skin to reduce errors.*

*Now it's on to the big party on South Beach; the chip is envisioned as the new age gold key to the VIP room.*

*You don't have to pull out your credit cards, your driver's licenses. You're part of a team. You're part of an elite family.*

*Instead of your credit card being scanned, YOU would be scanned.*

*The chip is currently the rage in clubs in Europe and implanting it is currently free.*

*So simple. I think that within 20 years, when you get born, you will get a chip. "*[16]

Wow! Sounds like the convenience factor is paying off big time, how about you? I mean, who wouldn't want to have their loved ones and property protected at all times and of course make financial transactions as well? Wouldn't it be common sense to get a microchip implant? And that's precisely what they want you to think! Recognize the days we live in. Don't be a *hypocrite*! They're preparing us *right now* to receive the Mark of the Beast, which means, we are about to see the Return of Jesus Christ!

**II. The 2nd way that we know we really are headed for this Mark of the Beast system is the Willingness Proof.**

You see, the Bible is clear. If you're going to pull off this Mark of the Beast System that the Antichrist is going to do, you not only have to condition the people on the planet repeatedly over and over again in a multitude of ways year after year after year, to warm them up to the idea to get an implant, but at some point, you're conditioning has to work, right? It has to get them to the point where they're willing to try it, right? Well, guess what? It has! For the first time in man's history, people are willing to take the Mark of the Beast! They're not just being conditioned, they're actually *willing* to take it right now! This shouldn't be a surprise to us because the Bible clearly says this is the exact same kind of cunningness and deceitfulness the Antichrist is going to use on people in the Last Days. But don't take my word for it. Let's listen to God.

**2 Thessalonians 2:1-10** "Concerning the coming of our Lord Jesus Christ and our being gathered to him, we ask you, brothers, not to become easily unsettled or alarmed by some prophecy, report or letter supposed to have come from us, saying that the day of the Lord has already come. Don't let anyone deceive you in any way, for that day will not come until the rebellion occurs and the man of lawlessness is revealed, the man doomed to destruction. He will oppose and will exalt himself over everything that is called God or is worshiped, so that he sets himself up in God's temple, proclaiming himself to be God. Don't you remember that when I was with you I used to tell you these things? And now you know what is holding him back, so that he may be revealed at the proper time. For the secret power of lawlessness is already at work; but the one who now holds it back will continue to do so till he is taken out of the way. And then the lawless one will be revealed, whom the Lord Jesus will overthrow with the breath of His mouth and destroy by the splendor of His coming. The coming of the lawless one will be in accordance with the work of satan displayed in all kinds of counterfeit miracles, signs and wonders, and in every sort of evil that deceives those who are perishing. They perish because they refused to love the truth and so be saved."

In other words, they didn't want to hear it! But according to the Bible, we clearly see that when the Antichrist is revealed, he's going to do so with what? False counterfeit signs, wonders and miracles, right? He's a *liar* and a *deceiver*! But that's not all. He's also, it says there, satanically inspired, which means he's also going to have the same character that satan has, right? When you look at satan's character, deceit and lying is just the tip of the iceberg.

**Accuser**: Revelation 12:10 "For the accuser of our brethren, who accused them before our God day and night, has been cast down."

**Adversary**: 1 Peter 5:8 "Be sober, be vigilant; because your adversary (enemy,foe) the devil walks about like a roaring lion, seeking whom he may devour."

**Deceiver**: Revelation 12:9 "So the great dragon was cast out, that serpent of old, called the devil and satan, who deceives the whole world; he was cast to the earth, and his angels were cast out with him."

**Enemy**: Matthew 13:39 "The enemy who sowed them is the devil, the harvest is the end of the age, and the reapers are the angels."

**Evil One**: John 17:15 "I do not pray that You should take them out of the world, but that You should keep them from the evil one."

**Father of Lies**: John 8:44 "You are of your father the devil…When he speaks a lie, he speaks from his own resources, for he is a liar and the father of it."

**Murderer**: John 8:44 "You are of your father the devil, and the desires of your father you want to do. He was a murderer from the beginning, and does not stand in the truth, because there is no truth in him."

**Power and Ruler of Darkness**: Colossians 1:13 & Ephesians 6:12 "He (God) has delivered us from the power of darkness and conveyed us into the kingdom of the Son of His love. For we do not wrestle against flesh and blood, but against principalities, against powers, against the rulers of the darkness."

**Ruler of Demons**: Luke 11:15 "But some of them said, 'He casts out demons by Beelzebub, the ruler of the demons.'"

**Tempter**: Matthew 4:3 "Now when the tempter came to Him, he said, 'If You are the Son of God, command that these stones become bread.'"

**Transformer**: 2 Corinthians 11:14 "And no wonder! For Satan himself transforms himself into an angel of light."

**Thief of Destruction**: John 10:10 "The thief does not come except to steal, and to kill, and to destroy."

**Wicked One**: Ephesians 6:16 "Above all, taking the shield of faith with which you will be able to quench all the fiery darts of the wicked one."

This is who we're up against and this is who is *inspiring* the Antichrist. How many of you would say that he's got a pretty evil rotten character, you know what I'm saying? Slightly! So here's the point. This is the same kind of evil satanically inspired character that we can expect to see from the Antichrist, which tells us the specific evil tactics he's going to use to dupe people in the Last Days to be willing to take the Mark. He's going to use lying, thieving, murderous, transforming seductive lies to get people to do it! Now you might be thinking, "Well so what! I don't care what kind of satanic tactics the Antichrist is going to use on people in the Last Days to get them to be willing to take the Mark. I'm not that dumb! Nobody's that dumb! I mean, come on! Everybody knows about the Mark of the Beast!" Really? Well, you ever wonder if all this lack of preaching on Bible Prophecy today is actually helping to keep people in the dark tomorrow when the Antichrist starts his tactics to get people to take the Mark? I kind of think so! In fact, that's why I keep saying I truly believe this lack of preaching on Bible Prophecy in the Last Days is a *spiritual warfare* issue. It's helping to keep people in the dark and ready to take the Mark. That's not by chance! They have no clue what to look for! They've already been made willing. Don't believe me? Let's take a look at the proof!

**1. The 1st proof we've been deceived by the Antichrist to be willing to take the Mark of the Beast is They've Already Put them Into Our Pets.**

Once again, put yourself in the Antichrist's shoes. I mean, here you are with your ultimate goal of tracking and tagging every single person on the whole planet and controlling what they "buy and sell." So how are you going to get people used to the idea of receiving an implant themselves? Wouldn't it make sense to implement a kind of Phase One, if you will and try it out on animals first? First get all the animals on the planet tagged and then once people accept that and get conditioned to that, then maybe Phase Two kicks into gear where people would be more willing to be treated like animals themselves and get their own implant too, just like Sparky! Wouldn't it be great? In fact as we saw before, that's not only happening, but now it's becoming *mandatory*. At first, they were voluntary through implant companies like INFOPET to keep track of stray animals, we can't allow that to happen! But that was just step one. Now, in many places across our country, it's mandatory to have your pet microchipped, or you're in big trouble, or in some cases you can't even get your pet back! In fact, right now whole countries are starting to require all pets, it's mandatory, to get an implant.

***Gillian Pensavalle:*** *You better microchip your dog or else! Hey! I'm Gillian on 560. All dogs in England will be fitted with a GPS microchip by 2016 or the owner will have to fork up 500 pounds.*

-----------

***BBC:***
*Just 13 weeks old, but it's a big day for Buddy. Time for him to be microchipped.*

***Vet:*** *So what we're going to do is we're going to implant the chip just in the skin in the back of the neck. We're just going to inject that through the skin- and you're the bravest puppy in the world.*

*It takes a few seconds and costs 20 pounds.*

-------------------

*Right now, about 60% of British pups already have microchips. That's 8 million dogs! No word on if the Royal Corgi's have microchips. But the Queen still has a few years until she's in danger of a fine.*"[17]

Well isn't that nice? At least the Royalty gets a choice...for now. But did you see what happened? First make it voluntary, then get us used to the technology, then *mandate* us to do it whether we want to or not! What's next? You're going to mandate it on people? Well, funny you should ask.

**2. The 2nd proof we've been deceived by the Antichrist and his evil tactics to be willing to receive the Mark of the Beast is They've Already Put Them Into Their Propaganda.**

You see, it's common sense. Just like they used propaganda for years and years and years to get us used to the idea of chipping our pets, so they've used the same propaganda to get us to think it's a good thing for people too! In fact, they've even been putting it in kid's cartoons to prepare the next generation!

**Clip from Futurama: Career displayed on screen: Deliveryboy**

*Fry: Deliveryboy? No! Not again. Please! Anything else!*

*[He grabs Leela's hand.]*

*Leela: Take your hands off me! You've been assigned the job you're best at just like everyone else.*

*Fry: What if I refuse?*

*Leela: Well that's tough! Lots of people don't like their jobs but we do them anyway. [She points at a poster of a man wearing a hardhat with the caption "You Gotta Do What You Gotta Do".] You gotta do what you gotta do. Now hold out your hand. I'm gonna implant your career chip. It'll permanently label you as a delivery boy.*

-------------------------------

**Scene from CSI Miami:**

*Horatio:We found this implanted in our victim's shoulder.*

*Wolfe: It's a Verichip. You scan it here. Information pops up there (on the computer screen) Your whole life on a grain of rice.*

*Horatio: Okay, hit more info and see if we get a driver's license.*

*Wolfe: <Clicks "more info" and up pops the driver's license of victim on the screen> Yeah, Jenny Price-18.*

*Horatio: Chase Shaw says this thing holds credit card information.*
----------------------------

*Medical Examiner: I excised this from her shoulder. I don't know what it is.*

*Detective Stabler: Ugh, that's an RFID chip and I think I know who put it there.*

*Medical Examiner: Naomi doesn't. I asked her. So whoever did this to her must have injected this into her while she was unconscious.*

*Stabler: A way to keep tabs on your cheating wife.*

---
*Stabler to "husband" Why would you implant an RFID chip in your wife's shoulder?*

*Husband: I was keeping tabs on her.*

*Stabler: Keeping tabs on her? She's a human being, you're aware of that, not a pet.*

*Husband: She was cheating on me.*

*Detective Benson: That doesn't give you the right to tag her.*

*Husband: RFID is the wave of the future, I'm just ahead of the curve. Fifteen years, everyone will be implanted with a chip.*

*Stabler: Really. Where do I sign up to opt out of that.*

Well, maybe that's just it. Right now, like the pets, it's voluntary, but maybe in a few years like that guy says, it's going to be mandatory. It's the way of the future! And you might be thinking, "Well, come on! Okay, so they're using the propaganda machines to get us used to the idea of getting a chip. But nobody is going to fall for this baloney! Nobody's going to be willing to do this!" Really? Well, according to a recent MSNBC poll, 20% of the American population right now is fully ready and *willing* to receive a microchip implant. Looks like the propaganda's working! Aren't you glad nobody's teaching on Bible Prophecy, keeping these people in the dark? In fact, so much so are people willing, that Scott Silverman, the president of Digital Angel said that, "He expects that in the next two to three years, it will be standard protocol for emergency room personnel to scan the upper right arm of every patient admitted." The next thing you know, all you gotta do is Google somebody's microchip and find out where they are! Don't believe me? Here's what one article's predicting.

*"Scientists tag animals to monitor their behavior and keep track of endangered species. Now some people are asking whether all of mankind should be tagged too. Looking for a loved one? Just Google his microchip.*

*Already, the government of Mexico has surgically implanted the chips in the upper arms of staff at the attorney general's office in Mexico City. Taiwanese researchers say that the tags could help save lives in the aftermath of a major earthquake.*

*Having one in every person could relieve anxiety for parents and help save lives."*[18]

Oh, isn't that wonderful? These propaganda machines are really helping this to pan out, aren't they?

**3.** The **3rd proof** we've been deceived by the Antichrist evil tactics to be willing to receive the Mark of the Beast is **They've Already Put Them Into Our Payments.**

You see once again, put yourself in the Antichrist shoes. Some people might have an inkling of Bible Prophecy and so we're not going to be willing to get a chip in our hand to buy or sell, right? So hey, if you're the Antichrist, what do you do with these people? Well why not use another evil tactic and warm them up to the idea first, right? I mean, just back up the train a little bit and first get them used to the idea of making a payment with their hand, period, and then later of course, make it mandatory with a chip! Don't believe me? It's already here! People right now are using something on the outside of their hand to make a payment, to warm them up to getting something on the inside of their hand to make a payment!

## Wristband Hand Payments

*Scene starts with RFID, Facebook banner*

*Scene goes to people wearing RFID wristbands scanning themselves to check into Facebook convention.*

*Scene shows people with RFID wrist bands paying for drinks at bar.*

*Switches to scene of guy who makes grocery purchase with RFID watch...*

*"Now we put money on this watch this morning. Which now it means we can use it on the trains, the trams, the buses, even the ferries. But that's not all. I can use this watch instead of cash at 3,000 service providers around the city. When it runs low I just add more cash. Or I can sync it with my credit card and have it automatically pop up. Let's go eat."*

*Switches to scene of concert goers who have RFID wrist bands. They scan wrist bands as they enter concert....*

Yeah! I made a payment with my hand! No more waiting in long lines! Now I'm ready for the Mark of the Beast concert! The younger generation, who knows squat about Bible Prophecy, just loves this stuff. Do you think that's by chance? I don't think so! In fact, lest you think this younger generation isn't going to move this technology on to the inside of their hand anytime soon...you're wrong! It's getting so commonplace now that they even have their own do-it-yourself home implant kits! Here's one guy doing it.

**Do-It-Yourself RFID Implant:**

*Man #1 getting implant gives directions: "So you're going to go down in that direction."*

*Man#2 with medical gloves pinching skin together on a man's hand and then with the other hand, injecting a syringe loaded with an RFID chip into the folded skin.*

*Man #1 "Go down, you're still at a good angle <referencing the syringe>."*

*Man #2 "Hey man, you're tough as heck."*

*Man #1 "Keep going, you got a lot of skin to go through. Keep going buddy."*

*Man #2: Yeah. This is so cool.*

*Man #1: More. More. You got to go past that about a 1/4 of an inch. There you go, it's in. Pull it out.*

*Man #2 <puts cotton ball on site of injection and pulls syringe out> Dude, you're tough! <laughs>*

*Man #1: Thank you. It's just like putting in an IV.*

Yup, just like putting in an IV. It's that simple. Don't you want to try? Why, the next thing you know, you're going to be able to buy gas with your hand? Don't believe me? Apparently this guy did!

*Bobbi Harley <reporter>Person with RFID in hand passes his hand in front of a speedpay on a gas pump and activates the pump."*[19]

Wow! This is not 50 years down the road folks! It's happening now! Who would have thought we'd be living in the days when people would not only be willing to get a microchip, but they'd already be using them to buy stuff! That's how close we are!

**4.** The **4**th **proof** we've been deceived by the Antichrist evil tactics to be willing to receive the Mark of the Beast is **They've Already Put Them Into Our People.**

As you just saw, at first, it's just the extreme fringe people who were willing to get these microchip implants. You know, like those young whipper snappers who don't know better. Then it was special dignitaries, if you've been paying attention, whose position put them in jeopardy of being kidnapped and so you can understand that. Then it was just those techy weird people like Kevin Warwick who said after he implanted himself, it changed him. *"After a few days I started to feel quite a closeness to the computer, which was very strange," he muses. "When you are linking your brain up like that, you change who you are. You do become a 'borg.' You are not just a human linked with technology; you are something different and your values and judgment will change."* Hmmm. Maybe even to the point where it'll change you to worship Antichrist with these implants!

But you might be thinking, okay, but maybe that's just those special dignitaries and those "special" people, those techies and those young whipper snappers. No normal adult person in their right mind would ever be willing to get an implant." Really? Well, haven't you been paying attention? In light of all those terrorist attacks and the recent rise of child abduction cases and of course, the FDA's approval, *for the 1st time in man's history*, whole families are lining up to get a chip. One family was the Jacobs family in Florida.

**CBS Eye on America:**

*A procedure that takes only seconds to carry out..*

**Doctor:** *And the chip is now extruded and we're finished.*

*Harley..has turned the Jacobs Family into medical pioneers. They are the first people to get chipped. Implanted with a tiny device called a Verichip that emits radio frequencies. It's a personal ID that also contains vital medical information.*

**Derek Jacobs:** *It can save a lot of lives, including my dad's-because he has a lot of medical problems and I want him to be around for awhile.*

**Harley:** *A handheld scanner reads the Verichip. Theoretically police, paramedics and hospital workers would use the information during an* *emergency. Thousands of Americans are already lining up to get them and Applied Digital Solutions-the company that developed the Verichip-says that this might only be the beginning. Company scientists are already working on a Global Positioning System similar to what you would use in your boat or your car-but to track people, and like the Verichip, it would be small enough to implant into someone.*

**Harley:** *Nathan Isaacson is in the early stages of Alzheimer's Disease.*

**Nathan:** *I couldn't find my way home. Kind of an embarrassing moment.*

**Harley:** *He already wears a beeper-like GPS gadget-and will also be injected with a Verichip. Implanting both devices would give him and his family more peace of mind.*

*Nate couldn't wait to be chipped.*

**Nathan:** *I'm ready.*

*I know you're ready.*

**Nathan's wife:** *I'm ready. I'm looking for the peace of mind.*

Peace of mind, if you'll just receive an implant. Looks to me like people are willing to get an implant in the Last Days, how about you? Why, the next thing you know, everybody will have one and life will be safe and secure at all times, like this article shares.

*"Worry no more, doting parents! Whether it's your little pumpkin's first day walking home from school by herself or the millionth time you've lost her at the mall, the Babysitter™ will track your sweetpea's location from a jelly bean-sized microchip implant, discreetly tucked under her collarbone.*

*Also available: The Constant Companion™ lets you keep a watchful eye on grandma or grandpa, even when you can't be by their side. Coming soon: The INS Border Patroller™; the Personal Private Eye™; the Micro-Manager™.*

*Alas, this is not as far-fetched or as futuristic as it sounds. The notion of surveillance chips being installed in human beings is poised to cross over from the realm of science fiction into everyday reality, and soon.*[20]

In other words, people are ready to do it…now! Just like the Bible said would happen when you're living in the Last Days! Aren't you glad nobody's been teaching on Bible prophecy? Folks, it's getting so apparent now that even secular reporters can put two and two together and see how this really is a satanic ploy to make us willing.

**PIX11/Lionel**
-------

*Sir Veillance*

*Well. Well. Well. It seems that everyone is scared about the I-Phone being able to track your every move. You do know I warned about this--last year. But here is what you should really worry about. Watch!*

*It will unfold like this. First! An RFID chip-Radio Frequency Identification-is already put into the BLINK credit cards, passports, License tags. They're everywhere. Watch for a full court press to have them implanted in your pets, not an ID chip, a tracker. They're beta tested but you'll start to see more of them at your vets' offices. OnStar for your pooch. You can track your little doggie. Peace of mind.*

*Next-if it's good enough for your dog, it's good enough for your child. A tiny, little RFID chip the size of a grain of rice. Completely "safe". Easy to remove. Your child is now kidnap proof. The placement of the chip is varied, so God forbid, some sicko doesn't look in one particular place so to forcibly remove it. OnStar for your child. No more Amber Alerts. No more kidnapping. No more parent's worst nightmare. After all, if it's good enough for your pet, it's good enough for your child.*

*Then the elderly! Forget the "I've fallen and can't get up" business. No, no, no. This RFID chip will have all of grandma's medical information and data on it! And if they have dementia, wander off-you'll be able to track them. After all, it's good enough for your dog.*

*Then once it's deemed cool-teens will insist on their own chip. They're already tattooing barcodes. It's "cool". It's their own number. And this will be your own chip. All of your information. Always stressing the medical information bit. What information. She's 20 years old. SHHHHHHH! It's for her own good.*

*And you can track them. And you know kids won't wear watches anymore. They got cell phones with the time on it and you're cool chip- no need for driver's licenses, credit cards, debit cards, keyless entry, ID-the RFID chip will have it all there. All of it. Goodbye wallet. After all, what's a wallet for? ID, cards...not anymore!*

*Oh! And money! We'll be completely cashless. Bank terminals will read your chip. Think EZ Pass and Metro Cards. No cash. No drug trafficking. No terrorism. Make any connection you want. No one's listening anyway. Then you'll beg for one! Everything's on the chip. Everyone's on the grid. The Grid is a 24/7 real-time tracking of you. Everyone will have this cool chip. Everyone's on the grid.*

*And if you're convicted of breaking some law. They don't take you to prison. They turn off your chip. POOF! You don't exist. No money. No identity. No existence. And you're worried about I-phones being tracked? You haven't seen anything yet!* "[21]

In other words, even a secular reporter gets it, get ready for your worst nightmare! What more does God have to do to get our attention? People right now are willing to receive the actual Mark of the Beast technology. What more does He have to do before we wake up and realize the days we live in?

**III. The 3rd way** that we know we really are headed for this Mark of the Beast system is the **Mandating Proof.**

You might be thinking, "Well hey, there's no way I'm going to line up and receive a microchip implant! That's crazy! That's nuts! You can't make me do that!" Oh yeah? You might want to read your Bible. That's precisely what the Antichrist is going to do to the whole planet! He's going to *make* you do it and if you don't do it you will *die!* But don't take my word for it. Let's listen to God.

**Revelation 13:11-18** "Then I saw another beast, coming out of the earth. He had two horns like a lamb, but he spoke like a dragon. He exercised all the authority of the first beast on his behalf, and made the earth and its inhabitants worship the first beast, whose fatal wound had been healed. And he performed great and miraculous signs, even causing fire to come down from heaven to earth in full view of men. Because of the signs he was given power to do on behalf of the first beast, he deceived the inhabitants of the earth. He ordered them to set up an image in honor of the beast who was wounded by the sword and yet lived. He was given power to give breath to the image of the first beast, so that it could speak and cause all who refused to worship the image to be killed.He also forced everyone, small and great, rich and poor, free and slave, to receive a mark on his right hand or on his forehead, so that no one could buy or sell unless he had the mark, which is the name of the beast or the number of his name. This calls for wisdom. If anyone has insight, let him calculate the number of the beast, for it is man's number. His number is 666."

Now according to our text, the Bible clearly says that the False Prophet, in the Last Days, is not only going to dupe the whole world into *worshiping* the Antichrist, or the beast, but he's what? He's going to make them do it, right? He orders them! In fact, so much so, if you don't worship the Antichrist, you're going to what? You're going to die! You're going to be killed, right? But he still goes on. He then says if you don't take this mark of the Antichrist, then what's going to happen to you? You're going to be forced into doing it, whether you want to or not, right? And so here's the point. The Bible clearly says this is all happening on a global scale which means in order for this to happen, for the Antichrist and the False Prophet to *make* and *force* and *order* people to do what they want them to do, including taking the Mark of the Beast, you have to at some point move from everything being an option or a choice under the guise of convenience of course, to at some point making this an *order*, right? At some point you have to mandate it. Now I don't know about you, but I am so glad that we see no signs of this happening any time soon. Yeah, right! It's already here! For the first time in mankind's history, we are moving towards the full mandating of the Mark of the Beast system whether we want it or not! Don't believe me?

**1. The 1ˢᵗ proof we've already started to have this Mark of the Beast System mandated on us is with a Universal ID.**

You see, once again, put yourself in the Antichrist's shoes. I mean, here you are with the ultimate goal of tracking and tagging every single person on the whole planet and controlling what they "buy and sell," right? As we just read, at some point, you're going to have to force them into doing it, right? So the question is, "How in the world are you going to get people used to the idea of being forced into receiving some sort of microchip technology into their bodies?" Wouldn't it make sense to implement a kind of Phase One *first*, where you mandate an external ID card that has a chip in it that people carry on the outside of them? Then once people get used to having that mandated, then maybe Phase Two would kick into gear where people would be mandated to receive a Universal ID Chip on the *inside* of them. I mean, we all know those cards can be lost or stolen so this would be much more secure, safe and convenient, don't you think? You might be thinking that's crazy, but I'm telling you, Phase One is already well under way. In fact, a Universal mandatory ID Chip Card is hidden in the new Immigration Bill. Ron Paul exposed it. Can you say, "Let me see your papers?" Hitler eat your heart out!

*Scene from an older black and white film:*

**Official:** *May I see your papers?*

**Man:** *I don't think I have them on me.*

**Official:** *In that case, I guess we'll have to ask you to come along.*

**Man:** *WAIT! I think it's possible (reaches inside in coat) YES! Here they are. (hands them to official)*

**2nd Official:** *These papers expired 3 weeks ago. You have to come along.*

**Man:** *(starts running)*

**Official:** *HALT! HALT! (both start in pursuit-then one of them pulls out a rifle and fires at the man)*

Man: *(hit by a bullet, falls to the ground)*
--------------------------
*Guiliano: (from 2008) Then we should develop a tamper proof ID card. And then as you got the tamper proof ID card- you'd be allowed to work, pay taxes, get online, become a citizen, follow the rules.*
--------------------------

**Sen. Ron Paul:** *It's by far the worst National ID scheme the statists have come* *up with yet. They're still hiding their true intentions. But in the wake of recent events, the statists believe they have the perfect excuse to ratchet up their attacks on our remaining liberties. Right now the so-called "Gang of Eight" in the United States Senate, including Senators John McCain, Lindsey Graham and Chuck Schumer- are working with President Obama to sneak this massive National ID Card power grab into a new "immigration reform" law that's being used as a cover for all sorts of statist madness. I hardly know where to begin.*

*The 844-page so-called "Immigration Reform" monstrosity is a statist's dream. Not only does this bill increase federal spending, it mandates every American carry a National ID card with their photo and creates a new federal database containing biometric information on every American, such as fingerprints and retinal scans. The card would be required for all U.S. workers regardless of place of birth, making it illegal for anyone to hold a job in the United States who doesn't obtain an ID card. All employers would be required to purchase an ID scanner to verify the ID cards by making sure the information on the card matches the information in the federal database. So every time any citizen applies for a job the government would know and you can bet it's only a matter of time until "ID scans" will be required to travel, attend public events or even make routine purchases, as well.*

Or in other words, what you can "buy or sell." This is happening right now! We've been totally duped! But you might be thinking, "Well hey, that can't happen! We've got to stand up and fight this! We can't go back to do what Hitler did! Let me see your papers! I mean, surely it's against the law to mandate a Universal ID Card." Well actually, as of 1986, with the passage of the Immigration Control Act, this now "gives the President the authority to implement whatever type of identification is necessary to control the population." And if people don't like it, that's too bad because all he needs to do is wait for another national emergency or crisis and *by law* the President can put it into action through FEMA to "restore order." In fact, an Executive Order that was signed allows the President to "Empower the Postmaster General to register all men, women and children in the United States." Hey! Go down to the Post Office and get your chip, kids! And as crazy as this is, I'm telling you, we've already been warmed up to this. If you think about it, it's not the first time we've seen a mandated card in the U.S. How about that ol' *Social Security Card*? First it was supposed to be just for tracking individual accounts for those who enrolled in the Social Security program and was *not* to be used for ID purposes...ever! But *now* try getting around in life without one, right? It's needed for almost everything, including "buying and selling" of certain items. Lest you think a government, even our own, would ever require people to receive a universal identification mark, well again, we saw Hitler do it with the Jews who many would say was a precursor to the Antichrist, and even more recently it's not just the U.S. but the whole world is preparing to do this. The European Union is preparing to give its citizens a universal identification so they can "freely move about from country to country." Japan has "launched a compulsory ID system" called Juki Net that links all citizens to a nationwide computer system, Germany is looking to do the same thing, as well as Mexico and even Israel is doing it too! I'm telling you, it's going global just like the Bible said!

But you might be thinking, "Well hey, this is crazy, there's no way in the world people can pull this off for the *whole planet*. I mean there's just way too many people and it would cost way too much and take too much time. It's just not feasible!" Really? Well, you might want to tell that to India. They're doing it right now with their 1.2 billion people, and wait till you hear what they won't be able to do if they don't get it!

**Biometrics in India:**

*Reporter: Fingerprint and eye scans of every person in India are being gathered in the biggest biometric database in the world. Well, the 1.2 billion people's data will be on the system which will give access to the welfare state.*

*This is an enormous task. The fingerprints and eye-scans of every Indian in the country are being taken and collected in an online data base. When complete, everyone will have a unique identity number. It will enable them to access India's vast and unweildy welfare-state.*

*Nandan Nilekani: There are a large number of Indians who don't have any form of identity whatsoever. So this is a way to include them into the society and give them the benefits.*

And get them ready for Stage Two and now everybody gets a chip! Feasible or not, looks to me like somebody's already doing it! In fact, in this program, it is envisioned to "facilitate everything from banking transactions to the purchase of goods and services." You know, buy and sell. Looks like the Antichrist's Stage One is working out great! In fact, that's not all. The United Nations has already outlined a scheme so that "every person in the world" would be "registered under a universal identification" and a "Global ID Card is being called for and issued to each person on the planet to not only identify themselves, but give access to all governmental services, health care services, allows them to drive a car, get a job, get insurance, gain access to buildings, and of course, pay for things."[22] First get this Universal Chipped ID Card mandated on the outside of you across the whole planet, then how about mandate it for on the inside of you with a chip. Sounds like a great plan for the Antichrist, how about you?

**2. The 2nd proof** we've already started to have this Mark of the Beast System mandated on us is with a **Universal Goal.**

Once again, put yourself in the Antichrist shoes. Some people, after all this time, might have an inkling of Bible Prophecy; we can see clearly where this Universal ID card is leading to. It's leading towards Stage Two, a Universal Microchip, right? So hey, if you're the Antichrist, what do you do with these people? They're going to let the cat out of the bag! What do you do? Well hey, doesn't it make sense to first warm them up to the mandate of a Universal Microchip incrementally by working at one end of the spectrum and then start moving towards your ultimate goal? Of course! And here's what you do. First get them used to having something mandated to be put in their bodies. You know, like with mandatory vaccinations like we're seeing across the country and mandatory blood samples taken from DUI suspects and mandatory DNA samples from people who get pulled over as we saw before. You are having something invasive put inside your bodies whether you like it or not! Then once people accept that, move to your ultimate goal, another invasive thing inside your body, the microchip! Makes perfect sense, right? Of course! But again, start at the end of the spectrum first, so people don't catch on and get warned up to it. You know, start with those *dangerous* people first like criminals and prisoners who "deserve" to have their rights taken away and micro-chipped. They should be forced to get one, right? Well, they are!

### KOMO 4 News/Tracking Trouble

*The trouble with tracking sex offenders has put a controversial plan before state law-makers. Instead of GPS bracelets, convicts would be forced to have a device implanted.*

**Luke Duecy:** *The thinking is this. You can track someone on their phone. You can even track your own pet if you want to. So why not track sex-offenders using a tiny radio chip.*

*David Torrence, a level 3 sex-offender, ripped his criminal tracking device from his ankle and disappeared. Authorities have no idea where he is. But soon, that might change. Instead of ankle bracelets, like Torrence was wearing, sex-offenders might have something like this <RFID chip> implanted.*

*It will be a little more difficult to take off.*

Yeah, I agree, it's stuck inside of you, now what are you going to do? So let me get this straight, the bracelets on the outside of prisoners were the first step of eventually getting a chip on the inside of prisoners. Hmmm, where have I heard that before? But hey, that's just those prisoners; who cares about those guys, right? They deserve to have this happen to them. Not! Oh, but that's not all. Now move a little closer away from the end of the spectrum and then try it out on those people behind bars. But what about those people who don't know better? You know, those who have lost their memory with Alzheimer's? I mean, if we put a chip inside of them, we could track them like the prisoners and it'll keep them safe; it's for their own good! Well, guess what? We're doing that too!

**GMA:**

*Reporter: Ida became one of 4 1/2 million Americans diagnosed with Alzheimer's.*

*Ida's husband David Frank: Well she was being very forgetful. She would ask the time and repeat the question over and over again.*

*Reporter: Which is why Ida is one of the first patients at this Alzheimer's Center in Florida to be implanted with a microchip.*

*Scott Silverman: (CEO VeriChip) When an Alzheimer patient enters an emergency room or is found wandering in a certain location, once their arm is scanned, it would immediately designate who they are-their identity and the fact that they are an Alzheimer patient.*

See? I told you it was for their own good! But that's right! Don't stop there! You're on a roll! Move a little closer now to your ultimate goal and how about mandating chipping not only for prisoners and Alzheimer's patients, but hey, how about policemen and soldiers! I mean, they're government property already anyway, right? I mean, if we just chip them too they'll be safe on the streets or the battlefield wherever they are! Believe it or not, that too is already happening!

*Reporter: Sgt. Bill Koretsky's implanted medical microchip may have saved his life. His story begins in the middle of a high-speed police chase in New Jersey.*

*Sgt. Bill Koretsky: The brakes on the police car overheated, the car wouldn't stop and I hit a telephone pole dead center at 40mph. The airbag did not deploy. I didn't have my seatbelt on and I hit the steering wheel.*

*Reporter: Paramedics rushed Koretsky to the Hackensack University Medical Center. Thanks to his implant, doctors immediately discovered Koretsky's diabetes.*

*Koretsky: I regained consciousness, full conscientiousness within an hour. But if I had not, I could have gone into a coma.*

*Reporter: If the VeriChip Corporation has it's way, Koretsky's story will become the norm.*

## CNN NEWS:

*Melissa Long: Keeping track of troops in Iraq. The military is already using some type of GPS on some soldiers, but what more can be done? CNN's Brian Todd takes a look in this week's Tech-Effect.*

*Brian Todd: One option, placing a tracking micro-chip under a service member's skin. Former Special Operations officers tell us they believe that's being developed. Current military officials won't comment on that.*

So first it was the external GPS tracker, then it moved to the internal microchip and they won't comment on it. I wonder why? Who wants to hear you're going to have a mandated microchip! But hey! Don't stop there! If it's good for your soldiers and policemen and Alzheimer's patients and prisoners to keep them safe, why not kids! I mean, they don't know any better and they get lost all the time! If we chip them they'll not only be safe from predators, but we can monitor them wherever they go! Won't it be great! Well, these people think so!

*"On my first instinct, it sounds like science fiction. The microchip is safe in humans.*

**Reporter:** *Dr. Jonathan Musher, who works for the company that sells the chip, says it will save lives.*

**Dr Musher:** *The FDA stands firmly behind this.*

**Reporter:** *He admits that there have been no long term studies on people but nonetheless, he's convinced it's safe. And there are some who see no problem using the chip for more than a medical ID. Parents are putting these chips in kids in Mexico where there is a higher risk of kidnapping. The scanners are put up at airports and bus stations, so if a chipped child is there, police know.*

**Dr Musher:** *"There's been over 10 million pets in 15 years that have had this microchip without any problems."*

There you have it! If it's good for Fido, it's good for Frankie and Johnny and little Susie and everybody! Won't it be great to have your mandated microchip! Now that we've allowed it to go on this far, why the next thing you know, if you don't want to take one willingly, they'll just make it a *necessity*, that is, if you want to keep your job! Don't believe me? It's already happening!

**Sean Darks:** *There's my chip right there.*

**Reporter:** *You can actually see it.*
*It's the size of about a grain of rice, and it feels like it too. But what that tiny chip can and can't do, has become the source of much concern and confusion.*

**Darks:** *I was in a grocery store and a couple of ladies said, "Hey you're the guy with the chip in you're arm, aren't you? Ride across the scanner to see if you can get us a discount on groceries."*

**Reporter:** *Sean Darks is the CEO of Citywatcher.com, a small company in Cincinnati. It's the first U.S. business to use chip implants in it's employees. Chip implants have been common in pets for several years. Giving the owner peace of mind that their lost animal could be identified. And for retail giant Wal-Mart, the chips are used as Smart-barcodes to keep track of thousands of products. But for use in people, well, privacy advocates think we shouldn't open that door. Like it* *or not, we're in that Brave New World and it might not be long before YOUR boss is literally getting under your skin.*

Now wait a second. You mean to tell me that even if I'm not willing to get a microchip implant, I might still have to just to keep my job? It's almost like we're getting boxed in, isn't it? Oh but that's still not all. They've covered all the bases. You see, if you're not willing to get an implant and even if you choose to lose your job over an implant, it might soon become mandatory from Congress. Don't believe me? This is what we saw before with the chilling quote from then Senator Joseph Biden talking to then candidate Chief Justice John Roberts. Let's take a look at that again!

**Joe Biden/Roberts Hearing:**

*Joe Biden: And we'll be faced with equally consequential decisions in the 21st Century. Can a microscopic tag be placed in a person's body to track his every movement? There's actual discussion about that. You will rule on that, mark my words, before your tenure is over.*

*Dr. Katherine Albrecht: I think the real concern that most people have is that at some point the government would say, "Line up and get your chip."*[23]

But hey, that'll never happen…"You will rule on that, mark my words." I don't know about you, but if the exact same two guys here who have now mandated for us to have healthcare are here talking about people being forced to be implanted with a microscopic tag to track their every move, whether they want to or not, uh, my guess is they're probably going to be forcing people to be implanted with microscopic tags to track their every move, how about you? And that lady is right! For the first time in man's history, we are seeing the Government say, "Line up and get your chip!" Gee, where have I heard that before!

Folks, this is how close we are! This is not a game and this is not 50 years down the road, it's happening now!

There are also plans to mandate this Mark for people with AIDS, "to monitor their activity, track their movements and to prevent them from infecting others." Two, people on food stamps, the USDA is now considering biometric identification for all individuals who will want to benefit from their Food and Nutrition Services. As one person stated, "The RFID chip may soon become a must for everyone who does not want to starve!" Three, some people are saying this needs to be done to babies the moment they are born. "Global warming alarmist Elizabeth Moon is calling for all babies to be forcibly implanted with a microchip to ensure that "anonymity would be impossible."

*"If I were empress of the Universe I would insist on every individual having a unique ID permanently attached – a barcode if you will; an implanted chip to provide an easy, fast, inexpensive way to identify individuals. It would be imprinted on everyone at birth. Point the scanner at someone and there it is."*

*And as one person said "Moon's proposal sounds like something out of Nazi concentration camps where prisoners were tattooed with five digit Hollerith numbers to identify them, using a punch card system developed by IBM."*

What? IBM was involved in the marking of the Jewish people for Hitler? Yup, and they're also involved with this new one involving RFID. It's an electronic marking as we saw before. In fact, I also got this email from a guy who said this forced micro-chipping, this mandate, is already starting in Mexico. Take it for what it is, I know it's just an email, but here's what he wrote.

*"Pastor Billy, the reason why I write to you is to inform you about something that happened when me and my wife went to Mexico to see her family. It was last March and we shared the Gospel with them not knowing if they really understood it. But to make the story short, we also informed them about the RFID chip that was coming.*

*My wife's family lives in a really small place in Central Mexico called Huejutla de Reyes. It is really a poor town and they do not have too much technology. But they participate in a program for poor Mexicans that is called Oportunidades (Opportunities) that gives them help for Medical Care and gives them money for food and their daily needs.*

*When we told them about the RFID chip, they told us that this program (Oportunidades) will implement soon (they did not give us a date) a chip in their body and they will not need money to buy or sell. But they will need to get a chip if they want to continue in the program and receive help from the Government."*[24]

Hey, that sounds like what the USDA is proposing for those who are on food stamps here? Are we getting close or what? This is exactly what the Bible says the Antichrist is going to do when you are living in the Last Days.

**IV. The 4ᵗʰ way that we know we really are headed for this Mark of the Beast system is the Optional Proof.**

You see, believe it or not, there is going to be one choice you're going to have when it comes to the Mark of the Beast and that is this, "Do you want this in your right hand, or your forehead? That's it. That's your choice! But don't take my word for it. Let's listen to God.

**Revelation 20:1-6** "And I saw an angel coming down out of heaven, having the key to the Abyss and holding in his hand a great chain. He seized the dragon, that ancient serpent, who is the devil, or satan, and bound him for a thousand years. He threw him into the Abyss, and locked and sealed it over him, to keep him from deceiving the nations anymore until the thousand years were ended. After that, he must be set free for a short time.I saw thrones on which were seated those who had been given authority to judge. And I saw the souls of those who had been beheaded because of their testimony for Jesus and because of the word of God. They had not worshiped the beast or his image and had not received his mark on their foreheads or their hands. They came to life and reigned with Christ a thousand years.(The rest of the dead did not come to life until the thousand years were ended.) This is the first resurrection. Blessed and holy are those who have part in the first resurrection. The second death has no power over them, but they will be priests of God and of Christ and will reign with Him for a thousand years."

Now maybe it's just me, but I think it's pretty obvious there's a great payoff for those who refuse to receive the Mark of the Beast, right? It says they're blessed, how? They get to rule and reign with Jesus Christ, personally, for 1,000 years and they will actually become priests of God! Isn't that cool? Yeah! How many of you guys would say that's much better than the alternative there? Yeah, the Lake of Fire usually isn't a great place to camp out at! Here's the point. Notice, not only the horrible penalty for those who receive the Mark of the Beast, but notice the placing. Apparently you've got only *two options*. Specifically the right hand or the forehead, right? It says it right there! In fact, as we've seen several times before, this isn't the only place where Revelation says it's these two specific options for the Mark.

**Revelation 13:16** "He also forced everyone, small and great, rich and poor, free and slave, to receive a mark on his right hand or on his forehead."

**Revelation 14:9-10** "A third angel followed them and said in a loud voice: 'If anyone worships the beast and his image and receives his mark on the forehead or on the hand, he, too, will drink of the wine of God's fury, which has been poured full strength into the cup of His wrath.'"

In other words, just like our opening text, you don't want to do it. Stay away from this thing! But again, the point is you're only given two options for this Mark, either it's taken in the right hand or the forehead, right? So the question is, "*Why*? Why specifically the right hand or forehead? I mean, why not the leg, why not the back of the neck, or something like that?

**1. The 1st reason** why I believe we're given the option of specifically the Right Hand or Forehead with the Mark of the Beast is the **Practical Issue.**

You see, in cold weather climates, the two parts of the body that just happen to be the quickest and easiest to expose for scanning purposes are the hands and the head. A large portion of the world wears these things called hats and coats to keep them warm and so if you're in line getting ready to buy and sell something, or get some government handout and you had the Mark on your back or your big toe or somewhere like that, it's going to be hard or cumbersome to get to it, right? But not if you had it in your right hand or forehead. Chances are even in cold weather climates these parts are already exposed, or you could just quickly remove your glove or lift up your stocking cap to reveal your forehead. Either way, it just so happens, these specific body parts make for a very practical place to put the Mark of the Beast in cold weather climates.

**2. The 2nd reason** I believe we're given the option of specifically the Right Hand or Forehead with the Mark of the Beast is the **Worship Issue.**

The Bible is clear. What goes along with the taking of the Mark of the Beast is an attitude of WORSHIP of the Beast. People are going to *worship* him. In fact, in Revelation 13 alone, it's mentioned 4 different times.

**Revelation 13:4** "…and they also worshiped the beast…"

**Revelation 13:8** "All inhabitants of the earth will worship the beast—all whose names have not been written in the Lamb's book of life."

**Revelation 13:12** "…and made the earth and its inhabitants worship the first beast, whose fatal wound had been healed."

**Revelation 13:15** "…so that the image could speak and cause all who refused to worship the image to be killed."

So this worshipful attitude towards the Beast with the Mark just happens to fit a HUGE portion of the planet when it comes to worshiping with the right hand or forehead. Different cultures today use these specific body parts to worship their deities. The first ones to do that are the Hindu and Asian populations with those red dots they put on their forehead called the "Tilaka" or the "Bindi." So, even though it might be weird to you and I here in the West, these people, a huge portion of the planet, would naturally opt to take the Mark of the Beast in their forehead in a worshipful attitude just like the text says. In fact, speaking of the West and a worshipful attitude, believe it or not, another huge portion of the planet may not have a problem with a Mark going on their forehead as well and that is the Catholics. Believe it or not, they already put a Mark on their foreheads every year on Ash Wednesday. In fact, Joseph Biden, a Catholic, did that himself. Gee, I wonder where this microchip to "track and tag a person's every move" that we saw Biden and Roberts were talking about is going to be placed? Forehead maybe?

Now you might be thinking, "Well I don't care what the Hindu, Asians, or Catholics think. There's no way I'm going to put something on my forehead! That's not cool! That's unsightly! That's ugly! What a fashion faux pas!" Well actually, guess what happens to be the latest fashion? It's called *Bagel Heads* and this is supposed to be the coolest thing ever for your forehead to be injected with saline and then push it in to make it look like a Bagel! Looks to me like those people aren't too worried about making a fashion faux pa or something being unsightly on their forehead.

But you might be wondering, "Alright, that's the forehead, but what about the right hand? What's that got to do with worship?" Well again, learn your history. We've seen even as recently as Adolph Hitler how the right hand was used to give him a heil Hitler in an attitude of *worship*, right? And if you think that attitude will never come back, you're wrong. We are also seeing

Palestinian soldiers do the same thing, you know, the ones who want to annihilate the Jews, they're using their right hands and we're even seeing Obama supporters, "being encouraged to mark their right hands with messages, press them over their hearts, to pledge allegiance to Obama."[25] Looks to me like we're seeing a resurgence of people using their right hands and foreheads in an attitude of worship, how about you? Just in time for the actual Mark of the Beast!

**3. The 3rd reason I believe we're given the option of specifically the Right Hand or Forehead with the Mark of the Beast is the Logistical Issue.**

You see, as we saw before, many skeptics today say that it's logistically impossible to Mark everybody on the planet at the same time. It would take too much time, cost too much…blah blah blah. It's just not feasible they say and what they do is they usually pick on the biometric version of the Mark that we've focused on in the bulk of our study, the tiny microchip the size of a grain of rice that can be implanted. What they say is this implant would take forever to get into people all over the planet. It's just too slow, it's too long of a procedure, it's too cumbersome, you'd never get the job done in time and I don't necessarily believe that what with all the advancements we've been seeing in technology (but be that as it may) even if you wanted to go there, it just so happens, for the first time in mankind's history, there's *another option* out there. As we saw before, they're using the exact same RFID implant technology, but they can now affix it to the outside of the body. They're called Epidermal Electronic implants and they can be affixed to the body externally very easy and quickly.[26] But here's the point. Just get one of those in the mail and put it "on" your forehead or right hand, real quick and you're good to go! It's that easy? No logistical problem here! Just send out a mass mailer and get the job done in one shot! For the first time in man's history, "on" or "in" it doesn't matter. *We can do both*! No need to debate, no need for a logistical problem.

Now for those of you who think people will never warm up to this new external marking system, you're wrong. Anyone just happen to know what the latest external marking rage is, young and old alike? Tattoos! External tattoos that you mark on your body! In my generation it wasn't that big of a deal, but now, they're everywhere! There's shows about them, they're everywhere being promoted and this of course led to the next phase of body piercings! In the tongue, in the nose, in the eyebrow, in the forehead, etc. In fact, it's even led to body implants in the head, horn implants are on the rise and the point is this: Once again, just in time for the Mark of the Beast, people are loving this external marking stuff, and it's getting darker I might add! But it's now led to another latest craze and that is getting your very own external bar code! It's the next big thing in body art.

**Scanning barcodes on your body with a verbal reader:**

Slaves
Bar Codes
For Sale
Peter
Anthony
Henrik Berg
Property of CRC
10408-045
08.26.2004
Dan The Man
Human
Sold
Scan Me

Man peels barcode off his forehead

Now, as creepy as that is, you might be thinking, "Well that's just a peel off version. Don't you think if this is the actual Mark of the Beast technology that it would be a little bit more *permanent*? Well yeah and they're not only working on it right now but they're busy beefing it up. They now have a new labeling technology out there called QR CODE and it's much more sophisticated than bar code. It allows you to not only identify any product including yourself anywhere on the planet, but it gives you the ability to *interact* with every product and person on the planet. Let's take a look at that new technology.

*"If you haven't heard or seen QR codes you soon will. QR or Quick Response Codes are two dimensional matrix codes that trigger responses in Smart phones. The response triggered might be a simple text message, a call to a telephone, a visual, or a trip to a website. QR codes have been in Japan and Europe for several years.*

*Very prevalent in Japan, they have been used in advertising to promote products, by sending customers to websites. Triggering information such as nutritional details or prompting a sale via coupon. They have even appeared in architecture. The Tokyo N Building, rather than having the typical billboards, was built with a QR code facade.*

*The QR code takes you to a site that gives you up to date information on the shops and services inside. The vision of the future includes the use of an I-Phone app that will allow users to see those inside who want to be seen and heard by clicking on them-you would see what they are tweeting.*

*QR codes are just starting to become popular in North America. A number of airlines like British Airways and United now allow users to download QR boarding passes to their phone to use at departure gates. Starbucks is piloting a QR enabled app that links customers to a store that allows customers to pay."*

So they not only connect you to the Matrix-like System, but you can use them to make financial transactions in the Matrix-like System. Now here's where it gets creepy. Can you guess what the next latest fashion craze is? Not only getting your own identifiable QR CODE so you can interact with the System, but to get a *permanent version* on your body. Move over temporary peel off bar code, the new permanent QR Code is here to stay!

**Machine Readable 2D Barcode Tattoo**

*You can make a statement about who you are with your own QR T-shirt, belt buckle, tattoo or business card.*
------
*Hi, today were going to do something that's never been done before. We are going to see a barcode/tattoo that can be read by a machine. My friend Livy, she got this tattoo about a week ago. <scans tattoo on her foot and info pops up on computer screen> There you go, and that is human tattoo barcode data.*
-------

*And if you think your food has escaped the code, think again! Your next birthday cake may have one. And if you buy a Clever Cupcake, it's code will send you to a sight to Aid World Poverty. There's no escape. Might as well relax on a beach somewhere <shows giant QR code in the sand>.*

Oh, and lest you think these external tattoos show no signs of becoming mandatory someday, the makers of the external RFID tattoos for cattle, a company called SOMARK, was launched to help fulfill the NAIS mandate where every animal has to have an electronic tag to supposedly ensure our safety. But the same company who makes these external RFID cattle tattoos has made some very interesting comments about our future.

*Mark Bydynowski: <Somark Innovations> Basically we make electronic ink tattoos. But the purpose of the electronic ink tattoos is actually to apply it to the food supply to identify and track them as they move throughout the food supply chain.*

*Ramos Mays: I was raised on a cattle farm in southwest Missouri. I grew up in the industry and I always heard my father speaking of the problems that were happening in the industry with identification and him being a small producer. You know, he was really feeling the economic hit from it and so I knew that. So you know when someone's getting pinched economically there's an opportunity there.*

*Bydynowski: I don't have a tattoo today. Ramos will probably be the first to have one himself.*

So it's cows now, but later it could be people. Sounds to me like we're being prepared for something, how about you? Oh, and it just so happens that this tattooing technology from SOMARK can be made *invisible* for those of you who are still worried about how this will look on your forehead or your right hand. They use a special ink that is only noticeable when exposed to UV light like they have in lines at places like Chucky Cheese, Bars, Amusement Parks, etc.[27] Looks to me like all options are covered! No need to worry whether the Mark goes on your forehead or hand! It still looks cool! It's invisible. But here's the point. Internal, External, both options are here for the first time in man's history. And one day they could not only become mandatory, but they present no logistical problem whatsoever!

**4. The 4th reason** I believe we're given the option of specifically the Right Hand or Forehead with the Mark of the Beast is the **Energy Issue.**

You see, what's really wild about these microchip implants, is they have a unique power source that recharges itself by converting electricity from the fluctuations of the person's body temperature, and it just so happens that a researcher, Dr. Carl Sanders, who worked for thirty-two years designing microchips in the Bio-Med field said that, *"Over one and a half million dollars was spent finding out the two places in the human body that temperature changes most rapidly."*[28] And can anyone guess just where these two best locations in the body might be? That's right, *in the forehead* right below the hairline and *the back of the hand.* Hey, that makes sense. That's how you check a child's temperature the old-fashioned way. But now that can be used to generate energy for the chip!

**5.** The **5th reason** I believe we're given the option of specifically the Right Hand or Forehead with the Mark of the Beast is the **Penalty Issue.**

You see the Bible says no matter how convenient it is, or how cool you might think it is, the Mark comes with a *penalty.*

**Revelation 16:2** "The first angel went and poured out his bowl on the land, and ugly and painful sores broke out on the people who had the mark of the beast and worshiped his image."

Now here's what interesting. Dr. Carl Sanders then went on to say that there was one drawback with this system. That is, if the chip broke down, the person would get a boil or grievous sore. Hmmm. Where have I heard that before? And if that still doesn't get you, maybe another advancement in this technology is why the text says in Revelation your fate is sealed when you take the Mark.

**Revelation 14:11** "He will be tormented with burning sulfur in the presence of the holy angels and of the Lamb. And the smoke of their torment rises for ever and ever. There is no rest day or night for those who worship the beast and his image, or for anyone who receives the mark of his name."

In other words, you go straight to hell. Why? Well, maybe the Antichrist is also going to make sure that if you try to change your mind after you take the Mark you will DIE and immediately go straight to hell. Believe it or not, that too, is already here!

**Mark of the Beast Killer Chip:**

*Fox News Host "Alright this story sounds like it's out of well, a Hollywood thriller. A Saudi inventor has created a killer microchip. It's designed to track terrorists and criminals and well, you can think of somebody. Not only does it include a GPS device, it also has a lethal dose of cyanide which can be activated at any time. You get my point?"*[29]

Who would have thought we'd be living in the days where we not only see the technology for the Mark of the Beast and the conditioning and willingness of people to take the Mark of the Beast, but who would have thought they would have actually figured out a way to kill you with the Mark of the Beast and send you straight into hell. Is that evil or what? And that's exactly what the Antichrist will do when you're living in the Last Days!

Yet, even with all this amazing evidence pointing to the signs of Christ's soon return, some people still have a problem recognizing what's going on, like this lady:

*"One day a blonde lady had finally had enough. She was tired of everyone assuming that she wasn't very smart just because of her hair color. So she decided to do something about it. She went to the hairdresser and had her hair dyed brown.*

*As she walked out of the beauty salon, she was feeling quite proud of her new look so she decided to go for a drive in the country. Well after she drove for awhile she suddenly came upon a shepherd.*

*She thought this was a perfect opportunity to test out her new look and demonstrate her intelligence. So she walked over to the shepherd and asked, 'If I can guess how many sheep you have, can I take one for a reward?'*

*Well, the shepherd thought for sure that this lady could never guess the exact number of sheep he had, so he took her bet and let her try. But to his surprise, amazingly she guessed 98, the exact number of sheep he owned.*

*So feeling rather good about herself, the lady picks up her reward and starts walking back to her car. But before she got to the car, the shepherd tapped her on the shoulder and said, 'Hey lady, if I can guess your natural hair color, can I have my dog back?'"*[30]

Now, that lady had a problem recognizing things, didn't she? But unfortunately, she's not alone. Many people today also have a problem recognizing what's really taking place in current events. They have no clue that the Rapture of the Church could happen at any time and that the Antichrist's wicked kingdom is being formed right before their very eyes and the warning that Jesus gave long ago still holds true today.

**Luke 12:54-56** "Then Jesus turned to the crowd and said, 'When you see clouds beginning to form in the west, you say, Here comes a shower.' And you are right. When the south wind blows, you say, Today will be a scorcher. And it is. You hypocrites! You know how to interpret the appearance of the earth and the sky, but you can't interpret these present times.'"

I hope you're not one of those who have bought into this lie that man can somehow have his own heaven on earth by implementing The Mark of the Beast. Why? Because you might wake up one day and discover that you've been left behind, and do you know what? God doesn't want you left behind. Because He loves us, He has given us the warning sign of The Mark of the Beast to show us that the 7-year Tribulation is near and that Christ's Coming is rapidly approaching. Jesus Himself said this:

**Luke 21:28** "When these things begin to take place, stand up and lift up your heads, because your redemption is drawing near."

Like it or not, we are headed for *The Final Countdown*. We don't know the day or the hour. Only God knows. The point is, if you're a Christian, "You must never forget the warning recorded for posterity by Martin Niemoeller, the Lutheran minister who lived in Hitler's Germany during the 1930s and 1940s. His words echo down to us over succeeding decades: '*In Germany they came first for the Communists, and I didn't speak up because I wasn't a Communist. Then they came for the Jews, and I didn't speak up because I wasn't a Jew. Then they came for the trade unionists, and I didn't speak up because I wasn't a trade unionist. Then they came for the Catholics, and I didn't speak up because I was a Protestant. Then they came for me, and by that time no one was left to speak up.*'" Folks, it's high time we Christians speak up and declare the good news of salvation to those who are dying all around us. But please, if you're not a Christian, give your life to Jesus today, because tomorrow may be too late! Just like the Bible said!

# How to Receive Jesus Christ:

1. Admit your need (I am a sinner).

2. Be willing to turn from your sins (repent).

3. Believe that Jesus Christ died for you on the Cross and rose from the grave.

4. Through prayer, invite Jesus Christ to come in and control your life through the Holy Spirit. (Receive Him as Lord and Savior.)

# What to pray:

Dear Lord Jesus,

I know that I am a sinner and need Your forgiveness. I believe that You died for my sins. I want to turn from my sins. I now invite You to come into my heart and life. I want to trust and follow You as Lord and Savior.

In Jesus' name. Amen.

# Notes

---

## Chapter Six · *The Rise of Apostasy*

1. *Story of Man with Hearing Problem*
   (Email story) – Source Unknown
2. *Statistics on the Rise of Apostasy*
   (http://www.barna.org/)
   (http://peacebyjesus.witnesstoday.org/RevealingStatistics.html)
3. *Quote Larry the Phony Believer*
   (http://www.bluefishtv.com/Store/Downloadable_Video_Illustrations/1230/
   Unbelief_Going_through_the_Motions)
4. *Quote Pastors Admitting They're Phony Believers*
   (http://www.albertmohler.com/2010/03/18/clergy-who-dont-believe-the-
   scandal-of-apostate-pastors/)
5. *Story Pesky Squirrels*
   (Email Story – Source Unknown)
6. *Quote Number One Cause of Atheism*
   (http://www.preceptaustin.org/titus_116.htm)
7. *Quote Counterfeit Bill*
   (http://www.famci.com/hearthstone/hstone012001.htm)
8. *Story Dead Church*
   (Email Story – Source Unknown)
9. *Quote An Interview with an Atheist*
   (http://www.youtube.com/watch?v=yLRFKxWcVFo)
10. *Quote False Teachings on Wealth & Health*
    (http://www.bereanfaith.com/heresy.php?action=tquote&id=18)
    (http://www.bereanfaith.com/heresy.php?action=tquote&id=12)
    (http://www.intotruth.org/wof/sayings.html)
    (http://www.bereanfaith.com/heresy.php?action=tquote&id=17)
    (http://www.whereisgod.net/guarantee.htm)
    Hank Hanegraaff, *Christianity In Crisis*
    (Eugene: Harvest House Publishers, 1993, Pgs. 11, 21, 24-25, 26-27)
11. *Examples of Fake Miracle Trinkets*
    (http://www.bible.ca/tongues-photogallery-pentacostal-trinkets.htm)

(http://www.youtube.com/watch?v=WjU5LZu6btE&feature=related)
(http://www.youtube.com/watch?v=P4_CYVGN15E)
(http://www.youtube.com/watch?v=QCbADp9Xh4A&feature=related)

12. *Quote Kenneth Copeland Says God a Failure*
    (http://www.bereanfaith.com/heresy.php?action=tquote&id=32)
13. *Quote Benny Hinn Exposed*
    (http://www.youtube.com/watch?v=NSxqFE_hmcE)
14. *Quote Benny Hinn Holy Ghost Machine Gun*
    (http://www.youtube.com/watch?v=mPB3a8FbeJY)
15. *Quote Marjoe Gortner the Fake Evangelist*
    (http://www.youtube.com/watch?v=KxfThlCcfHI)
16. *Quote Prosperity Pimps*
    (http://www.youtube.com/watch?v=nIdTFSIj8AI)
17. *Quote John Piper on Prosperity Gospel*
    (http://www.youtube.com/watch?v=PTc_FoELt8s)
18. *Church Growth Teachings Versus the Bible*
    (http://www.fundamentalbiblechurch.org/Foundation/fbcsdlbk.htm)
19. *Quote Theotainment in the Church*
    (http://www.gosanangelo.com/news/2009/jun/26/pop-cultures-new-role-in-the-church-thats/?print=1)
20. *Ignatius the New Youth Leader*
    (http://www.youtube.com/watch?v=wLGLBVSpBzY)
21. *Adult Theotainment in the Church*
    (http://www.raidersnewsupdate.com/proctor.htm)
    (http://www.qctimes.net/articles/2005/05/26/local/export93493.txt)
    (http://www.orthodoxytoday.org/articles5/LaymanClownEucharist.php)
    (http://abcnews.go.com/GMA/story?id=809937&page=1)
22. *Story Cows in the Corn*
    (Email story) – Source Unknown
23. *Corporate Worship Songs in the Church*
    (http://www.youtube.com/watch?v=aYaTSbCGY50)
24. *AC/DC Sung in Church Service*
    (http://www.youtube.com/watch?v=2vUt4pJgHZQ)
25. *Steve Harvey Introduces Jesus Christ*
    (http://www.youtube.com/watch?v=ZDpmBfncbjw)
26. *Quote Pastors Preachers Fluff*
    (http://www.youtube.com/watch?v=TGisLq9DA6U)
    (Various Video Interviews) – Sources Unknown
27. *Quote Good for Nothing Christians*

(http://www.newswithviews.com/baldwin/baldwin520.htm)
28. *Quote Paul Washer on Joel Olsteen*
(http://www.youtube.com/watch?v=pXcPLnKmBRQ)
(http://www.youtube.com/watch?v=igKhXFAfnzI)
29. *Quote Pastors Preaching False Gospel*
(http://www.youtube.com/watch?v=ihnGEV-q1gw&feature=related)
(http://www.youtube.com/watch?v=IXYNqVdcgEI)
(http://www.youtube.com/watch?v=oMr9OxcKXno)
(http://www.youtube.com/watch?v=0pW7IQxEqLg)
(Various Video Interviews) – Sources Unknown
30. *Quote Wake Up Church*
(http://www.youtube.com/watch?v=RzyGrcCv-fk)
31. *Quote New & Improved Emotional Church Services*
(http://www.youtube.com/watch?v=vTPowYQ-jVU)
(http://www.youtube.com/watch?v=rEcmoSy5op8)
(http://www.youtube.com/playlist?list=PL37A3882DD1906EDD)
(http://www.youtube.com/watch?v=pxunCIEI-18)
(http://www.youtube.com/watch?v=RKUrUUvpMxE&feature=fvwrel)
(Various Video Interviews) – Sources Unknown
(http://www.bible.ca/tongues-audio-video-documentation.htm)
(http://www.tzemach.org/articles/torbless.htm)
32. *Quote How Hindu Gurus Induce Altered State of Consciousness*
(http://www.youtube.com/watch?v=k7ca7Cm-QEY)
(http://www.youtube.com/watch?v=BcMnKYlk6UU)
33. *Quote How Yoga Induces Altered State of Consciousness*
(http://www.carylmatrisciana.com/site/index.php?option=com_content
&view=article&id=96&Itemid=70)
34. *Quote Churches Promoting So-called Holy Yoga*
(http://holyyoga.net/)
(https://holyyoga.net/media-hy-media/)
35. *Quote Chart of Signs & Wonders Movement Behavior Versus Occult*
(http://www.bible.ca/tongues-kundalini-shakers-charismatics.htm)
36. *Quote Evidence of Kundalini Spirit in the Church*
(http://www.youtube.com/watch?v=eBpw2oQrvMM)
(http://www.youtube.com/watch?v=BCcGaTRwG_4)
(http://www.youtube.com/watch?v=dWeUNoR30_0)
37. *Quote Me Church Services*
(http://www.youtube.com/watch?v=cGEmlPjgjVI)
38. *Quote the So-called New & Improved Services*

(http://www.christianpost.com/news/new-zealand-pastors-create-sports-bar-church-service-complete-with-beer-drinking-79293/)
(http://www.christianpost.com/news/california-church-preaches-gospel-at-the-bar-beer-replaces-coffee-59980/)
(http://wayback.archive.org/web/*/http://www.informationageprayer.com)
(http://content.usatoday.com/communities/Religion/post/2009/11/cash-for-churchgoers-what-incentive-did-jesus-have/1)
(http://news.yahoo.com/pastor-opens-tattoo-parlor-inside-michigan-church-194456243.html)
(http://www.fox10tv.com/dpps/news/strange_news/pastor-opens-tattoo-parlor-inside-michigan-church-ob12-tvw_4033498)
(http://www.theglobeandmail.com/technology/nova-scotia-priest-plans-to-bless-the-faithfuls-cellphones/article1378845/)
(http://life.nationalpost.com/2010/07/26/dog%E2%80%99s-anglican-communion-leaves-tongues-wagging/)

39. *Quote the So-called New & Improved Services*
(http://www.nytimes.com/2008/02/10/us/10manga.html)
Ravi Zacharias, *Deliver Us From Evil*
(Dallas: Word Publishing, 1996, Pgs. 52-53)
(http://www.worldnetdaily.com/news/article.asp?ARTICLE_ID=54518)
(http://www.worldnetdaily.com/news/printer-friendly.asp?ARTICLE_ID = 44563)
(http://web.archive.org/web/20090106183410/http://deathby1000paper cuts.com/2008/12/gay-bible-set-to-publish-aida-and-eve-christian-backlash-needed/)
(http://web.archive.org/web/20090121003341/)
(http://www.guardian.co.uk/world/2008/dec/01/princess-diana-gay-bible)
(http://www.wnd.com/2008/12/82520/)
(http://www.youtube.com/watch?v=XFJVn_82Eak)

40. *Quote the So-called New & Improved Services*
(http://www.aolnews.com/2011/03/25/former-exotic-dancer-crystal-deans-teaches-pole-dancing-for-jesu/)
(http://www.thebereancall.org/content/hundreds-queue-erotic-church-service)
(http://articles.chicagotribune.com/2012-07-07/news/sns-rt-us-usa-religion-transgenderbre8660ix-20120707_1_first-openly-gay-bishop-episcopalians-gene-robinson)
(http://www.wnd.com/2011/07/320969/)

(http://religion.blogs.cnn.com/2012/06/13/unbelieving-preachers-get-help-to-come-out-as-open-atheists/)
(http://books.gather.com/viewArticle.action?articleId=281474977005 360)
(http://www.dailymail.co.uk/news/article-1370694/Church-England-row-cathedral-opens-doors-tarot-card-readers-crystal-healers-new-age-festival.html)
(http://www.telegraph.co.uk/culture/harry-potter/8083870/Harry-Potter-is-Christ-like-claims-theologian.html)
(http://www.wnd.com/2011/10/360365/)
(New Age Church Service Video) – Source Unknown
41. *Quote Run Church Run*
    (http://www.youtube.com/watch?v=6A6lWl_XzKA)
42. *Story of Hockey Rivalry*
    (Email story) – Source Unknown

# Chapter Seven    *One World Religion*

1. *Story of Ten Dollar Airplane Ride*
    (Email story) – Source Unknown
2. *Chronology of One World Religion*
    (http://www.endtimeinfo.net/religion/religiousleader.html)
    (http://bible-prophecy.com/religions.htm)
    (http://www.bible-prophecy.com/religions2008.htm#Current)
    (http://www.bible-prophecy.com/2010/religions2010.htm#Current)
    (http://www.bible-prophecy.com/2012/religions2012.htm#Current)
    (http://www.fastboot.com/one_world_religion.html)
    (http://www.lamblion.com/prophecy/signs/Signs-06.html)
    (http://www.millenniumpeacesummit.org/summit_outcomes.html)
    (http://www.orthodoxinfo.com/ecumenism/video2.htm)
    (http://www.understandthetimes.org/topics/oneworldreligion_archive.shtml)
    (http://www.understandthetimes.org/topics/oneworldreligion.shtml)
    (http://www.worldpeacesummit.net/)
    (http://www.swarthmore.edu/Library/peace/DG051-099/DG078WCRP.html)
    (http://www.religionsforpeace.org/)
3. *Quote Global Warming is a Lie*
    (http://www.youtube.com/watch?v=Eyj4vu2v31k)

4. *Quote What Would Jesus Drive?*
   (Video Transcript of a CNN Report called "What Would Jesus Drive" – Source Unknown)
5. *What Really Causes Wars?*
   (http://www.forcingchange.org/under_war's_bloody_banner)
6. *Various People Promoting One World Religion*
   (https://docs.google.com/viewer?a=v&q=cache:MpsGzaKLPpcJ:www.phmu ltifaithsociety.ca/pdf/Chief_Rabbi.pdf+Chief+rabbi+advocates+a+un+of+reli gion&hl=en&gl=us&pid=bl&srcid=ADGEESjPwjIXHQxh7snB0-r9ZIFbr3JKnH-mC_HUtdw5BlFWFdXNFdFv_SKpP5H7XaQxSBsCs CnvVqBoXzXauhIu9H6dmi8sf5ndGiUcuX8atXASwz-uWMy3rpUyrYM48PPMlR4tPnLH&sig=AHIEtbRfC93TEMzOWci6lG5Sp EZK7gXBfw)
   (http://www.christianpost.com/news/saudi-king-abdullahs-interfaith-center-in-vienna-to-unify-the-worlds-religions-58241/)
   (http://www.wnd.com/2009/08/105938/)
   (http://bible-prophecy.com/religions.htm)
   (http://www.jeremiahproject.com/prophecy/ecumen01.html)
   (http://www.youtube.com/watch?v=Eo3TklNaFrc)
   (http://www.youtube.com/watch?v=EZ9To30Hz7A)
   (http://www.youtube.com/watch?v=t_8GoF9Slas)
   (http://www.youtube.com/watch?v=IY7Rp94Z5xE)
7. *Definition of Ecumenicalism*
   (http://www.jeremiahproject.com/prophecy/ecumen01.html)
8. *Quote United Religions Initiative Promo*
   (http://www.youtube.com/watch?v=guUKh7GuTVg)
9. *Quote New Definition of Tolerance*
   (Josh McDowell, *The Tangled Web of Christian Tolerance*, Video (Coeur d' Alene: Compass International, 1998)
10. *What Schools Are Teaching Our Kids*
    (http://www.youtube.com/watch?v=ifnJEFRvYus)
11. *Quote Schools Have Become Pagan Indoctrination Centers*
    (http://www.newswithviews.com/Turtel/joel46.htm)
12. *Quote Humanist's Agenda for Schools*
    (http://www.lunarpages.com/stargazers/endworld/signs/occult.htm)
13. *Quote One Click Away from Hell*
    (http://www.youtube.com/watch?v=IaruFiU8uqg)
14. *Quote Michael Jackson Funeral*
    (http://www.youtube.com/watch?v=MVgjMwOPJYc)

15. *9-11 Memorial Services*
    (http://www.cephasministry.com/ecumenism_and_the_soul_of_america.
    Html)
16. *Quote Salad Bar Religion*
    (http://www.gospelcom.net/apologeticsindex/c43.html)
17. *Christians Blending with Other Religions*
    (http://www.wnd.com/2007/08/43066/)
    (http://walkingwithintegrity.blogspot.com/2007/04/christians-celebrate-
    religious.html)
    (http://www.wnd.com/2011/06/314661/)
    (http://www.christianpost.com/news/many-born-again-christians-hold-
    universalist-view-barna-finds-49883/)
    (http://ww2.onenewsnow.com/church/2011/02/23/christian-churches-
    welcoming-muslim-worship)
    (http://global.christianpost.com/news/christians-muslims-buddhists-gather-
    to-remove-fear-stereotypes-47625/)
    (http://www.sacbee.com/2010/09/11/v-print/3022701/doves-roses-mark-
    blessing-of-quran.html)
    (http://www.mlive.com/news/muskegon/index.ssf/2010/06/spring_lakes_chri
    st_community.html)
    (http://www.wnd.com/2010/06/170585/)
    (http://www.youtube.com/watch?v=viTgXt1ZlCI)
    (http://www.youtube.com/watch?v=KcIrdZKbA00)
18. *Feminism Promoting Female Deity*
    (http://www.thebereancall.org/content/goddess-and-liberal-church)
    (http://wwwcalcatholic.com.newsArticlePrintable.aspx?id=ecf48aa8-
    8c1b-479f-9f08-c14a1a185fdd)
    (http://www.ltwinternational.org/fact_sheet.htm)
    (http://www.crossroad.to/articles2/08/shack.htm)
19. *European Union Symbols*
    (http://warsrumourswars.blogspot.com/2011/04/europe-rides-beast-official-
    eu-symbols.html)
    (http://www.jesus-is-savior.com/End%20of%20the%20World/seat_666
    .htm)
    (http://static.urbantimes.co/wp-content/uploads/2012/05/euro-coin-a-woman-
    rides-the-beast.jpg)
    (http://www.proxywhore.com/invboard/index.php?showtopic=188258)
    (http://pomoland-en.blogspot.com/2012/10/eussr-symbol-of-moral-
    deafness.html)

20. *People Worshipping a Political Figure as god*
   (http://www.wnd.com/2009/06/101217/)
   (http://www.wnd.com/2009/01/87040/)
   (http://www.wnd.com/2009/04/96417/)
   (http://www.wnd.com/2009/09/111399/)
   (http://www.wnd.com/2009/01/86695/)
   (http://christiannews.net/2013/01/21/newsweek-hails-obama-as-messianic-second-coming/)
   (http://www.examiner.com/article/newsweek-cover-depicts-president-obama-as-god-of-all-things)
   (http://www.youtube.com/watch?v=G2Tcy-9XnrM)
   (http://www.youtube.com/watch?v=J1sqx5uZBq8)
21. *People Calling for Global Religious Authority*
   (https://docs.google.com/viewer?a=v&q=cache:MpsGzaKLPpcJ:www.phmu ltifaithsociety.ca/pdf/Chief_Rabbi.pdf+Chief+rabbi+advocates+a+un+of+reli gion&hl=en&gl=us&pid=bl&srcid=ADGEESjPwjIXHQxh7snB0-r9ZIFbr3JKnH-mC_HUtdw5BlFWFdXNFdFv_SKpP5H7XaQxSBsCs CnvVqBoXzXauhIu9H6dmi8sf5ndGiUcuX8atXASwz-uWMy3rpUyrYM48PPMlR4tPnLH&sig=AHIEtbRfC93TEMzOWci6lG5Sp EZK7gXBfw)
   (http://www.christianpost.com/news/saudi-king-abdullahs-interfaith-center-in-vienna-to-unify-the-worlds-religions-58241/)
   (http://www.youtube.com/watch?v=GmdoGoCvsW0)
   (http://aclj.org/united-nations/update-u-n-defamation-of-religions)
   (http://www.youtube.com/watch?v=Z_vM1NiWLpI)
22. *Quote What Hell is Like*
   (Joe Schimmel, *They Sold Their Souls for Rock-n-Roll*,
   (Simi Valley: Fight the Good Fight Ministries, 2001, Video)
23. *Mock Christian Interrogation*
   (Video) – Source Unknown
24. *Accusation of Christians Being Intolerant*
   (http://www.jeremiahproject.com/prophecy/warxian.html)
25. *Anti-Christian Propaganda Quotes*
   (http://countdown.org/end/apostasy_03.htm)
   (http://www.jeremiahproject.com/prophecy/warxian.html)
   (http://www.cuttingedge.org/NEWS/n1861.cfm)
26. *Quote Janet Reno*
   (http://kenraggio.com/KRPN-UnitedReligions.htm)
27. *Christians Being Called New Terrorists*

(http://www.wposfm.com/HTML%20files/Darwin%20Sunday.htm)
(http://www.youtube.com/watch?v=1av8aFnc9t4)
(http://www.theadvertiser.news.com.au/common/story_page/0,5936,1714209
7%255E911,00.html)
(http://www.google.com/hostednews/afp/article/ALeqM5iTlqdnMHtY3e-
py5a-QUJFFstAGg?docId=CNG.1190a3922bd18461a04843016770
69d5.371)
(http://lubbockonline.com/stories/051907/rel_051907087.shtml)
(http://endoftheamericandream.com/archives/14-conspiracy-theories-that-
the-media-now-admits-are-conspiracy-facts)
(http://www.wnd.com/2011/05/298017/)
(http://www.onenewsnow.com/Politics/Default.aspx?id=1628344)
(http://www.prisonplanet.com/law-would-encourage-americans-to-report-on-
each-other.html)
(http://www.paulmcguire.org/articles/articles_the_coming_persecution_of_c
hristians_1.html)
(Various Videos) – Sources Unknown
28. *Christian Persecution Statistics*
(http://www.666beast.com/countdown.htm)
(http://www.jeremiahproject.com/prophecy/warxian.html)
(http://www.lunarpages.com/stargazers/endworld/signs/persecution.htm)
29. *Quotes on Christian Persecution*
(http://www.sconews.co.uk/latest-edition/7407/christian-persecution-is-
rising/)
(http://www.timesofisrael.com/merkel-calls-christianity-worlds-most-
persecuted-religion/)
(http://blogs.telegraph.co.uk/news/cristinaodone/100078209/christianity-
isn%E2%80%99t-dying-it%E2%80%99s-being-eradicated/)
(http://www.patheos.com/Jewish/Christians-New-Jews-Yitzchok-Adlerstein-
02-21-2013.html)
(http://www.freerepublic.com/focus/f-news/2926611/posts)
(http://www.charismanews.com/culture/32479-will-true-christians-churches-
be-forced-underground-in-america)
(http://www.onenewsnow.com/2007/12/ministry_founder_us_christians.php)
(http://www.christianpost.com/news/michael-youssef-christians-more-
persecuted-today-than-at-any-time-70222/)
30. *Examples of Modern Christian Martyrdom*
(http://www.youtube.com/watch?v=BI8-LhnnpQQ)
31. *Quote Who Jesus Is*

(http://www.sitski.com/wgod.htm)
32. *Removing Monotheism Photo & Concept*
    (By Billy Crone)
33. *Quote CNN God's Warriors*
    (http://amanpour.blogs.cnn.com/2012/08/24/gods-warriors/)
34. *Quote Jesus Camp*
    (http://www.youtube.com/watch?v=6RNfL6IVWCE)
35. *Evidence of Global Beheadings*
    (http://www.thefullwiki.org/Decapitation)
    (http://christianpersecution.wordpress.com/2007/10/27/the-sole-survivor-of-a-radical-muslim-attack-on-four-christian-high-school-girls-in-indonesia/)
    (http://www.wnd.com/2006/09/38008/)
    (http://www.worthynews.com/6391-somalia-islamic-militants-behead-four-christian-orphanage-workers)
    (http://www.bosnewslife.com/8123-somalia-militants-behead-christian-fathers-sons)
    (http://forum.prisonplanet.com/index.php?topic=232886.0)
    (http://www.worthynews.com/11576-laos-detains-thai-lao-christians-for-bible-study)
    (http://www.wnd.com/2012/07/70000-christians-locked-in-concentration-camps/)
    (http://www.christianpost.com/news/young-woman-killed-in-eritrea-for-refusing-to-renounce-jesus-christ-29233/)
    (http://www.worthynews.com/1415-death-of-pastor-in-india-remains-unsolved)
    (http://www.worthynews.com/1409-vietnam-christian-dies-after-torture-for-refusing-to-recant-faith-reports)
    (http://www.persecution.org/2007/07/10/pentecostal-pastors-shot-dead-in-colombia/)
    (http://www.wnd.com/2007/07/42623/)
    (http://www.zenit.org/en/articles/pakistani-christians-die-in-violent-attack)
    (http://www.worthynews.com/6241-news-alert-militants-kill-11-christians-in-iraq-somalia)
    (http://www.wnd.com/2008/11/81564/)
    (http://www.persecution.org/2007/04/25/turkish-believers-satanically-tortured-for-hours-before-being-killed/)
    (http://www.persecution.org/?p=7883&upm_export=print)
    (http://midnightwatcher.wordpress.com/2012/05/17/kenya-two-christian-pastors-burned-to-death-after-visiting-muslim-family/)

(http://www.worthynews.com/10648-vietnam-massacre-hmong-christians-pastors-beheaded)
(http://www.worthynews.com/10412-taliban-execute-man-for-leaving-islam-for-jesus-christ)
36. *Quote Will You Die for Jesus?*
(http://www.youtube.com/watch?v=QdY1Uxut5NE)
37. *Quote Hate Crime Law in America*
(CBN News Video Report – Source Unknown)
38. *Statistics on Homosexual Movement*
(http://www.bpnews.net/bpnews.asp?id=39514)
(http://www.christianpost.com/news/church-touts-homosexuality-as-a-gift-not-a-sin-50010/)
(https://www.thebereancall.org/content/descending-societys-level)
(http://www.thebereancall.org/content/no-hell-bell-comes-out-support-homosexuality)
(http://www.christianpost.com/news/uk-churches-fear-being-forced-to-perform-same-sex-ceremonies-81749/)
(http://www.dailymail.co.uk/news/article-2052619/Christian-faces-losing-home-opposing-gay-weddings-churches.html)
(http://www.catholicnewsagency.com/news/british-court-says-christian-couple-cant-adopt-due-to-beliefs/)
(http://www.wnd.com/2010/12/242021/)
(http://www.citizenlink.com/2013/04/11/bill-rescinds-tax-breaks-for-groups-with-christian-views-on-sexuality/)
(http://www.theblaze.com/stories/2013/04/10/army-email-allegedly-labels-christian-organizations-that-oppose-gay-marriage-as-domestic-hate-groups/)
39. *Quote What Homosexuality is Leading To*
(http://www.wnd.com/2011/07/320969/
(http://www.rethinksociety.com/government/pedophilia-is-a-sexual-orientation-under-ca-bill/)
40. *Quote Homosexual Manifesto*
(http://www.youtube.com/watch?v=65RGfRlSoH8)
41. *Evidence of Christian Persecution in America*
(http://countdown.org/end/apostasy_03.htm)
(http://countdown.org/end/apostasy_05.htm)
(http://www.jeremiahproject.com/prophecy/warxian.html)
(http://www.lunarpages.com/stargazers/endworld/signs/fallaway.htm)
(http://www.wnd.com/2012/07/fined-60-days-in-jail-over-arizona-bible-studies/)

(http://www.christianadc.org/news-and-articles/440-top-10-anti-christian-acts-of-2009)

(http://powerpointparadise.com/endworld/signs/fallaway.htm)

(http://conservativechristianvoice.blogspot.com/2012/01/why-is-this-ok-and-this-isnt.html)

(http://www.worthynews.com/7531-news-alert-street-preachers-killed-in-united-states)

(http://endoftheamericandream.com/archives/texas-public-school-curriculum-teaches-students-to-design-a-socialist-flag-and-that-christianity-is-a-cult)

(http://www.foxnews.com/us/2010/07/23/legal-challenges-prayer-rise-1410541964/)

(http://www.wnd.com/2010/07/182441/)

(http://exposingliberallies.blogspot.com/2010/07/chaplain-fired-for-speaking-name-of.html)

(http://www.afa.net/Blogs/BlogPost.aspx?id=2147494186)

(http://www.foxnews.com/us/2010/07/09/pastor-yanked-capitol-jesus-prayer/)

(http://www.wnd.com/2012/06/refuse-to-photograph-lesbians-get-fined-7000/)

(http://radio.foxnews.com/toddstarnes/top-stories/group-calls-military-bibles-threat-to-national-security.html)

(http://radio.foxnews.com/toddstarnes/top-stories/court-jesus-prayers-can-be-banned.html)

(http://radio.foxnews.com/toddstarnes/top-stories/vanderbilt-tells-group-leaders-can%E2%80%99t-be-followers-of-christ.html)

(http://www.thedailybeast.com/newsweek/2007/11/07/so-long-gideons.html)

(http://www.foxnews.com/us/2012/11/01/texas-woman-forced-to-cover-up-vote-bible-t-shirt-at-polls/)

(http://radio.foxnews.com/toddstarnes/top-stories/school-orders-child-to-remove-god-from-poem.html)

(http://radio.foxnews.com/toddstarnes/top-stories/teacher-faces-suspension-for-sharing-bible-verse.html)

(http://radio.foxnews.com/toddstarnes/top-stories/professor-makes-students-stomp-on-jesus.html)

(http://www.wnd.com/2011/09/340353/)

42. *Quote Odds of Revolutionary War*
    (http://www.wnd.com/2013/04/can-liberty-win-do-the-math/

43. *Quote President of Uganda Repents*

(http://www.wnd.com/2012/11/ugandan-president-repents-of-personal-national-sins/)

44. *Quote Machine Gun Story*
    (Email story) – Source Unknown
45. *Quote Story of Alexander Ogorodnikov*
    (http://www.youtube.com/watch?v=H4IpnQOJzP0)
46. *Story of Driver's Day Going from Bad to Worse*
    (Email story) – Source Unknown

# Chapter Eight *One World Government*

1. *Story of Not Getting Worms*
   (Email story) – Source Unknown
2. *Chronological Timeline of a One World Government*
   (http://www.bible-prophecy.com/2010/nwo2010.htm#Current)
   (http://www.bible-prophecy.com/2009/nwo2009.htm#Current)
   (http://www.bible-prophecy.com/nwo2.htm#Current)
   (http://www.bible-prophecy.com/nwo.htm#Current)
   (http://www.khouse.org/articles/political/19970301-90.html)
   (http://en.wikipedia.org/wiki/New_World_Order_(conspiracy)#New_World_Order_timeline)
   (http://www.threeworldwars.com/nwo-timeline2.htm)
   (http://www.understandthetimes.org/topics/oneworldgov_archive.shtml)
   (http://www.understandthetimes.org/topics/oneworldgov.shtml)
   (http://news.yahoo.com/pope-urges-religions-those-no-church-ally-justice-154731915.html)
   (http://www.onenewspage.us/video/20130409/1219626/UN-chief-hails-pope-as-global-spiritual.htm)
   (http://www.youtube.com/watch?v=SISUIhprOa8)
   (http://www.youtube.com/watch?v=lCRdKiYGbWo)
3. *Evidence of Anti-God and Anti-Christian Administration*
   (http://www.wnd.com/2008/10/77629/)
   (http://www.sba-list.org/obamarecord)
   (http://www.wallbuilders.com/LIBissuesArticles.asp?id=106938)
   (http://www.youtube.com/watch?v=1RWHdQBMgb4)
   (http://www.youtube.com/watch?v=bjFvvoFcD3o)
   (http://www.youtube.com/watch?v=ujwH6BXfP8E)
   (http://www.youtube.com/watch?v=CQ-ovHVG4TU)

4. *New World Order Quotes*
   (http://www.lunarpages.com/stargazers/endworld/fin-
   signs/news/globalnews.htm)
   (http://bible-prophecy.com/nwo2.htm)
   (http://babylonmysteryreligion.com/unitednationsagenda.htm)
   (http://www.arewelivinginthelastdays.com/com/quotes.html)
   (http://www.youtube.com/watch?v=Rc7i0wCFf8g)
   (http://www.youtube.com/watch?v=Ptcp07v_w-w)
   (http://www.youtube.com/watch?v=Q8uzxEHFDkw)
   (http://www.youtube.com/watch?v=ksy2yrUNd9Q)
   (http://www.youtube.com/watch?v=8BtuSioq-pU)
5. *Quote Aaron Russo Microchip*
   (http://www.youtube.com/watch?v=YGAaPjqdbgQ)
6. *Quote Franklin Graham*
   (http://www.wnd.com/2013/01/franklin-graham-warns-wicked-america/)
7. *Quote of Everything is a Crisis*
   (http://www.jeremiahproject.com/prophecy/nworder.html)
8. *Information on the Earth Charter*
   (http://www.earthcharter.org)
   (http://www.contenderministries.org/articles/arkofhope.php)
   (http://www.green-agenda.com/earthcharter.html)
   (http://www.arkofhope.org/)
   (http://www.crossroad.to/articles2/2002/ark.html)
   (http://www.youtube.com/watch?v=3pFIpdEAJIk)
9. *Information on the Constitution for the Federation Earth*
   (http://www.wcpagren.org/cnfdeart.dir/contents.html)
10. *Information on the World Criminal Court*
    (http://www.portal.telegraph.co.uk/news/main.jhtml?xml=/news/2002/06/26/
    wicc26.xml&sSheet=/news/2002/06/26/ixworld.html&secureRefresh=true&
    _requestid=97738)
    (http://www.newsmax.com/archives/articles/2002/5/6/154932.shtml)
    (http://www.youtube.com/watch?v=zfo7lMnR4O8)
11. *Quote Tony Blair*
    (http://www.freedaily.com/articles/990424n1.html)
12. *Information on the Word Heritage Protection Program*
    (http://whc.unesco.org/nwhc/pages/home/pages/homepage.htm)
    (http://www.crossroad.to/text/articles/whpwans97.html)
13. *Information on the World Food Summit*
    (http://www.fao.org/wfs/index_en.htm)

(http://www.radioliberty.com/kjos3.htm)
14. *Information on Agenda 21*
    (http://www.un.org/esa/sustdev/agenda21text.htm)
    (http://wwwcrossroad.to/text/articles/la21_198.html)
    (http://americanpolicy.org/2013/04/15/connecting-the-dots-from-
    the-united-nations-to-your-state-government/)
    (http://www.teaparty911.com/issues/what_is_agenda_21.htm)
    (http://www.youtube.com/watch?v=rwQNvjQSOsE)
    (http://www.youtube.com/watch?v=SkGVYt-1Zhk)
15. *Information on the Biodiversity Treaty*
    (http://www.epi.freedom.org/mapmabwh.htm)
    (http://www.epi.freedom.org/mapwild.htm)
16. *Information on Ten Global Kingdoms*
    (http://www2.ministries-online.org/biometrics/rome.html)
    (http://ec.europa.eu/world/where/index_en.htm)
    (http://en.unpacampaign.org/news/354.php)
17. *Mexico Using RFID Implants to Cross It's Border*
    (CNN News Video Report Kitty Pilgrim/Lou Dobbs Report – Source
    Unknown)
18. *Congress Talking About Ruling on Implants to Track Every Move*
    (http://www.youtube.com/watch?v=wKMDeTcShXQ)
19. *Fears Over Our Food Supply*
    (http://www.washingtontimes.com/news/2009/mar/15/obama-forms-group-
    to-protect-us-food-supply/)
    (http://www.wnd.com/2009/03/92002/)
    (http://www.crossroad.to/articles2/08/swat-team.htm)
20. *Fears Over Our Obesity*
    (http://usatoday30.usatoday.com/news/health/story/2012-05-07/obesity-
    projections-adults/54791430/1)
    (http://www.newswithviews.com/DeWeese/tom172.htm)
    http://www.telegraph.co.uk/health/3793719/New-York-planning-fat-tax-on-
    drinks.html)
    (http://usatoday30.usatoday.com/news/health/2006-12-04-trans-fat-
    ban_x.htm)
    (http://articles.mercola.com/sites/articles/archive/2007/11/03/you-might-lose-
    your-job-if-you-smoke-or-eat-junk-food.aspx)
    (http://cnsnews.com/news/article/federal-fat-police-bill-would-require-
    government-track-body-mass-american-children)

(http://www.dailymail.co.uk/news/article-1291470/Big-Brother-row-food-police-secretly-photograph-schoolchildrens-packed-lunches.html)
(http://www.naturalnews.com/040214_seeds_European_Commission_registration.html)
(http://cnsnews.com/news/article/obesity-rating-every-american-must-be-included-stimulus-mandated-electronic-health)
(NBC Video News Report – Source Unknown)

21. *Fears Over Our Water Supply*
(http://www.infowars.com/collecting-rainwater-now-illegal-in-many-states-as-big-government-claims-ownership-over-our-water/)
(http://www.youtube.com/watch?v=6jjxg8f3Gq0)
(http://www.newswithviews.com/Devvy/kidd102.htm)
(http://usatoday30.usatoday.com/news/nation/2008-03-10-drugs-tap-water_N.htm)
(http://www.youtube.com/watch?v=ej9YzFkbIjk)
(http://www.newswithviews.com/NWV-News/news220.htm)
(http://www.blueplanetproject.net/)

22. *Fears Over Our Health Supply*
(http://www.newswithviews.com/Lane/lauren104.htm)
(http://www.wnd.com/2009/07/104719/)
(http://visiontoamerica.com/5583/next-item-on-obama-agenda-live-patients-as-organ-donors/)
(http://www.newswithviews.com/McGuire/paul136.htm)
http://www.gpo.gov/fdsys/pkg/USCODE-2010-title21/pdf/USCODE-2010-title21-chap9-subchapV-partA-sec360i.pdf)
(http://www.lodinews.com/opinion/letters/article_ce3d223d-8b86-5aee-8993-968e835d2a6e.html)
(http://www.thenewamerican.com/usnews/politics/item/2881-global-obamacare-and-world-population-control)
(http://www.youtube.com/watch?v=pBGphLzwo6w)
(ABC Channel 7 News Report – Source Unknown)

23. *Evidence of Controlling the Information System*
(http://countdown.org/end/big_brother_13.htm)
(http://countdown.org/end/big_brother_12.htm)
(http://countdown.org/end/big_brother_13.htm)
(http://countdown.org/end/big_brother_09.htm)
(http://www.khouse.org/articles/political/20010801-360.html)
(http://countdown.org/end/big_brother_02.htm)
(http://www.mvcf.com/news/cache/00065/)

(http://countdown.org/end/big_brother_06.htm)
(http://theweek.com/article/index/229508/acxiom-corp-the-faceless-organization-that-knows-everything-about-you)
(http://www.dailyfinance.com/2010/09/24/who-is-watching-you-nine-industries-that-know-your-every-move/)
(http://www.godlikeproductions.com/forum1/message635711/pg1)
(http://www.youtube.com/watch?v=KU80hFAxwd4)
(http://www.youtube.com/watch?v=DIGdWsxHJlM)

24. *Evidence of Controlling the Communication System*
(http://countdown.org/end/big_brother_08.htm)
(http://www.khouse.org/articles/currentevents/20000401-213.html)
(http://www.mvcf.com/news/cache/00065/)
(http://www.youtube.com/watch?v=0G1fNjK9SXg)
(News on 6 News Report – Source Unknown)
(History Channel Big Brother Program – Source Unknown)

25. *What Life Will Be Like in 2017*
(http://www.youtube.com/watch?v=IqzmETqwLuA)

26. *Tracking & Mood Map of the U.S.*
(http://live.wsj.com/video/a-god-eye-view-of-the-world/9403A74F-92AD-434F-8E69-2384F101992A.html#!9403A74F-92AD-434F-8E69-2384F101992A)

27. *Satellite Tracking Technology*
(http://www.crossroad.to/text/articles/nis1196.html)
(http://countdown.org/end/big_brother_12.htm)
(http://countdown.org/end/big_brother_13.htm)
(http://countdown.org/end/big_brother_09.htm)
(http://www.khouse.org/articles/political/20010801-360.html)
(http://countdown.org/end/big_brother_02.htm)
(http://www.mvcf.com/news/cache/00065/)
(http://countdown.org/end/big_brother_06.htm)

28. *Onstar Tracking Technology*
(http://www.youtube.com/watch?v=GKWvosvq2B8)
(http://www.infowars.com/your-car-set-to-become-part-of-the-internet-of-things/)
(http://cbs13.com/local/video.cameras.cars.2.1849626.html)
(http://redtape.nbcnews.com/_news/2011/10/14/8308841-govt-cameras-in-your-car-e-toll-patent-hints-at-big-brotherish-future?lite)
(http://www.infowars.com/dhs-funds-real-time-spy-cams-on-sf-buses/)
(http://www.telegraph.co.uk/news/newstopics/howaboutthat/7608153/)

New-speed-cameras-trap-motorists-from-space.html)
(http://www.wired.com/threatlevel/2012/12/public-bus-audio-surveillance/)
(http://www.dailytech.com/IBM+Patent+Application+Describes+Intelligent+Stop+Lights+That+Turn+Off+Cars/article18514.htm)
(Various Videos – Sources Unknown)

29. *Camera Tracking Technology*
(http://www.crossroad.to/text/articles/nis1196.html)
(http://countdown.org/end/big_brother_12.htm)
(http://countdown.org/end/big_brother_13.htm)
(http://countdown.org/end/big_brother_09.htm)
(http://www.khouse.org/articles/political/20010801-360.html)
(http://countdown.org/end/big_brother_02.htm)
(http://www.mvcf.com/news/cache/00065/)
(http://countdown.org/end/big_brother_06.htm)
(http://www.usatoday.com/life/cyber/tech/cti856.htm)
(http://www.usatoday.com/life/cyber/tech/cti856.htm)
(http://www.thetruthseeker.co.uk/article.asp?ID=1421)
(http://countdown.org/end/big_brother_05.htm)
(http://countdown.org/end/big_brother_12.htm)
(http://www.islandpacket.com/2010/03/15/1173660/us-forest-service-admits-putting.html)
(http://www.infowars.com/federally-funded-street-lights-capable-of-recording-conversations/)
(http://www.computerworld.com/s/article/79572/Smart_Dust)
(http://www.youtube.com/watch?v=GvdGggusRYU)
(Various Videos – Sources Unknown)

30. *Ordering Pizza Under Big Brother*
(http://www.youtube.com/watch?v=o6UFX5j915w)

31. *Maxine Water Admits Secret Database*
(http://www.liveleak.com/view?i=b68_1360281969)

32. *Big Brother Peering Through Walls*
(http://www.crossroad.to/text/articles/nis1196.html)
(http://countdown.org/end/big_brother_13.htm)
(http://countdown.org/end/big_brother_12.htm)
(http://countdown.org/end/big_brother_13.htm)
(http://countdown.org/end/big_brother_09.htm)
(http://www.khouse.org/articles/political/20010801-360.html)
(http://countdown.org/end/big_brother_02.htm)

(http://www.mvcf.com/news/cache/00065/)
(http://countdown.org/end/big_brother_06.htm)
33. *Ratters Control Your Computer*
(http://www.youtube.com/watch?v=jwo5xIZtrg0)
34. *ACTA Controls Your Computer*
(http://www.youtube.com/watch?v=rrRuuSlCCOc)
35. *Cash for Clunkers Control Your Computer*
(=http://www.youtube.com/watch?v=KZxaWDqUmho)
36. *Your TV is Watching You*
(http://www.youtube.com/watch?v=souFJ_v6AZA)
37. *Dictators Who Advocated Gun Control*
(http://www.alipac.us/f19/bradlee-dean-gun-control-dictator-style-268189/)
(http://patdollard.com/wp-content/uploads/2013/01/Gun-control-experts1-600x350.jpeg)
38. *Doctors are More Dangerous than Guns*
(http://www.rense.com/general62/gns.htm)
(http://www.youtube.com/watch?v=x1Vu6fWro68)
39. *Smart Guns*
(http://www.youtube.com/watch?v=wtRP8h6FENE)
40. *Drones Being Used on Americans*
(http://www.youtube.com/watch?v=HYETraMg_mM)
41. *U.S. Census Took GPS Positions on American Homes*
(http://www.wnd.com/2009/05/97208/)
42. *MAV Drones*
(http://www.youtube.com/watch?v=vVDh-spS50A)
43. *Information on the City of Petra*
(http://www.swrc.com)
(http://www.radioliberty.com)
44. *Quote from Martin Niemoller*
(http://www.radioliberty.com/pca.htm)
45. *Story of Clown in Pain*
(Email story) – Source Unknown

# Chapter Nine   *One World Economy*

1. *Story of Funeral Procession Get in Line*
(Email story) – Source Unknown
2. *Timeline of the One World Economy*

(http://www.bible-prophecy.com/2013/economic2013.htm#Current)
(http://www.bible-prophecy.com/2012/economic2012.htm#Current)
(http://www.bible-prophecy.com/2011/economic2011.htm#Current)
(http://www.bible-prophecy.com/2010/economic2010.htm#Current)
(http://www.bible-prophecy.com/2009/economic2009.htm#Current)
(http://www.bible-prophecy.com/economic2008.htm#Current)
(http://bible-prophecy.com/smart2.htm)
(http://www.khouse.org/articles/political/19970301-90.html)
(http://www.globalcommunity.org)
(http://www.globalexchange.org)
(http://www.mvcf.com/news/cache/00356/)
(http://www.understandthetimes.org/topics/oneworldgov_archive.shtml)
(http://www.understandthetimes.org/topics/oneworldgov.shtml)
(http://www.understandthetimes.org/topics/techmoney.shtml)
(http://www.youtube.com/watch?v=5GmMyfcUQ3E)
(http://www.youtube.com/watch?v=OJI01b8ir_4)
(http://www.youtube.com/watch?v=22Ydqd_DEYc)

3. *Quote British Guys on Bailouts*
(http://www.youtube.com/watch?v=I5QwKEwo4Bc)

4. *Proof of a Universal Banking Institution Already in Place*
(http://www.worldbank.org)
(http://www.imf.org)
(http://www.swift.com)
(http://www.wto.org)
(http://www.mvcf.com/news/cache/00438/)
(http://www.euro.gov.uk/home.asp?f=1)
(http://www.mvcf.com/news/cache/00035/)
(http://www.mvcf.com/news/cache/00185/)

5. *World Leaders Calling for a One World Economy & Currency*
(http://mobile.reuters.com/article/businessNews/idUSTRE4A900K20081110
?src=RSS-BUS)
(http://news.bbc.co.uk/2/hi/business/7678577.stm)
(http://infowars.net/articles/october2008/161008New.htm)
(http://abcnews.go.com/International/story?id=7156932&page=1)
(http://www.telegraph.co.uk/finance/currency/6152204/UN-wants-new-
global-currency-to-replace-dollar.html)
(http://goingglobaleastmeetswest.blogspot.com/2012/03/april-2011-russia-
calls-for-new-global.html)
(http://news.xinhuanet.com/english/2009-04/01/content_11109506.htm)

(http://www.wnd.com/2010/10/213953/)
(http://www.prlog.org/10141522-single-global-currency-assn-urges-g20-to-initiate-research-and-planning-for-single-global-currency.html)

6. *Calls for a Global Tax*
(http://www.youtube.com/watch?v=7za1y-BNzwU)
(http://americanpolicy.org/2002/03/13/global-taxation-moves-closer/)

7. *Baja Beach Club Implants for Payment Purposes*
(http://www.youtube.com/watch?v=wgmraKtx7XI)

8. *Information on the Economic Unions*
(http://www.euro.gov.uk/home.asp?f=1)
(http://www.his2ndcoming.org/joomla/?option=com_content&view
=article&id=70&Itemid=79)
(http://themustardseed.home.mindspring.com/n16-11.htm)

9. *The Creation of a Revived Roman Empire*
(http://www.youtube.com/watch?v=EtdCtoA5J9E)

10. *Quote Super European President & Willingness to Follow an Antichrist*
(http://news.prophecytoday.com/2012_04_27_archive.html)
(http://www.arewelivinginthelastdays.com/article/owg/owg.htm)

11. *Is America Found in Bible Prophecy?*
(http://www.lamblion.us/2013/05/current-prophetic-events-united-states.html
(http://www.Raptureready.com/featured/gillette/bg53.html

12. *Proof of the Amero*
(http://www.youtube.com/watch?v=QYXx1ZL28UE)

13. *Proof of NAFTA Superhighway*
(http://www.youtube.com/watch?v=ildAhfMzEL4)

14. *Proof that Bush Wants a North American Union*
(http://www.youtube.com/watch?v=z3E4s4JTzsY)
(http://www.youtube.com/watch?v=oyINJcU1ToA)

15. *Proof that Mexico Wants a North American Union*
(http://www.youtube.com/watch?v=hsYz6xwFVTQ)

16. *Proof that Canada Wants a North American Union*
(http://www.youtube.com/watch?v=xDdlY3vqmzg)

17. *Proof that Obama Wants a North American Union*
(http://www.youtube.com/watch?v=JgGEv-cdoms)

18. *Various Uses for Smart Cards*
(http://bible-prophecy.com/smart2.htm)

19. *Who Will They Tax Next?*
(http://www.youtube.com/watch?v=kofaprF1Cpk)

20. *Various Implements of Smart Cards*

(http://bible-prophecy.com/smart2.htm)
(http://www.egov.vic.gov.au/index.php?env=-categories:m1397-1-1-8-s-0&reset=1)

21. *Quote on Decreased Crime from the Usage of Smart Cards*
(http://www.sfasu.edu/finance/FINCASH.HTM)
22. *Quote on Radio Frequency Burgers*
(http://www.endtimeinfo.net/cashless/cellphone.html)
23. *Cell Phones Being Used as a Form of Payment*
(http://bible-prophecy.com/smart2.htm)
24. *Sweden & Other Countries Going Cashless*
(http://www.youtube.com/watch?v=fQ6bK3OTA1o)
(http://www.perthnow.com.au/news/cash-may-be-victim-of-war-on-deflation/story-e6frg12c-1225737543536)
(http://www.news.com.au/news/cash-to-become-extinct-as-chips-take-off/story-fna7dq6e-1225734965479)
(http://www.globalresearch.ca/the-cashless-society-arrives-in-africa-the-multipurpose-biometric-national-identity-smart-card/5335292)
25. *Proof that Smart Cards are Not Secure*
(Internet Video – Source Unknown)
26. *MythBusters Bust RFID's Security Flaws*
(http://www.youtube.com/watch?v=X034R3yzDhw)
27. *IBM Propaganda for Cashless Shopping*
(http://www.youtube.com/watch?v=HehiILaFiOQ)
28. *Quotes of Cashless Payment Ideas from MasterCard & Visa*
(http://bible-prophecy.com/smart2.htm)
(http://www.geocities.com/Heartland/Pointe/4171/profeticword.html)
(http://www.mondexusa.com)
29. *Example of People Wanting an RFID Implant*
(Internet Video – Source Unknown)
30. *What is RFID?*
(http://archive.epcglobalinc.org/aboutthecenter_video1.asp)
(http://www.future-store.org/servlet/PB/-s/c5e2bv4km1mq1fo22l7edyn5y1rgzs4m/menu/1002197_l2/index.html)
(http://www.accenture.com/Global/Services/By_Subject/Radio_Frequency_Identification/R_and_I/TechnologySolutions.htm)
(http://archive.epcglobalinc.org/aboutthecenter_video1.asp)
(http://www.spychips.com/what-is-rfid.html)
(http://www.boycotttesco.com/about.html)
(http://www.spychips.com/faqs.html)

Katherine Albrecht, *Spychips*,
(Nashville: Thomas Nelson Inc., 2005, Pgs. 13,14,15,16,18)
(http://www.aimglobal.org/technologies/rfid/resources/shrouds_of_
time.pdf)
(http://en.wikipedia.org/wiki/RFID)
(http://www.rfidjournal.com/article/articleprint/1338/-1/129/)
(http://www.ti.com/tiris/docs/manuals/whtPapers/manuf_dist.pdf)
(http://www.zebra.com/id/zebra/na/en/index/rfid/faqs/rfid_basics.html)
(http://www.informit.com/articles/article.asp?p=413662&rl=1)
(http://www.citizen.com/apps/pbcs.dll/article?AID=/20051211/NEWS
01/112110062/-1/CITIZEN)
(http://www.news-leader.com/apps/pbcs.dll/article?AID=/20050828/
BUSINESS/508280361/1092)

31. *Proof RFID Tags are Not Turned Off*
(http://www.katherinealbrecht.com/index.php?Itemid=122&id=
99&option=com_content&view=article)

32. *Proof RFID Companies are Not Trustworthy*
(http://www.rsasecurity.com/rsalabs/node.asp?id=2117)
(http://en.wikipedia.org/wiki/RFID#Controversy)
Katherine Albrecht, *Spychips*,
(Nashville: Thomas Nelson Inc., 2005, Pgs. 43-46, 154-155)
(http://www.theregister.co.uk/2003/11/13/walmart_turns_customers
_into_rfid/)
(http://www.spychips.com/metro/scandal-coverup.html)
(http://www.accenture.com/Global/Services/Accenture_Technology
_Labs/R_and_I/PersonalAssistant.htm)

33. *Tracking Patents for RFID*
(http://www.accenture.com/Global/Services/Accenture_Technology_
Labs/R_and_I/PersonalAssistant.htm)
(http://www.worldnetdaily.com/news/article.asp?ARTICLE_ID=46697)
(http://www.accenture.com/Global/Services/Accenture_Technology_
Labs/R_and_I/PersonalAssistant.htm)
Katherine Albrecht, *Spychips*,
(Nashville: Thomas Nelson Inc., 2005, Pgs. 33-35, 61-70)
(http://www.newsreview.com/issues/Sacto/2005-12-15/sidebar.asp)

34. *Tracking Quotes for RFID*
Katherine Albrecht, *Spychips*,
(Nashville: Thomas Nelson Inc., 2005, Pgs. 9,23,24,37,55,85,135,
145,153, 167,218)

(http://www.boycotttesco.com/spychips.html)
(http://www.spychips.com/rfid_overview.html)
(http://www.wired.com/wired/archive/12.07/shoppers.html)
(http://www.rfidjournal.com/article/articleview/1508/1/1/)
(http://www.channelregister.co.uk/2004/09/30/rfid_tag_pulldown/)
(http://www.citizen.com/apps/pbcs.dll/article?AID=/20051211/NEWS01/
112110062/-1/CITIZEN)
(http://news.zdnet.com/2100-1009-5843867.html)
(http://news.com.com/2100-1029_3-5065388.html)
35. *Quote IBM Commercial The Boxes Told Me*
(http://www.youtube.com/watch?v=sgFLDfo7f5g)
36. *RFID is Good for the Companies*
(http://www-5.ibm.com/e-business/uk/tv_spot/?tactic=305A
X03W)
(http://www.accenture.com/Global/Services/Accenture_Technology_Labs/R
_and_I/PhysicalTracking.htm)
http://www.expresscomputeronline.com/20050905/management02.shtml)
(http://www.rfidjournal.com/article/articleview/1230/1/14/)
37. *RFID is Good for the Consumers*
(http://news.softpedia.com/news/RFID-between-spying-and-utility-868.shtml)
(http://wistechnology.com/article.php?id=2445)
(http://www.star.niu.edu/articles/?id=11932)
38. *RFID Creates Personalized Pricing*
(http://www.spychips.com/media/media_clips.html)
Katherine Albrecht, *Spychips*,
(Nashville: Thomas Nelson Inc., 2005, Pgs. 28,50,51,52)
(http://www.spychips.com/documents/Albrecht-Denver-Law.pdf)
(http://www.accenture.com/Global/Services/By_Subject/Radio_
Frequency_Identification/Services/BenefitsVideos.htm)
(http://www.accenture.com/Global/Services/Accenture_Technology_
Labs/R_and_I/ProductProfiler.htm)
(http://www.accenture.com/Global/Services/Accenture_Technology_
Labs/R_and_I/TechnologyList.htm#reality)
Katherine Albrecht, *Spychips*,
(Nashville: Thomas Nelson Inc., 2005, Pg. 160)
(http://www.accenture.com/Global/Services/Accenture_Technology_
Labs/R_and_I/PersonalizedPricingTool.htm)
(http://www.expresscomputeronline.com/20050905/management02.
shtml)

Katherine Albrecht, *Spychips*,
(Nashville: Thomas Nelson Inc., 2005, Pgs. 66-69,74-75,78-81)
39. *RFID Creates Personalized Tracking*
(http://www.accenture.com/Global/Services/Accenture_Technology_
Labs/R_and_I/RealWorldShowroom.htm)
(http://www.sundex.com/video.asp)
Katherine Albrecht, *Spychips*,
(Nashville: Thomas Nelson Inc., 2005, Pgs. 93-94,98-99,104-106)
40. *RFID Invasion of Privacy*
(Canadian News Report Video – Source Unknown)
41. *Quote IBM Commercial Farm to Fork*
(http://www-5.ibm.com/e-business/uk/tv_spot/?tactic=305AX03W)
42. *RFID Will Keep Your Food Fresh*
(http://www.future-store.org/servlet/PB/-s/pl98on1hjzd1v7xlltmbl
22eqn3r85s/menu/1007084_l2/index.html)
(http://atpos.com/product.php?productID=150)
(http://www.foodproductiondaily.com/news/ng.asp?n=62116-rfid-
epcglobal-fresh-produce)
(http://www.rfidjournal.com/article/articleview/1539/1/1/)
(http://www.rfidjournal.com/article/articleview/1775/1/1/)
Katherine Albrecht, *Spychips*,
(Nashville: Thomas Nelson Inc., 2005, Pgs. 73, 81-82)
43. *RFID Will Keep Your Food Safe*
(http://www.can-trace.org/About/?langid=e&pageid=standards)
(http://www.worldnetdaily.com/news/article.asp?ARTICLE_ID=48237)
(http://www.itworldcanada.com/a/Communications-Infrastructure/
262fc2f9-f3bf-4723-a11e-33f6f3c39579.html)
(http://www.cattlenetwork.com/content.asp?contentid=5226)
(http://www.suntimes.com/output/news/cst-nws-amish26.html)
(http://www.aimglobal.org/members/news/templates/aimpress.asp?
articleid=472&zoneid=1)
(http://www.rfidjournal.com/article/articleview/1623/1/1/)
(http://www.foodproductiondaily.com/news/news-ng.asp?n=62320-
idtechex-wal-mart-rfid)
(http://www.thewisemarketer.com/briefs/archive.asp?action=read&
bid=1392)
(http://www.supplychainreview.com.au/index.cfm?li=displaystory&
StoryID=24965)
(http://www.researchandmarkets.com/reports/304482)

(http://www.primezone.com/newsroom/news.html?d=90110)
(http://www.morerfid.com/details.php?subdetail=Report&action=details
&report_id=1003&display=RFID)
(http://nonais.org/but-what-is-nais/)
(http://www.forbes.com/video/?video_url=http://www.forbes.com/video/
fvn/business/tm_dangl&id=murphy_digital&title=Video%3A+Tech+
Guardians&tab=Technology)
44. *ABC News Reporting RFID Implants*
(http://www.youtube.com/watch?v=BWgUTrvRlA4)
45. *Story of Man Telling a Blonde Joke*
(Email story) – Source Unknown

# Chapter Ten            *The Mark of the Beast*

1. *Story of Nasty Bug*
(Email story) – Source Unknown
2. *Quote President Calvin Coolidge*
(http://adage.com/century/rothenberg.html)
3. *Chronological Media Promotion of the Mark*
(http://www.newswithviews.com/guest_opinion/guest54.htm)
(http://www.bible-prophecy.com/2013/mark2013.htm)
(http://www.bible-prophecy.com/2012/mark2012.htm#Current)
(http://www.bible-prophecy.com/2011/mark2011.htm#Current)
(http://www.bible-prophecy.com/2010/mark2010.htm#Current)
(http://www.bible-prophecy.com/2009/mark2009.htm#Current)
(http://www.bible-prophecy.com/mark2008.htm#Current)
(http://bible-prophecy.com/smart2.htm)
(http://www.understandthetimes.org/topics/oneworldgov_archive.shtml)
(Internet Video – Source Unknown)
(http://www.youtube.com/watch?v=VuFVsaFCzsw)
(http://www.youtube.com/watch?v=Dyk9Xnj4_5U)
4. *Signs the Internet is Being Controlled*
(http://www.dailytech.com/PostOlympics+China+Turns+Its+Back+on+Inter
net+Censorship+Promises/article13716.htm)
(http://www.smh.com.au/articles/2008/11/12/1226318695554.html)
(http://www.theregister.co.uk/2008/12/03/berlusconi_g8_internet/)
(http://news.xinhuanet.com/english/2009-01/06/content_10613478.htm)
(http://rt.com/usa/new-internet-itu-us-160/)

(http://rt.com/usa/un-internet-itu-packet-385/)
(http://www.prisonplanet.com/enemies-of-free-speech-call-for-internet-licensing.html)
(http://www.newsmax.com/newsfront/obama-seize-internet-emergency/2012/07/11/id/445083)
5. *Information on Google Glass*
(http://www.youtube.com/watch?v=4EvNxWhskf8&feature=c4-overview&list=UUxqyBoACUss6OxFdmFvxcXQ)
(http://www.youtube.com/watch?v=6BTCoT8ajbI)
6. *Information on Google Brain Chip*
(http://www.independent.co.uk/life-style/gadgets-and-tech/features/inside-google-hq-what-does-the-future-hold-for-the-company-whose-visionary-plans-include-implanting-a-chip-in-our-brains-8714487.html)
7. *Quote of Various People Promoting the Mark*
(http://www.bible-prophecy.com/mark2.htm)
(http://countdown.org/end/big_brother_07.html)
(http://wwwadsx.com/news/2002/042602.html)
(http://wwwadsx.com/news/2002/081602.html)
(http://www.blacklistednews.com/The_Beast:_Tracking_You_and_Your_Family_Just_Got_a_Whole_Lot_Easier/20129/0/0/0/Y/M.html)
(http://www.youtube.com/watch?v=WDW4CAAbvA4)
(http://www.youtube.com/watch?v=Y3m1N8Hrz0I)
(http://www.youtube.com/watch?v=DAmOPim8Jyg)
8. *Quote Pastor Who Promotes the Mark*
(Internet Video – Source Unknown)
9. *Information on Databases Already in Existence*
(http://countdown.org/end/big_brother_13.htm)
(http://countdown.org/end/big_brother_12.htm)
(http://countdown.org/end/big_brother_13.htm)
(http://countdown.org/end/big_brother_09.htm)
(http://www.khouse.org/articles/political/20010801-360.html)
(http://countdown.org/end/big_brother_02.htm)
(http://www.mvcf.com/news/cache/00065/)
(http://countdown.org/end/big_brother_06.htm)
(http://theweek.com/article/index/229508/acxiom-corp-the-faceless-organization-that-knows-everything-about-you)
(http://www.dailyfinance.com/2010/09/24/who-is-watching-you-nine-industries-that-know-your-every-move/)
(http://www.godlikeproductions.com/forum1/message635711/pg1)

(http://www.youtube.com/watch?v=KU80hFAxwd4)
(http://www.youtube.com/watch?v=DIGdWsxHJlM)

10. *Information on Biometric Databases*
(http://betabeat.com/2013/07/eyeball-scanning-is-now-a-reality-coming-to-a-middle-school-near-you/)
(http://www.washingtonpost.com/wp-dyn/content/article/2007/12/21/AR2007122102544_pf.html)
(http://singularityhub.com/2010/09/26/iris-scanning-set-to-secure-city-in-mexico-then-the-world-video/)
(http://usatoday30.usatoday.com/tech/news/surveillance/2010-09-13-1airis13_st_n.htm)
(http://www.nowtheendbegins.com/blog/?p=12776)
(http://www.wired.com/dangerroom/2013/01/biometrics/?pid=1775&viewall=true)
(http://www.wired.com/threatlevel/2013/05/immigration-reform-dossiers/)
(http://www.theblaze.com/stories/2013/03/28/eye-trackers-wrist-bands-posture-seats-mood-meter-a-close-look-at-the-tech-proposed-to-track-your-kids-in-schools/)
(http://www.foxnews.com/tech/2013/06/17/florida-school-district-reportedly-scans-childrens-eyes-without-parents/)
(http://countdown.org/end/big_brother_13.htm)
(http://countdown.org/end/big_brother_12.htm)
(http://countdown.org/end/big_brother_13.htm)
(http://countdown.org/end/big_brother_09.htm)
(http://www.khouse.org/articles/political/20010801-360.html)
(http://countdown.org/end/big_brother_02.htm)
(http://www.mvcf.com/news/cache/00065/)
(http://countdown.org/end/big_brother_06.htm)
(http://theweek.com/article/index/229508/acxiom-corp-the-faceless-organization-that-knows-everything-about-you)
(http://www.dailyfinance.com/2010/09/24/who-is-watching-you-nine-industries-that-know-your-every-move/)
(http://www.godlikeproductions.com/forum1/message635711/pg1)
(http://www.youtube.com/watch?v=KU80hFAxwd4)
(http://www.youtube.com/watch?v=DIGdWsxHJlM)
(http://countdown.org/end/big_brother_04.html)
(http://countdown.org/end/big_brother_02.html)
(http://www.mvcf.com/news/cache/00440/)
(http://www.countdown.org/end/mark_of_the_beast_05.html)

(http://www.mvcf.com/news/cache/00400/)
(http://countdown.org/end/big_brother_11.html)
(http://www.mvcf.com/news/cache/00431/)
(http://www.endtimeinfo.net/mark/eyeball.html)
(http://www.privacy.org/pi/reprots/biometric.html)
(http://www.endtimeinfo.net/cashless/fingerprint.html)
(http://www.youtube.com/watch?v=jADItDHOHOA)
(http://www.youtube.com/watch?v=aCa9-AmfLi8)
(http://www.youtube.com/watch?v=SFWYvXsB_eA)
11. *Information on Biometric Head Parts*
(http://www.slate.com/blogs/future_tense/2012/12/12/surveillance_ecuador_i mplements_speech_technology_center_s_facial_and_voice.html)
(http://www.infowars.com/14-incredibly-creepy-surveillance-technologies-that-big-brother-will-be-using-to-spy-on-you/print/)
(http://www.washingtonpost.com/wp-dyn/content/article/2007/12/21/AR2007122102544_pf.html)
(http://www.brandchannel.com/home/post/2011/07/27/Facial- Recognition-Comes-to-the-Social-Web.aspx)
(http://techcrunch.com/2013/05/31/google-wont-approve-glass-apps-that-recognize-peoples-faces-for-now/)
(http://www.huffingtonpost.com/x-prize-foundation/billboards-and-tvs-detect_b_1756778.html)
(http://www.dailymail.co.uk/sciencetech/article-2187801/Were-watching-The-camera-recognise-Facebook-picture-time-walk-shop.html)
(http://www.dailymail.co.uk/news/article-2212051/Powerful-CCTV-cameras-track-faces-half-mile-away-breach-human-rights-laws.html)
(http://rt.com/usa/fbi-recognition-system-ngi-640/)
(http://www.wired.com/dangerroom/2013/01/biometrics/)
(http://gizmodo.com/you-wont-need-a-pin-when-you-pay-for-everything-with-y-805487185)
(http://www.dailymail.co.uk/sciencetech/article-2365166/Next-generation-cash-machines-set-replace-bank-cards-facial-recognition.html)
(http://countdown.org/end/big_brother_04.html)
(http://countdown.org/end/big_brother_02.html)
(http://countdown.org/end/big_brother_13.html)
(http://www.mvcf.com/news/cache/00440/)
(http://www.countdown.org/end/mark_of_the_beast_05.html)
(http://www.mvcf.com/news/cache/00400/)
(http://countdown.org/end/big_brother_11.html)

(http://www.mvcf.com/news/cache/00431/)
(http://www.endtimeinfo.net/mark/eyeball.html)
(http://www.privacy.org/pi/reprots/biometric.html)
(http://www.endtimeinfo.net/cashless/fingerprint.html)
(http://www.newswithviews.com/guest_opinion/guest54.htm)
(http://www.bible-prophecy.com/2013/mark2013.htm)
(http://www.bible-prophecy.com/2012/mark2012.htm#Current)
(http://www.bible-prophecy.com/2011/mark2011.htm#Current)
(http://www.bible-prophecy.com/2010/mark2010.htm#Current)
(http://www.bible-prophecy.com/2009/mark2009.htm#Current)
(http://www.bible-prophecy.com/mark2008.htm#Current)
(http://www.bible-prophecy.com/2013/economic2013.htm#Current)
(http://www.bible-prophecy.com/2012/economic2012.htm#Current)
(http://www.bible-prophecy.com/2011/economic2011.htm#Current)
(http://www.bible-prophecy.com/2010/economic2010.htm#Current)
(http://www.bible-prophecy.com/2009/economic2009.htm#Current)
(http://www.bible-prophecy.com/economic2008.htm#Current)
(http://bible-prophecy.com/smart2.htm)
(http://www.understandthetimes.org/topics/oneworldgov_archive.shtml)
(http://www.youtube.com/watch?v=03QG-xMojb0)
(http://www.youtube.com/watch?v=3l9FRSMIEF0)
(http://www.youtube.com/watch?v=lDp9ewD2dXY)
(http://www.youtube.com/watch?v=c2n5ki54mqs)
(http://www.youtube.com/watch?v=sLOxUVvcjwE)
(http://www.youtube.com/watch?v=900yiMyIFo8)
(http://www.youtube.com/watch?v=xDO4hdfY11U)
(Various Internet Videos – Sources Unknown)
12. *Information on Biometric Hand Parts*
(http://www.infowars.com/14-incredibly-creepy-surveillance-technologies-that-big-brother-will-be-using-to-spy-on-you/)
(http://www.wired.com/dangerroom/2013/01/biometrics/?pid=1775&viewall=true)
(http://www.10news.com/news/fingerprints-now-required-at-poway-skate-park)
(http://www.cnn.com/2010/WORLD/europe/07/05/first.biometric.atm.europe/index.html)
(http://www.popsci.com/technology/article/2012-06/fingerprint-scanner-captures-prints-20-feet-away)
(http://www.economicvoice.com/people-like-buying-with-a-fingerprint/

50038161)
(http://www.mainenewssimply.com/content/bangor-daily-news/umaine-using-hand-scanners-dining-halls-deter-sharing-id-cards)
(http://www.wkbn.com/2013/06/06/hospital-implements-palm-scan/)
(http://countdown.org/end/big_brother_04.html)
(http://countdown.org/end/big_brother_02.html)
(http://countdown.org/end/big_brother_13.html)
(http://www.mvcf.com/news/cache/00440/)
(http://www.countdown.org/end/mark_of_the_beast_05.html)
(http://www.mvcf.com/news/cache/00400/)
(http://countdown.org/end/big_brother_11.html)
(http://www.mvcf.com/news/cache/00431/)
(http://www.endtimeinfo.net/mark/eyeball.html)
(http://www.privacy.org/pi/reprots/biometric.html)
(http://www.endtimeinfo.net/cashless/fingerprint.html)
(http://www.newswithviews.com/guest_opinion/guest54.htm)
(http://www.bible-prophecy.com/2013/mark2013.htm)
(http://www.bible-prophecy.com/2012/mark2012.htm#Current)
(http://www.bible-prophecy.com/2011/mark2011.htm#Current)
(http://www.bible-prophecy.com/2010/mark2010.htm#Current)
(http://www.bible-prophecy.com/2009/mark2009.htm#Current)
(http://www.bible-prophecy.com/mark2008.htm#Current)
(http://www.bible-prophecy.com/2013/economic2013.htm#Current)
(http://www.bible-prophecy.com/2012/economic2012.htm#Current)
(http://www.bible-prophecy.com/2011/economic2011.htm#Current)
(http://www.bible-prophecy.com/2010/economic2010.htm#Current)
(http://www.bible-prophecy.com/2009/economic2009.htm#Current)
(http://www.bible-prophecy.com/economic2008.htm#Current)
(http://bible-prophecy.com/smart2.htm)
(http://www.understandthetimes.org/topics/oneworldgov_archive.shtml)
(Various Internet Videos – Source Unknown)
13. *Information on World Pay Biometric System*
(http://www.olivetreeviews.org/news/new-world-order/item/3626-biometric-payments-are-top-option-for-security-concious-shoppers-survey-finds-june-13)
14. *Examples of Being More Pampered with Implants*
(http://www.spychips.com/blog/2007/02/rfid_a_journal_labels_verichip.html)
(http://www.thefamily.org/endtime/article.php3?id=12)

(http://countdown.org/end/big_brother_06.html)
(http://www.bible-prophecy.com/smart2.htm)
(http://countdown.org/end/big_brother_04.html)
(http://countdown.org/end/big_brother_02.html)
(http://www.lunarpages.com/stargazers/endworld/fin-signs/news/ chip.htm)
(http://countdown.org/end/big_brother_06.html)
(http://countdown.org/end/big_brother_04.html)
(http://blog.cleveland.com/metro/2010/08/city_of_cleveland_to_use_high-
.html)
(http://www.dailymail.co.uk/news/article-1255565/Spy-chips-hidden-2-5-
million-dustbins-council-snoopers-plan-pay-throw-tax.html)
(http://washingtonexaminer.com/new-recycling-bins-with-tracking-chips-
coming-to-alexandria/article/14336)
(http://www.zdnet.com/blog/emergingtech/rfid-tags-help-you-to-choose-
clothes/719)
(http://www.rfidjournal.com/articles/view?3503)
(http://www.engadget.com/2011/05/30/nutrismart-prototype-embeds-rfid-
tags-directly-within-food-trac/)
(http://www.geekosystem.com/nutrismart-rfid-food/)
(http://www.informationweek.com/rfid-tagged-umbrellas-track-shoppers-
mov/199703913)
(http://www.cio.com/article/164679/RFID_Chips_in_Your_Magazines)
(http://www.stockhouse.com/companies/bullboard/v.si/stratton-resources-
inc?postid=15561691)
(http://www.medgadget.com/2009/03/high_speed_rfid_to_help_set_new_rec
ords.html)
(http://www.prweb.com/releases/vehicle/system/prweb538891.htm)
(http://www.youtube.com/watch?v=sDyqhcy1L-0)
(http://www.geekosystem.com/nutrismart-rfid-food/)
(Various Internet Videos – Source Unknown)
15. *Examples of Being More Productive with Implants*
(http://www.bible-prophecy.com/mark.htm)
(http://countdown.org/end/big_brother_05.html)
(http://countdown.org/end/big_brother_03.html)
(http://www.digitalangel.net/medical.asp)
(http://www.lunarpages.com/stargazers/endworld/fin-signs/news/
chip.htm)
(http://countdown.org/end/big_brother_01.html)
(http://countdown.org/end/big_brother_07.html)

(http://www.dvice.com/archives/2008/01/rfid_clothing_t.php)
(http://www.itbusiness.ca/news/an-rfid-tag-in-your-nike-shoes-can-win-you-that-marathon/1308)
(http://gizmodo.com/231578/gps-shoes-let-mommy-know-where-you-are)
(http://www.cbsnews.com/8301-204_162-57593147/smart-diaper-with-qr-code-may-track-tots-urinary-health/)
(http://www.youtube.com/watch?v=63zbHBs-UX8)
(http://www.youtube.com/watch?v=rcokYRf1lAc)
(http://www.youtube.com/watch?v=SOkGYqEiMF0)
(http://www.youtube.com/watch?v=cHPSckL5RDI)
(Various Internet Videos – Source Unknown)
16. *Examples of Being More Protected with Implants*
    (http://www.digitalangel.net/consumer.asp)
    (http://countdown.org/end/big_brother_03.html)
    (http://www.geocities.com/Heartland/Ridge/1428/mark.html)
    (http://www.popsci.com/technology/article/2010-08/fraunhofer-wants-tag-trees-wood-based-rfid-chips)
    (http://www.reuters.com/article/2010/10/11/us-brazil-forestry-idUSTRE69A1XX20101011)
    (http://www.youtube.com/watch?v=6RRgN83bxcQ)
    (http://blogs.discovermagazine.com/80beats/?p=29515)
    (http://www.doritex.com/products-detail.php?recordID=01)
    (http://www.digitaltrends.com/lifestyle/never-lose-socks-with-rfid-chips/)
    (http://jalopnik.com/334858/rfid-embedded-bicycles-traffic-lights-saddens-scumbag-lawyers)
    (http://www.informationweek.com/baggage-bots-rfid-will-track-and-transfe/202300796)
    (http://www.theverge.com/2013/6/7/4405274/airbus-bag2go-smart-luggage-prototype)
    (http://www.simplyrfid.com/blog/2009/10/9/tracking-laptops-with-rfid.html)
    (http://www.nbcnews.com/id/29509303/ns/technology_and_science-tech_and_gadgets/t/radio-id-chips-help-stem-cacti-theft/)
    (http://www.youtube.com/watch?v=aJGfZvg0TUI)
    (http://www.youtube.com/watch?v=Ar2gZiT5dDM)
    (http://www.youtube.com/watch?v=poSikw_yNB0)
    (Various Internet Videos – Source Unknown)
17. *Pets Promoting Implants*
    (http://countdown.org/end/big_brother_03.html)
    (http://www.youtube.com/watch?v=PbtF0hHN0HE)

(http://www.youtube.com/watch?v=h0dnwGC5tVw)

18. *Propaganda Promoting Implants*
    (http://www.foxnews.com/tech/2010/05/14/radio-frequency-rfid-implant/)
    (http://www.newswithviews.com/guest_opinion/guest54.htm)
    (http://www.msnbc.msn.com/id/15221100/)
    (http://www.miami.com/mld/miami/business/3240630.htm)
    (Various Internet Videos – Source Unknown)

19. *Payments Promoting Implants*
    (http://www.youtube.com/watch?v=xWTPKdyrygc)
    (http://www.youtube.com/watch?v=cffBi1qst08)
    (Various Internet Videos – Source Unknown)

20. *People Receiving Implants*
    (http://countdown.org/end/big_brother_06.html)
    (http://www.abcnews.go.com/sections/scitech/TechTV/techtv_chipfamily020
    510.html)
    (http://www.millenniumhope.info/article1023.html)
    (http://countdown.org/end/big_brother_07.html)
    (http://www.youtube.com/watch?v=vevFqVbIwvg)
    (http://www.youtube.com/watch?v=9XtS440GOoo)
    (Various Internet Videos – Source Unknown)

21. *Reporter Exposes Tactics of Implants*
    (http://www.youtube.com/watch?v=CZUqWOLAE4I)

22. *Proof of a Universal ID*
    (http://www.youtube.com/watch?v=O6W1a8gjslQ)
    (http://www.youtube.com/watch?v=oeBiZGU23SY)
    (http://www.endtimeinfo.net/mark/rfid.html)
    (http://www.geocities.com/SouthBeach/Lagoon/1780/exec.html)
    (http://www.fema.gov)
    (http://www.endtimeinfo.net/mark/euid.html)
    (http://asia.news.yahoo.com/020805/reuters/asia-118809.html)
    (http://www.smh.com.au/breaking/2001/12/14/FFX058CU6VC.html)
    (http://www.activistpost.com/2013/08/forget-real-id-global-smart-id-is-
    coming.html)
    (http://www.blacklistednews.com/The_Beast:_Tracking_You_and_Your_Fa
    mily_Just_Got_a_Whole_Lot_Easier/20129/0/0/0/Y/M.html)
    (http://www.bible-prophecy.com/2012/mark2012.htm)
    (http://www.dw.de/germany-set-to-introduce-smart-id-cards-in-2010/a-
    5012697)
    (http://www.ynetnews.com/articles/0,7340,L-3816629,00.html)

(http://siouxcityjournal.com/news/mexico-to-issue-citizens-national-identity-card/article_597ce72e-e48b-5045-99e5-d75b828784c4.html)
(http://en.wikipedia.org/wiki/List_of_national_identity_card_policies_by_co untry)
(http://www.naturalnews.com/038223_forced_vaccinations_children_court_r uling.html)
(http://www.globalresearch.ca/the-cashless-society-arrives-in-africa-the-multipurpose-biometric-national-identity-smart-card/5335292)
(Various Internet Videos – Source Unknown)
23. *Proof of a Universal Goal*
(http://www.youtube.com/watch?v=bqDBg6AuqiI)
(http://www.youtube.com/watch?v=qYUlCKFHeAQ)
(http://portland.indymedia.org/en/2005/09/325974.shtml)
(Various Internet Videos – Source Unknown)
24. *More Evidence of a Microchip Mandate*
(http://www.reuters.com/article/2008/11/24/us-indonesia-aids-idUSTRE4AN3U620081124)
(http://www.infowars.com/usda-wants-rfid-tracking-technology-to-be-mandatory-in-us-food-stamp-program/)
(http://www.infowars.com/eco-fascism-bares-its-teeth-global-warming-alarmist-wants-to-barcode-babies/)
25. *Evidence of Forehead & Right Hand Worship*
(http://www.jesus-is-savior.com/False%20Religions/Roman%20 Catholicism/beast.htm)
(http://en.wikipedia.org/wiki/Tilaka)
(http://en.wikipedia.org/wiki/Bindi_(decoration))
(http://en.wikipedia.org/wiki/Bagel_head)
(http://www.paulmcguire.org/articles/articles_the_coming_persecution_of_c hristians_1.html)
(http://www.americanthinker.com/blog/2012/09/an_obama_revelation_suppo rters_marking_their_right_hands.html)
26. *Epidermal Electronic Tattoos*
(http://www.redicecreations.com/article.php?id=26320)
(http://www.technologyreview.com/news/512061/electronic-sensors-printed-directly-on-the-skin/)
27. *Human Barcode & QR Code & Somark Tattoos*
(Various Internet Videos – Source Unknown)
(https://www.youtube.com/watch?v=lOirF9Vv87U)
(http://www.informationweek.com/invisible-rfid-ink-safe-for-cattle-and-

p/196802844)
(http://www.somarkinnovations.com/)
(http://nyisdkiaszemed2012.blogspot.com/2012/12/invisible-rfid-tattoo-planned-for-humans.html#!/2012/12/invisible-rfid-tattoo-planned-for-humans.html)

28. *Quote from Dr. Carl Sanders*
(http://www.lunarpages.com/stargazers/endworld/fin-signs/news/chip.htm)
(http://meltingpot.fortunecity.com/chicon/321/mark_of_the_beast.htm)
29. *The Invention of a Killer Microchip*
(https://www.youtube.com/watch?v=iZoyflO3HVs)
30. *Story of Blonde Woman and Shepherd*
(Email story) – Source Unknown